THE PILGRIMAGE OF FA HIAN

THE PILGRIMAGE OF FA HIAN

FA-HIEN

GYAN

Published by

Gyan Publishing House
5, Ansari Road
Daryaganj, New Delhi-110002
Phone: 011-47034999, 9811692060
E-mail: books@gyanbooks.com

Distribution Network
gyanbooks.com
India, USA, Canada, UK, Australia

ISBN: 978-93-7014-438-5 (PB)

First Published, 1848

2nd Impression 2025

Printed at: Gyan Press, Delhi.

THE PILGRIMAGE OF FA HIAN
Author: FA-HIEN

THE

PILGRIMAGE OF FA HIAN.

THE

PILGRIMAGE OF FA HIAN;

FROM THE

FRENCH EDITION

OF THE

FOE KOUE KI

OF

MM. REMUSAT, KLAPROTH, AND LANDRESSE.

WITH

ADDITIONAL NOTES AND ILLUSTRATIONS.

CALCUTTA:

PRINTED BY J. THOMAS, BAPTIST MISSION PRESS.

1848.

ADVERTISEMENT.

THE original purpose of the Editor on undertaking the present version of the FOE KOUE KI, was to furnish the text of the Chinese Author with only so much of the commentary as was indispensible for its easy comprehension. But on reconsidering the subject, and reflecting how greatly the value of the work would be impaired by the contemplated omissions, he determined to publish the notes of the learned French Editors not only entire, but with such additions and corrections as the critical labours of Wilson, Lassen, and others, as well as his own research, should enable him to supply. The reader will find accordingly, that with the exception of a slight attempt at condensation in the earlier chapters, and a very few unimportant omissions elsewhere, the whole of the notes of MM. Remusat, Klaproth, and Landresse have been preserved; while the additional matter amounts to not less than fifty or sixty pages.

This great extension of his original plan compels the Editor to reserve for the present an introductory chapter on Buddhism for which he had collected ample materials. He trusts however that the work in its present state will be found useful to the antiquarian, and not devoid of interest to the general reader. His chief object was to promote and assist the labours of such as are engaged in exploring the ancient monuments of India, to many of whom the original edition is not easily accessible; and he cannot avoid remarking how greatly the same object might be promoted could we obtain through the instrumentality of our countrymen in China versions of other Chinese authors who treat of the history and geography of India; and especially of such as, like Fa hian, Houan thsang, Soung yun and Hoeï sing, have actually visited this country and recorded the results of their travels. Such works are doubtless procurable with the utmost facility in every part of China, and their translation into English might be effected with the same ease at any of our Anglo-Chinese Schools or Colleges, as that of a Persian or Urdu Manuscript in Calcutta.

The Editor regrets that many typographical errors have escaped correction as the sheets passed through the press. These are for the most part of no great importance; but there are a few in the subjoined list which the Reader is requested to correct with his pen.

E R R A T A.

Page 10, line 30, *for* " Note 22," *read* " Note 19."
,, 51, ,, 11, *for* of King *read* of the King,
,, 116, ,, 24, *for* like as *read* like.
,, 120, ,, 9, *for You feou thi read Yan feou thi.*
,, 129, ,, 27, *for Long (Agama) read Long Agama.*
,, 153, ,, 27, *for Fou lau na, read Fou lan na.*
,, 161, ,, 10, *for* tours *read* towers.
,, 183, ,, 16, *for Gina read Jina.*
,, 203, ,, 8, *for* that tribe *read* the tribe.
,, 215, ,, 5, *for* Asoka *read* Ajatasatru.
,, 115, ,, 14, *for* then *read* thero.
,, 221, *last line but one, for* south-west *read* south-east,
,, 225, ,, 4, *for* edentification *read* identification.
,, 241, *dele foot note.*
,, 243, ,, 32, *for Kivi read Kiui.*
,, 251 first note, *for* 6 miles *read* 16 miles.
,, 252, ,, 25, *for* 305 B. C. *read* 280 B. C.
,, 264, ,, 4, *for* south-west *read* south-east.

THE

PILGRIMAGE OF FA HIAN.

CHAPTER I.

Departure from Chhang'an.—The Loung Mountains.—Western Tsin.—South Lian.—North Lian.—Thun houang.—The Desert of Sand.

FA HIAN,[1] when in the olden time at Chhang'an,[2] was distressed to observe the Precepts and the Theological Works[3] on the point of being lost, and already disfigured by lacunæ. For this reason, in the second year *Houng shi*,[4] distinguished by the cyclical characters *Ki haï*, he set forth with *Hoeï king*, *Tao ching*, *Hoeï ying*, *Hoeï wei*, and sundry others,[5] to search in India for the Laws and the Precepts of Religion.

They departed from Chhang'an, and having crossed the Loung[6] Mountains, arrived at the kingdom of *Khian koueï*,[7] where they sojourned. This sojourn[8] ended, they proceeded onward, and arrived at the kingdom of *Neou than*.[9] They passed the mountains *Yang leou*,[10] and reached the military station of *Chang y*.[11]

The country of *Chang y* was at that time the theatre of great disturbances, which rendered travelling impracticable. The king of *Chang y*, out of interest amd affection, retained the travellers, and proved himself their benefactor.[12] It was then that they fell in with *Chi yan*, *Hoeï kian*, *Seng shao*, *Pao yun*, *Seng king*,[13] and several others. Delighted to find themselves united to these by identity of purpose, they dwelt together; and when the term of their sojourn was come, they set forth once more, and arrived at *Thun houang.* At this place are vast entrenchments which may extend 80 *li* from East to West, and 40 *li* from North to South. They halted here one month and some days. Then Fa hian and five others set out again in the suite of sundry ambassadors, separating from *Pao yun* and his companions. The Governor of *Thun houang,*[14] *Li hao,* furnished them with the necessary means of crossing the River of Sand.[15]

There are Evil Spirits[16] in this River of Sand, and such scorching winds, that whoso encountereth them dies, and none escape. Neither birds are seen in the air, nor quadrupeds on the ground. On every side as far as the eye can reach, if you seek for the proper place to cross, there is no other mark to distinguish it than the skeletons of those who have perished there; these alone serve to indicate the route!

They travelled there seventeen days, and the distance passed ere they reached the kingdom of *Shen shen* may be estimated at 1500 *li*.

NOTES.

(1) *Shy fa hian;* that is, "Manifestation of the Law of Shy" (Sákya); a name adopted in compliance with the practice of Chinese Buddhists, who, upon entering a religious career, lay aside their family name, and, in token of renewed life, adopt another of moral or religious significance.* *Fa hian* is the abridged form of his name generally employed by our pilgrim, who in the course of his narrative invariably speaks of himself in the third person. R.

(2) *Chhang'an (perpetual repose)*; the name of the province now known by that of *Si'an*, in *Shen si.*—R.

(3) *The Precepts and the Theological Works.*—In the original *Liú, Tsang liú* signifies precepts; *tsang*, a collection. The body of the theological works is in general called *Sang tsang*, the three collections, or rather the *three receptacles* (in Sanscrit *the three Pitaka*); and this expression applies equally to the doctrine set forth in them. The three parts of this triple collection are the *King*, or sacred books, the *Precepts*, and the *Discourses* (*Lun*); in Sanscrit *Sutra, Vinaya, Abhidharma.*†—R.

* *Wen hian thoung khao*: book CCXXVI. page 4 et seq.
† *Fan y ming i*; book IV.

For a summary of the contents of the great collection of Bauddha Theology here referred to, we are indebted to the late M. Csoma de Körös, whose analyses of the *Kah-gyur* were published in the Journal of the Asiatic Society, Vol. I. pp. 1 and 374, and in the Asiatic Researches, Vol. XX. The Tibetan words *Kah-gyur* (བཀའ འགྱུར b*kah*-h*gyur*), signify 'translation of commandment,' these works being versions of Indian originals most likely compiled in the first instance in Pali or Magadhi, but very soon after systematised and perpetuated in Sanscrit, the classical language of all Indian theology. (See Hodgson, Journ. As. Soc. Vol. VI. p. 682.) This great compilation, consisting of a hundred volumes, was translated into Tibetan betwixt the seventh and the thirteenth centuries of our era, but principally during the ninth. It consists of seven grand divisions, which are indeed so many distinct works; namely, 1st—*Dul vá* (Sans. *Vinaya*), "Discipline," in 13 volumes. 2d—*Sher ch'hin* (Sans. *Prajnyápáramitá*), "Transcendental wisdom," in 21 Vols. 3d—*Phal ch'hen* (Sans. *Buddha·vata Sanga*), "Bauddha community," in 6 Vols. 4th—*Dkon séks* (Sans. *Ratnakúta*), "Gems heaped up," in 6 Vols. 5th—*Do-dé* (Sans. *Sútranta*), "Aphorisms or tracts," in 30 Vols. 6th—*Nyáng-dás* (Sans. *Nirvána*), "Deliverance from pain," in 2 Vols. 7th—*Gyut* (Sans. *Tantra*), "Mystical doctrine or charms," in 22 Vols.

The entire collection is sometimes spoken of under the title of *Dé-not-sum* (Sans. *Tri pitaka*), the "three vessels or repositories;" namely, 1st, *Dul va* (Sans. Vinaya), treating principally of education or discipline; 2d, *Do* (Sans. *Sutra*), the fundamental principles or aphorisms of the Bauddha faith; and 3d, *Ch, hos-non-pa* (Sans. *Abhidharma*), the Discourses.

We learn from the text of the *Vinaya*, as well as from other sources, that these works were, in the first instance, compiled by the immediate disciples of Sákya, under whose authority the "first convocation on religion" was held at Rajagriha shortly after the demise of Buddha, to fix and perpetuate the doctrine of the faith as orally propounded by its author. (As. Res. Vol. XX. p. 42.) The *Abhidharma* was compiled on this occasion by Kásyapa; the *Sutra*, by Ananda; and the *Vinaya*, by Upálí. `In the course of a hundred years from the date of this convocation, so many heresies and schisms had arisen among the priesthood, especially at Vaisali, that it was deemed necessary to assemble another Council in the reign of Asoka, to determine the canon of Scripture once more. At this "second convocation" seven hundred priests assisted; and the edition produced under their auspices was designated B*dun*-B*rgyas-yang-dag-par*-B*rjod-pa*; "that has been very clearly expressed by the seven hundred." (Csoma de Körös, As. Res. Vol. XX. p. 92.) Lastly, about four hundred years after the death of Sákya, a " third convocation" was held in the reign of Kaniska (Ibid, p. 297,) for a further revision of these scriptures. It was from this third edition, according to MM. Burnouf and Lassen, that the Tibetan version was made. *Introduction a l'Histoire due Buddhisme Indien*, p. 579 ; and *Zeitschrift für die Kunde des Morgenlandes*, Vol. III. p. 157.)

In the Pali Buddhistical Annals the times and circumstances of these convocations are differently stated. See Turnour, J. A. S. Vol. VI. p. 505 ; and the 3d and subsequent chapters of the *Mahavanso*, in which an interesting account is given of the heresies that led to these revisions of the canon.

For further information on this subject, the curious reader is referred to the works above quoted, and to the ample illustration afforded in the subsequent notes of the present volume.—J. W. L.

(4) *Houng shi.*—The name applied to the years of the reign of *Yao heng*, a prince of the later *Thsin* dynasty, who reigned in *Shen si* towards the end of the fourth and the beginning of the fifth century.* The *first* year *Houng shi* corresponds with the cyclical year *Ki haï*, (399 A. D.) There is thus a contradiction in the narrative of Fa hian in making the cyclical year *Ki haï* and the second year *Houng shi* the date of his departure. If this arise not from a mere error of the text, the supposition is not improbable that the petty princes of Tibetan origin, who in those times of trouble and distraction reigned on the frontiers of the empire, were not very careful of observing the nicities of the Chinese calendar, and noted the commencement of the *political* year on the first day of the *astronomical* year. Fa hian might thus leave *Chhang'an* towards the close of A. D. 399, when the name of the years *Houng shi* had been re-adjusted, although they might still reckon the cyclical year *Ki haï*.—R.

(5) *Hoeï king, Tao shing, Hoeï ying, Hoeï weï and sundry others.* —It was the common practice of Buddhist priests to associate themselves in companies for the performance of pilgrimages from town to town, and from temple to temple ; from India to China, and from China to India. The four names here recited are adoptive ones of religious significance : *Hoeï king*, 'Splendour of Intelligence ;' *Tao shing*, 'Ornament of the Doctrine ;' *Hoeï ying*, 'Eminent Perspicacity.'—R.

(6) *The Loung Mountains.*—These hills are situated in the western part of *Shen si*, N. W. of the district of *Thsin'an*, and east of the river *Thsing*. They are distinguished as the great and the little *Loung*. In recent Chinese maps this name is found in latitude 35° N. and 10° W. from Pekin.—R.

(7) *The Kingdom of Khian koueï*, was sitituated beyond the Loung

* *Histoire des Huns* ; Vol. I. p. 162.

Mountain. *Khian koueï* is the name of a petty prince of the race of the *Sian pi*, appertaining to the dynasty of the western *Thsin* or of *Loung si*, who reigned in the western parts of *Shen si*, at the end of the fourth and the beginning of the fifth century.* *Khian koueï* ascended the throne A. D. 388.—R.

(8) *Sojourn;* in the text *hia tso*, *to stay in summer;* but the expression must be taken in a more general sense, as a halt or temporary rest merely, and not as a summer sojourn. The expression occurs frequently in Fa hian with this import.—R.

(9) *The kingdom of Neou than.*—This too, is the name of a prince and not of a country.† *Neou than* ascended the throne of *Ho si*, to the west of the Yellow river, so late as the year *Jin yin* of the Cycle (A. D. 402); which would lead us to infer that Fa hian and his companions had met with great detention in advancing even this short distance upon their journey.—R.

(10) As Fa hian proceeded from *Si ning* to *Kan cheou*, he must necessarily have crossed the great chain of mountains covered with perpetual snow, which separates the districts of Kan cheou and Liang cheou from the great valley of the river called *Oulan mouran* by the Mongols, and *Houang shoui* or *Ta thoung ho* by the Chinese. This lofty chain was anciently called *Khi lian shan.* At present its most elevated summit, which consists of a colossal glacier, is named in Tibetan by the neighbouring Mongols, *Amiye gang gar oola*, or the "grandfather's mountain, white with snow."—Kl.

(11) *Chang y*, hodie *Kan cheou*, was, at the period of Fa hian's transit, under the dominion of the dynasty of the northern *Liang.* The disturbances to which Fa hian alludes, and which for a time prevented his progress, arose from the incessan wars waged by these petty states against each other, which eventually led to their extinction. The king of Kan cheou then reigning was either *Touan nieï*, who died in A. D. 401, or his successor *Meng san*, who succeeded in A. D. 402.‡ It is a matter of regret that Fa hian does not mention his benefactor's name, which would have fixed the date of his passage through Kan cheou with precision.—R.

(12) *Benefactor.*—In the original text *tan youeï*, a Chinese word of Sanscrit origin, such as the Buddhists frequently introduce. *Tan* or *tan na (Sans. dâna)*, alms, or gifts presented with a religious feeling, one of the ten means of salvation (pâramita); *youei*, a Chinese syllable signifying to surmount, to pass over or beyond; implying "that he who practices beneficence, passes the sea of poverty."§—R.

* *Histoire des Huns;* Vol. I. p. 200. *Li taï ki sse;* book XLIV. p. 18 v.

† Called *Jo than* by Deguignes, *Hist. des Huns;* Vol. I. p. 198. *Li taï ki sse;* book XLIV. p. 13.

‡ *Histoire des Huns;* Vol. I. p. 224.

§ *San tsang fa sou;* book XXXIII. p. 25 v. et alibi.

(13) *Chi yan, Hoeï kian, Seng shao, Pan yun, Seng king and others:* all names of religious significance as before, and meaning the Majesty of Prudence;—the Reserve of Perspicacity;—The Union of the Monks; the Precious (divine) Clouds; the Splendor of the Clergy.—R.

(14) *Thun houang;*—a place of great military importance from the times of the *Han* to those of the *Thang* dynasty. Under the five petty dynasties which succeeded the *Thang*, it bore the name of *Sha cheou*, or the *Town of Sands*, which it retained till the times of the *Ming* dynasty. The present town of *Sha cheou* is situated five or six leagues more easterly, on the right bank of the river *Sirgaldzin gol.*—Kl.

Li hao took this kingdom from the petty dynasty of the *Northern Liang*, and established an independent principality, under the name of the *Western Liang*, assuming the title, not of king, but simply of prince (Koung).—R.

(15) *The River of Sand;*—in the text *Sha ho*. The description given by our traveller of the Great Desert is very correct, and coincides closely with that of Marco Polo, except that Fa hian exaggerates its extent, which cannot be more, betwixt *Sha cheou* and the Lake of *Lob*, than 110 leagues, or 1100 *li*, instead of 1500. Possibly, however, the establishments visited by the pilgrims were not in those days immediately on the Lake of Lob, but more to the westward, on the rivers of Khaïdon and Yarkand daria.—R.

(16) *Evil Spirits.*—Not less credulous on this subject was Marco Polo, who records and adopts the same superstition. "It is asserted as a well known fact, says he, that this desert is the abode of evil spirits, which amuse travellers to their destruction with most extraordinary illusions. If during the daytime any persons remain behind on the road, whether overtaken by sleep, or detained by their natural occasions, until the caravan has passed a hill, or is no longer in sight, they unexpectedly hear themselves called by their names in a tone of voice to which they are accustomed; supposing the call to proceed from their companions, they are led away by it from the direct road, and not knowing in what direction to advance, are left to perish. * * * * Marvellous indeed and *almost passing belief* are the stories of these spirits of the desert, which are said at times to fill the air with the sounds of all kinds of musical instruments, and also of drums, and of the clash of arms, obliging the travellers to close their line of march and to proceed in more compact order." *Marsden's Marco Polo*, p. 159. It is not improbable after all that these sounds may really exist, and be referrible to natural causes. See Sir A. Burnes, on the *Reg Rawán*, J. A. S. Vol. VII. p. 324.—J. W. L.

CHAPTER II.

The Kingdom of Shen shen.—Ou hou.—Kao chhang.

The kingdom of *Shen shen*[1] is a rugged and very unequal country. Its soil is poor and sterile. The manners of its inhabitants and their dress are coarse, and similar to those of the land of Han.[2] The only difference consists in the use of felt and stuffs.

The king of this country honoreth the Law.[3] There may be in his dominions some four thousand ecclesiastics, all devoted to the study of the *less translation.*[4] The laity[5] in all these kingdoms, as well as the *Sha men,*[6] all observe the Law of India,[7] with differences partaking more or less of coarseness or of refinement.

Henceforward, all the kingdoms that you traverse in journeying towards the west, resemble this in a greater or less degree, save that each hath its peculiar barbarous tongue;[8] but all the clergy apply themselves to the study of the books of India and the language of India.[9]

Fa hian and the rest sojourned here one month and some days, then setting forth again, and travelling fifteen days in a north-westerly direction, they reached the kingdom of *Ou i.*[10] The ecclesiastics of the kingdom of *Ou i* are also about four thousand in number, and all of the *less translation.* They are, as to the Law, exact and well ordered. The *Sha men* of the land of Thsin[11] who arrive in this country are not prepared for the customs of these ecclesiastics. Fa hian, being provided with a passport, proceeded to the encampment of *Koung sun,* who then reigned, and who detained him two months and some days. He then returned to Pao yun and the rest. They all found that the inhabitants of the kingdom *Ou i,* were by no means intent upon the practice of the rites and of justice, and evinced but small hospitality to strangers. For this reason *Chi yan, Hoeï kian*, and *Hoeï wei*, returned straightway to the country of *Kao chhang*,[18] with the purpose of soliciting assistance for their journey. Fa hian and the others had obtained a patent; *Koung sun* had furnished them with provisions; and they were thus in condition to set out at once, and advance in a south-westerly direction.

The country which they traversed is desert and uninhabited. The difficulty of crossing the rivers was extreme. Nothing in the world can be compared with the fatigue they had to endure. After a journey of one month and five days they succeeded in reaching *Yu thian*.

NOTES.

(1) *The kingdom of Shen shen.*—This country, at first named *Leou lan*, is situated in the neighbourhood of the Lake of Lob: it is sandy and sterile, and its government never acquired much influence. The name of *Leou lan* was changed for that of *Shen shen* in the first century before Christ. (See Deguignes, *Histoire des Huns*, tom. II. p. x.) R.

(2) *The Land of Han*; that is, China; so called after the dynasty of Han, the remembrance of whose power is influential to this day. A Chinese is still called *Han jin*, and the Chinese language *Han iu*, although the *Han* have ceased to reign these sixteen hundred years. R.

(3) *The Law*, i. e. the law of Foe, Buddhism.

(4) *Four thousand ecclesiastics all of the less translation.*—The ecclesitics, or monks, are here denominated by the term usually applied to the Buddhist priests, *Seng*, in Sanscrit *Sanga* (united, joined by a common bond.)*

The *Sangas* are distinguished according to their moral characteristics, into four orders: 1st, *Those who accomplish justice*, that is the Buddhas the *Lokajyesthah* (Honorables of the Age) the Bodhisattwas, the Pratyeka Buddhas, the Shrâwakas, &c. whose virtue transcends the law itself, and who surmounting every obstacle accomplish their own deliverance (mukti). 2nd, The *ordinary Sangas of the age*: that is, men who shave their beards and heads, who dress themselves with the *kia sha* (a kind of cape worn by Buddhist priests) who embrace monastic life and its obligations, and observe the precepts and the prohibitions of Buddha. 3dly, The *dumb-sheep Sangas, Ya yang seng*; those dull and stupid characters who are

* *Journ. Asiat.* Vol. VII. p. 267.

unable to comprehend the distinction betwixt the commission and the non-commission of the fundamental sins, (murder, theft, fornication, lying) and who when guilty of crimes of less enormity make no show of repentance. 4th, and last, The *shameless Sangas*, who having embraced monastic life, unscrupulously infringe the precepts and observances enjoined upon them, and devoid of all shame and chastity, are indifferent even to the bitter fruits of their wickedness in ages to come.*

The *less translation* and the *great translation* are expressions of such frequent recurrence in the narrative of Fa hian, that it is well to explain their import once for all. *Ta ching*, in Chinese, means the *great revolution; Siao ching*, the *little revolution. Ching* signifies *translation, passage from one place to another, revolution, circumference;* and also the *medium* of transport, as a *car*, or *riding horse.* Its exact Sanscrit equivalent is *yána*, the significations of which are identical.† But each of these acquires, with reference to the doctrines of Buddhism, a characteristic and peculiar significance. They are mystical expressions indicating that influence which the individual soul can and should exercise upon itself in order to effect its transference to a superior condition. As this action, or influence, and its results are of different kinds or degrees; so they are distinguished into two, three, or more *yânas*—(in Chinese *ching*, in Mongol *kulgun*); and according as his efforts are directed to the attainment of greater or less perfection, the Sanga belongs to the *less*, the *mean*, or the *great translation.*

The *vehiculum*, which is common to all the *translations*, is the contemplation of the *four realities*, namely, *pain, reunion, death*, and the *doctrine;*‡ and that of the *twelve concatenations.*§ By this means man is transported beyond the boundary of the three worlds and the circle of birth and death.‖ Strictly speaking, there is but one translation, that of Buddha, the practice of which is enjoined upon all living beings, that they may escape from the troubled ocean of birth and death and land on the *other shore*, namely, that of the *absolute.*¶ Buddha would at once have spread abroad the knowledge of the Law, and taught mankind the *one translation;* but he found it indispensible to adapt his instructions to the various faculties of those who receive them, and hence arose the different *Yânas*, or means of transport. We may in the first place distinguish the translation of *disciples* or *auditors, (Shing*

* *Ti tsang shi lun king*, Book V.
† Wilson's *Sans. Diction.* h. v.
‡ The four verities, or realities, are explained in several ways. See notes to Chap. XXII.
§ See *Nouvean Journ. Asiat.* Vol. VII. p. 291.
‖ *Hoa yan king sou;* book I.
¶ *Fa houa king;* book I.

ven ; in Sanscrit, Shrávaka), and that of *distinct understandings**(*Youan kió ;* in Sanscrit, *Pratyeka Buddha.*)† To these must be added a third, that of the *Bodhi-sattwas*, who are beings far more nearly approaching to absolute perfection. Again, there is another classification under five different heads, to wit ; 1st, the translation of *Men ;* 2nd, that of *Gods ;* 3rd, that of *Shráwakas*, or *hearers ;* 4th, that of *Pratyeka Buddhas*, or distinct intelligences ; 5th, that of *Bodhi-sattwas ;*‡ or a little differently, 1st, the less *Yána*, or translation of men and Gods ; 2nd, that of the *Shrawakas ;* 3rd, that of the *Pratyeka Buddhas ;* 4th, that of *Bodhisattwas ;* 5th, that of *Buddhas* or the *great translation, Maha Yána.*§ The triple division however is the most usual and that which most frequently occurs in ordinary Buddhist writings.

It is to the *Tri yana* that the double metaphor is applied of the *three cars* and the *three animals* swimming a river. The *car* is to be taken here as the emblem of that which *advances by revolving*, or that which serves as a vehicle ; and the idea is connected with that attached to *Yána*, and the means by which man may escape from the world, and enter upon *nirvána.* To the first car is yoked a *sheep*, an animal which in flight never looks back to observe whether it be followed by the rest of the flock. And thus it represents the *Shráwakas*, a class of men who seek to escape from the three worlds by the observation of the four realities ; but who occupied solely with their own salvation, pay no regard to that of other men. The second car is drawn by *deer ;* animals which can look back upon the herd that follow them. This is typical of the *Pratyeka Buddhas*, who, by their knowledge of the twelve *Nidánas*,‖ effect their own emancipation from the circle of the three worlds, and at the same time neglect not the salvation of other men. The third car is drawn by an *ox*, which typifies the *Bodhisattwas* of the doctrine of the three *Pitakas*, (see note 22, Chap. XVI.) who practice the six means of salvation, and seek the emancipation of others without regard to themselves, as the ox endures with patience whatever burthen is imposed upon him.¶

The three animals swimming a river, are the *elephant*, the *horse*, and the *hare*. The river is emblematical of *pure reason ;* the three classes above noted, the Shrávakas, the Pratyeka Buddhas, and the Bodhisattwas, equally emerge from the three worlds, and bear testimony to pure reason ; but their faculties and their dignity vary in extent. Thus

* See *Nouveau Journ. Asiat.* Vol. VII. p. 260.
† *Hoa yan king sou ;* book I. *Thian taï sse kiao yi tsi chu ;* book VII. p. 3.
‡ *Yu lan pan king sou ;* book XXII. p. 17. v.
§ *Hoa yan, ki ching kiao i ;* book XXII. p. 16.
‖ *Observations sur quelques points ;* p. 58.
¶ *Fa houa king ;* book II.

when an elephant, a horse, and a hare cross a river together, they each sink to greater or less depths in the stream : the *elephant*, touching the bottom, resembles the *Bodhisattwa*, practising the six means of salvation, and benefitting all creatures by ten thousand virtuous actions; suppressing the errors of sight and of thought, the effects of custom and of passion, and making manifest the doctrine (*bodhi*). The *horse* sinking deep, but not reaching the bottom of the stream, is the *Pratyeka*, who by the means aforesaid, suppresses the errors of sight and thought, as well as the effects of prejudice and passion, and manifests the nature of the true vacuum without attaining to absolute purity. The third is the *hare*, which floating on the surface of the stream without the power of penetrating deep, typifies the *Shráwaka*, who practises the four realities, and suppresses the errors of thought and sight, without being able to emancipate himself entirely from the influence of passion and prejudice.*

A complete exposition of all that is understood by the observances of these various classes would be nothing short of a treatise of Buddhism, and would far exceed the limits of a note; suffice it that these modes of *translation* are so many probationary steps by which men are led to a higher or a lower grade in the psychological hierarchy extending from inferior beings to the absolute. The *less translation* consists in the observance of the precepts and the rites of religion. The five precepts and the ten virtues are the *vehiculum* of this *translation*, by which men and Gods escape the four *evil grades*, namely, the condition of *Asura*, that of demons, that of brutes, and that of hell, remaining still, however, in the whirlpool of transmigration. In the *mean translation* three orders of persons effect their emancipation from the circle of the three worlds, either by listening to the oral instructions of Buddha (*Shráwakas*), or in meditating upon individual vicissitudes and the true void of the soul (*Pratyeka Buddhas*), or by the help of the ten means of salvation which draw all men along with them beyond the circle of the three worlds (*Badhisattwas*). Lastly, in the *great translation* the understanding, arrived at its highest point of perfection, conducts all living beings to the condition of Buddha.† Explained according to European notions, the *less translation* consists in morality and external religious observance; the *mean*, in traditional or spontaneous psychological arrangements; and the *great translation* in an abstruse, refined, and highly mystical theology.

* *Thian taï sse kiao i*, and *Fa houa hiuan yi*, quoted in *the San tsang fa sou*; book XI. p. 12.

† *Hoa yan*; the chapter upon *The One Revolution*, quoted in the *San tsang fa sou;* book XXII. p. 16.

It may be readily conceived that Buddhist nations would attain to higher or lower degrees on the *translation* scale as their dispositions might be more or less contemplative, or their intellectual condition more or less refined. Those to the north of the Himálayan range preferred, according to the Chinese, the *less translation*, that is morals and mythology, as most consistent with their nomadic and warlike habits; while the softer people of the south, devoted to speculative reveries under the influence of a more genial climate, generally aspired to the higher study of the *great translation*, and sought to propagate its doctrines amongst the neighbouring nations.* We thus see how the monks of any monastery might devote themselves at option to the study of either, and may comprehend how the Buddhists distinguished their sacred works into those which contained the most exalted and refined dogmas of their theology, and those of mere morality and symbolical myths. Hence the nine kinds of Books (*Sutra*, *Geya*, *Gathá*, *Itihasa*, *Jataka*, *Adbhutadharma*, *Udana*, *Vaipulia*, *Vyákárana*), were divided into two classes; those appertaining to the *great* and those to the *less* translation. Finally, this explains the distinction vaguely alluded to by previous writers, of a popular and an esoteric doctrine in Buddhism, both attributed to Sákya Muni himself.† We shall hereafter have occasion to recur to this subject. R.

(5) *The laity*,—in Chinese *Soú jin*, common people. This word occurs already in the preceding sentence, but its religious application in this place is evident from its antithesis to *Sha men*, Samaneans. R.

(6) *Sha men*,—the Chinese transcription of the Sanscrit word *Srámana*, in its Pali from *Sámana*. The meaning of the word, according to Chinese authors is, *one who restrains his thought*, or *one who strives and restrains himself*.‡ According to others it is the common name of Buddhists or heretics. The ancients knew the term and transcribed it with exactness.§

The *Sha men* are characterised by the following denominations:—1st, *Shing tao Sha men;* those who accomplish the doctrine, that is to say, in sight of Buddha embrace a religious life, attain to the extinction of all cupidity, the dissipation of ignorance and of all other imperfections, and so work out the principles of the doctrine. 2d, *Shoue tao Sha men;* those who having obtained for themselves its advantages, are in a condition to promulgate the

* *Chi tou lun*, book XXXIII.

† See Marini, *Relation du royaume de Tunquin*; p. 197. Georgi, *Alph. Tibet.* 223, &c. *Geschichte der ost Mongolien*, p. 16. 356. *Hist. des Huns*; Vol. II. p. 224. Hodgson, *Transact. Roy. As. Soc.* Vol. II. p. 254.

‡ Klaproth, *Asiatic Journal*, new series; Vol. VI. p. 263. *San tsang fa sou*, book XVI. p. 7 v. and XXXIII. p. 24 *et pass.*

§ Strabo, Lib. XV. Porphyr. *de Abstin*, &c.

true Law, and to induce others to enter upon the path of Buddha. 3d. *Hoai tao Sha men*, those who overthrow the Law by infringing its principles, practising all manner of wickedness, and boasting of *conducting themselves Bráhmanically*, when they do quite the reverse. 4th, *Ho tao Sha men;* those who revive the doctrine, or who are the *living doctrine;* inasmuch as having extinguished desire, dissipated ignorance, and practised all manner of good deeds, they aggrandise the established law and subdue their senses by knowledge (*prájna*).*—R.

"*Shama*, is a word of the Sanscrit language, signifying compassionate feeling; that is to say, to feel compassion for those who walk in the wrong way, to look benevolently on the world, to feel universal charity, and to renovate all creatures. This word means also, to observe one'sself with the utmost diligence, or to endeavour to attain Nihility."—*Laws of the Shamans, translated from the Chinese by Neumann.*—J. W. L.

(7) *The law of India,*——*Thian chu fa Thian chu*, is the ordinary name of India in Chinese books. It is written with a character which is most likely an abbreviation of *tü*, and should therefore be read *Thian tou*, which is one form of the many names *Shin tou*, *Hian teou*, *Sin theou*, *Youan tou*, *Yin tou*, all transcriptions more or less altered of *Sin theou*, Sinde, Hind, Hindú, which according to the Chinese, signify the *moon.*†—R.

The word *Thian chu*, designating India, is quoted for the first time in Chinese annals in the 8th year of the reign of the emperor *Ning ti*, of the Han dynasty; corresponding with 65 B. C. This name is found neither in the *King*, nor in any work anterior to that period.—Kl.

(8) *A barbarous language;*—in the text *hou yu.* This expression is usually applied to the language of the Tartars and other partially civilized people. Fa hian's remark would lead one to believe that the people who inhabit the country to the west of the Lake of Lob, belonged to separate races, having each peculiar idioms, without reference to the Indian tongue which religion had introduced into these countries. These languages must have been the Tibetan, the Turkish, and certain Getic and other unknown dialects. It is doubtful whether at that period any Mongul nation had advanced in this direction.—R.

(9) *The books of India and the language of India;*—in all probability the Sanscrit. We are ignorant whether in those times the works of the Buddhists were written in Pali. The latter idiom is well distinguished from the Sanscrit by differences of which the nature of the Chinese language did not permit the representation in the transcript. We are led to infer therefore that

* *Yu kia sse ti lan*, quoted in the *San tsang fa sou*, Book XVI. p. 7.

† *Pian i tian*, Book LVIII.

the *Fan** language was indifferently the Sanscrit or the Pali. There is reason further to believe that the books which the Chinese obtained in the northern parts of India were in Sanscrit, those from the south, in Pali. Fa hian, who studied the language to enable him to understand and copy the sacred works, throws no light upon this point, although he visited so many monasteries from the north of India to Ceylon.—R.

As the religion of Sákya, unlike that of Bráhmanism, was one of conversion, and not of exclusion, and as it was propagated with ardour by its founder and his immediate disciples, it necessarily follows that the language in which they addressed the multitude must have been that best understood by the latter. Was it then the Sanscrit? At the time of penning the foregoing note, the lamented Remusat was necessarily ignorant of James Prinsep's splendid discoveries, which satisfactorily establish the fact that the most ancient epigraphic monuments in all parts of India, from Girinar in Guzerat to Dhaulí in Cuttack, are Buddhist in substance, and Pálí in language. The inference from this is irresistible, and scarcely needs confirmation from other sources, that the Pálí, (the present and the traditional sacred tongue of Buddhism,) was the popular language of that faith in its earliest ages, and was anciently spoken, or at least understood, throughout all India. This conclusion is further borne out by the internal evidence of the language itself, which, so far being rude and uncultivated as prejudices imbibed from bráhmanical sources led European scholars to suppose, (and amongst others the accomplished Colebrooke, see As. Res. Vol. VII. p. 199) appears to have attained a very high degree of refinement, even so far back as the time of Sákya Muní himself. But upon this subject, I cannot do better than quote the opinion of that most competent authority, the Hon. Mr. Turnour, who thus sums up a short historical and critical notice of the Pálí: "The foregoing observations, coupled with the historical data, to which I shall now apply myself, will serve, I trust, to prove that the Pálí or Magadhi language had attained the refinement it now possesses, at the time of Gotamo Buddha's advent. No unprejudiced person, more especially a European who has gone through the ordinary course of a classical tuition, can consult the translation of the Báláwátáro, without recognizing in that elementary work, the rudiments of a precise and classically defined language, bearing no inconsiderable resemblance, as to its grammatical arrangement, to the Latin; nor without indeed admitting that little more is required than a copious and critical dictionary, to render the acquisition of that rich, refined, and poetical language the Pálí, as facile as the attainment of Latin." (*Mahavanso; Introd.* p xxvii.)

The Buddhists of Ceylon are apt, however, to claim for their venerated

* *Pian i tian*, page 2.

Pálí both *greater antiquity* and *higher refinement* than the Sanscrit ; and "in support of this belief," says Mr. Turnour, "they adduce various arguments which, in their judgment, are quite conclusive. They observe that the very word 'Pálí' signifies original, text, regularity; and there is scarcely a Buddhist Pálí scholar in Ceylon, who in the discussion of this question will not quote, with an air of triumph, their favorite verse,—*Sa Mághadi ; múla bhásá, naráyéyáde kappiká, brahmánó chassuttálápá, Sambuddháchápi bhásaré : 'There is a language which is the root (of all languages) ; men and bráhmans at the commencement of the creation, who had never before heard nor uttered a human accent, and even the Supreme Buddhas, spoke it : it is Magadhi.'* This verse is a quotation from Kachcháyanó's grammar, the oldest referred to in the Pálí literature of Ceylon." (*Ibid*, p. xxii.)

The superior antiquity of the Pálí has been maintained with great ingenuity of argument by Lieut.-Col. Sykes, "On the Religious, Moral, and Political state of ancient India," (J. R. A. S. Vol. VI.) but we must beware of adopting his opinions, which are adverse to those of every Sanscrit scholar of eminence, and are especially untenable, since the publication of the Behistun inscriptions by Major Rawlinson, in which we have monumental evidence of the high antiquity of a language clearly derived from the Sanscrit.—J. R. A. S. Vol. X.

The Pálí continues to this day to be the sacred language of religion in all Buddhist countries, at least in those south of the Himálayas. Even in China, according to Mr. Gutzlaff, that tongue is employed in the daily service of the temples ; although Medhurst, perhaps erroneously, states it to be the Sanscrit ; a language which, except in a very corrupted form, the organs of the Chinese are wholly unable to pronounce. (*China, its State and Prospects ;* page 206.)—J. W. L.

(10) *Ou i ;*—the barbarians of *Ou :* the Ouigours.—R.

In a letter recently received from my friend Capt. Alexander Cunningham, now in command of the Expedition to Chinese Tartary, that gentleman identifies the country of the *Ouigours* with the *Serica* of classical authors, and gives several reasons for so doing. "The first of these is, says Capt. C., that the road leading to Serica lay over the Komedan mountains, at *the source of the Oxus*. This name still existed in A. D. 640, when Hiuan thsang visited India ; for he mentions *Kiu mi tho* on the northern bank of the Oxus, along with *Po mi lo*, or Pamer, and *Po lu lo*, or Bolor. The next is that the Essedones (*magna gens*, as Ptolemy calls them), derive their name from the Gallic word *Esseda*, a chariot, or wagon. Now the people of the country around Beshbalik were called by the Chinese *Kio chchang* from *Kio che*, a high-wheeled wagon, (*quære*, origin of *coach?*) These people call themselves *Ouigours*, who are the Ουιγουροί of the time of the emperor Justin, and the Ιθαγουροί or Ηταγουροί of Ptolemy, which we may safely change to Ουιγουροί, the Ouigours, who, as their Chinese appellation of Kio tshang, (wagoners,) intimates, were the same as the Essedones. The Sera metropolis must have been Beshbalik, the capital of the Ouigours. The Psitaras river of Pliny, must simply be the *Sutarini*, or the river Tarini, that is the united streams of the Kashgar, Yarkand, and Khoten rivers." See also Wilson, *Ariana Antiqua*, pp. 212, 213.—J. W. L.

(11) The *Land of Thsin*.—By this name the whole of China is designated; it is also the name of a dynasty of the third century before our era, the first known to Western nations, who thence derived the various denominations of Sinæ, Θίναι, China, Chinistan. But in the time of our traveller, a number of petty dynasties established in Shen si, revived the name of *Thsin* in that country, where it originated. Fa hian having set out from Shen si, without doubt alludes to these dynasties when he gives to these Chinese monks the name of monks of *Thsin*.—R.

Although Fa hian evidently alludes to China proper upon this occasion, yet it must be remembered that the names *Thsin, Thsi, Chin, Tsin, &c.* were applied to other countries long prior to the dynasty of Thsin, which occupied the throne of China from B. C. 245 to 208. This is a point of great importance to keep in mind; for Klaproth and, after him, Col. Sykes (J. R. A. S. Vol. VI. p. 435) infer from the mention of the *Chinas* in the Laws of Menu (Chapter X. v. 44) that the date of that work was subsequent to the Thsin dynasty. Lassen has learnedly discussed this subject in the *Zeitschrift für die kunde des Morgenlandes*, Vol. II. p. 30—33 (a volume, I regret to say, missing from our shelves); and has shown that the word *Thsin* is not necessarily derived from the dynasty of that name, but was applied to various states about the time of the Emperor Wou Wang, B. C. 1122. In the Rámáyana the *Chinas* are associated with the nations inhabiting the neighbourhood of Kashmír. (See Troyer *Esquisse du Kachmír*, affixed to his edition of the Rája Taringini, p. 322, note 10.) Wilson (*Vishnu Purana*, p. 376, note 18.) in vindicating of the antiquity of Menu and the Rámáyana, supposes the word *China* to be a modern interpolation. But Lassen's researches seem very satisfactorily to establish the integrity of the text; and so demolish at a blow all theories built upon the supposed anachronism.—J. W. L.

(12) *Kao chhang*.—The country of the Ouigours, corresponding pretty accurately to the site of the present town of the Turfan, began to bear this designation under the Weï,* that is about the third century.—R.

* *Wen hian thoung khao*, Book CCCXXXVI. p. 13, v.

CHAPTER III.

The Kingdom of Yu thian.

Happy and flourishing is the kingdom of *Yu thian.*[1] The inhabitants live in the midst of great abundance. All, without exception, honor the Law, and it is the Law that ensures them the felicity they enjoy. Several times ten thousand ecclesiastics are reckoned amongst them, many of whom are devoted to the *great revolution.*[2] All take their repast in common. The people of the country determine their abode according to the stars. Before the gate of every house they erect little towers.[3] The smallest of these may be about two toises in height. They erect monasteries[4] of a square form, where strangers are hospitably entertained, and find every thing requisite for their comfort.

The king of this country lodged Fa hian and his companions in a *Seng kia lan.*[5] This *Seng kia lan* is called *Kiu ma ti.*[6] It is a temple of the *great translation*, containing three thousand ecclesiastics. These take their meals in common on a signal struck.[7] On entering the refectory their countenances are grave and sedate. They sit, each according to his rank, in order and in silence. They make no noise with their cups or their platters. These pure persons speak not to each other during meals, but signalise with their fingers.

Hoeï king, Tao ching, and *Hoeï tha,*[8] departed in advance and directed their steps to the kingdom of *Kie chha.*[9] Fa hian and the rest, who were anxious to witness the Procession of Images, remained behind for three months and some days. There are in this kingdom fourteen great *Seng kia lan,* and it is impossible to reckon the number of smaller ones. On the first day of the fourth moon[10] they sweep and water all the streets of the town, and they adorn and set in order the roads and the squares. They spread tapestry and hangings before the gate of the city. All is ornamented and magnificently arranged. The king, the queen, and many elegant ladies are stationed at this place. The monks of *Kiu ma ti*, being those devoted to the study of the *great translation*, are most honored by the king, and take, therefore, the lead in the Procession of Images. At the distance of three or four *li* from the town is constructed a four-wheeled car for the Images, about three toises[11] in height, in the form of a moveable pavilion, adorned with the seven precious things, with hangings, and curtains, and coverlets of silk. The Image[12] is placed in the middle; on either side are two *Phou sa*;[13] while around and behind are the images of the Gods. All are carved in silver and in gold, with precious stones suspended in the air. When the Image is one hundred paces from the gate, the king despoils him of his diadem, dresses in new garments, and advancing barefoot, and holding in his hands perfumes and flowers, issues from the town accompanied by his retinue to march in front of the Image. He prostrates himself at its feet, and adores it, scattering flowers and burning incense. At the moment when the Image enters the town, the ladies and the young damsels in the pavilion above the gate, scatter from all sides a profusion of every variety of flowers, so that the car is completely concealed with them.

There are different kinds of cars for each ceremonial, and each *Seng kia lan* enacts the Procession of Images on a particular day. This ceremony commences on the 1st day of the 4th moon, and the Procession of the Images is concluded on the 14th day, when the king and his ladies return to the palace.

At seven or eight *li* west from the town there is a *Seng kia lan*, called the *New Temple of the King*. Eighty years were occupied in building it, and the reigns of three kings were required to complete it. It may be twenty-five toises[14] in height. There are to be seen many ornaments and sculptures on plates of gold and of silver. The most precious materials were brought together for the construction of the tower. A chapel, dedicated to Foe, has since been erected, and exquisitely adorned; the beams, the pillars, the folding doors, the lattices, all are overlaid with plates of gold. Cells for the ecclesiastics are constructed separately, so beautiful and so highly decorated, that words fail to describe them. The princes of the six kingdoms situated to the east of the chain of mountains,[15] send thither as oblations every thing precious in their possession, and alms so abundantly, that but a portion only is called into requisition.

NOTES.

(1) *The kingdom of Yu thian.*—This is the town of Khotan, one of those in Tartary which adopted the religion of Buddha and observed its rites with the greatest magnificence. The name of this town is not derived from the Mongol word *Khotán* (a town), as was long supposed; but from two Sanskrit words, as I have elsewhere shown, *Kou Stana*, signifying the breast (mamma) of the earth. Many names and expressions borrowed from Sanscrit, and naturalised by religion, begin to show themselves already.—R.

(2) *The great translation.* See note 4, chapter II.

(3) *Small towers.*—The Chinese term here translated tower, corresponds with the Sanskrit word *sthupa,** signifying *tumulus:* but in the language of the Buddhists, this term is applied to buildings of seven, nine, and even thirteen stories, erected on spots where the relics of saints or of gods were deposited. Such towers are frequently mentioned in the course of his narrative by Fa hian. Other accounts, itineraries, and legends, make frequent allusion to similar towers. Their dimensions vary greatly; those here spoken of were but two Chinese toises high, or 6.120 metres (about 20 ft.) Many far smaller ones, miniature models of these, are also mentioned, and were perhaps used for the purposes of private devotion. On the other hand, a tower is spoken of in Gandhára, 700 Chinese feet high, or 216 metres, twice the height of the Pinnacle of the Invalids at Paris.—R.

(4) *Monasteries,*—in the original *Seng fang,* "a house for the ecclesiastics." Other expressions are more common. See next note.—R.

(5) *Seng kia lan.*—This word, borrowed from the Sanskrit, appears here for the first time, and must be explained. Chinese authors explain it to mean *gardens,* or *garden of several,* or *garden of the community.*† *Garden* implies habitation in the language of Buddhism. *Kia lan* is also used by abbreviation; but it cannot mean the *garden of several,* whatever the dictionary of Khang hi may assert to the contrary. I have submitted these transcriptions and interpretations to M. E. Burnouf, who proposes the restoration of *Seng kia lan* by the Sanscrit word *Sangá gáram* the *house of the*

* *Khang hi Tseu tian* ad verb. *Tha,* rad. XXXII.
† *San tsang fa sou,* passim.

union, or of *united priests*. However this may be, the *Seng kia lan* is the abode of the *Feou thou*,* that is of Buddha and the Sangas; it is at once temple and monastery, in Sanscrit *Vihára;* and the part of the building where objects of worship are exposed to the adoration of the faithful, is denominated a *Chaitya*. The Tibetans call their monasteries d*Gan-pa*. A description of these temples may be found in the work of Georgi,† and representations of them in the plates annexed to Mr. Hodgson's Memoir.‡—R.

Wilson, whose authority on such a subject is of great weight, suggests. (J. R. A. S. Vol. V. p. 110) other and more probable etymologies of *Seng kia lan*, in the Sanscrit words *Sangáloya*, or *Sankhyalaya ; álaya* signifying habitation or receptacle; and *Sanga*, a community, or *Sankhya*, number; or *Sangavihára :* which Chinese organs would pronounce *vehala*. To judge from the analogy of sound, the first of these appears the most plausible etymology. —J. W. L.

(6) *Kiu ma ti*.—Evidently a Sanscrit word; perhaps Gômati, from *Go*, a cow. This is the original name of the river Goomty (Gómati) in Oude.—R.

(7) *A signal struck*.—In the text *Khian chhouï ;* meaning either a plate of metal, stone, or wood, which emits a sound on being struck, and thus serves to summon an assembly.—R.

Wooden bells are used to this day in China. Neumann "visited the Hoe chung monastery at Canton when another European wished to try the effects of this wooden roller. The Chinese *Ciceroni* however, recommended the gentleman by all means to avoid it, lest it might bring all the priests of the monastery into the refectory." *Catechism of the Sramans*, p. 105. Wooden bells with clappers are elsewhere described by the same author. Porphyry (Lib. IV.) speaks of the Samaneans (Σαμαναῖοι) regulating their actions by the sound of a bell.—J. W. L.

(8) *Hoeï thá :*—one of the companions of Fa hian, whose name, not enumerated before, signifies *Intelligent Penetration*.—R.

(9) *The country of Kié chha*. See note 7, Chapter V.

(10) *The 1st day of the fourth moon*.—If, as is not improbable, Fa hian reckons after the Chinese calendar, this ceremony must have begun on the 4th June, and continued to the 18th.—R.

Or if Fa hian be supposed to have adopted the Indian calendar, it began on the *first of the moon of Assar ;* a matter of some little importance, as will be seen by and bye. At the time of our traveller's passage through India the year commenced in the month of Chaitra. (Prinsep's Tables, 2d part, p. 18.)—J. W. L.

* *Kang hi Tseu tian* ; vide *kia*.

† *Alph. Tibet*. page 407.

‡ *Trans. R. A. S.* Vol. II. pp. 245, 257.

(11) *Three toises,* about 9.180 m. or about 30 English feet in height. The cars used in India at the present time have, according to the testimony of travellers, fully this elevation.—R.

(12) *The Image.*—Fa hian does not particularise the divinity whose image was paraded on this occasion; most probably it was that of a Buddha; but we have not sufficient information on the state of Buddhism at Khotan in the fifth Century to enable us to decide whether this object of worship was a terrestrial Buddha, like Sákya Muni, or divine one, like Amitabha; or in short, whether it was BUDDHA par excellence. The circumstance to be spoken of in the next note, renders the last supposition the more probable, in as much as *Kiu ma ti* was a monastery of the great revolution.—R.

(13) *Two Phou sa.*—The principal image had on each side those of two *Phou sa* or *Bodhisattwas.* Taking this account literally, it would appear that the God was accompanied by two inferior divinities, perhaps Bodhisattwas; but it is more probable that Buddha had on each hand the two acolytes of the Supreme Triad, *Dharma* and *Sanga.** Others of the abundant triads of Buddhism may also be adduced, as the three Bodhisattwas, *Manjusri, Vajrá pani* and *Padmapani;* or else *Amitabha, Sakya muni,* and *Maïtreya,* &c. The gods whose images were placed at a greater distance from the principal figure, are called *Thian* in the text; these are the *Devas* of the Hindus, the *Lha* of Tibet, the *Tægri* of the Mongols; such as *Indra, Brahma,* and other divinities of the Brahmanical pantheon, far inferior in the system of the Buddhist, to the pure or purified Intelligences, the Buddhas, Bodhisattwas, &c.—R.

The reader cannot fail to be struck with the very close resemblance betwixt the Bauddha procession here described and that of Jagannáth, of which indeed it requires no great stretch of the imagination to suppose it to be the model and prototype. The time of the year at which the ceremony took place, corresponds, as we have seen above, very closely with that of the Rath Játrá, and the duration of the festival was about the same. The principal image with its supporters on either hand, seems the very counterpart of Jagannáth, Balarám and Subhadrá; and when we further bear in mind that the famous temple at Púrí is supposed to stand on the site of an ancient Buddhist Chaitya; that the annual festival is accompanied by that singular anomaly, the *suspension of all caste* for the time being; and lastly, that the image contains the *supposed relics* of Krishna,—a feature entirely abhorrent from Hindúism, but eminently characteristic of

* See the plates accompanying Mr. Hodgson's Memoir, *Trans. R. A. S.,* Vol. II.

Buddhism,—I think we can scarcely doubt that the procession of Jagannáth had its origin in the observances of the latter faith.—J. W. L.

(14) *Twenty-five toises*, about 76.500 metres; a little less than the height of the Pantheon at Paris.—R.

About 250 English feet. Although the great size attributed to these monasteries and *Sthupas* may have an air of exaggeration, yet the good faith of our simple-minded pilgrim must not be lightly impugned upon these grounds. The remains of Buddhist structures visible to this day, go far to confirm Fa hian's statements. The height of the *Ruanwelle Dagoba* in Ceylon, originally 270 feet, was still 189 feet when visited by Major Forbes in 1828; that of the *Abhayagiri* is 240 feet; and that of the *Jaitauanarámaya* (originally 315 feet high) the same. (See Knighton, *on the Ruins of Anuradhapura, in Ceylon;* J. A. S. Vol. XVI. p. 213.)—J. W. L.

(15) *The chain of mountains.*—The mountains here spoken of are the *Tsoung ling*, or the Onion Mountains, to the west of Khotan, a chain which crossing in a north and south direction, rejoins the mass of the Himalaya. It will be seen further on that Fa hian gives a name equivalent to that of Himalaya, to various ranges ordinarily bearing different denominations. As to the six kingdoms situated to the east of the chain, the princes of which sent to the *new temple of the king* magnificent offerings, Fa hian designates them in no precise manner; but without doubt *Shen shen*, *Ou hou*, and *Kao chhang*, countries he had traversed, and in which Buddhism was established, were three of them; the remaining three were probably situated between the Desert and the Onion Mountains.*—R.

CHAPTER IV.

Kingdom of the Tseu ho.—Tsoung ling mountains.—Kingdom of Yu hoeï.

After the fourth moon, the ceremony of the Procession of Images being concluded, *Seng shao* set out alone in the suite of a barbarian priest[1] proceeding to *Ki pin*.[2] Fa hian and the rest proceeded towards the kingdom of *Tseu ho*.[3] They travelled for twenty-five days, and at the end of that time arrived in that

* *Wen hian thoung khao*, Book CCCXXXVI. p. 6.

kingdom. The king is firmly attached to the faith.[4] There are in this country about one thousand ecclesiastics, for the most part adherents of the *great translation.* The travellers sojourned there fifteen days, and then proceeded southward; and having marched four days, entered the *Tsoung ling*[5] mountains, and arrived at the kingdom of *Yu hoeï*,[6] where they halted. Having refreshed themselves, they resumed their journey, and in twenty-five days they reached the kingdom of *Kie chha,* where they rejoined *Hoeï king* and the others.

NOTES.

(1) A *barbarian priest.*—*Tao jin* is a synonyme of *Tao sse;* a name given to the sectarians of *Lao tseu* and of the doctrine of *Tao,* or *Supreme Reason.* I know not why M. Remusat has translated this word, a barbarian priest.—Kl.

On showing the original characters to a Chinese friend, he unhesitatingly explained them to mean a *priest,* ("padre,") and not a *traveller*, as MM. Klaproth and Landresse would rather interpret them. See the last note to Chapter XL.—J. W. L.

(2) *Ki pin,*—Cophene, or the country watered by the Cophes. Rennell supposed the affluent of the Indus, so named by the ancients, to be identical with the *Cowmull;* Saint-Croix believes it rather to be the *Merhamhir.* The syllable Cow is probably a remnant of the ancient appellation. *Ki pin,* which Chinese authors confound with Cashmere,* and which Deguigne has taken for Samarcand, supposing the latter to be identical with *Kaptchak,* corresponds with the country of Ghizneh and Candahar. It is celebrated in Chinese Geography, and appears to have been a flourishing seat of Buddhism.—R.

The *Gômal,* (not *Cowmull*) rises at *Durchelly,* in the country of Ghizneh, to the south of Sirefza; and runs at first towards the south-west, but soon turning to the south, pursues that course towards *Domendi,* where it receives the river *Murrunye* and the *Kondour,* which has its source in the neighborhood of Tirwa. Thence the Gômal proceeds easterly to Sirmâgha, where it is joined by the *Zhobi;* a river nearly as large as the Gômal itself, rising in the mountains of *Kend,* east of *Berchori,* and running to a district to which it gives its name. A little to the east of Sirmâgha, the Gômal crosses the chain of the Suliman mountains, passes before Raghzi, and ferti-

* *Pian i tian,* Book LIII.

lises the country inhabited by the tribes of Daulet Khaîl and Gandehpur. It dries up in the defile of Pegou, and its bed is supplied with water only in the rainy season, when it rejoins the right of the Indus to the south east of the town of Paharpour.—Kl.

The Cophen of the ancients is not, as Rennell and the French Editors suppose, the Gômal, an inconsiderable mountain stream, dry all the year except at the season of the periodical rains. The Cabul River is the only one that corresponds with the accounts given of the Cophen by the historians of Alexander, particularly Arrian, who describes it as falling into the Indus in the country of Peukelaotis and carrying along with it the tributary waters of the Malantus, Suastus, and Garæus. (Indica IV. 11.) Some of these names will be identified hereafter from the narrative of our pilgrim and the Itinerary of Hiuan tshang.

It will be seen from the text that there were two routes to the country watered by the Cophen ; *Seng shao* most probably took the westerly or more direct one ; while Fa hian and the rest proceeded to the same country by the more circuitous route of the Indus and Peshawar. Why this separation took place is not stated, nor does it appear that Seng shao ever after rejoined the little band. He was one of those whom our pilgrim overtook at *Chang y.*—J. W. L.

(3) *Tseu ho.*—This country is placed by Fa hian at the distance of twenty-five days march from Khotan ; but the direction is not stated. On considering the route which our travellers would in all probability follow, and the positions they afterwards attained, I have traced this portion of their journey south-westerly from Khotan. Chinese Geographers identify the name of *Tseu ho*, which seems to signify the "*unions of sons*," with that of *Chu kiu pho*, or *Chu kiu phan*, words apparently derived from the Sanskrit. In the absence of other information I shall here transcribe the details touching this subject, found in the Chinese collections.*

"The country of *Tseu ho* has been known since the time of the latter Han, (3d century). It formerly constituted a single kingdom with that of *Si ye* ("*western night*"), but at present the two states have independent kings. The residence of the king of Tseu ho is called the *Valley of Kian* ; it is 1000 *li* (100 leagues) from *Sou lé* and Khachgar ; and contains 350 families and 4000 soldiers.†

"Under the Weï of the north, in the third year *King ming* (502) in the 12th moon, there came tribute from the country of *Chu kiu phan.* This country is to the west of *Ju thian* (Khotan). Its inhabitants live in the midst of

* *Pian i tian*, Book LX.
† *Notice of Western Countries*, quoted in the *Pian i tian*, p. 1.

mountains. There are corn and plenty of wild fruits. The whole population observes the Law of Foe. The language is the same as that of Khotan. This state is subject to the *Ye tha* (Getæ). Another tribute came in the 4th year, *Young phing* (511) 9th moon.*

"The *Chu kiu pho*, called also *Chiu kiu phan*, sent tribute in the years *Wou te* (618—626); this is the country designated *Tseu ho*, under the Han dynasty. There are four countries, known since the time of the Han, which are united to it, namely, *Si ye*, *Phou li*, *Y naï*, and *Te jo*. It is exactly 1000 *li* west from Khotan, and 300 *li* north of the *Tsoung loung* mountains. On the west it is coterminous with the country of *Kho phan tho*; to the north at the distance of 900 *li* is the frontier of *Sou le* (Kashgar). To the south at 3000 *li*, is the Kingdom of Women. It contains 2000 soldiers. The law of *Feou thou* is held in honour. The characters used are those of the bráhmans.†—R.

The position of the kingdom *Tseu ho* is determined in the last edition of the *Tai thsing y thoung chi* (Section 419). It is the present canton of *Kouke yar* (blue scarped bank) situated to the south of Yerkiyang, 70° 40‡ E. of Paris, and 37° 30′ N. Lat. on the right bank of the river *Kará sou* which runs northerly and falls into the *Tiz âb*, or *Tingsa âb osteng*, a right affluent of the *Yerkiyang deria*. This canton being distant five degrees of longitude west from Khotan, and the roads being indirect, it is not surprising that Fa hian should occupy twenty-five days upon the journey. The kingdom of *Chu kiu pho* extends from *Ingachar*, or *Yanghi hissar*, in the present territory of Kashgar, to *Youl arik*, in that of Yerkiyang. It is therefore identical with *Tseu ho*.—Kl.

(4) *Firmly attached to religion.*—The author employs a peculiar expression, borrowed from the ascetic vocabulary of his faith; *tsing tsin*, signifying properly, *efforts towards purity*, *progress in subtle, or holy things*; in Sanskrit *vírya*. It is one of the ten means of attaining absolute perfection, or in the language of Buddhism, of *attaining the other shore*. I have had occasion before to speak of this means or *páramitá*§ (see in particular *Journal Asiatique*, tom. VII. p. 250). Further details will be found in the *Commentaire sur le Vocabulaire Pentaglotte*, by M. E. Burnouf and myself.—R.

(5) *The Tsoung ling mountain.*—We have already seen (Chap. III. note 17) that this chain of hills, detached from the great mass of the Himalaya, runs, according to Chinese Geographers, in a direction nearly due north. Fa hian speaks here no doubt of some branch detached from the great eastern

* *Life of the Emperor Siouan wou ti* quoted in *Pian i tian*, B. LX. p. 1 v.
† *Desc. of Western Countries* quoted in the *Pian i tian*, p. 2.
‡ Quære, 74°?—J. W. L.
§ *Nouv. Jour. Asiatique*, Vol. VII. p. 25 v.

range. Our travellers on, leaving *Tseu ho,* fell in with it after having proceeded four days in a southerly direction. They were fifty-five days in crossing it; and of these thirty were spent in marching towards the west. In the very midst of these mountains they found, as will be seen further on, a kingdom named *Kie chha.*—R.

(6) *The kingdom of Yu hoeï.*—This word is apparently the transcription of some local name; further we know nothing,* nor is the country our travellers describe sufficiently known to furnish us with the means of comparison.—R.

In a subsequent note (7 of Chapter V.) M. Klaproth endeavours to identify *Yu hoeï* with Ladakh, but not very satisfactorily; for if *Tseu ho* be identical with *Kouke yar* it cannot be less than 250 miles direct distance from Ladakh, rendering it thus impossible that our pilgrims should reach the latter place in the short space of four days.—J. W. L.

CHAPTER V.

The kingdom of Kie chha.

The king of *Kie chha* celebrates the *pan che yue sse.*[1] *Pan che yue sse* signifies in Chinese the *great quinquennial assembly.* At the time of this assembly the *Sha men* are invited from all directions. They gather like the clouds, with pomp and gravity. At the place where the clergy sit are suspended hangings, flags, and canopies. A throne is prepared and adorned with lotus flowers of silver and of gold, and elegant seats are arranged below it. Thither the king and his officers repair to perform their devotions according to the Law. This ceremony lasts one month, or two, or three; and generally takes place in spring time.[2] When the king rises from the assembly, he exhorts his ministers to perform their devotions in turn. Some occupy one day in this duty, some two, and some three or five. When all have finished their devotions, the king distributes[3] the horse which he rides, his saddle and his bridle, the horses of the principal officers of his kingdom and of other persons of distinction, as well

* *Pian i tian,* Book LXIII. § 2 and Book LIV.

as all kinds of woollen stuffs and precious things, and all that the *Sha men* may require. All the officers bind themselves by vows, and distribute alms; they then redeem from the ecclesiastics all these donations.

This country is cold and mountainous. No other grain but corn arrives at maturity. As soon as the clergy have received their annual provision of grain, the weather, however fine before, becomes cloudy; the king is accustomed, therefore, to ordain that these shall not receive their annual provision till the harvest arrive at maturity.

There is in this kingdom a vase into which Foe spat; it is of stone, and of the same colour as Foe's begging pot.[4] There is also a tooth of Foe,[5] and in honor of this tooth the people of the country have erected a tower. There are more than a thousand ecclesiastics, all attached to the study of the *less revolution*.

To the east of these mountains the natives dress in coarse habiliments, similar to those of the land of Thsin, except the difference of stuffs of wool and of felt. The *Sha men* conformably to the Law, make use of wheels,[6] the efficacy of which is not to be described.

This kingdom is in the midst of the mountains *Tsoung ling*.[7] On advancing to the south of these mountains, the plants and fruits become quite different; there are but three plants,—the bamboo, the pomegranate, and the sugar-cane,—that resemble those of China.

NOTES.

(1) *Pan che yue sse.* This word is evidently of Sanskrit origin, and means, according to our author, *the great quinquennial assembly.* It is a compound of the Sanskrit radical *pancha*, five [and *yukti*, re-union, assembly. Kl.]—R.

To this etymology Professor Wilson objects that *yukti* is never used to denote an assembly or meeting of men; and he suggests *pancha-varsha*, as the probable reading; *pancha*, five, and *varsha*, a year. The difficulty with regard to this restoration is, that *yue sse* does not appear a very likely transcript of *varsha*; perhaps a more probable Sanscrit etymon is *ayu*, a word employed to signify either a year or the age of a man. Thus the ordinary salutation or blessing of a bráhman of the present day is शतायुभव, 'live a hundred years.' The commentator on the Raghu Vansa in explanation of a passage in the text, पुरुषायुष जीविन्यो, *purushayusha jíbinyo*, observes शतायु वै पुरुष, *Satayu vai purusa*. Hence *panchayusha* would be "five yearly."

As to the *great quinquennial assembly* here spoken of it, it was most probably the very religious festival ordained for perpetual observance in his own dominions by the emperor Asoka, and extended by his influence to neighbouring countries. In his third edict, he says—"Thus spoke the heaven-beloved king Piyadasi: By me after the twelfth year of my anointment, this commandment is made! Everywhere in the conquered provinces among the faithful, whether my own subjects or foreigners, *after every five years*, let there be a public humiliation for this express object, yea for the confirmation of virtue and the suppression of disgraceful acts. Good and proper is dutiful service to mother and father;—towards friends and kinsfolk, towards bráhmans and srámans, excellent is charity; prodigality and malicious slander are not good. All this the leader of the congregation shall inculcate to the assembly with appropriate explanation and example." (Journal As. Soc. Vol. VII. p. 250.) In the original of the foregoing the words signifying every five years are 𑀧𑀁𑀘𑀲𑀼 𑀧𑀁𑀘𑀲𑀼 𑀯𑀲𑁂𑀲𑀼 *panchasu panchasu vasesu*; words which might also very well form the original of the awkward Chinese transcription in our text.—J. W. L.

(2) I believe that this passage should be translated, "either the first month, or the second, or the third, but generally in spring."—Kl.

(3) *Distribution, alms.*—The traveller here employs the consecrated word *pou shi*, equivalent to the Sanscrit term *dána*. This is the first of the ten *páramitá* or means of salvation. See above, Ch. I, note 12, and Ch. IV. note 4.—R.

(4) *The pot of Foe.*—The alms pot is one of the characteristic utensils of a religious mendicant. That used by Sákya Muni during his terrestrial existence, became a very precious relic. It will be spoken of again, Chap XII.—R.

(5) *A tooth of Foe.*—The teeth of Foe are amongst the most celebrated reliques of Buddhism. The history of this religion preserves many facts connected with those precious remains of the body of Sákya Muni.—R.

(6) *Wheels.*—In the text *chhouan*, a circular and revolving object, and not *lun*, (*chakra* in Sanscrit, h*Gorlœ* in Tibetan, and *kurdou* in Mongal.)

The passage may be differently understood, but it probably refers to *praying wheels*, or cylinders to which prayers are affixed, and which are made to revolve with the utmost practicable rapidity, to obtain for the devotee at every revolution, the same merit as the recital of the prayer. A description of this practice may be found in accounts of travellers who have visited Tartary.* The idea of a *wheel*, or of *circular revolution*, is moreover, one of those which recur most frequently in the metaphorical language of Buddhism. We have already seen that this is the proper meaning of the mystical expression *yána* (Chap. II. note 4.) The *wheel* is one of the eight symbols (*vítarâgas* in Sanscrit; *naïman takil*, in Mongol) observed in Buddhist temples.† It is the symbol of supreme power in the hands of those monarchs who are held to have exercised universal dominion, and who are for this reason termed *Chakravarti*, or *turners of the wheel*; it is the emblem of the *transmigration of souls*, which, like a circle, is without beginning or end. It is also the emblem of preaching; and to announce that a Buddha has begun to preach the doctrine, it is said that he has begun to *turn the wheel of the Law.*

Lastly, the different branches of a doctrine, or the different systems embraced by those who adopt them, receive also the name of *wheel*; thus, *the precepts of the wheel of the superior law, of the wheel of the middle law, and of that of the inferior law.* This expression, when it occurs in the narrative of Fa hian, refers most probably to the use of *praying wheels*, which appear at present to be peculiar to the Buddhists of the northern countries. I have found no mention of them in any Indian books that have fallen under my notice; which justifies the remark made by Fa hian in the passage that has elicited this note.—R.

These ingenious and *efficacious* instruments are still used in the countries where Fa hian first saw them, and their construction seems to have attained very great perfection. "On a stream falling into the rivulet," says Moorcroft, "was a small stone building, which at first appeared to be a water mill; but which proved to be a *religious cylinder*, carved and painted, and *turned round by the current.*" (Travels in the Himalayan Provinces, Vol. I. p. 234.) —J. W. L.

(7) The position of *Kie chha*, or according to vulgar pronunciation, *Kiet chha*, or *Ket chha*, is the more difficult to determine, inasmuch as the name is not to be found in any Chinese author known in Europe. M. Remusat thought that in this name he recognised that of Kashmír; but this country is not so cold as Kie chha according to Fa hian's description.

* Pallas, Vol. I. p. 568. Klaproth, *Reise in den Kaukasus*, Vol. I. p. 181, &c.
† Pallas, *Sammlungen hist. Nachrichten*, Vol. II. p. 158. *As. Res.* XVI. p. 460.

It produces, according to Moorcroft, wheat, barley, buckwheat, millet, maze, vegetables, panicum and rice: the last of which, as most cultivated, may be regarded as the principal cereal of the country. Besides, to reach Kashmír from *Tseu ho*, or *Kouke Yar*, Fa hian must have crossed the upper branch of the Indus, which flows from Tibet, and at present bears the name of *Sing chu*, or *Sing dzing Khampa*, and is much more considerable than that which, coming from the north, takes its rise at the southern base of the immense glacier, *Poushti kher*, and is called the *Khámeh* river. In all the mountainous regions of central Asia, the roads which lead across glaciers, or which avoid them by detours, remain almost always the same; rendering it thus probable that the route followed by our traveller, is no other than that which still leads from Khotan and Yerkiyang to western Tibet. This route ascends the upper part of the *Tiz âb* to its source, passes the defile of *Kará koroum*, to the south of which it follows the course of the *Khamdan*, a feeder of the *Shayuk*, and then the course of the latter to Leh, or Ladakh. From this town the traveller proceeds to Baltistan, keeping to the north of the Tibetan branch of the Indus, and we shall see that he only passes the Kámeh much further. Fa hian on leaving *Tseu ho*, or *Kouke yar*, must therefore have followed a southerly direction, the *Kára sou*, to its sources in the Tsoung ling mountains. Thence having first turned to the south-east to reach and ascend the *Tiz âb*, he must have followed the course of the Khamdan and the Shayuk to Ladakh, which appears to be his kingdom of *Yu hoei*. From *Yu hoei* he marched twenty-five days, doubtless in a westerly direction, to *Kie chha*. We must look therefore for this country in Baltistan, which is the *little* or *first* Tibet; or in its neighbourhood.—Kl.

Were M. Klaproth's assumption correct, that there is but one pass towards northern India across this mountain range, and that it proceeds viâ Ladakh, we should be driven to suspect some error in the Chinese narrative which allows but four days for the journey from *Tseu ho* to *Yu hoei*. But such is not the case; it is well known that there are more direct routes towards India from *Kouke yor*, and by one of these we may reasonably infer that our travellers would approach India in preference to that viâ Ladakh, which would lead them so greatly out of their way. In the absence of fuller details we may never be able to determine this portion of Fa hian's course with certainty; but we may conjecture *Yu hoeï* to lie in a southerly or south-westerly direction from *Kouke yar*.

As to *Kie chha*, it were vain to attempt its identification with Kashmír, as this would lead our travellers a yet more unnecessary detour to the eastward, altogether incompatible with their subsequent course. *K'ha-chhé-yul*, or *Kha-chhul*, is indeed the Tibetan name of Kashmír, (Csoma de Körös,

Geograph. Sketch of Tibet, J. A. S. vol. I. p. 122); and *Katch*, or *Katchi* simply, is that applied to the same country by the Bhotees and Kunawarees. See "Notes on Moorcroft's and Gerard's travels," by Capt. J. D. Cunningham, who proceeds to observe—"Mr. Vigne enlarges on the frequent occurrence of the word *Kash;* but without giving it the many geographical positions he does, and even *he* omits some, it is *probable that a tribe of that name once possessed the whole course of the Indus*, if indeed the word has not a more general meaning, and a wider application." (Journal Asiatic Society, Vol. XIII. p. 229.) The emperor Baber, also, mentions a people, named *Kash*, inhabiting the same locality, and suggests this word as the etymology of Kashmír. It is by no means improbable that in these we have the original of *Kie chha ;* a supposition which the concurrence of situation (somewhere near Skardo) seems in some degree to confirm.

Are the people inhabiting this country the *Khasas* of Menu, (B. X. sl. 44, where they are mentioned immediately after the *Daradas ;*) and the *Khasiras*, *Khasikas*, or *Khasakas*, of the Vishnu Purana? (Wilson's translation, page 195.) Troyer (*Esquisse du Kachmir*, page 324) endeavours to identify these people with the *Cesi* of Pliny, whose position as described by that writer, corresponds very well with the supposed situation of *Kie chha*, —*hos includit Indus, montium coronâ circumdatos et solitudinibus.*— J. W. L.

CHAPTER VI.

Tsoung ling Mountains.—Perpetual snow.—Northern India.—The kingdom of Tho ly.—Colossus of Mi le Phou sa.

From the country of *Kie chha*, you advance towards the west in approaching India of the North. It takes one month to cross the *Tsoung ling* mountains. On those mountains there is snow both in summer and in winter. There are also venomous dragons which dart their poison if they happen to miss their prey.[1] The wind, the rain, the snow, the flying sand, and the rolled pebbles oppose such obstructions to travellers, that out of ten thousand that venture there, scarce one escapes! The natives of those parts are designated *Men of the Snowy Mountains.*[2]

On crossing this chain you arrive in India of the North.[3] Immediately on entering the boundaries of this region, you find the kingdom of *Tho ly*,[4] where nearly all the ecclesiastics are of the *less translation*.

There was formerly in this kingdom a *Lo han*,[5] who by an effort of supernatural power,[6] transported a sculptor to the heaven *Teou shou*,[7] to study the stature and the features of *Mi le Phou sa*,[8] and to make on his return, an effigy of him carved in wood. The artist ascended three successive times to contemplate that personage, and afterwards executed a statue eight toises[9] high, the foot of which was eight cubits[10] long. On festival days this statue is always effulgent with light; the kings of the country ardently render all homage to it. It still exists in the same locality.[11]

NOTES.

(1) In the original the passage signifies, as I understand it, "There are also venomous dragons, who if discontent spit their venom." He probably alludes to the vapours and poisonous exhalations which infest the valleys of the Himálaya and the mountains of Tibet.—Kl.

(2) *Men of the Snowy Mountains.*—We recognise in this name that of the mountains of the Indian Caucasus, covered with perpetual snow; in Sanscrit Himálaya. The remainder of the Chinese text is confused, and perhaps corrupted; it is literally: Occurrentium his ærumnis, decies mille, non unus servatur. Istius terræ homines nomine vocantur niveorum montium homines. The difficulty arises from the repetition of the word *jin* (homines.)—R.

I think that the character *yu*, (to meet, fall in with, rencontre) belongs to the preceding sentence, and refers to the wind, rain, snow, the flying sand, and the rolling stones, which the travellers *fell in with;* the meaning then would be, "These obstacles, though innumerable, are none to the people of the country: and these people are called the *people of the Snowy Mountains.*"—Kl.

(3) *India of the North.*—The country called India of the North, *Pe thian chu*, by the Buddhists and the Chinese Geographers who succeeded them, was not comprised in the present limits of Hindostan; the name applies to the countries situated to the N. E. of the Indus, south of the Hindu Kosh

in the eastern part of the country now called Afghanistan. India of the north contains besides *Tho ly* (Darada ?), *Udyana*, *Gandhára*, and other countries to be named further on.—R.

(4) *Tho ly.*—This little country is elsewhere wholly unknown.—R.

M. Remusat has conjecturally identified it with Darada, as will be seen in the preceding note ; upon what grounds, except its situation, I know not. The itinerary of Hiuan Thsang throws no light upon the subject. Professor Wilson, however, seems to concur in Remusat's identification, which, he says, "is better founded than perhaps he is aware ; for Chilas or Dardu, the capital of the Dard country, is situated among the mountains where the Indus enters the main range."—J. W. L.

(5) *Lo han.*—*Lo han*, or more exactly *A lo han*, is the Chinese transcript of the Sanskrit word *Arhan*, venerable. *A lo han* signifies, according to the Chinese, "he who is no more subject to birth, or who has no need of study *(wou seng, wou hio).*" The Arhan is one who has himself arrived at perfection, and who knows how to direct others to it.* He is ten million times superior to the Anágámí ; and a million times inferior to a *Pratyeka Buddha*, according to the scale of merit applied to the different classes of saints ; a scale attributed to Sákya Muni himself.† The Arhans play a very conspicuous part in the Buddhic legends. The Tibetans call them g*Nas-hrtan*, and reckon eighteen principal ones, who figure also in Chinese mythology. Sixteen others are also described, to whom they give the epithet *great*, and who reside in different islands of the terrestrial world.‡ The Arhan here spoken of is called *Mo thian ti kia*, (in Pali *Madhyántika)* according to the report of Hiuan Thsang. See sequel. Chap. VIII.—R.

(6) *Supernatural power,*—literally "*the sufficient strength of the Gods.*" The perfect knowledge of the verities of Buddhism obtains for the saints of this religion ten kinds of power. 1st, They know the thoughts of others. 2d, They possess the pure and piercing sight of the *eyes of heaven* ; i. e. they behold clearly, know without difficulty or obscurity, whatever occurs in the universe. 3d, They know the past and the present. 4th, They know the uninterrupted succession, without beginning and without end, of the *Kalpas* or mundane ages, present and future. 5th, They possess the delicacy of the *ears of heaven*, that is, they hear clearly and distinctly without obstacle or effort, every voice and every sound uttered in the three worlds and the ten parts of the universe, and discern their origin without difficulty. 6th, They are not restricted to corporeal conditions, but can assume at will the forms best adapted for the accomplishment of their purposes. 7th, They distin-

* Hodgson, T. R. A. S. Vol. II. p. 245.
† *Foe shoue sse shi eul chung king*, pp. 4, 5.
‡ *Fa chu ki*, quoted in *San tsang fa sou*, B. XLV. p. 17.

guish with delicacy words of lucky or unlucky import, whether near or distant. 8th, They have the knowledge of forms; knowing that form is vacuity, they can assume all forms; and knowing that vacuity is form, they can annihilate material bodies. 9th, They possess the knowledge of all the Law. 10th, They possess the science of contemplation.*

Amongst the ten great disciples of Sákya Muni, the sixth, named *Moa kian lian*, acquired the greatest amount of supernatural power. The rest shone by the exact observation of the precepts, or the mode in which they preached the doctrine, or expounded spiritual things.†

Supernatural power is called *riddi khoubilgan* by the Mongols. Sanang Setsen reports several instances of its possession.—R.

(7) The *Heaven Teou shou*.—This word, usually transcribed *Teou Sou*, or more correctly *Teou sou tho*, represents the Sanskrit word *Tushita*, and signifies the *abode of joy*. It is one of the paradisaical mansions raised above the material world, and termed in Sanskrit *bhuvana*. *Tushita* is the fourth of these mansions comprised in the *world of desires*, according to the most general classification, and the third of the *Káma vachara* of the Buddhists of Nepaul. As Mr. Hodgson, in his *Sketch of Buddhism*, gives a more ample account of these mansions, I substitute it for the remainder of M. Remusat's note. It is instructive as showing the intimate connection between Bráhmanism and Buddhism, as well as giving a general idea of Buddhist cosmogony.

"With respect to the mansions *(Bhuvanas)* of the universe, it is related that the highest is called *Agnistha Bhuvana;* and this is the abode of A'DI BUDDHA. And below it, according to some accounts, there are ten, and according to others, thirteen *Bhuvanas*, named *Pramóditá, Vimalá, Prabhákarí, Archishmatí, Sudúrjayá, Abhimukhí, Dúrangamá, Achalá, Súdhúmati, Dharma-meghá, Sumant prubhá, Nirúpamá, Jnyánavati.* These thirteen *Bhuvanas* are the work of *A'di Buddha;* they are the *Bodhisatwa-Bhuvanas;* and whoever is a faithful follower of Buddha, will be translated to one of these mansions after death.

Below the thirteen *Bodhisatwa Bhuvanas*, are eighteen *Bhuvanas*, called collectively, *Rúpya Vachara*. These are subject to BRAHMA', and are named individually, *Bramhá Káyiká, Brahmá púróhitá, Brahmá prashádyá, Mahá Brahmaná, Paratabha, Apramánábhá, Abháswará, Parita-subhá, Subha-Kishná, Anabhraká, Púnya-prasavá, Vrihat-phulá, Arangi-Satwá, Aarihá, Apayá, Sudrishá, Sudarsaná*, and *Sumúkhá*. Pious worshippers of Brahmá shall go to one of these eighteen Bhuvanas after death.

* *Hoa yan king*, quoted in the *San tsang fa sou*, Book XXXVIII. p. 18 v.
† *Fan y ming i*, ibid. B. XLI. p. 12 v.

And below the eighteen mansions of Brahmá, are six others, subject to Vishnu', called collectively *Káma-Vachara*, and separately as follows: *Chatúr-Mahá-rája-Kayika, Trayastrinsá, Tushitá, Yamá, Nirmánavatí, Paranirmitá-Vásavarti*. And whoever worships Vishnu with pure heart shall go to one of these. And below the six *bhuvanas* of Vishnu, are the three Bhuvanas of Mahade'va, called generally *Arúpya Vachará*, and particularly as follows: *Abhógá-Nitya-yatnópagá, Vijnyá-yatnópagá, Akinchaya-yatnópagá*; and these are the heavens designed for pious *Siva Márgis*. Below the mansions enumerated, are *Indra Bhuvana, Yama Bhuvana, Surya Bhuvana*, and *Chandra Bhuvana*; together, with the mansions of the fixed stars, of the planets, and various others, which occupy the space down to the *Agni Bhuvana*, also called *Agni-kúnd*. And below *Agni-kund* is *Vayu-kund*; and below *Vayu-kund* is *Prithví*, or the Earth; and on the Earth are the seven *dwípas, Jambu-dwípa*, &c. and seven *Ságaras* or Seas, and eight *Parvatas* or mountains, *Suméra parvata*, &c. And below Prithví is *Jala-kund*, or the world of waters; and the earth is on the waters as a boat. And below Jala-kund are seven Pátálas, as *Dharani*, &c.; six of them are the abodes of the *Daityas*; and the seventh is *Naraka*, consisting of eight separate abodes; and these eight compose the hell of sinners; and from the eighteen *Bhuvanas* of Brahma, down to the eight chambers of *Naraka*, all is the work of Manju'sri. Manjúsri is by the *Bauddhas* esteemed the great architect, who constructs the mansions of the world by A'di Buddha's command, as Padma-Páni by his command creates all animate things." Transactions Roy. As. Soc. Vol. II. pp. 233, 234.—J. W. L.

(8) *Mi le phou sa*, is the Chinese transcription of Maitreya Bodhisattwa. *Mi le* is the abbreviated and very corrupt pronunciation of *Maitreya*, a Sanscrit word, signifying, according to the Chinese, the *Son of goodness*, or *of tenderness*. This personage, who is to succeed Sakya Muni in the character of terrestrial Buddha, was under the name of *Ayi to*, a disciple of the latter. Others assert that he was born in heaven at the epoch of Sákya's entering the religious career, that is to say, at the period when the duration of human life was 100 years. Since then he has remained in the character of Bodhisattwa in *Tushita*, and will continue there till the time of his advent in that of Buddha. This advent, according to a prediction delivered by Sakya to his disciples in the town of *She weï*, will take place at a very remote period when the duration of human life shall extend to eighty-four thousand years; that is to say, after the lapse of five thousand six hundred and seventy millions of years.* The name of the town in which he shall be born, that of the prince his father, and that of the princess his mother,

* *Japanese Cyclopedia*, B. IV. p. 32.

are also announced by Sákya. His father will be named *Sieou fan ma*; his mother *Fau ma youe.* The latter will be the most lovely person in the world, with lips like the flower *ubara* and breath redolent of sandal wood. Maitreya, like Sákya, will be born from his mother's right side. Then the gods, inhabitants of Tushita, will break forth into singing,* &c. Maitreya will live eighty-four thousand years, and the law which he shall establish will have the same duration after his *pari nirvána.*—R.

(9) *Eight toises*;—about 80 English feet.

(10) *Eight cubits*; about 10 or 12 feet.

(11) *It still exists.*—Fa hian here speaks as one who had seen this colossal statue. We shall in the following Chapter see to what era he refers its erection.—R.

CHAPTER VII.

The River Sin theou.

They followed this mountain chain in a south-westerly direction for fifteen days. The road is extremely difficult and fatiguing, abounding in obstacles and dangerous steeps. In those hills are to be seen mural precipices of rock eight thousand feet in height. On approaching them the sight becomes confused; and should the foot of the traveller slip in passing those places, nothing in the world could save him.[1]

At the foot of these hills is a river named the *Sin theou.*[2] The ancients have perforated the rocks to open a passage, and have cut ladders of seven hundred steps. When you have passed these ladders you cross the river by (a bridge of) suspended ropes. The banks of the stream are about four score paces apart. Neither *Chang khian* nor *Kan yng,*[3] under the dynasty of

* *Shin i tian*, B. LXXVIII. p. 3.

the Han, ever reached this point in their travels, of which an account is given by the Interpreters[4] of the Cabinet of Foreign Affairs.

The ecclesiastics asked Fa hian if one might know when the Law of Foe began to spread in the East? Hian replied to them; "I learnt from the people of that country, and they all assured me, that according to the most ancient traditions, it was after the erection of the statue of *Mi le Phou sa* that the *Sha men* of India passed this river, carrying with them the sacred books and the collection of the Precepts." The statue was erected three hundred years after the *Ni houan* of Foe, which by calculation of the years, corresponds with the time of *Phing wang*,[5] of the family of *Cheou*. We may, therefore, affirm that the Great Doctrine began to be propagated and extended at the time of the erection of this statue. Without the assistance of this great master *Mi le*, who could have continued the labours of *Shy kia* and reduced his laws to practice? Who had been able to diffuse the knowledge of the Three Precious Ones,[6] and make it penetrate even to the inhabitants of the world's extremity, teaching them to know with certainty the origin of the mysterious revolution? This is no result of human endeavour. Nor was such the dream of *Ming ti*,[7] of the dynasty of the *Han*.

NOTES.

(1) *Nothing could save him.*—This description of the escarpments in the lofty chain of the Himalaya perfectly corresponds with the accounts of modern travellers, who corroborate this recital of the difficulties which render the passage equally painful and perilous; the peaked rocks, the steps cut in their precipitous sides, the chains extended across valleys, and the suspension bridges.—R.

(2) The river *Sin theou.*—This word signifies, according to Chinese interpretation, the *River of Testimony* (*or which serves for proof*). According to Buddhist cosmography, it issues from the south of the Lake *A neou tha*, passes through the mouth of the golden elephant, turns once (some

say seven times) round the lake, and thence proceeds to discharge itself into the sea of the south-west.*

We learn from this cosmography, that four rivers, starting from the same point, flow in opposite directions: 1st, the *Heng kia* or *Heng*, (Ganges) the name of which signifies in Sanscrit, *come from the celestial mansion*, because it takes its source in an elevated region. It issues from the eastern side of the lake *A neou tha*, so named from a Sanscrit word (*anawadata*) signifying *exempt from tumult*. This lake is situated to the east of the Mountain of Perfumes, and north of the great Snowy Range; it is eight hundred *li* in circumference, and its banks are adorned with gold, silver, glass, crystal, copper, iron, &c. The Ganges issues from the mouth of an ox of silver, and circumscribing the lake once, discharges itself into the sea of the south-east. 2d, The *Sin theou*, (Sind) of which we now speak. 3d, The *Fo thsou* (*Vach, Oxus* or *Jihon*), the Sanscrit name of which signifies the *pure stream;* it issues on the west side of the lake *A neou tha*, from the mouth of a horse of glass, or of sapphire, encircles the lake once, and discharges itself into the sea of the north-west. 4th, The *Si to*, from a Sanscrit word, (*síta*) which signifies *cold;* it issues on the northern part of the lake, from the throat of a lion of *Pho ti kia (sphatika*, rock crystal) encircles the lake once, and throws itself into the sea of the north-east."† Pallas,‡ following the Mongolian cosmography, *Ertundjin tooli*, names these rivers, the *Ganga, Shilda, Baktchou* (Wakshou, Oxus,) and *Aipara*. B. Bergmann,§ quoting the same work, names them the *Ganga, Sidda, Barkho* and *Baktchi*, or *Shida*. Father Horace names them after the Tibetans, m*Gan-hgis, Sindhou, Paktchhou*, and *Sida.*‖—R.

The *lake A neou tha*, or *Anawadata*, is the *Rawanhrada* of the Hindus, and *Mapam dalai* of the Mandchu-Chinese maps made under *Kang hi* and *Khian loung* * * *. M. E. Burnouf suggests another explanation of the word *A neou tha*. In Pálí the lake is named *Anavatatta*, which can be no other than the Sanscrit word *Anava tapta*, that is, "not brightened, or warmed (by the sunbeams):" an explanation that accords well with the opinion entertained of lake Râvanhrada.—Kl.

(3) *Chang khian* and *Kan yng.*—Chang khian, a Chinese general who lived in the reign of Wou ti of the Han dynasty, conducted in the year A. D. 122, the first memorable expedition of his nation into Central Asia. He was

* *Chang A han king*, quoted in the *San tsang fa sou*, Book XVIII. p. 21. v.
† *Ibid.*
‡ *Sammlungen*, Vol. II. p 37.
§ *Nomadische Streifereien*, Vol. III. p. 198.
‖ *Alphab. Tibet.* p. 186.

sent as ambassador to the *Yue ti*, but was detained by the *Hioung nou* and kept a prisoner for ten years by those people. During his residence among them, he obtained an extensive knowledge of the countries lying to the west of China. Having effected his escape, he travelled many days westward as far as *Ta wan* (Farghana). Thence he passed on to *Khang kiu* (Sogdiana), and the countries of the Yue ti and the Dahæ. To avoid on his return the obstacles that had before detained him, he passed by the mountains through the country of the *Khiang* (Tibet) ; but even thus he did not escape a second capture by the *Hioung nou ;* a circumstance, by the way, which shows that even then Tibet was exposed to the incursions of the northern tribes. Escaping again, he succeeded in reaching China, after an absence of 13 years, with no more than two out of the hundred followers with whom he set out. The countries visited by him in person were Ta wan, the country of the great Yue ti, that of the Ta hia (Dahæ) and *Khang kiu*, or Sogdiana. But besides these he had collected information of five or six other great states situated in their neighbourhood, of which he thus reported to the emperor on his return. "When in the country of the Ta hia," he observes, "*I* remarked the bamboos of *Khioung* and the fabrics of *Shu*. I asked whence these objects had been procured. The Ta hia replied, our merchants trade with the country of *Shin tou* (Sind) *Shin tou* is to the south-east of the *Ta hia*, distant several thousand *li*. The manners and dress of the inhabitants resemble those of the *Ta hia ;* but their country is low, hot and humid. The people make war mounted upon elephants. Their country extends to the sea. According to my calculation the country of the *Ta hia* is twelve hundred *li* to the south-west of China : and since *Shin tou* is several thousand *li* to the south-east of the *Ta hia*, and many articles from *Shu* are found there this country should not be very far distant from *Shu.* On this account I wished to pass by the country of the *Khiang ;* but in seeking to avoid the dangers which threatened me amongst those people, I proceeded somewhat too far to the north, and was captured by the *Hioung nou.* It would however be easy to issue by the country of *Shu*, and you would not be exposed to the attacks of brigands."

The emperor having learnt that these people formed powerful nations, and highly esteemed the merchandise of China, sanctioned the project of Chang khian, and dispatched several envoys in different directions from Shu. These found the roads closed to the north by the *Ti* and the *Tso ;* and to the south *Souï* and the *Kouen ning ;* tribes abandoned to a predatory life. Many of the Chinese emissaries were killed, so that the projected intercourse never took place. A few however, succeeded in reaching the kingdom of *Thian*, 1200 *li* to the west, to which the merchandise from Shu was conveyed. It was thus in seeking to establish an intercourse with the Dahæ that the Chinese obtained their knowledge of the kingdom of *Thian.*

Chang khian was afterwards advanced to an important office; but having failed in an expedition against the *Hioung nou* (B. C. 125) he incurred the penalty of death, commuted by special grace, to the entire loss of rank. He did not omit, however, to publish much useful information regarding the countries and people west of China, as such possessed great interest for his countrymen, who affected supremacy over Central Asia.* I have thought it right to enter upon these details because they refer to the earliest discovery of India by the Chinese. No mention whatever is made of this country, previous to this era, in any Chinese work with which we are acquainted. The other general, *Kan yng*, was sent in the year 97 A. D. as far as the borders of the Western, that is, the Caspian sea, with instructions to subject the Roman Empire. The information he derived from *Tiao chi*, (Tadjiks) and the *An tzu*, regarding the vast extent of this sea, and the time it would require to cross it, (three months with a fair wind, two years with an unfavourable one) induced him to abandon the expedition and return.†

It is evident from the foregoing that Fa hian had no exact idea of the distance or the direction traversed by either of these generals.—R.

(4) *The Interpreters.*—I have introduced a slight correction in this passage. *Kieou yi*, is the name of a kind of interpreters attached to the *Tian shou koue*, or bureau for the affairs of the foreign nations recently subjected to the Han dynasty ‡ It is to the reports of these employés that much of the geographic and ethnographic information of foreign countries is due.—R.

I think that M. Abel Remusat is mistaken in his correction of this passage, which should be translated, "The two banks of the river are at least 80 paces asunder; there are nine stations (where you pass it) It is related that neither *Chang khian*, nor *Kan yng*, reached this point."—Kl.

(5) *Phing wang of the dynasty of Cheou.*—Here we have a fact of the utmost importance in the history of Buddhism, determining the epoch when this religion spread beyond the Indus, into the eastern countries of Asia, into Tartary, and as far as China. It has been usual to fix the date of its introduction into the last mentioned country in the year 61 A. D. and to ascribe it to an event to be noticed in a subsequent note. But this was, in fact, merely the date of its official adoption; for it was then that the

* *Life of Chang khian* in the History of the Han, *Thsian han shou*, B. LXI. p. 1.

† *Ibid*, B. LXXXVIII. p. 6.

‡ *Ibid*, B. XXX. p. 7. v.

worship of Buddha was, according to authentic historians, admitted to the capital and professed with public solemnities. But there are isolated facts of which the memorials are incidentally preserved, which attest that Buddhism had nevertheless penetrated into various provinces at an earlier period, and had established itself unostentatiously, without exciting observation. It is even probable that this religion was preached in very early times, and that the destruction of the books under *Shi houang ti*, of the Thsin dynasty, was the cause of its decadence ;* and it is related that in the twenty-ninth or thirtieth year of the reign of that prince, a Samanean from the west, named *She li fang*, came to Hian yang, (a town near Sí an fou, in Shensi) with eighteen other ecclesiastics, bringing the sacred books in Sanscrit. They presented themselves at court ; but the emperor, shocked at their extraordinary customs, put them into prison. On that, Li fang and his companions began to recite the *Mahá prajna páramitá ;* a brilliant light filled the entire prison, and immediately after, a genius of the colour of gold, and sixteen feet in height, armed with a club, broke open the gates and liberated the prisoners. The Emperor was alarmed, and repenting his treatment of them, dismissed them with great honor.†

Towards the year 122 B. C. the campaign of the general *Hou khin ping* against the *Hioung nou*, brought the Chinese to a country named *Hieou thou*, situated beyond the mountains of Yarkand. The king of that country offered sacrifice to a golden statue of a man. This statue was captured and conveyed to the Emperor in 121 B. C.‡ Yan sse kou observes that it was made of gold to represent the prince of the celestial genii, and that it is the model of the statues of Foe now in use. The Emperor deeming it sacred, deposited it in the *palace of sweet springs*. It was more than one toise high. No sacrifices were offered to it, perfumes only were burnt in its honor.§ It is thus adds he, that the worship of Foe began to be introduced. Chang khian, on his return from his embassy to Ta hia, recounting what he had learnt of neighbouring nations, speaks of *Shin tou*, or India, and the worship of *Feou thou*.‖ Under 'Ai ti (2 years B. C.) a savant named Thsin king, received from an envoy of the *Yue ti*, named *I tsun kheon*, certain Buddhist works. China at this time, to adopt the expression of the historian of the Weï, understood this doctrine, but believed it not.¶ This is all that I can find regarding the introduction of Buddhism into China

* *Wen hian thoung khao*, B. CCXXVI. p. 3.
† *Foe fa kin thang pian*, quoted in the *Shin i tian*, B. LIX. p. 5.
‡ *Thsian han shou*, Life of *Wou ti*.
§ *Weï shou*, notice of the Sects of *Shy kia* and *Lao tseu*.
‖ *Ibid.*
¶ *Shin i tian*, B. XIX. p. 7.

prior to the year 61 A. D., which is the epoch usually accepted for that event. We shall presently learn further details of the part enacted by the Emperor Ming ti in connection with this subject.

As to the history of this religion, which the Chinese found in their earliest expeditions established in the north of Tibet and in Bucharia, Fa hian is the author who has preserved for us the most precise and interesting tradition. According to him, the Buddhists of the Indus asserted that their religion had been spread beyond that river by the labours of the Samaneans of India, at the time of the erection of the colossal statue of Maitreya Bodhisattwa, and that this event took place three hundred years after the nirvana of Sakya, in the reign of *Phing wang*, of the dynasty of Cheou. Now Phing wang began to reign in the year 770 B. C. and died in 720. This fact, en passant, would establish the death of Sákya, according to our author, 300 years before the erection of the statue, i. e. in the year 1020 B. C. or a little later. Now, without entering upon the discussion of the various dates assigned by the Buddhists to this event, so important to them, I may observe that the calculation most generally adopted by the Chinese places the birth of Sákya in the year 1027, or 1029 B. C. and his death in 950.* The date adopted by other Chinese authors well informed in Buddhist traditions,† differs yet more from the chronology of Fa hian, since it places the birth of Sákya, in the ninth year of Chouang Wang, (688 B. C.), which brings down his death to 609, more than a century subsequent to the date assigned to the erection of the statue. We may here remark on the expressions in the text, that they show that in the opinion of Fa hian, Maïtreya was not a mere mythological personage restricted to Tushita, but that his influence was effectual on earth in promoting the objects of Sákya's mission and in propagating his doctrine to the ends of the world. This passage must be compared with the other traditions, which fix the advent of a personage of the order of Bodhisattwas three centuries after Sákya, as a kind of reformer, or continuer of Buddhist predication, and a compiler of the sacred books, and which speak of him as engaged in this work in the western part of India. The colossal statue of the Bodhisattwa will be spoken of in the account of Udyana by Hiouan thsang.—R.

(6) *The knowledge of the Three Precious Ones;*—that is to say, of the *Tri ratna*, or *Buddha*, *Dharma* and *Sanga*. I have elsewhere collected many illustrations of this triad amongst the Buddhists ;‡ to these I will now

* *Melanges Asiatiques*, Vol. I. pp. 115—117.
† *Shin i tian*, B. LIX. pp. 1—3.
‡ Hodgson, *Sketch of Buddhism*.

add the following curious passage from a Muhammadan author :—" When the Tibetans make oath, they invoke the *Kandja soum* (d*Kon* m*tchhog soum*,) that is to say, the triple God ; *Kandja* meaning God, and *soum*, three. They assert however that there is but one God, and the other two are his prophet and his word, and that the combination of these three in the oath refers to but one God. There is moreover a great resemblance between the Lamas of Tibet and the monks of Christian nations, &c."* Buddhist travellers, when they would assert of a people or a prince that they practise the Samanean religion, simply remark that they are deeply attached to the *three precious ones*. The dogma of the *three precious ones* is with them the foundation of the doctrine ; a point which once admitted, involves all others with it. Not to believe in the *three precious ones* is an unpardonable sin. It would be difficult to understand these passages in the strict sense in which the words *Buddha*, the *Law*, and the *Clergy*, are generally accepted. It is evident that a Supreme Triad is spoken of, whose intelligence is manifest by speech and separate personality. Without entering here upon a metaphysical or theological discussion, which has found place elsewhere, I shall repeat an anecdote with which a Chinese book printed in Japan furnishes me. In the fifteenth year of the reign of a prince of *Sin ra*, (Sin lo in Corea) named *Fâ hing wong, the king*, promoter of the Law, 528 A. D. the religion of Foe began to spread in this country. Formerly in the reign of *No khi wang*, a Samanean named *Me hou tseu* arrived from *Kao li*, (Corea proper) at the town of *I chen na*. He excavated a grot for his dwelling. The Emperor of China, of the dynasty of the Liang, sent a present to the prince of *Sin ra*, consisting of all manner of perfumes ; but of these neither the prince nor his subjects recognised the use or even the names. *Hou tseu* instructed them. "These substances, said he, are designed to be burnt ; the exquisite odour which they emit extends to the sanctified spirits ; and amongst those designated sanctified spirits, there are none above the *three precious ones* ; the first is called *Foe tho* ; the second *Tha mo* ; the third *Seng kia*. If you make your invocations in burning these perfumes, Divine Intelligence will not fail to respond. At that moment the daughter of the king fell sick. They directed *Hou tseu* to burn the perfumes and repeat the formulæ. The princess was forthwith restored. The king was delighted, and munificently rewarded the Samanean."†

I will add, as the opportunity offers, that the images, the books, and the worship of Foe were introduced into Corea in the second year of the king *Siao sheou lin* (372) ; that the art of writing was introduced into *Pe*

* *Mir Izzut ullah*, J. R. A. S. Vol. VII. p. 292.
† *Japonese Encyclop.* B. XIII. p. 10.

tsi (another part of Corea) in the twenty-ninth year of the reign of *Siao kou wang* (374) and that a foreign ecclesiastic, named *Ma la nan kouei*, came from Tsin (China) to the same country in the tenth year of king *Kieou sheou*, (384); the king went out before him, led him to his palace and showed him the greatest honor. It was then that Buddhism was established in Pe tsi. The following year they began a temple to Foe upon Mount Han, and ten persons there embraced the monastic life.

I say nothing of the establishment of Buddhism in Japan. Titsingh, in his *Annals of the Daïris*, and M. Klaproth in the annotations he has added to that work, will no doubt give every necessary elucidation.—R.

(7) *The dream of Ming ti.*—*Ming ti*, of the Han dynasty, had a dream; he beheld a man of the colour of gold, and of lofty stature, and having his head surrounded by a luminous halo, soaring above his palace. He consulted his courtiers on the subject of his dream. They replied, "In the western countries there was a spirit named Foe." The Emperor therefore appointed a high officer named *Thsaï yn*, and a scholar named *Thsing king*, to proceed with sundry others to Hindostan, and gather information touching the doctrine of Foe; to draw, paint or depict the *Feou thou* (temples and idols) and to collect the precepts. Thsaï yn applied to the Samaneans, and returned with two of them, *Ma teng* and *Chou fa lan* to *Lo yang*. It was then that the Central Kingdom began to possess Samaneans and to observe the genuflexions. A prince of *Chou*, named *Yng* was the first to embrace the new religion. Yng also procured the book of Foe in forty-two chapters, and the images of Sákya. Ming ti caused paintings of religious subjects to be made, and placed them in the 'Tower of Purity.' The sacred book was deposited in a stone building near the tower of *Lan*; and as in returning to *Lo yang*, Thsaï yn had placed this book on a white horse, a monastery was constructed, called the '*Temple of the White Horse.*' Ma teng and Fa lan passed their lives in this monastery.—R.

CHAPTER VIII.

Kingdom of Ou chang.—Print of the foot of Foe.

On passing this river you are in the kingdom of *Ou chang*.[1] The kingdom of *Ou chang* forms the extreme northern portion of India. Here they actually speak the language of Central India.[2]

Central India is denominated the *Kingdom of the Middle.* The dresses of the people and their manner of living are also similar to those of the Kingdom of the Middle. The law of Foe is held in the highest reverence. At all the places where the ecclesiastics halted were *Seng kia lan.* There are about five hundred *Seng kia lan,* all devoted to the study of the *less translation.*[4] If any stranger, or *Pi kieou*[5] arrive, they receive him with eagerness and entertain him three days. After these three days they warn him to seek for another hospitium.

When tradition tells of the travels of Foe in the north of India, it is of this kingdom that it speaks. Foe here left the impression of his foot. The dimensions of this impression vary according to the thoughts of those who contemplate it.[6] It remains to this day. The stone upon which his clothes were dried in the sun,[7] and the place where the wicked dragons were converted, equally remain. The stone is one toise in height, two toises square, and flat on one side.

Three ecclesiastics, Hoeï kíng, Tao ching, and Hoeï tha, set out in advance to the kingdom of *Na kie,*[8] where is the shadow of Foe.[9] Fa hian and the others tarried a time in this kingdom; and when the term of their sojourn had elapsed, they descended towards the south, into the kingdom of *Su ho to.*[10]

NOTES.

(1) *The kingdom of Ou chhang.*—This name signifies *a garden;* in Sanscrit *Udyána;* the country was so named because the park of a *king of the wheel (Chakravarti raja)* was formerly there. Fa hian is the first Chinese by whom it is spoken of: according to his orthography, the name is *Ou chang;* Soung yun writes it *Ou chhang,* and Hiouan thsang *Ou chang na.* The last mentioned traveller preserves two other spellings, *Ou san chhang* and *Ou chha.* That which he has himself adopted is the most exact transcription the Chinese admits of, Oudyána, the *tch* or *dj* almost always being substituted for the soft dental in the transcription of Indian words.

The country of Udyána is very celebrated in Buddhist annals; but it is not from travellers of this creed alone that the Chinese derive their knowledge of it. They had political intercourse and relations with the princes of Udyána especially in 502, 518, 521, and 642, A. D. The historical existence of this country in A. D. 401 or 402, when visited by Fa hian, cannot be doubted, as also in the year A. D. 642, when its king addressed a letter to the Emperor of China. If we rely upon legends, it must have been known by the name of Udyána in the time of Sákya Muni ; but we are not yet in a position to enable us to adopt, or even to discuss such traditions.

Ma touan lin places this kingdom to the east of Kandahar, and there locates the Bráhmans, whom he designates *the first among the tribes of barbarians.* This country could not be far removed from Attock or Peshawur ; but the name is no longer found among the geographical denominations of that neighbourhood ; nor is there any resembling it among the ancient names of places in northern and western India, extracted from the Puránas by Wilford, or among those extracted by Ward from the *Márkandeya Purána.* This remark may be extended to the rest of our itinerary ; too many revolutions have overturned the institutions of India to admit of our tracing the names of places of more than fourteen centuries ago upon modern maps. The Hindus have no idea of the critical labours, by means of which, in China as well as in Europe, concurrent evidence is brought together as the groundwork of ancient geography ; and amongst learned Europeans, whom the study of Sanscrit has placed in a position to supply such materials, but a very small number have been attracted to researches so dry, thorny, and distasteful. The geography of the Puránas by Wilford, has not been sufficiently followed up ; it would nevertheless be most interesting to extend the investigations and correct the errors of that laborious but too systematizing writer. The perusal of those ancient compositions the Rámáyana, Mahábhárata, and other poems, such as the *Megha duta,* undertaken for the express purpose of despoiling them of their geographical information, would be a genuine service to learning. We justly admire in these works their graceful pictures and elegant descriptive ; but these beauties, however admirable, are the objects of exclusive interest only to superficial understandings. A few fugitive notes adapted to chronological purposes, or to elucidate the ancient Geography of India, would have infinitely more value in the estimation of the learned. There are some happy attempts in this way of late years ; but these do not grapple with the entire subject. Hence the determination of the places spoken of by Fa hian has been a laborious work ; and would have been impracticable in the time of Deguignes.

[Before the reader proceed to the sequel of M. Remusat's highly interesting note, it may be as well to apprise him that here begins the grand geographical error of the learned French commentators, who conduct our pilgrim as far west as Kandahar, while his actual route extended no further than the neighbourhood of Jellalabad. This error will be sufficiently apparent as we progress; meanwhile the insertion of the following observations of Professor Wilson, on *Ou chang*, will not be deemed inappropriate. "It is not correct to say that its name (*Ou chang*) is not traceable in Sanscrit authorities; and it is rather remarkable that we find the name in what may be considered rather its vernacular than its classical form. We have not Udyana, but Ujjana, the *Ou chang na* of the later Chinese traveller. Ujjana is named in the Mahábhárat, in the Vana Parva (Vol. I. p. 585), as one of the Tirthas, or holy places, of the north, and its mention follows close upon that of Kashmír, from which therefore its contiguity may be inferred. We have therefore the Sanscrit verification of its name and site, and this confirms its position on the upper part of the Indus, possibly on either bank, extending westward towards Cabul, and eastward towards Kashmír. Chinese authority, also, is not wanting for such a position, for *Ma twan lin*, as quoted by Remusat, states that it lies east of *Kian tho lo*, and in the Itinerary of Hiouan thsang, *Kian tho lo* is bounded on the east by the Indus. He places Ou chang 600 *li* to the north of *Kian tho lo*. In accounts extracted by M. Remusat, from Chinese Geographical compilations, *Ou chang* is evidently confounded with Kashmír; the description of its mountains, its valleys, its forests, its fertility, its irrigation, its rice, its lakes tenanted by dragons, the Nágas of the Rája Tarangini and the Kashmirian chronicles, and the character of its people as ingenious and gentle, but cowardly and crafty, as still perfectly applicable to Kashmír. At a later period, however, the Chinese knew Kashmír, by its own name; *Kia she mi lo*, is its appellation in the itinerary of Hiouan thsang. It is easy to understand, however, this seeming confusion. Kashmír had at various times a political boundary considerably exceeding its natural limits. At different periods, therefore, different districts, such as Ujjána, were or were not considered to be portions of Kashmír."—J. R. A. S. Vol. VII. pp. 115, 116. The identification is here complete; name and situation both concur in proving the *Ou chang* of Fa hian to be the Ujjána of Indian Literature; a country situated on the Indus, immediately west of Kashmír.—J. W. L.]

We see by the account of Fa hian that Buddhism was established in the 4th century in the eastern part of Afghanistan on the right bank of the Indus in a country now known by the name of Kafristan, or the country of idolaters; for this is incontestibly the country of Udyána, whatever may have been its extent towards the west. We learn elsewhere* that the same religion

* *Pian i tian*, description of *Ou chang*, p. 6.

flourished there in the seventh century although manifesting some symptoms of decline; that of more than fourteen hundred monasteries existing there in former times, several had fallen into ruins; that many of the ecclesiastics had removed elsewhere; and that those who remained had lost the orthodox understanding of the sacred books. These facts, preserved in books written previous to the invasion of the Muhammadans, are consistent with the testimony subsequently borne by the latter, and may even serve to explain it. Several facts connected with the kingdom of Udyána, and known to the Chinese during the dynasties of the northern Weï and the Thang, will be found in the following extract from the *Kou kin thou shou, Pian i tian,* Chap. LXIII. pp. 1, 15.

"In the third year *King ming*, of the reign of *Siuan wou ti*, of the dynasty of the northern Weï (502 A. D.) ambassadors from the kingdom of Ou chang brought tribute.

"This kingdom is to the south of *Siu mi* (*Su meru*): on its north is the chain of the Onion Mountains; on the south, it borders with India. The Bráhmans are, among foreigners, looked upon as the superior caste. The Bráhmans are versed in the science of the heavens and in the calculation of lucky and unlucky days. The kings do nothing without consulting their opinions.

"This country contains many forests and produces fruits. Water is led for the irrigation of fields. The soil is fertile, and produces rice and wheat in abundance. There are many followers of Foe. The temples and the towers are highly adorned and magnificent. When two parties have a dispute they submit themselves to the ordeal of drugs; he who is in the wrong experiences violent pain; but he who is in the right suffers no inconvenience. The punishment of death is not inflicted by their law; criminals who merit this punishment are simply banished to the S. W. of the mountains of '*Intelligence*,' where is the mountain *Tan the*, on which a temple has been constructed; food is conveyed to them by the help of asses, which go and return of themselves without the necessity of any guidance.

"The history of the monasteries reports the journey of two natives of *Thun houang (Sha cheou)* named *Soung yun tse* and *Hoeï seng*, who proceeded to the western lands. This kingdom is bounded on the north by the Onion mountains, and on the south by India. The climate is temperate. The country is several thousand *li* in extent, well peopled, and rich in productions. There is an isolated little hill, near a river whose waters are black, and the isle of the genii. The plains are very fertile. This is the dwelling place of *Pi lo shi eul*, where *Sa tho* abandoned his body. (This passage is mutilated; at all events unintelligible.)

"Although in former times their manners were far from perfect, nevertheless, following the example of the king, the people had made some advance in purity; they observed the fasts, lived on vegetables, and honored Foe morning and night: they beat the drum, sounded the conch, played on the guitar, the flute, and other wind instruments; and it was not till half the day had been so employed that they engaged in the affairs of the state. They never punished criminals with death, but exposed them on a barren mountain and there left them to seek their own means of sustenance. When any matter was involved in doubt, they appealed to drugs, and decided upon the evidence of these.

"The soil is good and fertile; the inhabitants live amidst abundance. All the cereals flourish there; and the five principal fruits, as well as many others, come to perfection. At night you hear the noise of bells which fills the air (literally, the world) on all sides. The richness of the soil gives birth to extraordinary flowers, which succeed in summer as well as in winter. The priests collect these as offerings to Foe.

"The king beholding the arrival of Soung yun, as envoy of the great kingdom of Weï, to salute him, and having received his credentials, asked Soung yun, if he were a native of the country where the sun rises? "To the east of our country," replied Soung yun, "there is a vast sea, from the bosom of which the sun rises; such is the will of the *Jou laï*." (Tathagáta). The king again asked, "Does that country abound in holy personages?" Soung yun then spoke of *Cheou koung*, *Confucius*, *Chouang tseu*, *Lao tseu*; pointed out their virtues; discoursed of the mountain *Pheng laï*, of the gate of silver, the hall of gold, and the genii and the immortals who inhabit there; he next came to the skilful astrologers and the diviners, to the physicians and the magicians; treating of all these things separately and in order. When he had done, the king observed—"If it be as you say, then is your's the country of Foe, and we should during the whole term of our lives, honour its inhabitants."

"Soung yun and Hoeï seng then issued from the town in search of traces of the doctrine of the *Jou laï*. To the east of the river is the place where Foe dried his garments. When the Jou laï was travelling in the kingdom of Ou chang, he converted the king of the dragons. The latter, in his rage, raised a violent tempest. The *Seng kia li* of Foe was wet through and through with the rain. When the storm was passed, Foe, seated at the foot of the rock, dried his *kia sha* (a species of cape worn by Buddhist priests over the shoulders) in the sun. Although many years have elapsed since this happened, the spots and markings are as clear as if quite recent. You see not merely the distinct traces, but the very slightest impressions of the threads. At the time of our visit it seemed as though they had scratched these lines.

" At the place where Foe sat, as well as at that where his garments were dried, they have erected towers to serve as a memorial of these events.

" To the west of the river is a tank, in which dwelt the king of the dragons; at its side is a temple containing fifty ecclesiastics. The king of the dragons frequently performed miracles. The king of the country, to conciliate him, cast into the tank gold, and pearls, and precious stones, which the king of the dragons caused to be ejected, and commanded the monks to gather up again. The clothing and the food of the servants of the temple are supplied by the dragons. The inhabitants call it the *temple of king of the dragons.*

" To the north of the town, distant 18 *li*, there is a print of the foot of Jou laï; they have erected a stone tower to enclose it. The place in the rock where the impression is, seems as if the print of the foot had been made in clay. Its measure is not determinate; it is sometimes large and sometimes small. There are at present attached to the temple seventy ecclesiastics.

To the south of the tower twenty paces, there is a spring issuing from a rock. Foe having purified himself, chewed the branch of a willow, and planted it in the ground : it has become a great tree, which the barbarians call *Phou leou.*

" To the north of the town is the temple of *Tho lo*, where there are many worshippers of Foe. The Feou thou (pyramid or obelisk enclosing the *saríra* or relics of Buddha) is grand and lofty, but the cells for the monks are very contracted. There are sixty gilt statues around the temple. Every year the king holds a great assembly in this temple; all the Samaneans in the kingdom assemble like clouds. Soung yun and Hoeï seng beheld these mendicants and admired their manners, their orderly conduct, and their pious austerities; and gave up to them a male and a female slave to make wine-offerings and to sweep the temple.

" To the south-east of the town, at the distance of eight days' journey is, the place among the mountains where Foe abandoned his body to a famished tiger. It is a very steep mountain, with precipices, caverns, and peaks that enter the clouds. The tree of happiness, *Kalpa daru*, and the mushroom, *Ling chi*, grow there in great plenty. The springs in the forest, and the agreeable mixture of flowers delight the eye. Soung yun and Hoeï seng gave money to erect a statue in the Feou thou in front of the mountain, and engraved upon the rock an inscription in the *li* character, recalling the great actions of the Weï dynasty. On this mountain is the temple of *the preserved gold*, containing more than three hundred monks.

"To the south of the town royal, at the distance of 500 *li*, is the place where Foé, being in the country of *Ma hieou* used a portion of his skin for paper and one of his bones for a pencil. The king *A yeou*, erected a tower in that place; it is ten *chang* high. At the place where the bone was removed, the marrow fell upon the stone, and you see the color of the grease and the oily spot as if it were quite recent!

"Five hundred *li* to the south of the royal city is the hill *Shen chi*, or *of good things:* there are sweet springs and delicious fruits, of which mention is made in the legend. The hills and the valleys are pleasingly diversified; and the trees on the mountains preserve their green foliage during winter. The rich vegetation, the delightful temperature, the spring in its bloom, the butterflies like fluttering flowers, produce an exquisite whole. In this seductive abode, so far from his own country, Soung yun was agitated by a thousand varying thoughts, and felt his heart throb with the emotions of olden times. He remained there a month, seeking from the Bráhmans charms to appease him.

"To the south-east of this mountain is a stone house, called *the Prince's*, having two chambers. Ten paces in front of the Prince's house there is a square stone on which it is said the Prince was accustomed to sit. The king, *A yeou,* caused a tower to be built to consecrate the remembrance of the fact. To the south of the tower one *li* is the place where the cottage of the Prince stood.

"In descending the mountain, at fifty paces to the north-east, is the place where the Prince and the Princess walked round a tree without separating, and where the Bráhmans flogged them so that their blood ran to the ground. This tree exists still, and preserves the drops of blood with which it was watered. There is a spring of water there.

"To the west of the house three *li* is the place where the king of Heaven, (Indra) changed himself into a lion and sat upon the road concealing *Man yun*. The traces of his hair, of his tail, and his claws exist to this day; as also the place where *A cheou tho khon,* and his disciple offered food to their parents. In these various places there are towers to preserve the memory of these events.

"In the mountains are the beds of five hundred ancient Arhans. They are placed in rows from north to south, and on the spot where the Arhans sat facing each other. At the second row there are a great temple where two hundred monks reside, and the spring of water at which the Prince drank. To the north the temple is always surrounded by a great number of asses; no one looks after them, and they go of themselves where they will. They go out at three in the morning, and at noon they eat. These are spirits who guard the tower, as commissioned by the immortal *Wo pho*. There was formerly in this temple a *Sha mi*, who was in the habit of throwing out the ashes, which by the will of the eight spirits, he attracted to himself. Insensibly his skin shrivelled up and his bones separated. The immortal *Wo pho*, succeeded him in the function of carrying away the ashes. The king raised a temple to *Wo pho*, in which is his image covered with leaves of gold.

" Near a little defile is a temple of *Pho kian*, built by *Ye cha*, and containing eighty ecclesiastics. It is said that the Arhan Ye cha frequently went there making offerings of wine, and sweeping, and gathering wood. Ordinary mendicants cannot remain in this temple. We, Samaneans of the great Wei dynasty, had the glory to come thus far; but we returned, not daring to remain.

" The third year *Young phing*, (510) at the ninth moon, the country of *Ou chang* sent tribute. In the fourth year, in the third moon, and in the tenth moon, there came another tribute from the same country. The same thing took place in the seventh intercalary moon of the first year *Chin koueï* of Hiao ming ti (518) and in the fifth moon of the second year *Ching kouang* (521).

" Under the dynasty of the *Thang*, in the sixteenth year *Ching kouan* (642) there came ambassadors from Ou chang. There is no mention of this in the life of *Taï soung*; but we read the following in the notice of the Western Lands: " *Ou chha*, also called *Ou chang na*, and *Ou chang*, is in the extreme south of India (an evident mistake for extreme north, as will be seen further on.) It is five thousand *li* in length. It borders on the east, with the country of Phou liu (Pourout) distant 500 *li*. To the west, at four hundred *li*, is *Khi pin* (Cophene) Mountains and valleys alternate with each other. They produce gold, iron, grapes, and the odoriferous plant *yu kin*. Rice comes to maturity there at the end of a year. The inhabitants are weak, fraudulent, and much addicted to superstition and magic. They do not award capital punishment in this country; criminals who deserve this penalty are banished to desert mountains. When any doubts arise as to the guilt of the supposed criminal, these are dissipated by the administration of a medicinal drink, which distinguishes truth from falsehood. There are five towns; the king dwells in that named *Shou meng pe li*, or otherwise called *Meng kie li*. To the north-east is the rivulet *Tha li lo;* this is the ancient country of *Ou chang*. In the sixteenth year *Chhing kouan* (642) the king *Tha mo in tho po sse*, sent ambassadors bearing *camphor*. An imperial rescript conveyed to him the satisfaction produced by his conduct."

We may observe that in passing the mountains to the north of the *Pho lo tou lou*, and proceeding 600 *li* you reach the tribe of Ou chang. The *Thse fou youan Kouï* then reports the letter of *Tha mo in to ho sse*:—" The most honourable sovereign, endowed with goodness and virtue, who reigns at once over the middle and the high, ascends the precious chariot of heaven, dissipates all darkness, and like the Lord Indra, is able to subdue the king of the *A sieou lo* (Asura). Your slave reposes at the root of your bounties, and as if he had obtained the living stock of Indra, salutes your most honourable person and offers you camphor." The emperor was flattered by homage from so distant a land, and caused a benevolent answer to be sealed with his seal."

According to the *Notice* of *Western Countries under the dynasty of the Thang*, the country of *Ou chang*, was not more than five hundred *li* in circumference. It is filled with mountains and valleys, succeeding each other, and streams and lakes connected at their sources. Cereals are sown there but seldom arrive at perfection. There are plenty of grapes, but few sugarcanes. The soil produces iron and gold, and is suitable for the *yu kin*. The forests are extremely dense; and flowers and fruits are abundant. The climate is temperate, and wind and rain alternate regularly. The inhabitants are timid and cunning; they love study, and transgress not the Law. Astrology is their habitual occupation. Their clothes are of white wool, and few possess garments of any other kind. Their language, although different, resembles that of *In tou*, as do their written character, their ceremonies, and their usages. They greatly honor the law of Foe, and their worship belongs to the *great translation*. On the river *Sou pho fa sou thou*, there were formerly fourteen hundred *Kia lan*, (monasteries) many have already fallen into ruin. In former times there were eighteen thousand ecclesiastics, but now their number has greatly fallen off. All study the ***great translation*** and yield themselves up to contemplation. They delight in the study of their scriptures, but understand not the occult sense thereof. The precepts are carried out in practice, and the conduct of the monks is pure. They observe the ceremonies, and the formulæ of incantation are in use among them. We learn from tradition that there are five sects among them; the first is that of *Fa mi* (silence of the law) the second, that of *Houa ti* (conversion of the world); the third, that of *Yn kouang*, or *Kasyapa* imbibed light) the fourth that of *Shoue i thsi yeou;* and the fifth, that of *Ta choung*, or the multitude. At least ten temples are inhabited pell-mell by the heretics. The towns are four or five in number. The king lives principally in *Meng kie li*, a town of sixteen or seventeen *li* in circumference. The population is very numerous. To the east of the town of Meng kie li is a great *Sou tou po*, (*stupa*, tumulus, mound of earth) where a great number of divine wonders present themselves. When Foe was alive he installed in this place the immortal *Jin jo*, king of *Ky li*,

(This word signifies in Chinese, *debate, discussion.*) To cut the limbs * * * (lacuna in the text.)

[Lassen *(Zur Geschichte der Griechischen und Indoskythischen Könige,* page 144) has given us the probable restoration of *Men kie li,* (called *Meng ho li,* by Hiuan thsang) in the Sanscrit word *Mangala,* 'fortunate.' —J. W. L.]

"To the north-east of the town of *Meng kie li,* some 250 or 260 *li,* you reach a great mountain and arrive at the fountain of the dragon *A po lo lo,* which is the source of the river *Sou pho fa sou thou.* The waters divide in running towards the south-west. Summer and winter the cold is great; it snows morning and evening. In the midst of snow and rain there is a light of various colors which shines on all sides.

"The dragon *A po lo lo,* was born while *Kia she pho Foe* was among men. He bore the name of *Keng khi,* and being profoundly skilled in magic, he prevented, by his incantations, the formation of rain-storms by the dragons. The natives of the country confided in him, and offered him the superabundance of their harvests; they were very grateful, and cherishing the remembrance of this benefit, set apart, each house, one bushel of grain as an oblation. Some years afterwards, it so happened that they failed in this duty. Keng khi, wrath at this, resolved to become a venomous dragon. He raised a tempest of wind and rain, which destroyed the harvests, and which when he ordained it to cease, became this lagoon, and the fount of the dragon, whence flows a white water that destroys the fruits of the earth. *Shy kia jou laï,* full of compassion for man, and governing the age, was touched with pity for the inhabitants of this country, who were exposed only to this single misfortune. He caused a spirit to descend for the conversion of this furious dragon; he took a diamond sceptre in his hand and struck the side of the mountain. The king of the dragons was terror-struck and made his submission. He listened to the doctrine of Foe, purified his heart, and believed the law. *Jou laï* immediately interdicted his injuring the harvests thenceforward. The dragon replied, "All those who eat, reckon on the fields of man; this day I receive your holy instruction; yet I fear that I can with difficulty secure myself against want. I entreat that every twelfth year one harvest he abandoned to me." The Jou laï had compassion upon him and granted it. It is thus that once in twelve years there is a disaster of the white water.

"To the south-west of the river of *A po lo lo,* about 30 *li,* there is a print of the foot of the Jou laï upon a large stone. The size of it varies according to the fortune or the strength of beholders. It is an impression of his foot after he had subdued the dragon. Men of subsequent times gathered together stones in this place for the erection of a temple. From far and near they go thither to offer flowers and perfumes. In descending towards the river about 30 *li*, there is a stone where Jou laï washed his garments; the marks of his *kia sha*, are as distinct as if they had been engraved.

"To the south of the town of *Meng kie li*, distant four *li*, are the mountain, and the valley of *Hi lo*. The river runs towards the west and turns back again to the east. Flowers and rare fruits are carried along by the stream. The banks are steep, and the hills are separated by deep valleys, into which torrents precipitate themselves. Travellers sometimes hear amongst them the sound of voices, or cries, and that of musical instruments. The rocks are squared like a bed, as if they had been wrought by the hand. They stretch out and prolong themselves, following each other in succession. These valleys and escarpments are the place where Foe, having listened to the half of a poem, made the sacrifice of his person and his life.

"To the south of the town of Meng kie li, about two hundred *li*, is the monastery of the *Ma ha fa na*, (*vana*, Sanscrit; the great forest.) It is the place where the Jou laï performed the labours of *Phou sa*, and was surnamed the king of *Fo tha tha* (a *Fan* word which in Chinese signifies *universal gift.*) Flying from his enemies, and abandoning his kingdom he arrived at this place. He fell in with a poor bráhman who besought him for alms; having lost his kingdom and his rank, and having nothing therefore to bestow, he directed that himself should be bound and delivered to the king of his enemies, in order that the price given for him should serve for alms.

"On descending from the hills 34 *li* north-west of the monastery of *Ma ha fa na*, you come to the kia lan of *Mo yu*. (This word signifies in Chinese, *bean.*) There is a sthupa there two hundred feet high. Behind it on a large square stone, is the mark of the foot of the Jou laï. Foe having stamped upon this stone, made the light *keou chi* shine from it and illumine the monastery *Ma ha fa na*; he related the adventures of his own birth in favour of men and Gods. At the foot of the sthupa there is a stone coloured white and yellow; it always emits a greasy juice. In the times when Foe enacted the part of *Phou sa*, in order that they might understand the doctrine in this place, he broke one of his bones wherewith to indite the sacred books.

"Sixty or seventy *li* to the west of the monastery of *Mo yu* there is a Sthupa erected by the king *Wou yeou*. It was there that the Jou laï, practising the actions of *Phou sa*, received the title of the king of *Shi pi kia*. (This *Fan* word signifies in Chinese *to give*; elsewhere *Shi pi*, is used for brevity.) He had prayed to Foe, and it was actually in this place that he hacked his own body to deliver it to the sparrow hawk instead of the pigeon.

"Two hundred *li* to the north of the place called '*for the pigeon*,' you come to the rivulet *Shan ni lo she*, and arrive at the monastery *Sa so sha ti*. (This word signifies in Chinese, the *medicine of the serpent.*) There is a *sthupa* there more than eighty feet high. It was in this place that Jou laï, when formerly Indra, met a crowd of starving and diseased people. The physicians could do nothing for them ; and those who died of hunger on the roads followed each other in uninterrupted succession. Indra, full of compassion for them, changed his form into that of a huge serpent. He summoned the corpses from the streams and the valleys ; hearing him, these all joyously began to flee and to run. He cured the famished and the sick.

" Not far, is the great sthupa of *Sou ma*. This is the place where the Jou laï, when Indra, out of compassion for the infected, changed himself into the serpent *Sou ma*. Of all those who eat of it, there was not one that was not relieved.

" On the edge of the rocks north of the stream *Shan ni lo she*, there is a sthupa. The sick who go there are cured and guaranteed against many maladies. The *Jou laï*, being formerly the king of the peacocks, came hither with his flock. Urged by heat and thrist, they searched for water, but no where found it. The king of the peacocks with one peck of his beak, struck the rock and caused water to issue, which immediately formed a lake. Those who drink of it are cured of their ailings. On the rock there is still the impress of a peacock's foot.

" To the south-west of *Meng kie li*, sixty or seventy *li*, to the east of the great river, there is a sthupa about sixty feet high, raised by the king of the High Army. In former times, the Jou laï, when on the eve of entering upon extinction, thus addressed all people : " After my *nirvána*, the king of the High Army, of the kingdom of *Ou chang na*, shall divide a portion of my reliques among all princes, to establish equality." When the king of the High Army was come, a consultation was held upon their value. Then the celestials and the crowd repeated the words of the prediction, and the command of the *Jou laï*. They divided the reliques, and each carried away his share to his own kingdom ; and in honor of them they erected this sthupa. On the bank of the great river there is a large stone of the form of an elephant. Formerly the king of the High Army placed the reliques on a large white elephant, and reached this place on his return. The elephant fell there and died ; he was changed into stone. At this place, they have constructed a sthupa.

" Forty or fifty *li* from *Meng kie li*, across the great river, you come to the sthupa *Lou hi ta kia*. (This word signifies *red* in Chinese : it is the Sanscrit word *lohitaka.*) It is more than fifty feet high, and was erected by the king *Wou yeou*. Formerly the Jou laï, when Phou sa, became king of a great kingdom, under the title *Tseu li*, ('power of goodness.') In this place he pierced his body and extracted the blood to feed five *yo sha* (Sanscrit, *Yaksha*, demons, who according to Hindu mythology, are specially attached to the God of riches, and invested with the care of gardens and treasures).

"To the north-east of the town of *Meng kie li*, 30 *li*, you come to a stone Sthupa named *Ko pou to*, (a word signifying 'unique wonder'); it is 40 feet high. In old time the Jou laï discoursed here upon the law in behalf of men and Gods, and opened the way to them. After he had departed, the crowd, afflicted at his departure, honored him by offering flowers and perfumes without interruption.

"To the west of the stone sthupa, on passing the great river, there is a temple containing an image of *A fou lou chi ti she fa lo Phou sa.* (This word signifies in Chinese, 'contemplating him who exists of himself;' it is a Chinese transcript of the Sanscrit words *Avalokiteswara Bodhisattwa*; that is the *Bodhisattwa, the master who contemplates with love.*)

"To the north-west of the statue of *Phou sa contemplating the being who exists of himself*, at the distance of 140 or 150 *li*, you come to the mountain *Lan pho lou.* On the summit of this mountain is the dragon's tank, which is more than 30 *li* in circumference. The water is pure, and forms a transparent sheet like a clear mirror.

"To the north-east of *Meng kie li*, you pass the mountains and traverse the valleys, and ascend again the *Sin tou.* The road is perilous and steep; the hills are lofty, the valleys deep and obscure. You walk along ropes, or on bridges of iron chains, or upon timbers, or on bridges constructed of spars joined together. You scramble thus more than 1000 *li*, and arrive at the streamlet *Tha lo li.* It is here you find the ancient capital of *Ou chang na*. Much gold and the perfume *yu kin* is brought from it. In the stream *Tha li lo*, near to a great monastery, there is a statue of the beneficent Bodhisattwa, sculptured in wood; it is of the colour of gold, splendid and majestic, and more than one hundred feet high. It was constructed by the Arhan, *Mo thian ti kia.* He completed it after he had himself thrice beheld his marvellous perfections. Since the erection of this statue the law has spread considerably to the east. To the east of this point, traversing the hills and the valleys, ascending the *Sin tou*, crossing flying bridges, logs of timber, precipices, and marshes, and proceeding in all 500 *li*, you come to the country of *Po lou lo* (limit of northern India.)—R.

Po lou lo is no doubt the Chinese transcription of Bolor; an identification happily confirmed by Capt. A. Cunningham, who writes (J. A. S Vol. XVII. pp. 97, 98.) "I have also been fortunate enough to discover another point of much interest and importance in the comparative geography of the countries to the northward of Kashmír; which is the identification of the ancient country of Bolor, with the present Balti or Little Tibet. The Bolor mountains have occupied an uncertain position in our maps for a considerable period, which I am now able to define with precision. They are in fact that chain of mountains called Muztak, which forms the northern boundary of the district of Balti. Amongst the Dards who speak the Shina language, namely, in Hasora, Gilgit, Chilas, Darel, Kohli, and Palas, all lying along the Indus, Balti is known only by the name of *Palolo*. What renders this identification more striking and complete is the mention by Hiuan thsang in A. D. 640, that the kingdom of *Po lou lo*, "produced much gold;" a production for which Balti or Palolo is still celebrated, and which produces much of its revenue."—J. W. L.

(2) *Central India.*—Apparently *Madhya desa*, or the middle region. It is remarkable that according to Fa hian, they made use of the very language of Mid-India, in Oudyana. The original expression is singular, "They employ altogether the language of Central India."—R.

I think it should be translated, *finem fecit linguæ Indiæ Mediæ*, or "thus far extends the language of Mid-India."—Kl.

(3) *The Central Kingdom;* in the text *Choung koue.* This is precisely the expression used to designate China; and care is required in reading Buddhist narratives, to avoid confounding passages referring to China, with those intended to apply to Mathura, Magadha, and other kingdoms of central India. This mistake cannot occur in the work of Fa hian, who always speaks of his native land as that of the Han, Thsin, &c. dynasties. —See notes on Chap. XVI.

(4) *Less translation.*—See notes to Chap. II.

(5) *Pi khieou,* Chinese transcript of the Sanscrit word *bhikshu* mendicant, as *Pi khieou ni* is its feminine form *bhikshuní.* This term is honorable, as applied to those who beg their subsistence from motives of devotion and humility. Those who have devoted themselves to this kind of life, have to practise twelve kinds of observances, named *theou tho*, from a Sanscrit word which signifies *to shake one's-self* because these observances help to clean away the dust and the foulness of vice. The mendicant should shun all causes of disturbance; eschew vain ornaments; destroy in the heart the germs of cupidity; avoid pride, and in purifying his life, search for supreme reason, rectitude, and truth. The twelve observances which are recommended to them with this view, have reference to the four actions or manners of being, named *Weï yi (gravity*, or *that which should be done gravely)*, namely, to walk, to stand, to sit, and to lie

down. The following is extracted from a book specially treating upon the twelve observances, and entitled *Shi eul theou tho king.**

1st.—The mendicant should dwell in a place which is *a lan jo*, (áranyaka,) that is to say a *tranquil place, a place of repose*. This is the means of avoiding disturbance of spirit, of escaping *the dust* of desire, of destroying for ever all the causes of revolt, and of obtaining supreme reason, &c.

2nd.—It is requisite that he always beg his subsistence (in Pali, *pindapátika*) in order to extinguish cupidity. The mendicant should accept no man's invitation. He should beg the nourishment necessary for the support of his material body and the accomplishment of his moral duties. He ought to recognize no difference in the food obtained, whether it be good or bad; nor to feel resentment if it be refused him, but always to cultivate the equanimity of a perfect spirit.

3rd.—In begging he should take his rank (in Páli, *Yáthâpantari*) without being attracted by savoury meats; without disdain for any one, and without selection betwixt rich and poor; with patience should he take his rank.

4th.—The mendicant who occupies himself with good works should thus reflect: "It is much to obtain one meal; it is too much to make an early repast (breakfast) and a second (after midday.) If I do not retrench one of these, I shall lose the merit of half a day, and my spirit will not be entirely devoted to reason." He therefore avoids multiplicity of meals, and adopts the custom of making but one (*eka pánika*).

5th.—The food which the mendicant obtains shall be divided into three portions; one portion shall be given to any person whom he shall see suffering from hunger; the second he shall convey to a desert and quiet spot, and there place it beneath a stone for the birds and the beasts. If the mendicant fall in with no person in want, he must not on that account himself eat all the food he has received, but two-thirds only. By this means his body will be lighter and better disposed, his digestion quicker and less laborious. He can then without inconvenience apply himself to good works. When one eats with avidity, the bowels and the belly enlarge, and the respiration is impeded; nothing is more injurious to the progress of reason. This fifth observance is called in Sanscrit *khalupaswaddhaktinka*.

6th.—The juice of fruits, honey and other things of the same kind, ought never to be taken by the mendicant after midday. If he drink of these his heart abandons itself to desire, and becomes disgusted with the practice of virtue.

7th.—The mendicant ought not to desire ornaments; let him seek no sumptuous dresses, but take the tattered raiments that others have rejected,

* *San tsang fa sou* B. XLIV. p. 10.

wash and clean them and make of them patched garments only for protection from cold, and to cover his nakedness. New and handsome vestures give rise to the desire of rebirth ; they disturb the reasoning, and they may moreover attract robbers.

8*th.*—*Traïchivarika*, or only three dresses. These words import that the mendicant should content himself with the *kia sha*, of nine, of seven, or of five pieces. He has few desires and is easily satisfied. He desires neither to have too much nor too little raiment. He equally eschews men dressed in white, who have numerous dresses, and those heretics who, from a spirit of mortification, go entirely naked, in defiance of all modesty : each extreme is contrary to reason. The three vestments hold the proper medium. Moreover, the word *kia sha* signifies of *divers colours*, because of the pieces which form the vestment of the first, second and third order.

9*th.*—*Smásánïka*, or *the dwelling amid tombs*, obtains for the mendicant just ideas of the three things which form the prime gate of the law of Foe ; *instability*, or the brief duration of bodies which, composed of five elements, return to their originals and are destroyed ; *pain*, which oppresses the body from the moment of birth till that of death ; and *vacuity*, since body is borrowed, formed by the reunion of the four elements, and subject to destruction. This is in fact the observation made upon this subject by Sákya Muni himself, who opened by it the road to supreme wisdom. By dwelling among tombs the mendicant beholds the exhibition of death and of funerals. The stench and the corruption, the impurities of every description, the funeral pyres, the birds of prey, awaken in him the thought of instability, and hasten his progress in goodness.

10*th.*—*Vrikshamulika*, or being seated under a tree. The mendicant who hath not attained wisdom amid the tombs, should go and meditate beneath a tree ; there let him seek for wisdom, as did Buddha, who accomplished under a tree, the principal events of his life ; who was there born, who there completed the doctrine, there turned the wheel of the law, and finally there attained his *parinirvána*. This is an effect of destiny. We learn besides that other Buddhas similarly placed themselves ; and the *tree* is so connected with these supreme operations that the word *bodhi*, equally means the *tree* and the *doctrine*.

11*th.*—To sit on the ground, *ábhyavakáshika*, is an additional advantage for the mendicant. Seated beneath a tree so as to be half covered by its shade, he enjoys the cool air. It is true that he is exposed to rain and moisture, that the droppings of birds soil him, and that he is exposed to the bite of venomous beasts ; but he also abandons himself to meditation ; seated on the earth, his spirit is recreate ; the moon, in shining on him, seems to illumine his spirit ; and he thus gains the power of more easily entering the extatic state.

12*th.*—*Naishadhika*; to be seated, not recumbent. The sitting posture is that best becoming a mendicant; his digestion and his respiration are more easy, and he thus more readily attains wisdom. Vices invade those who abandon themselves to idleness, and surprise them at disadvantage. Walking and standing set the heart in motion, and the mind is at rest. The mendicant should take his rest seated, and should not allow his loins to touch the ground."

It appears to me that the foregoing extract from a work consecrated to the habits of Buddhist mendicants, would supply the reader with more correct ideas of the sect than the repetition of what travellers have said upon the subject. The observances inculcated in the 8th paragraph may be noted as directly opposed to the manners of the *digambaras*, or gymnosophists.—R.

(6) *The dimensions of this impression vary.*—The text says, *sometimes long, sometimes short; this depends upon the thoughts of men.* This passage might be supposed corrupted, if the same fanciful idea were not expressed in yet more precise terms by other Buddhist pilgrims who saw the same object in Udyána.—R.

(7) *The stone where his clothes were dried.*—This event is detailed more fully by *Soung yun.*—R.

(8) *Na kie.*—This is the Chinese transcription of *Nagara* (a town), as we are enabled to affirm with certainty from the more correct orthography of the same name by Hiuan thsang; namely, *Na ko lo ho.* Lassen (*Zur Geschichte*, &c. pp. 139, 147) identifies this with the Νάγαρα of Ptolemy, and establishes its position very satisfactorily in the immediate neighbourhood of Jellallabad. See notes to Chap. XIII.—J. W. L.

(9) *The shadow of Foe.*—Regarding this prodigy, one of the most absurd mentioned in Buddhist legends, see notes of Chap. XIII.—R.

(10) Fa hian in proceeding to the south, traversed the country of Udyána for a distance which he has omitted to record, but which, to judge from the sequel, must have been very considerable. It must not be forgotten that he remained to the west of the Sind, in countries usually comprehended in Persia, but which then formed part of India, and which are, in fact, intermediate betwixt both, and distinct from each by the character of their population as well as their geographical position. It was there that he found a petty state, *Su ho to*, otherwise wholly unknown.—R.

See next Chapter, note 1.—J. W. L.

CHAPTER IX.

The kingdom of Su ho to.

Equally flourishing is the law of Foe in the kingdom of *Su ho to.*[1] In former times, Shy,[2] the celestial emperor, put the Phou sa[3] to the test. He changed himself into a hawk and a dove.[4] [The Phou sa] tore his flesh to redeem the dove. After Foe had accomplished the law, he passed by this place with his disciples, and said to them "Behold the place where formerly I tore my flesh to redeem the dove!" The people of the country learnt in this way of that adventure, and erected on the spot a tower enriched with ornaments of gold and of silver.

NOTES.

(1) *The kingdom of Su ho to.*—The form of this name would seem to establish its Indian origin; but it is elsewhere wholly unknown. All that is known of the country so called is that it lies to the south of Udyana, and five days' journey to the west of the Gandhara of Fa hian. The fabulous adventure here recorded may enable us to recover its Sanscrit name; but there can be no doubt that the latter has long disappeared in the country itself under Persian and Muhammadan influence.—R.

In the *Savat, Sewad, Swat,* of the Ayin Akbarí, and of our modern maps we have the restoration of *Su ho to,* the valley of the *Suastus* of the ancients, the *Suvastu* of the Hindus, and the *Sou pho fa sou tou* of *Hiouan thsang's* itinerary. The boundaries of this kingdom at the time of Fa hian's transit cannot now be determined. Wilson (J. R. A. S. Vol. V. p. 116) remarks that in the time of Baber the kingdom of Swát or Suvát extended on both sides of the Indus.—J. W. L.

(2) *Shy, the celestial emperor.*—Indra is thus designated in Chinese Buddhistical works when his name, *In tho lo,* is not itself transcribed.* He

* *San tsang fa sou,* Book XLVI. p. 11.

is also called *Ti shy*, the Lord of the Gods, and *Shy ti houan in*, (apparently *Shatamanyu*,) which signifies in Sanscrit the *powerful king of the Gods*.* We have seen that according to the order of Buddhist divinities, Indra is the Lord of the *Trayastrinsha*, or the abode of the thirty-three Gods, the second in ascending of the Bhuvanas in the world of desire. In Tibetan he is designated d*Vang-po*, Lord, and has many other denominations which are merely epithets. In Mongolian he is called *Khormusda*, and this name, coupled with the circumstance of the thirty-three Gods of whom he is chief, was with Mr. Schmidt, the occasion of a curious comparison with Hormuzd and the thirty-two Amshaspands. It is difficult to object to this analogy, and yet more so to explain it, seeing that the Mongolian nomenclature is its only ground, not a trace of such analogy being found among the Hindus, who more than any other people of Asia were likely to influence, or to be influenced by, the Persians.—R.

(3) *Phou sa* ;—Bodhisattwa. What is here said of Sákya Muni, refers to a previous existence, in which he had attained the rank of Bodhisattwa only. Personages of this order are distinguished during life by their extreme goodness, by universal benevolence, and by a self-abandonment which impels them to sacrifice themselves for the benefit of all other creatures, as in the present instance.—R.

(4) *He transformed himself into a hawk and a dove.*—This double transformation is by no means inconsistent with Buddhistical notions. The Gods and the saints could assume several forms at once, or could create several simultaneous appearances of them ; and this is what the Chinese expression signifies.—R.

The legend here alluded to, as well as those of the starving tiger, of the breaking of his bone for a pen and the shedding of his blood for ink, &c., belongs to an anterior existence of Sákya, "immeasurably distant ages ago," and may be found in the འཛངས་བླུན (H*dsangs* b*lun*), an elegant edition of which in Tibetan and German was published at St. Peterburgh in 1843, by M. I. J. Schmidt. In that work, however, the double transformation mentioned in the text is not alluded to : but Viswakarma personates the dove and Indra the hawk. Professor Wilson† seems to think that the legend is derived from Brahmánical sources ; and states that it is told at some length in the *Vana Parva* of the Mahábhárata of king Usínara, whose charity was similarly tested by Indra, on which occasion the dove was personated by Agni, the God of fire. The spirit of the legend appears to me, however, to be thoroughly Buddhist.—J. W. L.

* *San tsang fa sou*, B. XXXIII. p. 4.
† *Journal Royal As. Soc.* Vol. V. p. 116.

CHAPTER X.

The kingdom of Khian tho wei.

They descended from *Su ho to* towards the east; they were five days on the road, and arrived at the kingdom of *Khian tho wei.*[1] Here reigned *Fa i,*[2] the son of *A yu.*[3] In the times when Foe was *Phou sa,*[4] he gave his eyes in alms in this country. Here in like manner, they have erected a great tower with ornaments of gold and silver. Amongst the inhabitants of this kingdom many are devoted to the study of the *less translation.*

NOTES.

(1) The kingdom of *Khian tho wei.*—We are tempted to take this as the name of the province of *Gandháva*, recently introduced in our maps.* But the opinion of a Chinese author who visited these countries subsequently to Fa hian, and who has endeavoured to rectify the errors of his predecessors in transcribing Geographical names, would lead us to consider this as a corruption of the well known name *Khian tho lo.* Now this latter is evidently the Gandari of Strabo;† the *Gandhára* of the Purânas,‡ the *Kandahar* of Mussulman Geographers, and has finally attached itself to a celebrated town. The remote western position of this town must not be held as an exception to an incontestible synonyme. Many witnesses, amongst whom we must place the Chinese Geograpers of the dynasty of the *Thang,* testify that before the Muhammadan invasion the Gandháras formed a powerful and extensive state to the west of the Indus. We possess in the Chinese collections, a detailed description of this state, two centuries posterior to the Foe koue ki. Many most important Buddhist traditions had currency at this period among the Gandháras and neighbouring small states; some of them refer to the acts of Foe, *in the time when he was Bodhisattwa*, that is, as has been observed before, at one of the periods of his history which mythology places antecedent to his real life.—R.

* Pottinger's Travel's in Beluchistan. † Lib. XV.
‡ Ward, Vol. I. p. 11.

This identification of *Kian tho wei*, with the Gandhára of the Hindus is no doubt correct; but *Su ho to*, be the country watered, by the Punjkora or Suwat river, Fa hian's *easterly* route must have taken him in an opposite direction from *Kandahar*. The position of the *Gandháras*, is by no means difficult of determination. In the *Váyu Purána*, the *Sindhu* is stated to flow through the *Daradas, Kasmíras, Gandháras, Yavanas, &c.* (Wilford, *As. Res.* Vol. VIII. p. 331). "The *Gandaritis* of Strabo, says Wilson (*Hist. of Kashmír*), which furnishes an approximation to the *Gandarii* of Herodotus, is placed nearer even to the Indus than the modern city of Candahar; he observes it is watered by the *Choaspes* which falls into the *Cophenes:* he has also a *Gandaris*, which he places between the *Hydraotis* (Ravi) and the *Hydaspis* (Beyah), and consequently towards the eastern part of the Punjab. Ptolemy only notices the first position, bringing it rather more to the west, unless as Salmasius conjectures, his *Suastus* be the *Cophenes* of Strabo, and making the Indus the eastern boundary of the *Gandari: Inter Suastum et Indum sunt Gandari:*" a definition which corresponds with our pilgrim's position very well.

For further information on this subject the reader may consult Wilson, *Ariana Antiqua*, and the admirable dissertation of Lassen *Zur Geschichte der Griech. und Indoskyth. Könige*, p. 143.—J. W. L.

(2) *Fa i.*—This appears to be a significant name; meaning *extension of the law*. It may be a translation of the Sanscrit name *Dharma vardhana*, which was borne by several Indian princes. According to this tradition, the son of the king of Magadha, reigned in the country of Gandhára. This historical point might be settled by the examination of Sanscrit works, which, judging from extracts quoted by Wilson,* might furnish other proofs of some connexion betwixt Magadha and Gandhára at an early period of Indian history.—R.

Wilson has observed that the name *Dharma Varddhana* no where occurs in the catalogues of Indian princes.—J. W. L.

(3) *A yu.*—This king is more frequently designated *Wou yu*. His Sanscrit name is more accurately transcribed *A shou kia* (Asoka, sorrowless.) He was the great-grandson of king *Ping cha*, or *Pin po so lo* (Bímbására,) of whom more will be said hereafter, and flourished a century subsequent to the nirvána of Sákya Muni. In Mongolian he is called *Khasoloung ougei*,† a word of the same signification, which however Mr. Schmidt has failed to recognise. As the foundation of nearly all the religious edifices in ancient India is attributed to this sovereign, and referred to the 116 year after the

* *Mudra Rakshasa*, preface, p. 11.
† *Geschichte der Ost-Mongolen*, p. 16.

nirvána, the 9th year of the Regency *Koung ho*,* 833 B. C., we have here a synchronism of the utmost importance; and as it is grounded upon an epoch in the reign of Asoka, to which frequent reference will be made in the course of this narrative, we shall have occasion to recur more than once to the history of this monarch. We may particularly notice what Hiouan Thsang says of him in his description of Magadha.—R.

The mention of the son of Asoka, as having reigned in this kingdom is a circumstance of great importance to Indian history. The *Raja Taringini* (Book I. sl. 1. p.) mentions an *Asoka* as king of Kashmír; but in no part of the slight account there given of him do we discern any circumstance calculated to identify him with the Asoka of Magadha, save that of his conversion to Buddhism. He is described as the great-grandson of *Sakuní*, son of the paternal uncle of *Sachinara;* no notice is taken of either *Chandragupta* or *Bimbására*. Yet the impression on our pilgrim's mind is evidently that the Asoka whose son formerly ruled in this kingdom, was the famous patron of Buddhism in Magadha. Had it been otherwise he would scarcely have introduced an allusion so irrelevant and uninteresting as this would then be. Professor Wilson (*History of Kashmír*, As. Res. Vol. XV. p. 20) seems inclined to treat the Asoka of Kalhana, as an ideal personage. It will be observed that Fa hian speaks of the son of Asoka only (named *Jaloka* in the *Raja Taringini*) as having reigned in *Kian tho 'wei*, and not Asoka himself. That the latter had great power and influence in *Gandhára*, we have good evidence in his fifth Edict as translated by James Prinsep, in which he appoints ministers of religion to that country. (J. A. S. Vol. VII. p. 252.) Without being able to solve the difficulties of the case, historical and critical, I incline to think that our Chinese authorities can hardly be wrong on such a point. Asoka himself, according to the Mahavansa, reigned in Ujjain previous to his accession to the throne of Magadha.—J. W. L.

(4) *In the time when Foe was Phou sa*,—that is, in one of those states of existence which we recognise as anterior to his historical existence, in which Sákya Muni had already attained the highest point of moral and intellectual perfection, and acquired the rank of Bodhisattwa. This portion of the legend being but little known, and forming as it were the *introductory scene* of the life of Buddha, I proceed to give an extract from a sermon preached by Sákya Muni, in the kingdom of Kapila, in the chapel of the Sákya family, under a tree of the species *nyagrodha (ficus religiosa)*, at which were present, twelve hundred and fifty great mendicants all of the rank of Arhans, five hundred female mendicants, an infinite number of *Upásika* and *Upásikí* (faithful of either sex) of bráhmans; the four kings of Heaven,

* *Wa kan kwo to fen nen gakf oun-no tsou.* B. I. p. 17 v.

the king of Trayastrinsha (Indra), Yama, the gods of Tushita, the god Nimalothi, the god Pho lo ni mi, Brahma, and the gods also of Aganishta, with the princes of the Nagas, of the Asuras, of the Kia lieou lo, of the Chin tho lo, of the Ma hieou le, &c.; and, the king Pe tsing, the king Wou nou, the king Wou youan, the king Kau lou tsing, and nine hundred thousand grandees and magistrates of the kingdom of Kapila, who were all assembled to do honor to Sákya, in his recently recognised rank of Buddha. *Maha mou kian lian*, one of the favorite disciples of Sákya, was he who elicited the account of the antecedent fortunes of the latter delivered the following discourse, of which I limit myself to the transcription of the most prominent circumstances only.* "My real life has extended over innumerable *Kalpas*. I was at first but an ordinary man, searching for the doctrine of Buddha. My soul received a material form in passing by the five ways. When one body was destroyed, I obtained another. The number of my births and deaths can only be compared with the number of plants and trees in the entire universe. The bodies I have possessed cannot be reckoned. That period of time which comprises the beginning and the end of heaven and earth, is called a *Kalpa;* and I cannot myself relate the renewals and the destructions of heaven and earth that I have witnessed. The causes of painful emotions are earthly passions. I was a long time floating on, and as it were immersed in the ocean of desires; but I strove to trace these to their source: such was the object of my efforts, and thus I succeeded. Anciently, in the time of the Buddha *Ting kouang* ("light of the vase," Dípankara) there was a holy king named *Teng shing* ("abundance of lamps") who reigned in the country of *Thi ho 'weï.* His subjects were favoured with great longevity, and lived in the exercise of piety and justice. Their land was fertile, and they enjoyed profound peace. It was then that the prince *Teng kouang* was born; a prince endowed with peerless faculties. The holy king, who loved him, perceiving the approach of old age, would have resigned to him the kingdom; but the prince yielded in favor of his younger brother, embraced a religious life, founded the Samanean doctrine, and became Buddha. He traversed the whole world at the head of a band of numberless disciples. When he returned to the kingdom of Thi ho 'weï, to convert his family and the grandees of the country, the latter were alarmed at the multitude of his followers, and were about to oppose his progress by a great army. The Buddha, by means of the six supernatural faculties he enjoyed, penetrated their design, raised a strong and lofty wall, and then a second, and rendered these walls transparent as glass, so that six hundred and twenty thousand bhikshus, all equal to Buddhas,

* From the *Sieou hing pen keï king*, quoted in *Shin i tian*, Book LXXVII. p. 8.

were seen through them. The king saw his error; the Buddha was adored, and preparations were made for a mighty festival for his reception. For the space of 40 *li* the roads were made smooth, and watered with perfumed water; and tents and pavilions were erected, all adorned with gold and silver and precious stones. The king advanced to meet the Buddha, and the latter commanded the bhikshus to acknowledge the honors he received. Whilst this was enacting, there was a young *Fan chi* scholar (Brahmacharí) named 'Spotless light:' from his youth upward he had given indications of superior intelligence. His soul was already opened to the most rare knowledge. Retired amongst forests and mountains, he led a pure life, given up to contemplation, studying the scriptures; and there was nothing that he did not thoroughly understand. He had converted many, and among the rest, a Brahmacharí named *Pou tsi tho*, who served in a great temple, where throughout the year he performed ceremonies and sacrifice. The band of his disciples, amounting to eighty thousand, brought him at the end of the year, gold of the Dakshin, silver, precious stones, chariots, horses, sheep, rich dresses, stuffs, elegant shoes, canopies enriched with pearls, staves of brass (for the use of the mendicants) and ewers. The most able and the most intelligent are entitled to all these treasures. Seven days had not elapsed ere the young Bodhisattwa entered this company. He preached seven days and seven nights. His audience was enraptured, and more than all their chief, who wished to present the Bodhisattwa with a virtuous girl; but the Bodhisattwa would accept nothing but an umbrella, a staff, a ewer, some shoes, and a thousand pieces of money. He restored all the rest to the master, who desired, at any rate, to share it with him; but the Bodhisattwa still refused; and when on parting from his disciples, distributed to each a piece of money. Proceeding on his journey he came to a land the inhabitants of which seemed joyously making preparations on all sides for festivals. He enquired the cause of these festivals, and was informed that Ting kouang was coming to receive the homage of the people. The young Bodhisattwa leapt for joy on learning the advent of the Buddha, and asked what homage they were to pay him? "Nothing but offerings of flowers, they replied; perfumes, woollen stuffs, and flags." He hastened to the town; but the king had forbidden the sale of flowers for seven days to reserve enough for the ceremonies! The Bodhisattwa felt deeply mortified at this disappointment; but the Buddha penetrated the intentions of the young man. A girl happened to pass with a pitcher full of flowers: the Buddha illumined it with a ray of light; the pitcher became transparent as glass, and the Bodhisattwa, having bought the flowers, went away delighted.

"The Buddha arrived, an immense multitude accompanying him and forming around him many thousand times a hundred rows. The Bodhisattwa strove to approach and scatter his flowers, but was unable. The Buddha, perceiving his efforts caused a great number of men of clay to arise from the earth and assist him in penetrating the throng. The Bodhisattwa then threw forward five flowers, which remained suspended in the air and formed a canopy seventy *li* in circumference. Two other flowers fixed themselves on the shoulders of the Buddha, as if they had there taken root. The delighted Bodhisattwa spread his hair upon the ground and entreated the holy personage to tread upon it. After sundry compliments and fresh solicitations, the Buddha complied. There then issued from his smiling lips two rays of light of different hues, which separating at the distance of seven feet, thrice encircled his person; one of these then illumined the three thousand millions of worlds without omitting one, and returned to the vertex (of the saint); the other penetrated to the eighteen infernal regions and for a moment suspended the tortures of the damned. The disciples asked the Buddha, to explain the reason of that smile. "You see this young man, he replied; the Honorable of the Age announces to you, that the purity he has striven to attain during an infinite number of kalpas, in subjecting his heart, surmounting fate, and expelling his passions, hath obtained for him, from the present time, that supreme void which results from the accumulation of virtues, and which shall accomplish his desires." Then turning to the young man, 'In a hundred kalpas, continued the Buddha, thou shalt become Buddha; thou shalt be called *Shy kia wen*, (the pious, the humane). The name of the kalpa in which thou shalt appear shall be *Pho tho*, (wise); the world shall be called *Sha fou*. Thy father shall be *Pe tsing*, thy mother *Ma ye*, thy wife *Kieou i*, thy son *Lo*. Thy companion shall be *Anan*, thy right hand disciple *She li foe*, they left *Maha mou kian lian*. Thou shalt instruct the men of the five great worlds; thou shalt save the ten parts, in all respects like myself" Thereupon Bodhisattwa *the Pious*, whom this announcement overwhelmed with joy, lost the faculty of thought and fell into an extasy; while his body at the same moment was raised in the air and continued suspended at the height of fifty-six feet from the earth. He then came down and prostrated himself at the foot of the Buddha. He then ceforth became a Samanean, and when the Buddha preached the law, Bodhisattwa the Pious assisted. When Ting koung attained nirvána, this Buddha received the precepts and maintained the law in all its purity. He never ceased the practice of goodness, humanity, charity, and all the virtues. When he died, he was reborn in Tushita; but as he ever longed to save those who continued in blindness and darkness, he descended in the form of the *King turning the Wheel*, (Chakravarti) *the* *emperor who walks flying.** He was the owner of the seven treasures, each more precious than the other; the golden wheel, the divine pearls, the perfect wife (of jasper), the all-accomplished minister, a well disciplined army, the mane of a purple horse bedecked with pearls, and the equally graced tail of a white elephant." See XVII. 12.

"The age of man was at that time, eighty-four thousand years. He had in his palace eighty-four thousand wives. A thousand sons were born to him, all so brave and virtuous that each was equal to a thousand (ordinary men). The holy king reigned with the utmost wisdom, and caused virtue to flourish. He established peace throughout the universe. Wind and rain came at the fit moment for ripening the crops; and whoever eat of the latter experienced no sickness. Their savour was as a sweet dew, and ensured perfect health. There were but seven infirmities or imperfections; cold, heat, hunger, thirst, the two natural necessities, and the cravings of the spirit. When the holy king had fulfilled his time, he ascended to the heaven of Brahma and became Brahma. The duration of the life of a Brahma, is two regenerations of the world, or two thousand six hundred and eighty-eight millions of years. In heaven, he was Indra. The life of an Indra, is a thousand years, of which each day is equal to one hundred of our years; or thirty-six millions five hundred thousand years. Upon earth he was a holy king. These vicissitudes occurred thirty-six times; when again he experienced a desire to save men, and at an appropriate time, became once more Bodhisattwa. In subjection to pain he passed three *Asankya* of kalpas (three hundred quadrillion times sixteen million eight hundred thousand years). At the end of this time he longed to display his commiseration for all sufferers, and to turn the wheel in favor of all living beings. He abandoned his body to a hungry tiger, and passed nine kalpas devoted to the greatest efforts. In the ninety-one kalpas remaining (from the time of the Buddha, Ting kouang) he applied himself to the study of reason and virtue; introduced himself to the thoughts of Buddha, practised the six means of salvation, and united in his heart the truth of alms (dána), the observation of the precepts (Síla), the salutary confusion (Kshánti), and holy activity (vírya), with transcendental knowledge, (prájná) and subtlety (upáya). He accustomed himself to treat all living beings with the tenderness he would manifest to a new-born babe. Lastly, he acquired all the virtues of a Buddha; so that having in the course of those kalpas traversed the ten earths (or stations for unification)† with this endeavor, he found himself arrived at that point in his existence called ***ekavíchika***, when the soul has but one more obstacle to surmount in the attainment of

* *L'empereur qui marche en volant*, is the original of this absurd expression.
† *Vocabulaire pentaglotte.* Sect. XI.

supreme intelligence. His merit being then complete, and the immense circle of divine prudence having been entirely traversed, it remained for him to descend and become Buddha.

"He prescribed to himself in the heaven Tushita four subjects of contemplation; the country where he should be born, the parents from whom he (*I* in the text) should receive birth, and all that was requisite for the instruction and the conversion he projected. I knew beforehand (continued Sákya, speaking henceforward in the third person) that it was the king *Pe tsing* that should be my father in the present age. *Kieou li sha ti*, had two daughters, who were then bathing in a tank, in the ladies' garden. The Bodhisattwa stretched forth his hand and said, "Behold the mother that shall bear me in the age." When the time of my birth was come there were five hundred Fan chi, all enjoying the five supernatural faculties, who passed flying over the walls of the palace without the ability to penetrate them. Struck with astonishment they said to each other; "our divine faculties enable us to pass through walls; how is it that we cannot penetrate these?" The master of the Brahmacharís replied; "See you these two damsels? One of them shall give birth to the *great man*, possessor of the thirty-two *lakshana* (corporeal beauties) and the other shall nurse this same great man. This divine and formidable being is about to deprive us of our supernatural faculties." This news spread rapidly through the universe. The king *Pe tsing*, transported with joy and longing that the *emperor who walks flying* should be born in his house, sought the young girl in marriage; and came to receive her as his bride. The pious Bodhisattwa, mounted upon a white elephant, approached his mother's womb, and selected for his birth the eighth day of the fourth moon. The matron having bathed and perfumed herself, was reposing, when she beheld in a dream a white elephant shedding light throughout the universe. A concert of vocal and instrumental music was heard, flowers were scattered, and perfumes burnt. When the cortège, which traversed the atmosphere, approached above her, all suddenly disappeared. She awoke alarmed, and when the king asked the cause of her alarm, she narrated the circumstances of her dream. The king, disquieted in his turn, consulted the augurs, and was re-assured. "This dream," said they, "is the forerunner of your happiness, oh king! it announces that a holy spirit hath entered the womb (of the princess). Of this dream she shall conceive, and the son she shall give birth to shall be in your house (as prince) the *emperor that walks flying, turning the wheel*; and out of your house (i. e. as an ascetic) he shall study the Law, become Buddha, and deliver the ten parts of the world. The king was enraptured with this assurance; the matron experience its salutary influence on mind and body. The princes of the petty neighbouring states, learning that the king's wife had conceived, came to pay her homage; each of them brought tribute of gold, of silver, of pearls, of precious cloth, of flowers, and of perfumes; expressed their respect, and invoked a thousand blessings. The matron extended her hand and declined their gifts with civility. After the matron's conception the Gods presented her with the most savoury viands; a subtle vapor nourished her, superceding the necessity of all recourse to the royal kitchen. At the end of the tenth month the body of the prince being entirely formed, on the 8th day of the fourth moon, the matron went forth, passed through the throng, and placed herself beneath a tree. The flowers expanded, and a brilliant star appeared."

Here I interrupt the legend at the point where this holy personage begins an existence, during which he attained the rank of Buddha. Many particulars of his latter career will be found in subsequent notes; but we may here remark that the name of *Bodhisattwa*, is still applied to Sákya in relating the adventures of his terrestrial life previous to the time of his attaining Buddhahood; that is, up to his thirtieth year (see XII. 2.)—R.

(5) This proof of the charity of Buddha is spoken of in the other narratives.—R.

CHAPTER XI.

The kingdom of Chu sha shi lo.—The starving Tiger.

At the distance of seven days' journey to the east of *Kian tho wei*, there is a kingdom named *Chu sha shi lo*. The word signifies in Chinese the *Severed Head*.[1] Foe, while he was *Phou sa*,[2] bestowed his head[3] in alms at this place; and hence they gave this name to the country.

Further to the east you arrive at the spot where Foe abandoned his body to a starving tiger.[4] In these two places they have erected great towers, embellished with all manner of precious things. The kings of those countries, the grandees, and the people, all vie with each other in the performance of their devotions at this place; they never intermit the scattering of flowers and the burning of perfumes. These towers, and the other two spoken of above, are called by the people of the country *the Four Great Towers.*[5]

NOTES.

(1) *Chu sha shi lo,* apparently *chyutasira,* a Sanscrit word, having pretty nearly the signification indicated by Fa hian : the sibilant replacing the dental of the second syllable in the Chinese transcription. We have already seen this substitution, and will meet with it again. It is not to be wondered at that a denomination founded upon such an adventure should disappear with Buddhism itself from the locality. Our information does not enable us to determine the position of this country with exactness ; it should be not far from Sorawak and the present district of Sarawan.—R.

The place here named *Chu sha shi lo* by Fa hian is evidently identical with that called *Tan cha shi lo* in the itinerary of Hiouan thsang, where the mention of a monastery of the *alms gift of the head* places this point beyond all doubt. The latter name at once recalls the *Takshasila* of the Puranas and the *Taxila* of the ancients. Taksha and Pushkara were sons of Bharata, according to the *Vishnu Purana* (Wilson's Translation, p. 385,) and are stated in the *Váyu* to have been sovereigns of *Gandhára* residing at *Takshasila* and *Pushkaravatí.* The situation of *Chu sha shi lo,* seven days journey eastward from *Kian tho wei,* corresponds very well with the position of Manikyala. That village (now so celebrated for its tope) is situated on the ruins of a very ancient town, which from its extent and position, and the abundance of ancient coins found in the neighbourhood, may with much probability be assumed to have been the Taxila of the Greek historians. For further information on the subject of Manikyala and its relics, the reader is referred to the Journal of the Asiatic Society for 1834.—J. W. L.

(2) *When Foe was Phou sa ;* (See X. 4.)

(3) *His head in alms.*—This circumstance, as well as that of the *alms-giving of his eyes,* before alluded to, is found among the legends collected by Hiouan Thsang.—R.

(4) *Abandoned his body to a starving tiger.*—(See Chap. X. note 4.) Formerly Buddha, when prince, under the name of *Sa tho* (*Sattwa*) was walking among the hills ; he beheld a tiger perishing of hunger, and cast his own person before it to save its life.*—R.

(5) *The four great towers,*—to wit, that of *Su ho to,* where the Bodhisattwa rescued the dove at the expense of his own flesh ; that of *Gandhára,* or of the almsgiving of his eyes ; and the two spoken of in the present chapter.—R.

* *San tsang fa sou,* B. XXXVIII. p. 1 *v.*

CHAPTER XII.

The Kingdom of Foe leou sha.—The pot of Foe.

Proceeding to the south four days' journey from the kingdom of *Kian tho wei*, you arrive at the kingdom of *Foe leou sha.*[1] In days of old, Foe, when passing through this country with his disciples, addressed A nan[2] and said—"After my *pan ni houan,*[3] there shall be a king named *Ki ni kia,*[4] who shall raise a tower on this spot." Accordingly, the king *Ni kia* having appeared in the world, betook to travelling; and as he passed through this country, Shy, the celestial emperor,[5] sought to awaken a thought within him. He produced a young cow-herd erecting a tower on the road. The king asked him, "What doest thou?" He replied, "I am building a tower to Foe." The king praised him highly, and caused a tower to be erected over that of the young cow-herd. This tower is more than forty toises[6] high, and is adorned with all manner of precious things; all who behold it and the temple, admire their beauty and magnificence, to which nothing can be compared. Fame reports this tower superior to all the others of *Yan feou thi.*[7] When the king's tower was completed, the smaller tower appeared to the south of the large one, about three feet high.

The *pot of Foe*[8] is in this kingdom. In former times the king of the *Yue ti*[9] raised a powerful army and invaded this country. He longed to possess the pot of Foe. When he had subjected the kingdom, the king of the *Yue ti,* who was firmly attached to the Law of Foe, endeavoured to seize the pot and carry it away. For this purpose he commanded sacrifices to be made, and when he had sacrificed to the *three precious ones,*[10] he brought a large elephant richly caparisoned, and placed the pot upon the elephant. But the elephant fell to the earth, unable to advance. He then constructed a four-wheeled car, and placed thereon the pot, and eight elephants were yoked to draw it; but these were unable to move a step. The king then knew that the destiny of the pot[11] was not yet fulfilled. He experienced deep mortification; nevertheless he caused a tower and a *Sen kia lan*[12] to be erected on this spot. He left a garrison to protect it, and caused all manner of ceremonies to be performed. There may be in that place about seven hundred ecclesiastics. A little before mid-day, the ecclesiastics bring the pot forth from its retreat, and clad in white garments, pay it all manner of honour. They then dine, and when evening is come, they burn perfumes, and afterwards return home. The pot may contain about two bushels.[13] It is of a mixed colour, in which black predominates; it is well formed on all four sides, about two lines thick, bright and polished. Poor people come and, with a few flowers, fill it; whilst rich people bringing flowers as an offering, are unable to fill it with a hundred, a thousand, yea, ten thousand great measures.[14]

Only *Pao yun* and *Leng king* paid their devotions at the pot of Foe; they then returned. *Hoeï king, Hoeï tha,* and *Tao ching* had set out in advance to the kingdom of *Na kie* to worship there the Shadow and the Tooth of Foe, as also the bone of his skull. Hoeï king having fallen sick, Tao ching remained to attend him, and Hoeï tha returned alone to the kingdom of Foe leou sha. When he rejoined his companions, Hoeï tha, Pao yun and Seng king returned forthwith to the country of Thsin. Hoeï king was delighted in an extraordinary manner with the temple of the pot of Foe. Fa Hian alone proceeded to the place of the skull-bone of Foe.

NOTES.

(1) *The kingdom of Foe leou sha.*—There is scarce room to doubt that this is the most ancient record of the name Beluchí, under a form most probably borrowed from the Sanscrit. The town of *Pa leou sha*, which Hiouan Thsang places to the south-east of Gandhára, and that of *Fou leou sha*, which was inhabited by the *Yue ti*, seem to recall the same denomina-

tion. I hesitated at first to recognise the Beluchís, in the country of *Foe leou sha*, and thought that the name might be a corruption of that of *Pars* or *Fars;* but the geographical and religious considerations involved in the subject of *Foe lou sha* and *Pa lou sha*, forbid this conjecture.* It is singular enough that we should find this word in a Chinese narrative of the 5th century; and still more so to learn from such a source, particulars of the religious observances of the people not found elsewhere. The most magnificent tower in all *Jambudwípa*, that is of Indian architecture in the entire continent, was constructed by the *Foe leou sha*, in honor of Buddha; and in that tower was preserved his begging pot, an indispensible and characteristic utensil of the Buddhist recluse. The possession of such a treasure drew upon the country an invasion of the *Yue ti* or *Getæ*, of whom Fa hian preserves this tradition accompanied by fabulous details. Chinese Geographers are, moreover, unanimous on the subject of the domination exercised by the Getæ in these countries, and we shall by and bye see their name mixed up with a tradition relative to the same begging pot of Foe, noted by our traveller during his sojourn in Ceylon.—R.

Lassen *(Zur Geschichte, &c.* p. 145) has satisfactorily restored the true reading of *Foe lou sha*, (or as it is more correctly transcribed by Hiouan thsang *Pou lou sha pou lo.)* in *Purushapúra;* a reading so obvious that the acquiescence of MM. Klaproth and Landresse in Remusat's identification of *Foe lou sha* with *Beluchí*, is quite unaccountable. The situation of *Foe lou sha*, must have in the neighbourhood of Peshávar, if indeed it be not the same; an inference which the similarity of name would seem in some degree to justify, although Muhammadan historians ascribe the present name to Akbar, who imposed it with reference to the frontier situation of the town. Certain it is there are many splendid monuments of Buddhism in the immediate vicinity. "In the gorge of the Khyber Pass, says Dr. Gerard, which penetrates the country from Peshávar, stands a most magnificent edifice equal or exceeding that of Manikyala, and if I am not mistaken there are others." These remains sufficiently prove that *Foe lou sha*, was an eminently Buddhist country, such as it is here described by Fa hian. See also Burnes, J. A. S. Vol. II. p. 308; and Wilson *Ariana Antiqua*, p. 36, *et seq.* —J. W. L.

(2) *A nan*,—frequently *A nan tho* (*Ananda*) the meaning of which is explained to be *gladness, jubilation;*† one of the favorite disciples of Sákya Muni, and one of those most frequently mentioned in the legends. He

* *Pian i tian*, B. LXIII. p. 15.
† *San tsung fa sou*, B. XXXI. p. 10 *verso*.

was deemed the most learned (*to wen*)* and the best versed in the doctrines of the three *tsang* (*Pitaka*), that is, the sacred books, the precepts, and the discourses. When Buddha had accomplished the law, the king *Hou fan* (*Amitodana*) his uncle, sent a message to his elder brother, king *Pe tsing* (*Suklodana*) that a son had been born to him. Pe tsing, enraptured at the news, observed to the ambassadors, " Since it is a son, we must give him the name of *Joy* (*Ananda*)." This prince subsequently attached himself to Sákya Muni, when the latter embraced a religious life.

A notice of the life of Ananda, informs us that he was a Kshetriya, native of the *town of the kings* (Rajagriha) and son of the king Pe fan. This last point is at variance with the preceding text which makes Ananda son of king Amitodana. After the narvána of his cousin, Ananda proceeded to the banks of the Ganges. Five hundred Arhans, descended through the air; amongst them were *Shang na ho sieou*, and *Mo ti kiá;* he knew that all these personages were *receptacles* (*vases*) *of the great law*, and he called them to him. "Formerly," he said to them, " the Tathágata confided to the great Kashyapa, the treasure of *the eyes of the true law*. When the latter entered into extasy, he transferred it to me; and I, who am on the eve of extinction, am about to transmit it to you. Listen to the following verses:

> There exists a law which I am about to confide to you,
> And that law is non-existence (the absolute).
> It is essential to distinguish these two things,
> And understand the law of that which is not nihility.

The Arhan then raised himself in the air, and after undergoing eighteen transformations, allowed himself to be borne away by the breeze, and extinguished himself suddenly, sinking into *san mi* (extasy). They divided his reliques, (*sarira*) and erected towers to his honor. This happened in the time of *I wang* of Cheou (894-879 B. C.)†

A chronological calculation may be deduced from these data. Sákya was thirty years of age, when he accomplished the law near the town of Benares;‡ and it was at this epoch that Ananda was born. Mahá Kasyapa, the first successor of Sákya Muni, in the capacity of patriarch, withdrew to the hill Kukutapada to await the advent of Maitreya in the fifth year of Híao wang of the Cheou, 905 B. C. forty-five years after the Nirvána, when

* *Fan i ming i*, quoted in the *San tsang fa sou*, B. XII. p. 13 ; *Japanese Encyclop.* B. XIX. p. 8.

† *San thsaï thou hoeï jin we*, Book IX. p. 6. v.

‡ Or rather Rájagriha.—J. W. L.

Ananda was 94 years old. How long he exercised his functions of patriarch, is not narrated; but in order to make his death synchronise even with the first year of the reign of *I wang*, he must have lived one hundred and five years. This is not impossible; still there is the more reason to doubt the fact since all the Buddhist writers whose works we have access to leave us in ignorance of the data upon which they establish such synchronisms between the early events of Buddhism and the ancient history of China. The subjoined is a brief recapitulation of these, from the Chinese work quoted above.

Birth of Sákya ,.............	0—24th of Chao wang, B. C.	1029
Embraces a religious life, ...	19—43d....................	1010
Accomplishes the law. Ananda born,	30—3d	999
Enters Nirvána, ...	79—52d of Mou wang, ...	950
Mahá Kasyapa dies,...........	124—5th of Híao wang,........	905
Ananda dies,.................	in the reign of I wang,....	894-879

Other Chinese works furnish calculations attended with similar uncertainty. Japanese Chronology places the death of Kasyapa, in 905 B. C. and that of Ananda in the eleventh year of Li wang, 868, when he must have been a hundred and thirty years old.*—R.

See my notes 4, Chapter XXVI, and 1, Chapter XXXII.—J. W. L.

(3) *Pan ni houan;—ni houan*, or extinction, may be recognized without difficulty as the transcription of the Sanscrit word *Nirvána*. But the word is often preceded in Chinese books by the syllable *pan;* and this occurs always when the expression refers, not to annihilation or extasy in general, but to the passage from real and relative life to the state of absorption as effected by a Buddha. *Ni houan* is the state to which saints aspire; *pan ni houan*, is the act by which they attain it. Adopting this explanation, M. Burnouf, thinks that these words may be the transcription of *pari nirvána* which in Sanscrit are employed in the same sense and upon similar occasions.—R.

The words of the text are *ngo pan ni houan heou*. The word *pan*, or rather *pouan*, signifies, according to Chinese dictionaries, *to transport one's-self from one place to another*. It would thus appear not to be the transcription of a Sanscrit word in the passage quoted, of which the sense seems sufficiently clear, being, " after that I was transported into *Ni houan (nirvána)*." The *San tsang fa sou*, (Book XXXIX. folio 24 *verso*) nevertheless mentions that the words *Pan ni phan*, is a Sanscrit expression, meaning in Chinese *my tou*, that is, " the passage into a state of absorption."—Kl.

(4) *Ki ni kia*, or abbreviated as lower down, *Ni kia;*—the same prince who,

* *Wa kan kwó toó fen nen gakf oun no tsou*, p. 16.

according to *Hiouan thsang*, reigned four hundred years after the Nirvána of the Tathágata, and whom he names *Kia ni se kia.* This must be the *Kanika* of Sanangsetsen, whom this Mongolian writer places three hundred years after the Nirvána of Buddha, and whom he designates as the king of Gatchou, with the epithet, *prince of mercy, bestower of charity, beneficent.** —R.

This is no doubt the Kanishka of the *Lalita Vistára*; the monarch in whose reign, 400 years after the *nirvána*, the third revision of the Buddhist scriptures was completed. It is extremely probable that this prince is identical notwithstanding a chronological discrepance, with the Kanishka of the *Raja Taringini*, in which he and his immediate predecessors are spoken of as eminent Buddhists. "During the long reign of these kings, the country of Kashmír was for the greater part of the time in the hands of the Bauddhas, whose strength was augmented by their wandering habits. One hundred and fifty years had then elapsed since the emancipation of the blessed Sákya Sinha from this perishable world." *Raja Taringini*, B. 1. sl. 171, 172. Hiouan thsang confirms the chronology of the *Lalita Vistára.* It does not follow however that the territories of Kashmír extended to Foe leou sha at this time; for Fa hian simply speaks of Kanishka as travelling through that country; very possibly on a pilgrimage to the consecrated spots which attracted himself some centuries later.—J. W. L.

(5) *Shy*;—Indra.

(6) *Forty toises*;—about 400 English feet. For an account of a yet loftier *sthupa*, in the same country, see Chap. III. 3, and the account of Gandhára by Hiouan thsang.—R.

(7) *Yan feou thi.*—This is a corruption of *Jambu dwípa* sometimes more correctly rendered the *Island of Shen pou.* Buddhist cosmogony, like that of the bráhmans, divides the earth into four great *Dwípas*, or continents (islands) disposed around Sumeru. These continents are named,—

1. *Foe yu thaï*, or *Foe pho thi*, (Púrvavidehá ?) to the east of Sumeru. This word signifies *a body which surpasses*, because the extent of this continent exceeds that of the southern one. It is also translated *origin*, or *beginning*, because the sun rises in that country. This continent is narrow towards the east, and broad towards the west, having the form of a half moon. The faces of the inhabitants are also fashioned like a half moon. Their stature is eight cubits, of eight inches each; and they live two hundred and fifty years.

[This word is properly a synonyme of *Videha*, oriental.—Kl.]

* *Geschichte der Ost-Mongolen*, p. 16.

2. *Yan feou thí; yan feou*, in Sanscrit *Jambu; thi, dwípa*, an island. *Jambu* is the name of a tree. "In western lands there is a tree called *Jambu;* at its foot is a river, and at the bottom of this river is auriferous sand."* This continent is to the south of Sumeru; it is narrow to the south and broad towards the north, of the form of the body of a chariot; its extent is seven thousand yojanas. The faces of the inhabitants are of the same shape as the continent. The greater number of them are three and a half cubits high, and some so much as four cubits. The duration of their life is one hundred years, but many do not attain this age.

[Other Chinese authors say that Jambu dwípa signifies *the eastern isle of gold.*—Kl.]

3. *Kiu ye ni* (Gódhanya.) This Sanscrit word signifies *wealth of oxen*, because it is in oxen that the riches of the country consist. It lies west of Sumeru. Its form is that of the full moon; its diameter eight thousand yojanas. The faces of its inhabitants resemble the full moon. Their stature is sixteen cubits, and they live five hundred years.

4. *Yu tan yue* (*Uttara kuru*). This Sanscrit word signifies the '*Land of conquerors*,' because its inhabitants have subjected the three other continents.

[The Chinese text says that the word Yu tan yue signifies in Chinese, "The most elevated place, because this country is more elevated than the three other *Cheou*, or divisions of the world." The version of M. Remusat, "Land of Conquerors," &c. is incorrect; besides *uttaru* in Sanscrit signifies pre-eminent, or raised, and *Kuru* is the name of a tribe.—Kl.]

To the north is Sumeru. This continent is square like a tank; its size is ten thousand yojanas. The faces of its inhabitants are of the form of the continent. They are thirty-two cubits high, and live a thousand years. There is no such thing as premature death among them.†

The names of these four continents in Tibetan and Mongol are—

Tibetan.	Mongolian.
1. Char giï Lus pag dwíp.	1. Dorona Oulamdzi beyetou dip.
2. Jambu dwip, or Jambu gling.	2. Jambu dwíp.
3. Noub giï Balang bdjod dwíp.	3. Ourouna Uker edlektchi dip.
4. Bdja gra misnan dwíp.	4. Môh dôhtou dip.

Jambu dwíp evidently represents India in this cosmography, together with what other parts of the old continent were known to the Hindus. I shall hereafter have occasion to explain who were the *Kings of the Wheel* (Chakravarti raja) or universal monarchs. During the interval of the

* *Fan y ming i*, quoted in the *San tsang fa sou*, Book XX. p. 8.
† *Chang a han*, quoted in the *San tsang fa sou*, B. XVIII. p. 17.

dominion which these kings exercised over one or other of the great isles of which I am about to speak, Jambu dwípa was divided among four great lords: 1. To the east, the *king of men*, so called because of the vast population of those parts. The natives were refined in their manners; they cultivated humanity, justice, and science; the country was pleasant and agreeable. 2. To the south, *the king of elephants*. This country is hot and moist, suitable for elephants, and hence its name. The inhabitants are violent and ferocious, addicted to magic and the occult sciences; but they are capable also of purifying the heart, and, by casting off the trammels of the world, of emancipating themselves from the vicissitudes of life and death. 3. To the west, *the king of precious things*. This country extends to the sea, which produces plenty of pearls and precious things and thus gives rise to the name. The inhabitants are ignorant alike of the rites and of social duties, and hold nothing in esteem but riches. 4. To the north, *the king of horses*. This land is cold and hard, adapted to the nurture of horses. The inhabitants are bold and cruel, capable of enduring dangers and death.*—R.

I believe that this refers to the four chiefs who divided the empire of India, after the dismemberment of the ancient royalty of Delhi, and whom tradition names *Narapati*, chief of men; *Gajapati*, chief of elephants; *Chhatrapati*, chief of the umbrella; *Ashwapati*, chief of horses.—E. Burnouf.

(8) *The begging pot of Fo.*—The pot is one of the six indispensibles of a religious mendicant. It is with the pot that he asks alms, and it is in it that he holds his food. Its form is that of a small flat vessel, narrow at the top and broader at the bottom. Its material should be common and low-priced, like clay or iron; and it should contain a bushel and a half at least, and not more than three bushels. A figure of one may be seen in the little elementary Japanese Encyclopedia.† That represented in the great Encyclopedia is too much ornamented, and represents the State vase of some rich convent in Japan. The pot and the garments of Foe are looked upon as precious reliques, which should be preserved with religious solicitude and passed from hand to hand, so that the Chinese expression *i po*, (vestment and pot) have become synonymous with this mode of transmission.‡ It is pretended that the pot and the garments of Foe were brought to China, in the 5th century, by Bodhidharma, the last of the Buddhist patriarchs born in Hindustan.§ We shall see in the course of the present narrative, many other facts connected with the pot of Buddha. The

* *Fa youan chu lin*, i. e. *the forest of pearls in the garden of the law*, quoted in the *San tsang fa sou*, Book XVI. p. 12 v.

† *Huin meng thou louï*, Book XI. p. 6.

‡ *Khang hi tseu tian*, ad verb *Po*.

§ Id. ibid.

Chinese word *po* (pot) is an abridgment of the Sanscrit *po to lo,* (pátra). The Manchous have formed of it their word *badiri.* The Burmese သပိတ်.*—R.

(9) *The king of the Yue ti.*—The *Yue shi, yue chi,* or as M. Klaproth thinks, the word should be read the *Yue ti,* or *Youtti,* are one of the most celebrated nations of ancient Tartary. According to the Chinese, they originally led a wandering life in the country lying between *Thun hoang* (Sha cheou) and the Khi lian Mountains. A war waged against them in the second century before Christ by their northern neighbours, the Hioung nou, compelled them to fly towards the west. They established themselves in Transoxania beyond Ferghana; and having overcome the Ta hia, halted on the northern bank of the *Weï* (Oxus), subjecting at the same time the *Anszu,* who in those times had no supreme chief. They occupied at the time when Chang khian was among them as ambassador (See Chap. VII. note 4) five towns, the names of which it is not easy to recognise, owing to the penury of geographical information connected with that country at the epoch in question. These towns were *Ho me,* capital of the tribe of *Hieou mi; Shouang mi,* occupied by a tribe of the same name; *Hou tsao,* subject to a prince of *Koueï shouang*; *Po mao,* inhabited by a tribe of the *Hi tun,* and *Kao fou* (Cabul) where dwelt a tribe so named. The town of *Lan shi,* is quoted as the residence of their king. In the first century of our era the prince of the Koueï shouang subjected the other four states, became very powerful, mastered the countries of the An szu, of Cabul, of Han tha (Kandahar), of Ki pin (Cophene). His successor yet further increased in power and possessed himself of India. The kings of the Yue ti continued their authority in these countries up to the third century. Their incursions into India are spoken of even to the fifth century, and the situations of their settlements pointed out. *Pho lo* (Balkh) to the west, Gandhara to the north, and five kingdoms to the south of the latter, recognised their authority. It was the merchants of this nation that instructed the Chinese in the art of making glass from melted flint. A branch of the Yue ti, which remained behind at the period of their emigration, inhabited the N. E. of Little Tibet, under the name of the Little Yue ti. Another branch, bearing the same name, but very distinct, detached itself at a subsequent period (in the fifth century) from the bulk of the nation, and occupied the town of *Foe leou sha,* situated to the S. W. of *Pho lo,* (Balkh), and which must be the *Pa lou sha,* of Hiouan thsang, (see Chap. XII.), or the country of the Beluchís. It is reported that at ten *li* distance from this town

* Judson, *Burm. Dict.* p. 362.

there was a tower dedicated to Foe, which was three hundred and fifty paces in circumference and eighty toises high. From the date of the erection of this gigantic tower, called the *tower of a hundred toises*, to the eighth year of the *Wou ting* (550 A. D.) eight hundred and forty-two years were reckon-ed; which gives 292 B. C. as the date of its erection, and consequently at an epoch previous to the emigration of the Yue ti.

There can be no doubt that the *Yue ti* were one of those nations of upper Asia, who settled in Batriana and conquered the eastern provinces of Persia, modern Afghanistan, Beloochistan and the western parts of India. Their name, of which traces exist among all these nations, leads us to the opinion that they are of the Gothic stem, notwithstanding their oriental origin. It is not a little remarkable to find this race so attached to the religion of Buddha as the fact here narrated by Fa hian, and other circumstances to be noted hereafter, would evince.—R.

(10) *The three precious ones.*—See Chap. VII. note 6.—R.

(11) *The destiny of the pot.*—The word *Yuan*, which I translate *destiny*, signifies perhaps not that which has been irrevocably fixed beforehand by a free and infinitely powerful being, but the inevitable concatenation of all cause and all effect. As to the fate of the pot of Buddha, we shall see a curious tradition on this subject in Fa hian's narrative connected with Ceylon.—R.

(12) *Seng kia len.*—See Chap. III. note 5.—R.

(13) *Two bushels.*—The *teou* or bushel, contains ten pounds of rice or 140 ounces of our ordinary weight (French).—R.

(14) *Great measures.—Hou*, the decuple of a bushel.—R.

CHAPTER XIII.

Kingdom of Na kie.—Town of Hi lo.—Skull-bone of Foe.—Tooth of Foe.—Staff of Foe.—Mantle of Foe.—Shadow of Foe.

Travelling westward the space of sixteen *yeou yan*,[1] you arrive at the frontier of the kingdom of *Na kie*[2] and the town of *Hi lo*.[3] In this place is the chapel of the skull-bone Foe. It is gilded all over and covered with the most costly ornaments.[4] The king of the country entertains the greatest veneration for the bone; and in the dread lest any one should purloin it, has chosen eight chiefs of the principal families of his kingdom, each of whom has a seal which he sets on the gate of the chapel. Early in the morning the whole eight proceed to verify the seals, and then open the gate. When it is opened, they wash their hands in perfumed water, take up the skull-bone of Foe, and bear it out of the chapel to a throne provided with a round stone table and all kinds of precious things. The table of stone which is below, and the bell-glass which covers it are equally adorned with pearls and fine gems. The bone is of a yellowish white colour; it is four inches in circumference, and has an eminence on the upper part. Every day at sunrise the attendants of the chapel ascend an elevated pavilion, beat great drums, sound the conch, and strike the copper cymbals. As soon as the king hears these, he repairs to the chapel, where he performs his devotions, offering flowers and perfumes. This service concluded, each, according to his rank, places the relique on his head[5] and goes away. You enter by the eastern gate and go out by the western. The king adopts this practice every morning, and it is only after he has paid his devotions and completed the ceremony of adoration, that he engages in the affairs of the state. The grandees and the principal officers begin with the same act of adoration before engaging in their private affairs. It is the same every day, and this particular duty admits of no intermission or abatement of zeal. When all have finished their devotions, the skull-bone is taken back again to the chapel. There are *towers of deliverance*,[6] adorned with all manner of precious things, some open, the others shut, and about five feet high. To supply these, there are constantly every morning, dealers in flowers and perfumes before the gate of the chapel, that such as wish to perform their devotions may buy of every variety. The kings of neighbouring countries are likewise in the habit of deputing persons to perform the ceremonies of worship in their name. The site occupied by the chapel is forty paces square. Were the heavens to fall down and the earth to open up, this spot would never be removed!

From this place, proceeding northward one *yeou yan*, you arrive at the capital of the kingdom of *Na kie*. It was here that the *Phou sa* bought with silver money flowers wherewith to do homage to *Ting kouan Foe*.[7] In this town there is a tower erected over a tooth of Foe.[8] They perform the same ceremonies there as in honor of the skull-bone.

At the distance of one *yeou yan* to the north-east of the town, at the entrance of a valley, is the staff of Foe.[9] In this place also is a chapel erected, and are similar ceremonies performed. The staff is surmounted with a bull's head in sandalwood; it is about six or seven toises long. It is placed within a wooden tube, whence a hundred, or even a thousand men, could not withdraw it.

Entering the valley, and proceeding four days' journey towards the west, you arrive at the chapel of the *Seng kia li* of Foe,[10] where the ceremonies of adoration are performed. When there is great drought in the kingdom, the inhabitants proceed together, draw forth the *Seng kia li*, and adore it. The heavens then shower down rain in abundance.

To the south of the town, about half a *yeou yan*, there is a stone building backed by a mountain and facing the south-west. It was here that Foe left his shadow.[11] When you contemplate it at the distance of ten paces, it is as if you saw the veritable person of Foe himself, of the colour of gold, with all its characteristic beauties, and resplendent with light. The nearer you approach the fainter the shadow becomes. It is a representation perfectly resembling the reality. The kings of all countries have sent painters to copy it, but none have succeeded. The people of the country have a tradition according to which a thousand Foes will eventually leave their shadows here.

At about a hundred steps to the west of the shadow, Foe, while in the world, cut his hair and his nails; and in concert with his disciples erected a tower seven or eight toises[12] high, to serve as a model for all towers to be erected thereafter. It subsists to this day. Near it is a monastery in which are about seven hundred ecclesiastics. In this place is the tower of the *Lo han* and the *Py chi Foe*,[13] where have dwelt a thousand (of those sanctified personages.)

NOTES.

(1) *The space of six yeou yan.*—The length of the *yeou yan*, or *yojana* of India, is estimated at 4 kros, that is 4½, 5, or even 9 English miles. The employment of this measure, foreign to China, shows that Fa hian adopted Indian estimations of distance. From the correspondence of many of these mentioned by him with the actual distances upon our maps, it would appear that he faithfully delivered the estimations of geographers or of travellers in India during the 5th century. Nevertheless, the greater part of his distances whether expressed in *li*, or in marches, or in *yojanas*, appear somewhat too great, and even exaggerated. The sinuosities of the roads, and the variations of the standard of measure may in some degree account for too high an estimate. On some occasions he was misled by false and almost fabulous reports; but this is only when he speaks of places which he had not himself visited, or of distances which he was not himself in a condition to verify; and his errors of this kind are of less consequence. We are inclined to adopt as the mean value of the *yojana*, of the Foe koue ki, the least of those mentioned by Wilson; that is 4½ English miles, or 15 to a degree, as applicable with exactness to the most celebrated localities, the synonymy of which will hereafter appear incontestible.

I may here adjoin some literary and historical observations. This metrical term is written in Chinese, *yeou yan*, *yeou siun*, or *yu chen na*, the threefold transcript of *yojana*, and is translated *measure*, *goal*, or *station*. The *Ye sou** ascribes its origin to the stations established by the *kings of the wheel* (*Chakravarti raja*) when they visited the different parts of their dominions. "They are," says a Chinese writer, "the relays of the post in that country." And the writer estimates the yojan at 40 *li* in the times of the *Tsin*.† The translators of Buddhist works distinguish three kinds of yojan according to the *Ta chi tou tun*;‡ the *great yojana* of 80 *li*, which is used in the measurement of level countries, where the absence of mountains and rivers renders the road easy; the *mean yojana* of 60 *li*, when

* *San tsang fa sou*, Book XIII. p. 5.
† *Youan kian louï han*, Book CCCXVI. p. 6.
‡ *Fan y ming i*, quoted in the *San tsang fa sou.*—*ibid.*

rivers and mountains oppose some difficulties to the traveller, and the *little yojana* of 40 *li*, adapted to those countries where the mountains are precipitous and the rivers very deep. For the Indian valuation of the *yojana*, the reader may consult Wilson (Sanscrit Dictionary) and the Ayin Akbarí ; and for that deduced from the distances given by Fa hian what has been said above. It may be inferred that our traveller obtained the distances he sets down from the mouths of the natives, or perhaps from some Indian geographical work which he had within reach. In either case an approximate determination only can be expected, sufficient for the historical geography of a country almost entirely unknown. We may further observe that Fa hian begins to use this measure in the country of *Na kie*, having employed the Chinese *li* throughout the previous portions of his journey. This is another of those facts which attest the predominance of the language and customs of Hindustan beyond the present limits of that country towards the north and north-west.—R.

(2) *The kingdom of Na kie.*—The position of this country is not easy of determination, as well from the few points of comparison as because Fa hian and Hiouang thsang followed different routes to reach it. The former arrived there after a journey of sixteen *yojanas* to the west of the Beluchí country: the second goes viâ Cabul, after crossing a great river, which must be one of the affluents of the Indus, and thence proceeds westerly to the country of the Gandharas. We cannot, however, be far from the truth in placing *Na kie*, to the east of the present Ghazni and Kandahar. But confining our attention here to the names only, that of *Na kie*, written *Na kie lo ho*, by Hiouan thsang, is written *Na kia lo ho*, by the two Chinese travellers Soung yun, and Hoeï sang. A legend is given in the *Si yu ki*, which may explain its origin. The kingdom of *Na kie lo ho*, sent tribute to China in A. D. 628. It was then a dependence of that of *Kia pi she*.

As China had, under the dynasty of the Thang, political intercourse with the kingdom of *Na kie*, the latter must have had an existence of some duration. We learn that at the period in question it was not subject to one prince, but was divided among several tribes, each of which had its own chief; the ordinary condition of Scinde, Belúchistan, and Afghanistan. The country was rugged, unequal, scooped into valleys, and surrounded by mountains. This description applies equally to all parts of that country. Finally, five hundred *li* to the south-east, bring us back to the country of Gandhára. This indication, though vague, places *Na kie* in the centre of Afghanistan, and the town of *Hi lo* must be situated on the confines of that country and Persia. The number of hermits there had greatly diminished, and many religious structures had fallen to ruins. Shy kia (Sákya) in his condition of Bodhisattwa, had left traces of his passage through this country.—R.

I here transcribe Lassen's luminous critique of this portion of our pilgrim's route:—

"*Na kie* lies sixteen yojanas westward of *Foe leou sha*, (Peshawur). Its name is more correctly transcribed *Na ko lo ho* by Hiouan thsang, who approached it from *Lan pho* or Lamghan, crossing the great (or Cabul) River, from which it was distant a hundred *li*, or somewhat more than five geographical miles. *Na ko lo ho* lay in the valley of the river *Hi lo*, about a mile from the capital of the same name, and close to a hill likewise called *Hi lo*.

"The latter river, on the south side of the Cabul, can be no other than the Súrkhrúd, and on this supposition we must search for *Na ko lo ho* in Balabagh. The Buddhist remains said to be in the neighbourhood of the *Hi lo*, are identical with those on the Súrkhrúd from Balabagh to Jellalabad.

"In the river *Hi lo*, I think I recognise the *Hir* of D'Anville and Rennell's maps, at the confluence of which with the Nilab the town of Nagara must have stood; only there is another *Hir* to be accounted for, which in other narratives is said to flow past Cabul. If then *Hi lo* be the Chinese transcription of Hir, *Na ko lo ho* seems as certainly that of Nagara.

"This leads us back to the *Nagara* of Ptolemy, which was unquestionably to the south of the Kameh river. Now the obvious similarity of names leaves little room to doubt that his Nagara was no other than *Na ko lo ho*. His *Artoartar* must be identical with the Purushapura of the Chinese travellers. * * * * * *Na kie* was in the year 628 subject to the kingdom of *Kia pia she*, on the Gurbend, and was the boundary betwixt Gandhára and western Cabulistan. This town was sixteen yojanas distant from the capital of the Gandháras, or according to others, 500 *li* north-west from thence over the hills; say twenty-five geographical miles. The distance from the Súrkhrúd to Jellalabad is, according to Tieffenthaler, twenty-four miles; and the capital of Gandhára could not have been much more easterly than Jellalabad. The route of Hiouan thsang, however, was not by the river, but across the hills, and therefore more direct.

"To verify the geography of western Cabulistan, we must begin with Hiouan thsang's entrance into the country from the northward. He proceeds from Bamian eastwards over the snowy hills, then over the Black Mountains to *Kia pi she*. The distance is not given; but as the town of *Kia pi she* was also in the mountains, it is probable that it lay in the next valley east of Bamian, where a pass leads to the valley of the Gurbend, as described by Baber. I refer to Burnes's corrected map. Two hundred *li* to the north of the capital are the Great Snowy Mountains and the Hindu Kosh, so that it cannot be Cabul, as M. Landresse supposes. It was, in 632, an independent State, to which several neighbouring countries belonged, as we see was the case with Na kie. Here was the old kingdom of the Gandháras, not indeed of the Indians, but of the Scythians, who at a later period took possession of the Indian Gandhára. Ptolemy has a town named *Kapisa* two and a half degrees to the north of *Kabura*, and Pliny, when enumerating the countries to the west of the Indus, observes, "a proximis Indo gentibus montana Capissene habuit *Capissam* urbem, quam diruit Cyrus. This is without doubt the *Kia pi she*, of the Chinese." (Lassen, *Zur Geschichte der Griechischen und Indoskythischen Könige*, pp. 147—150.)—J. W. L.

(3) *The town of Hi lo.*—This town was not the capital of the kingdom of Na kie, but was situated thirty *li* to the south-east of the capital, and appears to have been particularly remarkable for the number of reliques of Buddha which it possessed.—R.

(4) *All sorts of precious ornaments.*—More literally, the *seven precious things*, an expression frequently employed in an indeterminate sense, *definitum pro indefinito*. The designation of *the seven precious things* is very various: the following are two series of them, with details which appear curious enough. 1st. *Sou fa lo*, (Suvarna) the Sanscrit word for gold. According to the *Fa chi tou lun*, gold is drawn from mountains, stones, sand, and red copper. It has four properties; it never changes its color; it alters not; nothing prevents it resuming its form (sense of the text doubtful); and it makes man opulent. 2d. *A lou pa* (rúpya) the Sanscrit name of silver. According to the same work, silver is extracted from melted stones; it is commonly called *white gold*. It has the four properties of gold. 3d. *Lieou li*, the Sanscrit word for a blue stone. The *Kouan king sou*, or "*Explanation of the Book of Comtemplation*," calls it also *feï lieou li ye*, which signifies, *not far;* a name given in consequence of its being found in the western countries *not far* from Benares.

[It is without doubt the Sanscrit word *Vaïdurya*, or lapis lazuli. *Vidura*, which signifies *not far*, is the name of the mountain where it is found.—E. Burnouf.]

The blue or green colour of this precious substance cannot be changed by any other matter. Its lustre and hardness are unrivalled in the world. 4th. *Pho li*, otherwise *Se pho ti kia*, (*sphathika*, spath) is the Sanscrit name of *Shouï yu*, or rock crystal. Its transparence and lustre are unique in the world. 5th. *Meou pho lo kie la pho;* this Sanscrit word designates a precious substance of a blue or white colour; its form is that of a wheel, with a nave, and rays. (I think this must be a species of ammonite.) Its hardness and beauty of colour cause it to be greatly in request in the world. 6th. *Mo lo kia li*, or agate, a stone of mixed colors, white and red, resembling the brain of a horse, whence its (Chinese) name *ma nao, equi cerebrum*. It may be polished, and made into vases; and hence its value. 7th. *Po ma lo kia* (padmarága), a Sanscrit word signifying a *red gem* (more correctly *colour of the nelombo*). The *Foe ti lun* ("Discourse on the land of Buddha") says that it is the produce of red insects. The *Ta chi tou lun* says, that it is a stone found in the belly of a fish, and in the brain of a serpent. Its red color is extremely bright and lustrous, which causes it to be sought after. [*Padmarága* is the Sanscrit for ruby.—Kl.]

The second series is composed exclusively of precious stones. 1st. *Po lo so* (Sanscrit *prabála*, Bengalí *palá*) coral. The *Ta chi tou lun* calls it the *tree of sea-stone*. They say that in the sea of the south-west, distant 7 or 8 *li*, (this is an evident error,—perhaps it should be 7 or 8 thousand *li*) there is a coral isle, the foundation of which is a stone upon which this substance grows. The coral is detached from it with iron nets. 2d. *A chy ma kie pho* (*asmagarbha?*) or amber. It is of a red colour and transparent. 3d. *Ma ni* or *mo ni* (*mani*) a word which signifies *spotless*, and designates a pearl. This substance is brilliant and pure, free from spot and stain. It is on this account that the *Yuan kio chhao* (Manual of the Pratyéka Buddhas) calls it also *jou i (conformable to the desires or intentions)*; the wealth one desires to possess, vestments, food, in short, all necessary things are to be procured by means of this precious thing, *conformably with one's desires*; and hence its name. 4th. *Chin shou kia*; this Sanscrit word designates a precious stone of a red colour. According to the history of the western countries, there is a tree named *Chin shou kia (kimsuka, Butea frondosa)* the flowers of which are red and as large as the hand. The substance to which this name is also given is of the same colour with these flowers. 5th. *Shy kia pi ling kia*. This Sanscrit word signifies a *conqueror, one that excels*, because this substance surpasses all other precious stones in the world. 6th. *Mo lo kia pho (marakata*, emerald*)*. The *Ta chi tou lun* names thus a precious stone of a green colour. It comes from the beak of a bird with golden wings, and is a charm against all sort of poisons. 7th. *Pa che lo* (*vajra*), or the diamond. This substance is born in gold; its color is similar to that of the amethyst; it is incorruptible and infusible, extremely hard and sharp, and capable of cutting jade.

For seven other precious things appertaining to the monarch of the earth, See Chap. X. note 4.—R.

(5) *Places the relique on his head.*—This phrase is obscure in the text and may be variously translated. *Thing thaï* signifies *to carry to the head,*

and *that which is borne on the head*, as the button on the bonnet which distinguishes rank and those who enjoy such distinction. *Tsou ti* signifies *per ordinem*.—R.

(6) *Towers of deliverance.*—This word *tower*, in Sanscrit *sthupa*, applies not merely to great religious buildings, but likewise to those miniature structures which are the model of the former on a reduced scale. Several kinds are distinguished by different names; such as *sthupa*, *ta pho* (eminence), *feou thou* (acervus), *sou theou pho* (precious tower), *teou seou pho*; but many of these denominations are derived from the Sanscrit radical *sthupa*, and their various significations seem altogether arbitrary. These little structures are built of stone or brick, in the form of a tower without capital. They are of one, two, three, or four stories, for the *sravakas* or auditors of Buddha of the first four ranks. The *pi phao tha*, are consecrated to the reliques of Buddha anterior to his entering upon nirvána. Those of the Pratyéka Buddhas have eleven stories; those of Buddha thirteen, to show that he had passed the twelve *nidánas*, or conditions of relative existence; but no stories are observable on those erected to ordinary mendicants, or virtuous persons.*

According to the *Fa houa wen kiu*, towers or *sthupas* were never erected over the tombs of either monks or laymen; but simple stones, which by their form symbolise the five elements, ether, air, fire, water, and earth, and consequently the human body which is compounded of these. These too are called sthupa by analogy. The annexed cut may give some idea of the figure assigned to each element.

The lowest, or the earth, is rectangular. Water, immediately above, occupies a circle; fire, a triangle; air, a crescent; and ether a smaller accuminated circle. Instead of Chinese names, Sanscrit letters, being the abbreviation of the Sanscrit name of each element, are inscribed on these different parts of the sthupa: thus *kha*, ether; *ka*, air; *ra*, fire; *va*, water; *a*, earth (?). On joining thereto a fifth syllable, *ma* or *sa* for *knowledge*, or *thought*, we have the names of the six elements, and a formula of immense efficacy. Another species of tower is spoken of, called *a look-out sthupa*;† and a formula which has the power to ensure against the three evil ways (hell, the condition of brutes, and that of demons). Many boast of it; but this formula is not found in the sacred texts; it is an invention of subsequent times and of unknown origin.

* *Shy shi yao lan*, quoted in the Japanese Cyclopedia, Book XIX, p. 14.

† *Sthupa a vue.*

The *towers of deliverance* spoken of by Fa hian, would appear to have been hollow altars, adapted to receive offerings of flowers and perfumes. The word *deliverance* signifies the *final emancipation* of the soul, its return to original perfection ; in Chinese *Kiaï thou ;* in Sanscrit ***mukti***.—R.

(7) *Ting kouang Foe*.—The adventure to which allusion is here made, is given in detail, Chap. X. note 4. We see that the country of ***Thi ho weï***, where the father of this ancient Buddha reigned, must be situated in the eastern part of Persia ; so that, while reserving to Sákya himself the local traditions of northern and central India, the Buddhists did not hesitate to transport the scene of the mythological deeds of their saints beyond the limits of Hindustan, to countries which they designate 'India of the North,' and where their religion very probably did not penetrate till an age very recent when compared with that of its origin.—R.

(8) *A tooth of Foe*.—A relique of this nature has already been mentioned in Chapter V. and others will yet come before us, particularly in our pilgrim's account of Ceylon. An observation to be made in the following note, and which is equally applicable to the tooth here spoken of, would induce us to suppose that these precious remains appertainied to another personage than the historical Buddha, Sákya Muni ; possibly to ***Ting kouang Foe***, spoken of in note 7. The tooth here mentioned had disappeared before the journey of Hiouan thsang, two hundred and twenty seven years subsequent to that of Fa hian.—R.

(9) *The staff of Foe*.—The *staff*, like the *begging pot*, is an essential attribute of the Buddhist mendicant. Its Sanscrit name is *hi ki lo ;* in Chinese it is called *sy chang* (tin staff), *chi chang*, *tě chang*, *shing chang*, the staff of prudence, of virtue, *the talking staff*, because of the noise occasioned by the rings with which it is ornamented ; in Manchou it is called *douldouri*. There is a '*Book of the Staff*,' (*Sy chang king*) in which Buddha is made to say to his disciple Kásyapa, "Tin is the lightest (among the metals) ; the staff is at once a support, and a preservative against vice, by the help of which escape is effected from the boundary of the three worlds." The staff of Kásyapa Buddha had a head with two openings, in which were fixed six rings. That of Sákya Buddha had four openings and twelve rings. The modern *douldouri* has nine. What is said here of the dimensions of the staff of Foe, that it was of six or seven Chinese toises (18 to 21 metres) would prove, unless there be some error in the text, that our author speaks of the staff, not of Sákya, but of one of those Buddhas who were born at an epoch when the life of man was of prodigious length and his stature colossal. For example, Kásyapa was born in the age when the life of man extended to twenty thousand years, and his stature was sixteen toises (48m.

80); Vipasyi, born in the time when men lived eighty thousand years, was sixty yojanas high, and the glory encircling his head, one hundred and twenty. It must have been to some giant of this order that a staff of eighteen or twenty metres belonged.—R.

(10) *The seng kia li of Foe.*—*Seng kia li*, or more correctly *Seng kia ti*, is the Chinese transcription of *Sanghâti*. Buddhist ascetics have three kinds of dresses. 1st. The *Seng kia li*, so called from a Sanscrit word signifying *joined* or *doubled*, because it is made of pieces cut and united together again. The *I ching fa sse* states that the Sanscrit word *Seng kia ti* signifies a doubled dress; but the *Suian liu sse* assures us that the names of the three garments can not be very exactly translated; that the great garment is named *Tsa souï i*, because of the number of pieces of which it is composed. As to its use, it is called, 'a dress to enter the palace of kings,' or 'a dress for a public place,' because it is worn on the occasion of preaching the law in palaces, as well of begging in the cross-ways. The *Sa pho to lun*, distinguishes three sorts of *full dress;* the lower, which consists of nine, eleven, or thirteen pieces; the middle, which is of fifteen, seventeen and nineteen pieces; and the upper, which has twenty-one, twenty-three, or twenty-five. 2d. *Yu to lo seng (uttarasanghati);* a Sanscrit word signifying the *upper garment, surtout;* it consists of seven pieces. The *Siuan liu sse* calls this garment of seven pieces the *dress of the middle order*, and according to its style, '*the dress for going to the assembly.*' It is worn on the occasion of ceremonies, prayers, festivals, and preaching. 3d. *An tho hoeï;* this Sanscrit word means an inner vesture, used in sleep and worn next the body. The same work calls it the *nether garment*, and states that it is composed of five pieces. Its use is defined to be 'a garment formed of several pieces worn in-doors by those who practise the law.' Its Sanscrit name is *antaravâsaka*.—R.

(11) *His shadow.*—This singular relique was also seen by Hiouan thsang, and as we cannot question its existence, must be accounted for as the effect of some optical contrivance, dexterously used to deceive these superstitious pilgrims. The characteristic beauties here spoken of are the thirty-two *lakshana*, of the visible and transfigured body of Buddha. Hiouan thsang explains the occasion on which the Tathágata left his shadow in this place, and confirms the prediction that all the *Shi tsun* (*Lokajyestha, illustrious of the age, Buddhas*) of the *period of sages*, or the present cycle, would imitate in this respect the example of Sákya Muni.—R.

(12) *Seven to eight toises.*—Betwixt 70 and 80 English feet.

(13) *The Lo han and the Py chi foe.*—We have already seen that *Lo han*, or more exactly *A lo han*, is the transcription of Arhan; and that this San-

scrit term designates one of the superior orders in the scale of saints or purified intelligences. The degree immediatly below these is the *Py chi foe*, or *Py chi kia lo*, the name of which is interpreted *simple*, or *complete intelligence*, and represents the Sanscrit term *Pratyeka Buddha*, *separate* or *distinct Buddha*. Without entering upon the almost infinite distinctions which Buddhists have established in the different degrees of perfection at which it is possible to arrive by contemplation and the exercise of virtue, I shall here transcribe a passage from a sacred book which will explain the rank of the Pratyeka Buddhas in the Buddhist hierarchy.

"We call the *five fruits*, those fruits to which the *Siu tho wan*, the *Sse tho han*, the *A na han*, the *A lo han*, and the *Py chi foe* bear witness; implying that these five classes of men in passing through the world, do not tarry for the entire suppression of their moral imperfections before directing their souls towards the great purification, and culling the fruits of the (tree) *bodhi*, or reason."

"1st. The *first fruit* is that of the soul whose return lasts eighty thousand kalpas; it is obtained by the *Siu tho wan*, (*Srotápanna*). Their name imports that they *come* by *flowing*; that is, that they have escaped from the general stream (of worldly beings) and have attained the stream of saints. They have cut the three knots (which bind the body to the three worlds) passed the three inferior conditions (that of asuras, of brutes, and of the damned) and after having been born seven times among gods and men, delivered from all pain, they enter upon *nirvána*, or attain *bodhi* of the most exalted kind, above which there is nothing.

2d. "The *second fruit* is that of the soul whose return lasts sixty thousand kalpas. It is obtained by the *Sse tho han* (*Sakridágámi*). Their name signifies *a going and coming*, because after they are born once among men and once among the gods, they obtain the *nirvána* that makes perfect. They have suppressed the six classes of errors attached to the actions of the senses and the desires which these originate; and after being re-born once among the gods or among men, they are delivered from all pain, and pass sixty thousand kalpas in *nirvána*, to obtain eventually supreme *bodhi*.

3d. "The *third fruit* is that of the soul whose return lasts forty thousand kalpas. It appertains to the *A na han* (*Anágámih*); personages whose names signify that they '*come no more*,' that is, that they are not again born in the world of desires. They are emancipated from the five inferior bonds and the necessity of re-birth, so that after forty thousand kalpas, they obtain supreme *bodhi*.

4th. "The *fourth fruit* is that of the soul whose return lasts twenty thousand kalpas. It is the lot of the *Arhans*, who having suppressed all the imperfections which are produced in the three worlds, of desires, of anger, of hatred and of ignorance, after twenty thousand kalpas, obtain supreme *bodhi.*

5th. "The *fifth fruit* is that of the soul whose return lasts ten thousand kalpas. It belongs to the *Py chi foe* (*Pratyeka Buddhas*), who obtain after ten thousand kalpas, the supreme bodhi they have merited by the suppression of the imperfections which arise from the desires of the three worlds, of rage, of hatred, and of ignorance."*

It would thus appear that there is no expressed difference between the deserts of the Pratyéka Buddhas and the Arhans. Another passage in the same book places the Pratyéka Buddhas in an intermediate station betwixt the *Sravakas* and the *Bodhisattwas* by reference to their progress in knowledge and the science which consists in contemplating the uninterrupted succession of the twelve *nidánas*, or conditions of individual existence, in recognising their continuous concatenation, and consequently the unreality of what is called birth and death, in destroying the errors of thought and vision, and ascending to the true condition of things, which is vacuity. More ample explanations regarding the Pratyéka Buddhas will be found hereafter.—R.

CHAPTER XIV.

Little Snowy Mountains.—Kingdom of Lo í.—Kingdom of Po na.—River Sin theou.

In the second moon of the winter,[1] Fa hian and the rest passed to the south of the *Little Snowy Mountains.*[2] The snow gathers in these hills as well in summer as in winter. On their northern side the cold is excessive, and its severity is such that one is almost frozen. Only Hoeï king, however, was unable to endure its rigour, and became unfit to proceed. A white foam issued from his mouth. He said to Fa hian—"It is impossible that I should survive! Proceed at once; it must not be that we all perish here." And thereupon he expired! Fa hian had

* *Sacred Book of the Nirvana, Ni phan king,* quoted in the *San tsang fâ sou,* Book XXII. p. 3 *verso.*

comforted him with all manner of consolation; he wept for him, and regretted bitterly that their common project had proved so contrary to destiny; but unable to help it, he gathered his remaining strength, and proceeding to the south of the chain,[3] arrived in the kingdom of *Lo i.*[4]

There are in this country three thousand ecclesiastics belonging both to the *great* and to the *less translation*. They halted and sojourned there; and when this sojourn was ended, they proceeded to the south, and after a ten days' march reached the kingdom of *Po na.*[5]

In this kingdom also there are three thousand ecclesiastics, all attached to the *less translation*. Thence going to the east three days' journey, you pass again the river *Sin theou,*[6] on both sides of which is a smooth and level country.

NOTES.

(1) *The second moon of winter.*—If this date is set down according to the Chinese calendar, the spring commencing with the new moon nearest the day upon which the sun enters the 15° of Aquaries, the second moon of winter had begun two months before, that is to say, on the 5th December, omitting reductions. It is rather surprising that our pilgrims should undertake a journey across these snow-covered mountains at such a season; nor is there any room for wonder at the accident that occurred to one of their number.—R.

(2) *The Little Snowy Mountains.*—These can be no other than the range which bears at present the name of the *Suleiman-koh*, in Afghanistan. The denomination of the 'little mountains of snow' has no doubt reference to that of the *Himálaya*, following the meaning in the Sanscrit tongue then employed in those countries. It frequently occurs in the narrative of Hiouan thsang.—R.

(3) *To the south of the chain.*—Apparently in the district of Gandhára, where the mountains leave, as far as the Indus, a space free to the occupation of the petty states of *Lo i*, and *Po na*, and which Fa hian traversed in the space of thirteen days.—R.

(4) *The kingdom of Lo i.*—A country otherwise wholly unknown. Fa hian mentions no circumstance which would enable us to restore this geographical name.—R.

Professor Wilson suggests that this may refer to *Lohita*, a name found in the Mahábhárata as that of a country, as is also that of *Loha*, the appellation of a people in the north of India, associated with the Kambojas and others in the same locality and subdued by Arjuna. The principal tribes of the Afghans betwixt the Suleimáni Hills and the Indus are known collectively as the *Lohanis;* and in them professor W. thinks we have *Lohas* of the Hindu geographers and the *Lo i* of the Chinese.* Capt. A. Cunningham identifies *Lo i* with the modern *Roh,* or *Rohi,* another name for Afghanistan.† Roh is stated in Persian authors to be the original seat of the Afghans and to have extended in length from Sewad and Bijore to the town of Sui in the dominions of Bukharast.‡ The word signifies in their language *mountainous.* Whatever may be the true restoration of *Lo i,* there can be no doubt that this kingdom was situated immediately south of the Sufēd Koh.—J. W. L.

(5) *The kingdom of Po na.*—Equally unknown.—R.

Capt. A. Cunningham has identified the *Pou na* of our pilgrim with *Banu,* which is situated exactly three marches west of the Indus, as Fa hian states.—J. W. L.

(6) *The river Sin theou.*—See Chap. VII. n. 2. The circumstance noted by Fa hian that the country on both banks of the river was level, shows that he speaks of the lower or the middle Indus. We have seen that this river should be crossed by our travellers about Bukker. The sequel of their itinerary will immediately confirm this supposition.—R.

CHAPTER XV.

The kingdom of Pi chha.

On crossing the river you arrive at a kingdom named *Pi chha.*[1] The doctrine of Foe is there honored and flourishing, both in the system of the *great* and in that of the *less translation.* The inhabitants were greatly touched to see among them travellers[2] from the land of *Thsin,* and they thus addressed us: "How became the people of the extremities of the earth acquainted

* J. R. A. S. Vol. V. p. 120.
† Ibid: Vol. VII. p. 243.
‡ Stewart, *Hist. of Bengal,* p. 127.

with sanctified life and the practice of reason? and how come they thus far in quest of the Law of Foe?" They gave us every thing necessary for our comfort, and treated us conformably with the prescriptions of the Law.

NOTES.

(1) *A kingdom named Pi chha.*—We may read ***Pi thou***; but I believe we should substitute *chha*, or even *thsa*, for *thou*; and then we shall have a slightly aberrant transcription of the name which it is natural to look for in that neighbourhood, whether we imagine it employed in its Persian form in the dialects of the country (*Panjáb*), or in its Sanscrit (*Panchála*). The position of the country admits of no doubt that this is the name that Fa hian picked up, and any discussion upon the point would be superfluous.—R.

If Fa hian and his companions had passed the Indus at ***Bukker***, or ***Pukor***, they could not have entered the Panjáb, a country much farther to the north. It derives its name from the five great rivers, Behat or Jylum, Chenab, Ravi, Beyah, and Sutledge, which traverse it, and fall into the Indus more than fifty leagues above Bukker. Fa hian therefore entered Sinde and not the Panjáb.—Kl.

The rectification of Fa hian's route removes M. Klaproth's difficulty. Moreover had Fa hian passed through the inhospitable desert as he must had he crossed the Indus at Bukker, he would scarcely have failed to record the difficulties and privations of such a journey, nor would he have described the country as abounding in small streams and watercourses.—J. W. L.

(2) *Travellers.*—In the text *men of the road.* This expression signifies travellers, and not *priests of Tao*, as in Chap. IV. n. 1.—Kl.

CHAPTER XVI.

Kingdom of Mo theou lo.—River of Pou na.

Proceeding thence towards the south-east, they travelled at least eighty *yeou yan.*[1] They passed a great number of temples, in which there lived ecclesiastics amounting to many tens of thousands.[2] After passing all those places they came to a kingdom ; this kingdom is named *Mo theou lo.*[3] They followed also (the course of) the river *Pou na.*[4] On the right and on the left of this river there are twenty *Seng kia lan,* which may contain three thousand ecclesiastics. The law of Foe begins again to be had in honor here.[5]

As soon as you leave the sands[6] and the river to the west, all the kings of the different kingdoms of India are firmly attached to the law of Foe, and when they render homage to the ascetics they first take off their tiaras.[7] They and the princes of their families, and their officers, present these with food with their own hands. When they have so presented them with food, they spread a carpet on the ground, and sit in their presence on a bench. In the presence of the clergy they would not dare to recline upon a couch. This custom, which these kings observe in token of respect, began at the time of Foe's sojourn in the world, and has been continued ever since to the present time.[8]

The country to the south of this is called the *Kingdom of the Middle.* In the Kingdom of the Middle the cold and the heat are temperate and moderate each other: there is neither frost nor snow. The people live in abundance and in happiness. They know neither registers of the population,[9] nor magistrates, nor laws. Those who cultivate the lands of the king alone gather the produce. When any wish to depart, they depart; when they wish to stay, they stay. To govern them the kings require not the apparatus of (painful) punishments. If any one be guilty of a crime, he is simply mulcted in money, and in this they are guided by the lightness or the gravity of his offence. Even when by relapse a malefactor commits a crime, they restrict themselves to cutting off his right hand without doing him any further harm. The ministers of the king and those who assist to the right and to the left, all receive emoluments and pensions. The inhabitants of that country kill no living being; they drink no wine, and eat neither garlic nor onions.[10] We must except only the *Chen chha lo;*[11] the name

Chen chha lo signifies *hateful.* These have dwellings separate from other men. When they enter a town or a market they strike upon a piece of wood to make themselves known; at this signal all the inhabitants avoid them, and secure themselves against contact. In this country they keep neither swine nor cocks. They sell no living animals; there are in the markets neither shambles nor wine shops. For money they use shells.[12] The *Chen chha lo* alone go to the chase, and sell meat.

After the *pan ni houan*[13] of Foe, the kings, the grandees and the heads of families erected chapels for the clergy; they furnished them with provisions, and made them grants of lands and houses, and gardens and orchards, with husbandmen and cattle to cultivate them. The deeds of these donations are engraved upon iron,[14] and no subsequent princes are at liberty to interfere with them in the slightest degree. This custom has been perpetuated to the present day without interruption. The ecclesiastics who reside in this country have houses to dwell in, beds and mattrasses to sleep upon, wherewithal to eat and drink, clothes, and in short every thing that they require, so that they lack nothing. It is the same every where. The priests are constantly engaged in good works and in acts of virtue. They apply also to the study of the Sacred Books, and to contemplation. When foreign ecclesiastics arrive the elders meet and conduct them, carrying by turns *their clothes and their pots.*[15] They bring them water to wash their feet, oil to anoint them, and an extraordinary collation.[16] After they have rested awhile, they are asked the number and the order of the sacrifices they have to perform; and on arriving at the dwelling, they are left to repose, after being provided with every thing necessary for them according to the law.

The places where the pilgrims halted are the tower of *She li foe,*[17] the towers of *Mou lian*[18] and *A nan,* and the towers of the *A pi than,*[19] of the Precepts,[20] and of the Sacred Books.[21] After they had enjoyed repose for one month, all the people who hoped for happiness, exhorted them to betake again to their pious duties.

They prepared an extraordinary collation,[22] when all the clergy held a great assembly and discoursed upon the Law. This conference ended, they proceeded to the tower of *She li foe* to make an oblation of all sorts of perfumes, and there kept the lamps burning the entire night. *She li foe*, was a bráhman who came to Foe in order to embrace ascetic life. The same may be said of the great *Mou lian* and the great *Kia che*. The *Pi khieou ni*[23] pay their devotions principally at the tower of *A nan*, because it was *A nan* who prayed the *Honorable of the Age*,[24] that he would grant to women the liberty of embracing ascetic life.[25] There is also a (prescribed) order in which the *Sha mi*[26] fulfil their religious duties. Those who have a master of the *A pi than*, pay their homage to the *A pi than ;* those who have a master of the Precepts, honor the Precepts. Every year there is a service of this kind, and all of these have their day. The devotees of the *Ma ho yan*[27] pay their homage to *Phan jo pho lo mi*,[28] to *Wen chu sse li*,[29] to *Kouan shi in*,[30] &c.

The pilgrims received the presents which it is customary to make at the end of the year.[31] The elders, the officials, the bráhmans and others presented them with dresses of different kinds, and all things essential to Samaneans, and which are offered in alms to the clergy. The pilgrims themselves in like manner presented alms. The rites and the ceremonies which that holy band[32] perform have thus continued without interruption since the *Ni houan* of Foe.[33]

After passing the river *Sin theou* in going towards Southern India, there are forty or fifty thousand *li*[34] to the Sea of the South. There are every where plains, where one sees neither great mountains nor great rivers, but merely streamlets and water-courses.

NOTES.

(1) *Four score yeou yans.*—From the point where our pilgrims passed the Indus to Mathura are eight degrees of a great circle ; which gives ten yojanas to a degree.—R.

(2) *Several tens of thousands.*—As Fa hian enters upon no details regarding these monks, and does not appear to have visited their monasteries, we may infer that they did not belong to the Samanean religion, but were very probably attached to the bráhmanical worship. Without some such supposition, it is not easy to explain how these pilgrims who traversed India purposly to visit temples where they could become acquainted with the minutiæ of their faith, and who in other parts of their journey, describe almost topographically such objects as merited their pious regard, should have met with none such in all this space of one hundred and twenty leagues. This inference will be confirmed in note 5.—R.

(3) *Mo theou lo,*—and in the narrative of Hiouan thsang *Mo thou lo*, is the most exact Chinese transcription that can be made of the word *Mathurá.*—R.

It is still a town in the province of Agra, on the right bank of the Jumna. It is celebrated among the Hindus as the birth-place and earliest sojourn of Krishna, on which account it is a place of frequent pilgrimage amongst them.—Kl.

(4) *The river Pou na.*—This name is greatly changed, but the position precludes mistaking the Jumna, or *Yamuna*, on the right bank of which is situated the town of *Mathura.*—R.

It may be the transcription of the last two syllables of *Jabuna*, a provincial name of the Jumna.—J. W. L.

(5) *Begins again to be held in honour.*—The Chinese text is susceptible of several interpretations; the most natural appears to be, 'the law of Foe revives;' but this revival may be understood in two senses, as referring either to time or to space. We may suppose that after having been persecuted or neglected, the religion of Buddha began, at the time of Fa hian's visit, to find a greater number of adherents; or that after having traversed countries where Buddhism prevailed, then other countries where bráhmanism predominated, the traveller found the former religion once more flourishing in the country of Mathurá, at which he had arrived. The latter explanation appears to me the more probable; for Fa hian expressly tells us that the observance of the ceremonies of Buddhism, and the privileges of its adherents had continued without interruption since the nirvána of Sákya Muni. We have just remarked (note 2) that the tract of country passed over by our pilgrim since leaving the Indus was most probably inhabited by Hindus of the bráhmanical sect, since he, whose quest was for objects associated with his own faith, had not found matter for a single observation, but passed over with so few words the space of eighty yojanas.—R.

(6) *The sands.*—The great salt desert east of the Indus, and which must be crossed on proceeding direct from that river to central India.—R.

(7) *Their tiaras*;—in the text, *celestial* or *divine cap*: that is, the ornament for a king's head, a tiara, diadem, or crown.

(8) *To the present time.*—This passage is very remarkable; it shows us that in the fifth century Buddhism had lost nothing of its superiority over bráhmanism, and that it had enjoyed this superiority since the time of Sákya Muni, i. e. the 10th century before Christ, according to Chinese chronology. Subsequent travellers, though animated with the same spirit as Fa hian, confess on the other hand that the Samanean religion began to show, in sundry places, symptoms of decline. Temples had fallen to ruin, celebrated reliques had disappeared, the number of ecclesiastics had diminished in several monasteries, and those who yet remained were mingled with the heretics, or bráhmans. The history of Indian Buddhism receives immense illustration from the comparison of these passages, which establish most important points in the chronology of these religions.—R.

(9) *Registers of population.*—These registers are used in China to fix the poll-tax; hence our author reckons it among the advantages enjoyed by the Hindus that they had no census amongst them.

(10) *Garlick or onions.*—Wine, garlick, and onions, are of the number of things from which Buddhists are, according to the fifth precept, to abstain. The five precepts are—

1st. Not to kill any living being.

2nd. Not to steal.

3rd. Not to commit adultery.

4th. Not to lie.

5th. Not to drink wine.

These five precepts answer to the five corresponding virtues;—humanity, prudence, justice, sincerity, and urbanity.*

Three others are added to these, making eight;

6th. Not to sit on a large bed, or a large or lofty seat.

7th. Not to wear flowers or ribbons on your dress.

8th. Not to become fond of songs, dances, comedies.†

The two following are likewise enumerated, completing the number of ten.

9th. Not to wear on the arms ornaments of gold or of silver.

10th. Not to eat after noon.

Such are the precepts which the aspirant to the rank of Samanean should observe. They are called '*the ten precepts of the ascetics.*'‡ There is another enumeration which extends the number to two hundred and fifty, called *sufficient*, because they suffice for the full and perfect exercise of religious life. They are distributed in the following manner:—

* *Sang tsang fá sou*, B. XXIII. p. 7 v. † *Ibid.* ‡ *Ibid*, B. VII. p. 15 v.

1st. Rules against *Pho lo i* (corruption, extreme wickedness). Four articles.

2d. Rules against *Seng kia pho shi sha;* this Sanscrit word signifies '*ruin of the Sanga ;*' because whoever infringes these precepts is as one who had been assassinated ; his body ever lives, but he is nevertheless lost. Thirteen articles.

3d. Indeterminate rules ; two articles.

The infraction of these articles is estimated either according to *Pho lo i*, or *Seng kia pho shi sha*, or *Pho y thi* (see below), and hence they are said to be indeterminate.

4th. Rules relative to *Ni sa khi* and *Pho y thi ;* thirty articles. The Sanscrit word *Ni sa khi*, signifies to *abandon :* the term is applied to the love of riches and to negligence, which lead to unwillingness to join the body of the *Sangas*. That of *Pho y thi* signifies *to fall*, intimating that if one does not *abandon* (the love of riches, &c.) he *falls* into hell.

5th. Rules relative to *Pho y thi*, ninety articles.

6th. Rules relative to *Pho lo thi thi she ni*, four articles. This word signifies to '*repent in presence of some one.*' According to the *Seng khi liu*, whatever faults have been committed should be acknowledged in open assembly. Hence this denomination.

7th. Rules prescribed for the studies of mendicants. A hundred articles.

8th. Rules for stifling controversies ; seven articles. These two hundred and fifty rules are enjoined for observance by monks and mendicants.*

(11) *The Chen chha lo.*—There is no difficulty in recognising in this transcription the Sanscrit word *Chandála*, the second syllable of which is altered by the substitution of a palatial for a dental, as we have had occasion to observe before in the representation of Sanscrit words by Chinese characters. The Buddhists seem to have partaken the contempt with which the bráhmans regarded the *Chandálas*, 'the lowest of mortals,' as Menu characterises them.† Wilson explains this word to mean *hateful*, as in the Foe koue ki. The Chinese pretend that it signifies a *butcher*, also *sævum signum*, because individuals who exercise the vocation of butcher and perform other wicked acts are compelled when they go abroad to ring a bell or hold up a piece of bamboo, that they may be readily recognised. There are five classes of persons from whom ecclesiastics ought to be careful to avoid seeking alms : 1st. Singers and comedians, who think of nought but jesting and merriment, and who disturb contemplation. 2d. Women of bad character, whose conduct is impure and whose reputation is bad, who are abandoned to libertinage, and who shut the good way. 3d. Dealers in wine ; for wine leads

* *San tsang fa sou* B. VII. p. 15. † Menu, Chap. X. 12, 16.

to all vice, excesses, and crimes. 4th. Kings, because their palaces are full of courtiers and attendants who interdict access, and whom it is necessary to avoid offending. 5th. Finally *Chen tho lo*, or *Chen chha lo*, (*Chandálas*,) that is butchers who delight in killing and tormenting living beings, and who in destroying sensibility, destroy virtue and good inclinations.—R.

It is known that the Chandálas pass for the mixed descendants of Sudras with females of the bráhman caste.—Kl.*

The following account of the origin of the Chandálas, is from a Burmese work, the *Dhammathat*, a Buddhist edition of the Laws of Menu, recently published at Maulmain. "In former times, before the god (Gaudama) appeared, a most wicked young bráhman killed his wife; and at the time of the murder his fellow bráhmans consulted together and agreed on, that this young bráhman had committed a crime which no one else had committed, and what they should do with him; so having shaved his head, they turned him out of society, and caused him to be called *Tsandala*, and from that the *Tsandala* class became a distinct one for the most wicked incorrigible bráhmans."†

In the same work we find the following statement of the "nine kinds of bráhmans. 1st. Those who live on alms in the jungle, who do not take wives, or accumulate property, called *bráhma-tsa-ree*; 2d. Those who take wives, but live on alms, called *bráhmanah*; 3d. The class from which kings are taken, called *khat-te-ya*; 4th. Those who support themselves by trade, and do not take alms, called *da ya*; 5th. Those who support their families by agriculture and who do not receive alms, *besha*; 6th. Those of pure descent, *yek-khi-ta*; 7th. Those who are of loose habits, *ba-ra-dwa-za*; 8th. Those who have broken the rules of their caste, degraded men, who have been turned out of the society of bráhmans, called *tsan-da-la*; 9th. Those who have left their families and subjected themselves to privations, *ta-pa-thee*. Under these nine classes, many are included; the Burman, the Kula, the Talien bráhman, the Kalay and the Hindu bráhmin," &c.‡ It is curious to observe how generally the bráhmans are spoken of by the Chinese and other foreigners as a nation or tribe and not as the priestly order. A *bráhman Buddhist*, however incongruous the terms now appear, is an expression that occurs oftener than once, and sounds not less strange than the *Tsandala bráhman* in the foregoing passage.—J. W. L.

(12) *Shells*.—M. Remusat had translated this passage, '*Shells and teeth*,' and he adds a note, "I translate it according to the correction of the *Pian*

* As. Res. Vol. I.

† *Dhammathat*, translated by D. Richardson, Esq. p. 130.

‡ Ibid. p. 317.

i tian. The text of the *Foe koue ki* is evidently erroneous. The shells here spoken of are the *cypræa moneta* (cowries) which are used as current money in India." Nevertheless there is not any difference between the text of the *Pian i tian*, and that of the *Foe koue ki*; they both import, "to carry on commerce; to make use of shells." The term *Peï chhi*, is employed to designate those shells employed as money, which are described in the great Japanese Encyclopedia as "shells with denticulations resembling the teeth of fishes."—Kl.

(13) *The pan ni houan of Foe.*—This expression has been explained already, Chap. XII. note 3. We gather from the traditions here preserved by Fa hian, that Buddhism had not suffered in Central India from the rivalry of bráhmanism, for fourteen centuries after its institution.—R.

(14) *Engraved upon iron.*—Deeds conveying grants of land (*grantha*) to Buddhist temples, are the most ordinary subject of inscriptions found in India. Such in particular are those translated by Mr. Wilkins;* that which M. Burnouf has published, and many of those in the collection of Col. Mackenzie. These grants are engraved upon copper or some other metal.—R.

(15) *Their dresses and their pots.*—That is their entire baggage.†—R.

(16) *An extraordinary collation.*—Literally '*an unseasonable broth.*' What the Buddhists call *time* in reference to meals, is thus explained: *the time of the Gods* is the early morning, the hour chosen by the Gods to take their repast. *The time of the law* is noon, the hour selected by the Buddhas, past, present, and to come for their refection. *The time of brutes* is evening, when animals feed. *The time of the genii* is night, during which good and evil spirits eat.‡ Thus all meals taken after mid-day are *unseasonable* for ecclesiastics, and all who observe the precepts rigorously abstain from such. Those however who are sick observe no distinction, but eat when they please.§ Breakfast is called among ecclesiastics *Chai*, (*abstinence*,) and supper, *Feï chi*, (*unseasonableness.*) Buddha has recommended all his disciples to observe the *kia lo*, that is, the *veritable* (time), and to avoid the *San mo ye*, or *false (Feï chi.)* The present *unseasonable collation* seems to have been given to our travellers on account of the fatigues they had undergone; but the same expression occurs again further on, in a passage which seems more difficult of explanation.—R.

(17) *She li foe*, whom they likewise name *She li tseù*; in the former the last syllable is the Chinese transcription of the Indian termination of the original name, *Sáriputra*, which signifies the *son of the Indian crane*, so

* *As. Res.* Vol. 1.
† See Chap. XII, note 8.
‡ *San tsang fa sou* B. XIX, p. 4 v.
§ Jap. Encyc. B. CV. p. 15.

called because the eyes of his mother resembled those of that bird.* He was one of the principal disciples of Sákya Muni, and the one who excelled in *Prajná*, or *divine knowledge*, in which he was instructed by Avalokiteswara.—R.

(18) *Mou lian.*—Another disciple of Sákya, reckoned amongst the most considerable. He is distinguished by the epithet *great.* His title is *Tsun che*, equivalent to *Arya.*—R.

(19) *A pi than*, or more correctly, *A pi tha mo* (Abhidarma), is the name given to the last of the three classes in which the sacred books are arranged, which contain the discourses, or conversation. These three classes are called the '*three comprehensives*;' in Chinese, *San tsang*; in Mongolian, *Gourban aïmak saba*,† and in Tibetan, s*Desnod* g*soum*. The words employed in these several languages, signify a *vase*, or *receptacle*, and are equivalent to the Sanscrit *Pitaka*, or *Kiu she* (kocha).‡ This name is given them because they *contain, include, embrace*, the various religious works mentioned in the three following classes :

1st. *Sieou tho lo* (*Sutra*). These are the principles or aphorisms which constitute the basis of the doctrine, the authentic and invariable texts (in Chinese *king*) ; in Tibetan this sense of immobility is rendered h*gyour*. These texts include, *above*, the doctrine of the Buddhas ; *below*, the duties, or faculties of all living beings.

2d. *Pi nai ye* (*Vinaya*). This word signifies, precepts, rules, laws, or ordonnances, or literally *good government*, such as should overrule the bad qualities of living beings, as worldly laws serve to restrain faults, whether more or less serious. The Tibetan word *b*Kah, expresses this meaning, and united to the Tibetan title of the sacred books, forms the compound b*Kah*-h*Gyour*, which is the title of the most celebrated collection commonly called *Gandjour*. The Precepts are called in the same collection h*Dul ba*, *books of conversion*, of *changing* evil to good ; in Mandchou *Weniboure no moun*, and in Mongolian, *Dzinaï*.

[M. Csoma De Koros explains b*Kah*-h*Gyur* to mean *translation of commandment*, because these works were translated from the Indian originals into Tibetan. See page 3.]—J. W. L.

3d. *A pi tha mo* (Abhidarma). This word signifies discourse, conversation ; these are, according to a Buddhist work (the *Iu kia lun*), treatises in which, by means of questions and answers, a deliberate choice may be made regarding the different procedures indicated by the law. The Abhidhar-

* *San tsang fa sou* B. XLI. p. 13.
† *Geschichte der ost Mongolen*, pp. 41—45.
‡ *San tsang fa sou* B. VIII. p. 2.

mas are called in Tibetan *Tsios mdon pa*, or the ***manifested law***; in Mandchou, *Iletou nomoun.*

The works of these three classes are divided into two species, as they happen to appertain to the *great* or the *less translation.* Among the ***Sutras*** of the *great translation* are quoted the *Hoa yan*, and other sacred texts which treat only of *Bodhi*, or *Intelligence conceived in the world of the law*, teaching and expounding the good actions of the Bodhisattwas of the *Mahá yaná*, and making manifest the fruits of moral conduct. The Vinayas belonging to the same *translation* are like the ***Fan kang***, ***(Bramajala, the thread of Brahma)***, books in which the laws are recorded as observed by the Bodhisattwas of the *great translation.* Lastly, amongst the ***Abhidharmas*** of the same class are cited the *Khi sin lun (Discourse to give birth to faith)* and other controversial works upon the conduct of Bodhisattwas of the *Mahá yaná.*

Among the sutras of the *less translation* are cited the ***Agama***, and other sacred works, in which the nature of the veritable void (spirit) and repose or annihilation (extacy) are treated of to explain the practice of the *Srávakas* and *Pratyekas*, and its fruits. *Agama* is a Sanscrit word signifying *peerless.* Among the *Vinayas* are included the ***rules for the four sections*** *(sse fen leu)* that is to say, for the conduct of mendicants, male and female, for *the observation of the precepts*, and for ***the extinction of disputes***. The discourses entitled *kiu che* (*kocha*, that which ***embraces, contains***; in Chinese *tsang)* are cited as belonging to the class of Abhidarmas of the *less translation*; they enlarge upon the conduct and merits of the Sravakas, Pratyekas, and Buddhas.

Another work, after defining the word ***Tsang*** (***that which contains*** *or includes a law and an immense significance*), distinguishes five of these. 1st. The *Sou ta lan*, (Sútram) or *Sicou to lo*, immutable doctrine to which all at once conform in the ten worlds, and of which not a tittle changes in the three times. 2d. The *Pin nai ye* (Vinaya) or rules. 3d. The *A pi tha mo* (Abhidarma), or discourses. 4th. *Pan jo pho lo mi to* (*Prajna paramita, the arrival on the other shore by knowledge.*) Men far separated from knowledge and detained within the circle of life and death, are designated as being on *this shore*; the Bodhisattwas who practise the ***prajna***, and attain nirvána, are on the *other shore.* According to the sacred books that being endowed with sensibility who applies himself to the true and solid science of the *Mahá yaná*, emancipates himself from the condition of ***self***; and the subtilties by which he attains this object constitute the ***Prajna*** *paramita.* 5th. *Tho lo ni* (*Dhárani*) that is to say, *what one takes, invocation, mysterious formula.* It means also that which, when a man cannot understand or observe the sutras, serves for his regulation and diminishes the weight of committed sin, procures deliverance sooner or later, and conducts to nirvána equally the ignorant and the enlightened man.

In general the Prajna paramitas and the Dharanis are not reckoned among the sacred books known by the title *San tsang*, or *the Three Collections*. This expression frequently occurs, and is found in the title of the work from which the principal part of these explanations is derived, namely, the *San tsang fa sou*, literally the *numbers of the law of the three receptacles;* because the substance of the sacred books is there distributed according to the subdivisions ascribed to each psychological notion. This title might be in Sanscrit *Tri pitaka dharma sankhya.* Many other and more particular classifications of these religious works will be found in the notes referring to those passages in which our Buddhist travellers speak of such as they had collected in their travels.

The custom of erecting towers for preserving the original of a sacred book, as well as for depositing a relique, or perpetuating the remembrance of some prodigy, is established by the passage which gives rise to this note. There were at Mathurá the tower of the *Abhidarmas*, that of the *Vinayas*, and that of the *Sutras*.—R.

(20) *The Precepts.*—That is the *Vinayas.* There are three kinds of precepts. 1st, The *Pi ni* (Vinaya); this word signifies *bonum regimen.* It is applied to that which is capable of regulating the desires, anger, ignorance, and other imperfections. It expresses the ideas of moderation and submission; because by the help of these precepts we may temper and restrain the *three acts;* that is, those of the body, the mouth, and the will; and govern and subjugate all evil propensities. 2d. *Shi lo* (Shíla), that which stays or restrains (evil), and renders capable (of good); or simply *prohibition*, that which suppresses the vicious acts of the body, the mouth, and the will. 3d. *Pho lo thi mou sha* (*Para adhi muksha*) or deliverance, because these precepts remove the bonds of wicked inclination, and render man master of himself.—R.

(21) *The Sacred Books.*—The word *king* in Chinese signifies that which is *invariable;* it conveys the idea of constant doctrine, 'revealed text.' Every sect introduced into China has borrowed this term from the school of the literati, who apply it only to the works compiled by Confucius. The Buddhists apply it particularly to the *Sutras*, because according to the explanation given in one of these books, they 'constitute law and are invariable.' They are conformed to in the *ten worlds* and are unchanged by the *three times.* The ten worlds are those of the Buddhas, the Bodhisattwas, the Pratyeka Buddhas, the Sravakas, the gods, men, asuras, *demons of hunger* (*pre-*

táh), and brutes ; and the infernal regions. The three times are the past, the present, and the future.—R.

(22) *An extraordinary collation.*—We have seen the explanation of this expression, which here seems somewhat out of place. It is not easy to understand why our travellers, invited by devout persons to resume their religious exercises, should prepare themselves for a theological conference by an infraction of the enjoined observances of their profession, such as taking meals at other than conventual hours. The passage appears to require correction ; but it is the same in each of the copies that I have access to.—R.

(23) *The Pi khieou ni,*—the feminine of *Pi khieou* (*Bhikshuni*). After Sákya had accomplished the law, his aunt *Maha pho she pho ti* (*Mahápraja-patí*) *Ta aï tao* (the friend of religion), sought permission to embrace religious life and study the doctrine. Sákya was unwilling to consent to this, when Ánanda pressed him to permit it. Buddha replied, " Be careful ; do not permit females to enter upon my law and become Samaneans ; when there are more daughters than sons in any family, you know that that family falls to ruin and can never regain its splendor." Ánanda renewed his importunity, when Buddha expounded to him what have been called the *eight respectful procedures.* " If they can observe these," added he, " I consent that they should become ascetics." The following are the *eight respectful procedures* imposed upon women by Buddha :

1st. A female ascetic, though a hundred years of age, owes respect to a monk, though he be in the very first year of his profession.

2d. A female ascetic should manifest respect towards mendicants, and never insult or calumniate them.

3d. If a monk happen to commit a sin, the female ascetic should not commend him ; but if a female ascetic sin, and hear the praises of a monk, she should turn, in self-examination, to herself.

4th. She should receive the precepts from a Sanga, or from some mendicant of exemplary virtue, to whom she should apply for that purpose.

5th. If she have sinned and feel herself unworthy to continue in the society of mendicants, she should humble herself, confess her fault, and put away pride and negligence.

6th. She should receive during half a month the instructions of the Sanga, and should apply twice each month to a mendicant of distinguished virtue for such instruction as shall promote her progress in the doctrine.

7th. She should, during the three summer months, abstain from repose and attach herself night and day to mendicants ; inquiring of them concerning the meaning of the law, and increasing her knowledge with a view to its practical application.

8th. After the three summer months have elapsed, from the 15th day of the 4th moon to the 15th of the 7th, she should follow mendicants to improve herself by the example of others, and if she commit any sin, she should repent and confess before all.*

The eight crimes by which female ascetics prove that they have abandoned the precepts, and should therefore themselves be abandoned by the world, as out of the pale of the law of Buddha, are these: 1st. Taking away the life of any living being, as all such beings cling to their body and existence; causing them pain and torturing them, instead of showing compassion for them. 2d. Stealing that which belongs to another; abandoning one's-self to avarice; taking instead of giving. 3d. Committing impurities. The female ascetic who knows not how to defend herself by the rites and protect herself by the precepts, conceives desire, and soils the purity which should preside over her conduct. 4th. Lying, concealing the truth, and deceiving others by crafty words. 5th. Permitting *contact*; this is said of a female ascetic who allows herself to touch the person of a man, which originates impure desires. 6th. The *eight*; committing any of the eight following acts: taking a man by the hands from any improper desire, touching his clothes, going with him to any retired place, sitting and conversing with him there, walking there with him, leaning against each other, and making criminal assignations. 7th. *Covering* or *concealing*; that is, when in the assembly where the precepts are expounded and the law observed, the female ascetic *conceals* the sins of others, and is unwilling to disclose her own. 8th. *Following* or resting *upon*; that is, not performing service in common at the great assembly of the Sangas, and following some private society.

(24) *The Honorable of the Age.*—This is one of the ten surnames given to human Buddhas, and of course to Sákya Muni among the rest. A Buddha, by the sublime science (Prajná) and the other perfections he has attained to, extinguishes desire, anger, ignorance, and every other imperfection,—the sorrows of life, as well as those of death, and obtains an intelligence transcending that of all others. Gods and men, all the saints, as well in the world as beyond it, recognise and honor him as the *Venerable*. This is the meaning of the Sanscrit surname *Lokajyestha*; the Tibetan translation of which is n*Djig* r*ten gyi* g*tso bo*.†—R.

(25) According to the Japanese chronology, entitled, *Wa kan kwo to fen nen gakf oun-no tsou*, preserved in the Bibliotheque du Roi, *She li foe* and *Mou lain*, embraced monastic life in 995 B. C. According to the same

* *Fan i ming y*, quoted in the *San tsang fa sou*, B. XXXII. p. 17.

† *Vocab. pentagl.* Sect. I. No. 11.

work, *A nan*, or *Ananda*, was instructed by Sákya Muni, became a monk in 975 B. C. and in 970 entreated his master to grant to women the privilege of becoming ascetics.—Kl.

(26) The *Sha mi*.—This is the name given to the disciples or aspirants of the religious profession. It is rendered by two words, which signify to *soothe* or *compassionate ;* to *compassionate* the sufferings of all living beings and to afford them assistance.* The more regular form of the word is *she li ma li lo kia*, but it is more usually employed in the abridged form *Sha mi*. The *Sha mi* must observe the ten precepts,† and when they have received the '*sufficient precepts*,' that is the two hundred and fifty, they are reputed *Bhikshus*. Different names are given to the Sha mis according to age. From seven to twelve or thirteen, they are called '*hunters of ravens ;*' from fourteen to nineteen, '*peculiar disciples of the law ;*' from twenty and upwards they obtain a name or title.‡ They must then suppress all evil inclinations, and practise every virtue, when they merit the title of *Sha mi*, that is *Sha mi*, as strictly defined. The word *Shabi*, which means disciple in *Mand chou*, is apparently derived from the Chinese *Sha mi*. Females bear the name of *Sha mi ni*, or more exactly *Sha li ma li kia*, which expresses their efforts to advance in the doctrines of Buddha. The author of the translation of the rules of the *Sha mi*, has made a singular mistake in taking the latter word as the equivalent of Sha men (*Sramana*) even in the title page of his work (*Catechism of the Shamans.*)—R.

(27) *Ma ho yan ;*—the transcription of the Sanscrit word, *Makáyána*, the *great translation*. The clergy of the *great translation* are termed *Maháyána deva ;* those of the *less*, *Moksha deva* (delivered gods.)—R.

(28) *Phan jo pho lo mí :*—an imperfect transcription of the Sanscrit *prajná páramita*, the act of attaining *the other shore* by science. *Páramita* is one of the ten means of final deliverance. The several religious books in which this divine science is inculcated are called *Prajna paramita*. These are ascribed to *Manjusri Avalokiteswara* (see next note.)—R.

(29) *Wen chu sse li*,—in Sanscrit Manjusri. The Chinese pretend that there are three modes of writing and interpreting this name ; 1st. *Wen chu sse li*, 'marvellous virtue ;' the being whom they so designate being endowed with admirable, subtle, infinitely varied, and innumerable merits. 2d. *Man chu she li*, 'admirable head or chief,' because by his wondrous, subtle, and infinite merits he is above all the Bodhisattwas. 3d. *Man chu she li*, 'admirable benediction,' (a formula of praise, adoration, or a happy omen)

* *San tsang fa sou*, B. VII. p. 16 v.
† See note 10.
‡ See note 1. Chap. I.

because by reason of those same merits his name is the happiest of auspices.* But there is reason to suppose that in transcribing in different Chinese characters the same Sanscrit word, they have, as is often the case, sought for meanings and allusions, and fortuitous coincidences and plays of words which the true etymology does not sanction. Manjusri signifies in Sanscrit the happy *Sri*, and Sri is the expression used in blessing gods and saints. The same personage is also called *Manja ghosha*, 'the happy sound,' 'the happy voice.' The Tibetans name him h*Djam* d*Vyang*. He is the mythological god of wisdom.†

He formerly animated the great golden tortoise before the beginning of the universe, whose foundations rest upon that tortoise ; and he will at some future period again appear in the world as its governor.‡ He is the great Demiourgos, the *Viswakarma*, the architect who, by the orders of the supreme Buddha, erected the different mansions, as well celestial as infernal, which constitute a *universe.*§

This would be quite sufficient to explain the theological part assigned to Manjusri, were my present object to give a sketch of the Buddhist pantheon ; but the extracts from Chinese books which are necessary to explain and elucidate this discussion will show how entirely philosophical ideas are denatturalized in mythology and lost sight of by legendary authors.

" Buddha, (Sákya Muni) traversed one day the mountains *Khi che khiu*, in the country *Lo yue khi*, (Rájagriha) with an immense multitude of mendicants, consisting of 1250 *bhikshu* and 32,000 Bodhisattwas. The Honorable of the Age was encompassed by an infinite assemblage of his adherents, reckoning by hundreds and by thousands. In the assembly was then seated a *son of the Gods* (Devaputra) named *Tsi shun lin* in (*Inquietè obsequens præceptorum voci* vel *vox quietè præceptis obsequens*) who rising from his seat, and performing a long genuflexion and joining together his hands, addressed the Honorable of the Age and said : " Where is the present habitation of Manjusri ?" The whole assembly, all those who compose the four classes, that is the male mendicants and the female, the Upasika and the Upayi, as also the gods, the nagas, the good and evil genii, Brahma, Indra, and the four kings of the gods, longed ardently to hear the wondrous communication of the veritable master and to receive his expositions of the Sacred Books. Buddha replied, that towards the east, at the distance of ten thousand Buddhic worlds from this, that is to say, ten thousand times

* *San tsang fa sou*, B. XI. p. 3. v.
† Schroeter, *Bootan Dictionary*.
‡ Sammburg *Historischer Nachricht*, Vol. II. p. 85.
§ *Hodgson's Sketch of Buddhism.*

the space of the world to which extended the happy influences of the preaching of a Buddha, there was a world named *Pao shi*, (precious family—perhaps *Ratneya*) where a Buddha named *Pao ing jou laï* (*pretiosi terminus Tathágata*) a pure and highly exalted intelligence, even then preached the doctrine, and that Manjusri was there listening to the instructions of the great master of all Bodhisattwas, who taught them to estimate their imperfections." The son of the gods once more addressed Buddha: "I would, oh mighty saint! that by an act of your power and goodness you would cause Manjusri to appear here, that he may instruct us in the means by which he expounds the doctrine of the sacred books, and enlightens with so lovely a light whatever difficulty is met with in them as to excel all the Sravakas and the Pratyeka Buddhas. When Manjusri preaches the great law every demon is subjugated, every error that may deceive man is dissipated, and there is not a heretic but returns to his duty. Already, Oh Tathágata! all exalt supreme truth; if your instructions be fortified by his holy teaching, the duration to the true law will be extended. Never has the Tathágata been assisted by an auxiliary so versed in the *Prajná*, so endowed with high faculties, so able to spread abroad and publish the doctrine, as Manjusri." According to the wish of the son of the gods, *Tsi shun liu in*, the Honorable of the Age, caused to flash from the down betwixt his eyebrows a ray of light which illumined the three thousand millions of universes and Buddhic worlds, and made the tour of ten thousand of those worlds, shedding a brilliant light over the world, *Pao shi*. The Bodhisattwas of that Buddhic world asked of their Buddha whence came this light, and what might be the cause of the prodigy? The Tathágata Pao ing replied, "Towards the west, after passing ten thousand *kshma* of Buddhas there is a world called the world of patience (Savaloka); its Buddha is called the Tathágata, *capable of goodness* (Sákya), a pure intelligence arrived at the supremacy of truth. At this instant he is preaching the law. A ray has emanated from the interval of his eyebrows, and in illuminating ten thousand Buddhic worlds it has reached even this *kshma*." "And what may be the wish of this *Lokajyestha?*" replied the Bodhisattwas. "Hundreds of thousands and millions without number of Bodhisattwas are assembled with this Buddha," replied the Buddha, "with the Indra and the Brahma of the world, and the four tribes; and all ardently desire that Manjusri would be pleased to show himself to them and expound the law. They have imparted their desire to the Buddha, who by this ray of light has engaged Manjusri to go. And thou," continued the Tathágata Pao ing, addressing Manjusri, "go to the world where the Tathágata, *capable of goodness*, awaits thee, and where innumerable Bodhisattwas sigh for thy presence." "I too," replied Manjusri, "have recognised the miraculous ray." And thereupon he paid homage to the Buddha Pao ing, and accompanied by ten thousand Bodhisattwas, passed three times to his right, and, stretching forth his arms like a valorous general, disappeared suddenly from the *kshma Pao shi.* In less than no time he found himself in the land of *patience*; and sustaining himself unseen in space, he let fall a shower of celestial flowers upon the assembly, reaching to their knees. Astonished at this prodigy, they all asked of Buddha what meant this fall of flowers? Buddha advised his relations and those about him that it was Manjusri who thus signified his advent with 10,000 Bodhisattwas, in conformity with his orders, and who from mid-air, rained down flowers in honor of his dignity. "Oh, how we long," exclaimed the assembly, "to behold Manjusri and the Bodhisattwas! What unutterable happiness to gaze upon that veritable master!" They had not finished speaking ere Manjusri and the Bodhisattwas showed themselves and were prostrate at the feet of Buddha. They circumambulated him seven times, and by the supernatural power with which they were endowed, they caused large nymphæas to blow, on which they seated themselves. Then the son of the Gods, *Tsi shun lin in,* said to Buddha that he desired from Manjusri such explanations regarding holy instruction as were necessary to assist the uncertain progress of the assembly. "Explain your thoughts," said Buddha, "and your questions shall be resolved." Then the son of the gods propounded a series of questions, which Manjusri amply satisfied, on the perfections of the Buddha whom he had just left, on the principle of truth, on the progress of religious mendicants, on the nature of the soul, and so forth." This theological conference is exceedingly curious, inasmuch as it touches upon the most recondite dogmas of Buddhism, the exposition of which is referred to an exalted Buddha, and placed in the mouth of divine wisdom itself. But it embraces matter of great obscurity, and as it extends to twenty-eight pages, I must reserve it to a future occasion.—R.

(30) *Kouan shi in.*—Another personage of Buddhist mythology, less celebrated, but better known than Manjusri. Under the form here seen his name signifies in Chinese *vox contemplans sæculum*; but this is a translation of the Sanscrit *Avalokiteswara*, which, although generally admitted in China, rests upon a mistake indicated by M. Klaproth.* The first authors who transcribed this name in their language, have taken the final *iswara* for *swara, vox, sound.* The true Chinese interpretation is *Kouan tseu tsaï*, the *contemplative lord.* They give to this mythological personage a host of names. In Sanscrit he is called *Padma páni*, the bearer of the nymphæa; in Tibetan

* *Nouveau Journal Asiatique*, Vol. VII. p. 190.

sDjan ras gZigs dVang tcchong; in Mongol ***Ergetou khomsun bodisatou.*** In the Buddhist system for the exposition of which we are indebted to Mr. Hodgson, Padmapáni is the Bodhisatwa, or active product of the fourth heavenly Buddha Amitabha, the creator of the present world, or at least of its animated inhabitants ; for the creation of the material world passes for the work of Manjusri. According to another system, Padmapáni, the celestial progeny of the divine Buddha of the present world, has in this quality entered upon his functions since the death of the terrestrial Buddha Sákya Muni, as his substitute, charged with the perpetual guardianship and propagation of the Buddhist faith revived by Sákya. It is for this reason that he is not limited to a single appearance, as the Buddhas, but he submits almost without interruption to a succession of births, which are to last till the advent of Maitreya, the future Buddha. It is further believed that he is incarnate in the Dalai Lama, and that he will appear in the character of Buddha for the thousandth part of the present age of the world. Tibet is his chosen land ; he is the father of its inhabitants, and the celebrated formula, *Om mani padma hom*, is one of his blessings.* The system to which this account of the part played by Avalokiteswara belongs, requires confirmation in various points; and for example, it does not appear whether it is to the order of philosophic ideas, or to the class of myths that we are to refer the supposition that in arriving at the perfection of Buddhahood, a Tathágata creates in the world of manifestions, a sort of reflex (*Abglanz*) of himself who is a Buddha of contemplation (*Buddha dhyani*) and that of such is born a Bodhisattwa like as Avalokiteswara. I shall not at present enter upon this theological labyrinth, but following the plan perscribed to myself I shall transcribe a few Chinese legends regarding the personage spoken of by Fa hian.

"In former times, ten quadrillion times a hundred quadrillions of Kalpas ago (the less Kalpa consists of 16,800,000 years, and the great here spoken of is a thousand and three hundred and forty-four millions of years) in a world named *Shan thi lan*, and in a Kalpa named the ***well kept*** (i. e. the precepts well observed,) there was a holy king Chakravarti, named ***Wou tseng nian***, who reigned over the four quarters of the world. It was then that the Tathágata *Pao tsang* (*Rutnagarbha*) appeared in the world. The king had a thousand sons, the eldest of whom was named ***Pou hiuan (non-oculos movens:*** animisha?) and the second *Ni mo*. His minister, ***Pao haï***, (Ratnákara) was the father of the Tathágata ***Pao tsang***. This minister exhorted the king, his sons, their relatives and allies, as also an infinite number of men and gods, to give their thoughts to ***Bodhi*** (Buddhic perfection), so that all might attain in the ten parts of the universe the rank of

* *Shin i tian*, B. XCVIII. p. 24.

pure intelligences. That minister, *Pao haï*, is the Sákya Tathágata of the present time. Then the king and his thousand sons paid homage to the Tathágata, and attaching themselves to that Buddha, embraced religious life and cultivated the doctrine. Buddha changed the name of the king to *Wou liang thsing tsing* (*immensa puritas;* Amitasudhi ?), and assigned him the dignity of Buddha, with the title *Wou liang sheou* (Amitabha) in the western world of the *Au lo* (in Sanscrit, Sukhávati, *the abode of tranquil joy.*) Then the eldest son, *Pou hiuan*, thus addressed the Buddha: "Honorable of the Age! my good dispositions, my contemplations and my vows, all tend towards the practice of the doctrine of the supreme *Bodhi*. The evils which afflict all beings, the terrors of which they are the prey and which divert them from the right path, their fall into the abode of darkness, the endless agony that torments them without hope of delivery or protection, cause them to invoke my name and my power. But their sufferings, patent to my celestial ken, and sensible to my ears, and which I cannot alleviate, disturb me so as to impede my progress towards pure intelligence. Honorable of the Age! permit me to renew a vow which I have heretofore made in behalf of all those beings. The holy king Chakravarti has now become Buddha in the world of *Tranquil Joy*, under the title of *Wou liang sheou (Amitabha)*. When, after an infinite number of Kalpas, he shall have accomplished his work of Buddha, he will enter the *pan ni houan*, and the law will be strictly observed. During this time I must fulfil the lot of Bodhisattwa; if I could accomplish the work of Buddha from the first night on which his immediate law shall be extinct, on the next night I shall attain Buddhahood." Then the Buddha, *Pao tsang*, assigning him the function he aspired to, replied; "Excellent young man! Thou hast reflected on men and gods, and the three bad conditions (that of brutes, of demons, and of the damned), and touched with perfect compassion, thou wouldst destroy the sufferings and the imperfections of all beings. Thou wouldst that all should be admitted to the abode of *Tranquil Joy;* and for that reason I award you the title of *Kouan shi in* (Avalokiteswara, *Contemplative Lord*). Whilst thou shalt excercise the functions of Bodhisatwa there shall be hundreds of thousands of *Wou liang* (i. e. five quintillions) of millions of *Na yeou tha* (i. e. billions) of beings who shall owe to thee their deliverance from pain. Thou shalt work the great work of Buddha and succeed the Buddha *Wou liang sheou* (Amitabha) under the title of the Tathágata, *King of the Hills, resplendent with the light of his merits (Y. thsy kouang ming koung te shan wang jou lai*)." The second of the princes presented himself before the Buddha, and expressed a desire of succeeding *Kouan in*, and of having the same kingdom and the same personal beauty. The Buddha assigned him the quality of Buddha, with the title of the Tathágata, *King of the precious hills where they excel in the observation* (of the law) (*Shen chu chin pao shang wang jou laï*). He then proceeded; "Excellent young man! as thou hast desired to take the great universe (under thy protection) I assign thee this title, and thou shalt be *Ta chi shi* (in Sanscrit, *Mahásthána prápta*, he who has acquired vast power; it is the title of a Bodhisatwa). The thousand sons of the king all came in like manner to make their request to the Buddha, who granted them all the rank of Buddhahood."

The foregoing legend, it will be seen, is opposed to the notion that Amitabha is a Dhyani Buddha, and Avalokiteswara a Dhyani Bodhisattwa; it seems contrary also to the opinion which connects these two personages with the human Buddha Sákya, the first in the character of a celestial radiance or reflex (*Abglanz*), and the second as an emanation from himself. It will be seen how difficult it is to form any just conception of the theological abstractions of Buddhism, if to appreciate them we were compelled to penetrate the veil of legends and allegories by which they are concealed.

For reasons which it were tedious to transcribe here, Avalokiteswara is generally represented with eleven heads and eight arms; sometimes he is described as having a thousand eyes and a thousand arms, and designated *Kouan shï in with the thousand eyes and thousand hands.* As representing in mythological arrangements, the productive faculty of supreme intelligence, Avalokiteswara is represented with some of the attributes of a female divinity.* The sweetness and beauty of his features,—barring the eight arms and eleven heads,—would admit of his being taken for a goddess. Hence many authors have been deceived into the belief that *Poussa*, (*Phou sa*, Bodhisatwa) was a female divinity, a Cybele, and have embellished this error with absurd explanations. What is very singular, the Chinese themselves have fallen into the same mistake; *Phou sa*, is feminine alike in their popular religion and their common language. The ornaments of the *Phou sa* are similar to those worn by the women of France; and the pictured idols, or those of metal or of porcelain, called *Phou sa*, bear unmistakeable characteristics of the sex to which, according to vulgar apprehension, they belong. Some mythologists who have drawn their information from corrupt sources, have not hesitated to repeat the most absurd fables upon this subject, totally at variance with the spirit of the Buddhist creed. A notice of this kind of *Kouan shi in*, is found in a little mythological work of no authority, the title of which would lead one to expect a treatise on the three doctrines, but which contains a mass of mere mutilated notions gathered here and there from writings of no weight, and reunited under the influence of that ignorant syncretism which

* *Alpha. Tibet*, p. 178.

predominates amongst the lowest populace of China. According to this author, ***Kouan in Phou sa*** is no other than the third daughter of the king ***Choung*** of Thsou (who reigned in the sixth century B. C. in the present province of ***Hou kouang***). This princess named *Miao shen*, (admirably good) merited divine honors by her virtue, her filial piety and her devotion to the ***Honorable of the Age***, five or six hundred years before her name was even known in the country she inhabited !* Her father, according to this absurd tradition, erected a statue to her honor under the name of the *most compassionate Phou sa*, (*Ta peï Phou sa*). This statue was held in honor under the dynasties of Han, Thsang, Soung, and Yuan; was destroyed by the *Red Caps* under the Ming dynasty; and re-established by public authority in the years *Siouan* (A. D. 1426-35).

(39) *The holy band.*—The Sanga—the Church—the Faithful.—R.

(40) *The ni houan of Foe.*—Whatever be the opinion entertained of the date of Sákyas death, it is extremely remarkable that a Buddhist of the 5th century of our era should maintain the pre-eminence of his religion in Central India, in the 8th and 9th centuries B. C., and the uninterrupted privileges granted by the kings of the country to the Samaneans up to his own times. The supremacy of the bráhmans must therefore be referred to other places. It is a question of the highest historical importance.—R.

(41) *Forty or fifty thousand li.*—The *li* employed in the vague enunciation of long distances was very short. The length of the Malabar coast from the mouths of the Indus is not therefore greatly exaggerated —R.

CHAPTER XVII.

Kingdom of Seng kia shi.

Proceeding thence in a south easterly direction you reach a kingdom called *Seng kia shi.*[1] This is the place where Foe, having ascended into the heaven of *Tao li*,[2] and for three months preached in behalf of his mother,[3] re-descended to the earth. When Foe ascended to the heaven of *Tao li*, he so employed his supernatural powers[4] that his disciples knew nothing of it

* *Seou shin ki*, B. IV. p. 10.

Seven days were yet wanting (of the time fixed for his return,) when these made use of their divine faculties.[5] *A na liu*,[6] who was endowed with the sight of the Gods,[7] perceived afar off the *Honorable of the Age*,[8] and said to that venerable personage, the great *Mou lian*,[9] "Go, enquire of the *Honorable of the Age*." *Mou lian* then proceeded to prostrate himself and worship the foot (of Buddha) and addressed the question that had been suggested. When he had spoken, Foe said to *Mou lian*; "In seven days hence I shall descend to *You feou thi*."[10] *Mou lian* returned, and on his return the great kings of eight kingdoms, their vassals and their people, who for a long time burnt with anxiety to behold Foe again, assembled like clouds in the kingdom (of *Seng kia shi*) to await there the *Honorable of the Age*. Then said the female mendicant *Yeou pho lo*[11] to herself—"This day the kings and the people await with adoration the advent of Foe; how shall I, who am a woman, obtain the first sight of him?" She then availed herself of the divine faculty to transform herself into the *holy king turning the wheel*;[12] and she was by much the first to render homage to Foe.

Foe descended from the heaven of *Tao li*. At the moment of descent he formed a triple ladder of precious steps. Foe descended on the middle ladder, adorned with the seven precious things.[13] The king of the Gods, *Fan*,[14] prepared also a ladder of silver; he was on the right side, holding in his hand a white chowry[15] and accompanying (Foe). The Lord *Shy*[16] constructed a ladder of burnished gold; he was on the left side, holding in his hand a parasol enriched with the seven precious things and accompanying (Foe). An innumerable throng of Gods[17] followed Foe whilst he descended. When he had descended, the three ladders disappeared under the ground, and nothing of them remained visible but the seven steps. Long after, the king *A yeou*[18] desired to behold the foundation of them, and sent people to dig down to the base. These reached a yellow spring, without being able to penetrate to the foundation. The king felt sensible of a great increase of his faith and veneration. He caused therefore a chapel to be raised over the steps, and upon the middle one erected a full length statue (of Foe), six toises high.[19] Behind the chapel was erected a pillar thirty cubits high,[20] and thereon was placed a lion. Within the pillar on the four sides were images of Foe. The interior and the exterior were polished and resplendent as crystal. There were heterodox philosophers[21] who contested with the *Sha men* the right of sojourn here. The *Sha men* submitted to a condition, and entered into a mutual convention. "If, said they, this place ought to be the abode of the *Sha men*, let a supernatural testimony proclaim it." They had no sooner finished this speech than the lion on the summit of the pillar uttered a loud roar.[22] On witnessing this testimony the heretics were overwhelmed with fear, and submitting their hearts to Foe, received the divine sustenance.[23] During three months their bodies exhaled a heavenly fragrance very different from that common to the men of the age;[24] and as they performed there their ablutions, men afterwards erected in that place a bathing-house; this bath exists still. A tower was also erected in the place where the religious mendicant *Yeou pho lo* rendered the first homage to Foe. At the time when Foe was in the world, they built a tower on the spot where he cut his hair and his nails;[25] on that where the three former Foes[26] sat with *Shy kia wen*;[27] in the places where he had journeyed, and where images of Foe were erected; every where have they constructed towers which remain to this day. At the place where the Lord *Shy*, and the king of the Gods, *Fan*, descended with Foe, they have likewise erected a tower. In these places there may be a thousand devotees, both male and female, who dwell together and eat in company, those of the *great* intermingled with those who study the *less* translation.

In the dwelling place of the ecclesiastics a dragon[28] with white ears was their benefactor. It is he who confers fertility and abundance on the country by causing gentle showers to fall upon the fields and securing them against all calamities. It is he who procures repose to the ecclesiastics, and these in gratitude for his benefactions have erected a chapel with an alcove to place him in. They prepare also *happy* food for the dragon and pay him homage. The clergy choose every day in their assembly three persons to dine in the chapel of the dragon. Their stay being ended, the dragon assumes the form of a little serpent with two ears bordered with white. When the ecclesiastics perceive him, they present him with cream in a copper vessel. The dragon descends from the throne and comes to the floor of the alcove, where he walks about with an air of enquiry. After going the round he disappears. He comes out once every year. This kingdom is fertile, and abundant in all kinds of produce. The people are numerous and rich; and beyond comparison happier than any other. The inhabitants of all other countries fail not to repair thither and receive whatever may be requisite for them.

To the north of the temple, fifty *yeou yans*,[29] there is a temple named the *Limit* or *Boundary of Fire*.[30] *Boundary of Fire* is the name of an evil spirit. Foe converted this evil spirit, and men of subsequent times have built a chapel in the place and made a gift of it to the *A lo han*. He (Foe) washed his hands with water of which some drops fell to the earth; you may see them still there; it were in vain to sweep the place; they would ever restore themselves, and they never dry up. There is also a tower of Foe in this place which a good spirit is in the habit of sweeping and watering so that there is no need of human labor A perverse king said, "Seeing that thou canst do this, I shall assemble a large army to dwell in this place: canst thou carry away in the same manner the filth and the ordure that will accumulate?" The spirit raised a great wind which carried away and purified all. There are a hundred little towers in this place; but one might pass the whole day counting them, and (yet) not know the number of them exactly. If they wish to know the number with precision, they place a man by the side of each tower, and afterwards count these men: but there are sometimes more and sometimes fewer; so that it is impossible to have an exact statement of them.

There is a *Seng kia lan*[31] which may contain six or seven hundred monks. It is here that a *Pi chi foe*[32] took his food. The spot of the *ni houan* is as large as the wheel of a car. Other spots produce grass. This alone produces none. The same may be said of the place where they dried their dresses; it produces no grass. The seams of the garments are marked upon the ground, and exist to this day as they did of old.

NOTES.

(1) *Seng kia shi.*—There can be no doubt that *Seng kia shi*, or *Seng kia she*, is the Chinese transcription of the *Samkassam* or *Samkassa*, of Pali books. Hiouan thsang, who visited the temple where the ladder of Buddha was preserved, as well as those erected to his companions Bráhma and Indra, names the country *Kia pi tha*; and thus establishes its identity with *Seng kia shi*. The position of this place with reference to Mathura and Kanouj, depends therefore upon the concurrent testimony of Hiouan thsang and Fa hian, and corresponds with that of the present Furrukabad.—R.

Captain Alexander Cunningham has had to good fortune to indentify the actual remains of this capital, and to trace the yet unextinct worship of the dragon mentioned by our pilgrim. "This capital," says Capt. C. "still exists in the village of Samkassa, situated on the north or left bank of the Kalí nadí, three quarters of a kos from Aghat Serai, twelve kos from Farakhabad, and twenty-five kos from Kanouj. The village consists of only 50 or 60 houses, on a high ground which has once been a fort; but all around it for a circuit of six miles there is a succession of high ruined mounds of brick and earth which are said to be the walls of the old city. My munshi's expression of wonder, after having visited these ruins, '*Kanouj se bará hy*,' "it is even larger than Kanouj," will convey some notion of their great extent." After describing some modern temples surmounting the ancient mounds of debris and some fragments of Buddhist sculpture, Capt. C. proceeds:—"Close by to the southward is the most interesting point in these ruins. It is a small mound of ruined brick dedicated to the worship of the *Naga*. Nothing whatever is erected there; but whenever rain is desired the people proceed to the spot and pray for it. The period of annual worship, however, is the month of Bysákh, just before the commencement of the seasonal rains, when the village women go there in procession and make offerings of milk which they pour out upon the spot. This is no doubt the identical dragon (Naga) which Fa hian mentions as appearing *once a year*, from whose favour the people of Seng kia shi obtained propitious rains and abundant harvests. It is most interesting thus to trace back with certainty this local worship for nearly fourteen centuries and a half, to A. D. 400, which though most probably not the period of its origin, yet undoubtedly must be close to the time of its engrafture upon Buddhism."

Capt. C. then records a tradition of the destruction of this capital in Samvat 1240 (A. D. 1183) by Raja Jayachandra of Kanouj, who at the instigation of the bráhmans, marched against it and ploughed it up into fields, on the borders of which the large bricks are piled in dykes to the present day. These old traditions and authentic dates are of infinite value in illustrating the medieval history of India.

Sankasya is mentioned in the Ramáyána and is one of the holy cities claimed by the Hindus.—J. W. L.

(2) *To the heaven of Tao li,*—the *Trayastrinsha*, or *heaven of the thirty-three,* that is the habitation of Indra and the thirty-two gods dependent on him. It occupies the second place in the inferior world, called the *World of desires*, as of course it does of the twenty-eight superimposed heavens which constitute a *universe.** The expression in the text is synonymous therefore with the second heaven to which Buddha is said to have ascended. These thirty-two gods were as many men who in preceding ages had merited by virtuous acts regeneration in this place with divine attributes.† The duration of their life is fixed at 1000 years, every day of which is equal to 100 of our years, which amount to thirty-six millions of years. At the end of this period they die, and are born again in a superior or an inferior condition, according as they may have advanced or receded in moral merit. It is thus that we meet in Buddhist legends with personages who have been Indras or Brahmas, or some other divinity, whose name does not indicate a fixed and definite condition, which when once acquired is forever attached to the same individual, but a transitory state at which all may arrive in their turn.

According to Tibetan cosmography, the town inhabited by the thirty-two gods, is of a square form ; its circuit is 10,000 *dPag thsad*, or 40 Roman miles ; the walls of pure gold are 2½ *dPag thsad* or 10 miles high. (Some error here.—J. W. L.) The palace is situated in the midst of the town, and is 1000 *dPag thsad* in circumference. At the four angles are delicious gardens, in each of which is an elephant with six trunks and a red head, leading a herd of a million animals of the same species. These gods have wives who bear them sons, who are conceived, born, and full-grown in the same moment. Their stature is 250 *Dom pa*, or quadruple cubits.

According to a Buddhist work, the summit of *Su meru* is the dwelling

* *Journal Asiatique*, tom VII. p. 314.
† *San tsang fa sou*, B. XLVII. p. 26. v.

place of the gods ; and there is the town named *Shen hian*, or *goodly appearance*, in which abides Indra.—R.

(3) *In favour of his mother.*—*Maha maya*, or the *Lady*, as she is called by the Buddhists, daughter of *Kieou li sha ti*, and wife of the king *Suddho dana*, died seven days after the birth of Sakya ; but in consideration of the merit of having borne in her womb the great Master of the Gods, she was born again in *Trayastrinsha*, and there received among the gods. One of the duties which the Tathágata had to perform was to preach the law to his mother. Thus then after he had accomplished the doctrine, he thought of nothing more than of the goodness of that mother who had cherished him (in her womb) ; but besides the depth of his affection he was bound by engagement to return to save his father and his mother. It was on this account that he desired to preach on her behalf and obtain her deliverance, and for this purpose that he ascended to the heaven *Trayastrinsha.*—R.

(4) *His supernatural faculties.*—We have already seen supernatural power ascribed to the Buddhist saints.* The expression in the text is the same that is applied to the faculties of *Bráhmacharis* in the treatise formerly quoted ;† and instead of the ten *powers*, six *faculties* only are reckoned. What was formerly advanced on that subject, may be compared with the following explanation taken from another religious treatise :—

" *Shin* (spiritual, supernatural, divine) is predicated of the soul or of the thoughts of the gods; *Thoung* (penetration, intelligence) of intelligent nature. That which enables one to penetrate, and see after the manner of the gods, is called *Shin thoung.*"‡

1st. *The divine eye.*—Thus is named the faculty of beholding all beings, living or dead, who belong to the six conditions, that is, of gods, of men, of *asuras*, of hungry demons, of brutes, and of the damned ; of seeing the sorrows and the joys of all these beings of whatever kind they be, and in all the worlds, without obstacle or impediment.

2ndly. *The divine ear,*—enables the possessor to hear every word, whether of sorrow or of joy, uttered by the beings of the six conditions, and all sounds and noises of whatever kind, and in whatever place they be.

3rd. *Knowledge of the thoughts of others.*—The faculty of knowing what is passing in the bottom of the heart of all the creatures of the six conditions.

4th. *The knowledge of existence.*—This is the faculty of knowing every thing connected with one's own existence, whether at the distance of one,

* Chap. VI. note 6.
† Chap. X. note 4.
‡ *Inglo king*, quoted in the *San tsang fa sou*, B. XXVI. p. 7. v.
§ *Fa kiaï tseu ti*, quoted in the *San tsang fa sou*, B. XXVI. p. 11.

two, or three generations, or a hundred, a thousand, or ten thousand; as well as that of all and each of the beings of the six conditions and all their actions.

5th. *The body at will.*—By this is meant the power of passing bodily by flight over seas and mountains without experiencing impediment; disappearing from this world, and re-appearing in another, and the reverse; of becoming great or small, and finally of changing the form of the body at will.

6th. *The end of the dropping.* (Stillationis finis).—This singular expression designates the errors of sight and of thought in the three worlds. By the errors of sight are understood the divisions or distinctions which arise from the connexion of the *root* of the mind (mens) with the *dust* of the law; and by the errors of the thought, the desires and affections which spring from the connexion of the *five roots* of the eye, the ear, the nose, the tongue and the body, with the *five dusts* of color, sound, smell, taste and touch. The Arhans, delivered from the errors of sight and of thought, obtain supernatural faculties, since they are no longer subject to birth or life in the three worlds.*—R.

(5) *Their divine faculties*, or the *sufficient strength of gods.*—See what has been said of the supernatural faculties, Chap. VI. note 6.

(6) *A na liu;*—one of the ten great disciples of Sakya, and renowned for his penetrating sight. He had the *divine eye.* His name is more correctly written *A na liu tho*, and signifies in Sanskrit *unextinguishable.* He was so named, because, having practised charity, he had merited re-birth among men and gods, and *unextinguishable* happiness. He was cousin of Buddha† and second son of the king Hou fan; and he embraced religious life in the suite of Sákya.—R.

(7) *Sight of the Gods.*—See chapter VI. note 6.—R.

(8) *The Honorable of the Age.*—In Sanscrit *Lokajyestha;* See Chap. XVI. note 24.—R.

(9) *Mou lian*, is the same as *Mou kian lian*, in Sanskrit *Mauggala-yana*, the sixth of the ten great disciples of Sakya.—R.

(10) *Yan feou thi*,—Jambudwípa. (See note 7, Chap. XII.)

(11) *Yeou pho lo*, perhaps a transcription of the Sanskrit *Utpala*, lotus, blue nymphæa. There is no mention of this incident either in the *Si yu chi*, or in any other of the Chinese legends in our possession.—R.

(12). *The holy king turning the wheel.*—This is the Chinese transcript of the Sanskrit *Mahá Chakravartti Rájá*, a title implying "universal monarch." The present is an appropriate occasion to explain this pompous title, which is nowhere completely defined, not even in the History of *Sanang Setsen.*

* *Great Japan, Cyclop.* B. XIX. p. 8.
† *San tsang fa sou*, B. LXI. p. 13.

The *Holy King of the Wheel* is he who reigns over the four continents, (see Chap. XII. n. 7.) He enjoys, four special advantages, decorated with the name of virtues : 1st. He is extremely rich, possessing a great abundance of treasure, fields, dwellings, slaves of both sexes, pearls and precious stones, elephants and horses ; none under heaven in this respect equalling him. 2ndly. His beauty is unrivalled. 3rly. He is never sick, and enjoys perpetual complacency. 4thly. His life is prolonged beyond that of other men. When he goes forth he is followed and guarded by four kinds of troops ; those mounted on elephants, those on horses, those in chariots, and infantry clad in cuirass and helmet.

The age of man, according to the Buddhists, is subject to a vicissitude of increase and diminution, the complete revolution of which constitutes a *small kalpa.* The greatest increase of human life is to 84,000 years. When this has lasted one hundred years, human life diminishes by one year, and so on in the same proportion, one year in every hundred, until it is reduced to ten years ; and this is called the *Kalpa,* or cycle, *of diminution.* Then after the lapse of one hundred years, it increases by one year ; or according to others *the son lives to twice the age of the father,* for if the latter have lived ten years the former will live twenty. This period is called the *Kalpa of prolongation.* The prolongation goes on till the age of 84,000 years is attained, when there appears a *King of the Golden Wheel,* who is born in a royal family and obtains supreme dignity on succeeding his father and being baptised in the water of the four oceans. For fifteen days he bathes in perfumed water, and fasts ; he then ascends an elevated tower surrounded by his ministers and courtiers. Suddenly there appears a golden wheel in the east, shedding a brilliant light and advancing to the place where the king is standing. If the king would proceed towards the east, the wheel turns in that direction, and the king accompanied by his troops follows. Before the wheel are four genii who serve as guides. Wherever it stops, there does the king in like manner. The same thing takes place in the direction of the south, the west, and the north ; wherever the wheel leads, the king follows ; and where it halts, he does the same. In the four continents he directs the people to follow the ten right ways, that is to say, not to kill, not to steal, not to commit adultery, not to lie, not to be double-tongued, not to calumniate, not to speak with elaborate refinement, not to abandon one's-self to lusts, not to entertain anger and hatred, and not to have immodest looks. He is called *the king of the golden wheel* or *the holy king turning the wheel*, and he possesses the seven precious things, viz :—

1st. *The treasure of the Golden Wheel.*—This wheel has a thousand rays (or spokes) ; its diameter is one toise and four feet (4m. 270 = to 14 English feet nearly). Its nave and felloes are sculptured and enchased with precious ornaments, shedding great splendour; it is the work of heavenly artists, and is unequalled by any thing in the world. The monarch who obtains it is called the *holy king who causes the wheel to turn*, because from the moment of his possessing it, the wheel turns and traverses the universe according to the thoughts of the king.

2nd. *The treasure of the White Elephant*, named also the *blue mountain*. The king of the wheel having come in the morning to his palace, there suddenly appears to him a elephant, the body of which is entirely white and the head of various colours; he has six teeth of the colour of the seven precious things. He is so powerful that he can traverse the air; and when the king has mounted him can make the tour of the universe, setting out in the morning and returning by evening, without experiencing pain or fatigue. If he cross a river, the water is not agitated, nor does it even moisten his feet. (We here see the reason why the kings of Ultra-India keep white elephants in their stables, and assume the title of '*Lord of the White Elephant*;' this title being synonomous with 'sovereign of the world.')

3rd. *The Purple Horse*, named also *strong and rapid wind.*—This horse is of a mixed tint of red and blue. The king having come to his palace, early in the morning, a purple horse suddenly appears before him. His hair is strung with pearls, which fall off when he is washed or combed and are instantly reproduced more beautiful and brilliant than before. When he neighs he is heard at the distance of a yojana. He has strength sufficient to fly; and when the king mounts to traverse the world, he sets out in the morning and returns by night without experiencing any fatigue. Every grain of dust which his feet touch is converted into gold.

4th. The *Divine Pearls*, called also, *clouds of hidden light.*—These pearls present themselves to the king's sight in the same manner as the preceding objects. Their colour and water are perfect without spot or blemish; suspended in the air during night they enlighten both great and little states; and within and without they emit light equal to the full day.

5th. The *treasure of the Jasper Girl*, otherwise called, *pure and admirable virtue*. Her body is warm in winter and cool in summer; from all its pores there exhales the perfume of sandal wood, as from her mouth that of the blue lotus. Her speech is sweet, her gait is dignified; whatever she eats is dissipated and evaporates; nor is she subject to any of the impurities of other women.

6th. The *Doctor of Wealth*, otherwise *vast wealth*, or the *doctor of treasures*. When the king of the wheel desires to possess the seven kinds of wealth, the magistrate in charge of the mines and treasures, turns to the earth, and the earth produces the seven precious things; or to the water, the mountains, and the stones, and these equally produce them. The work entituled *Agama*, adds that the functionary who occupies this charge is under the influence of great prosperity, and that he is able to perceive treasures hidden in the earth, whether having an owner or not. If they have one, he watches for their preservation; if not, he assumes them for his master's use.

7th. The *General of the Army*, called also *the spotless eye*, or the *officer charged with the command of the troops*. When the king of the wheel requires the four kinds of troops to the number of a thousand or ten thousand, or even an *asankya* (an innumerable amount), he has but to turn his eyes, and they are at once marshalled in perfect order. The book *Agama* adds, "this officer is able and prudent, brave and intrepid, and consummate in the stratagems of war. He presents himself singly and addresses the king: 'Lord! if you have enemies to combat be not uneasy. If you desire the four kinds of troops, men on elephants, or in war-chariots, or cavalry, or infantry, I will place them at your disposal.'"*

When *Siddartha* (Sakyá Muni) came into this world he exhibited, according to the judgment of astrologers, the signs of the happiest of alternatives in his physiognomy. "If this prince remain at home (that is continue a laic) he will become, said they, a holy king of the wheel, and lord of the four continents; for the kings of the wheel possessed, as this prince did, the *thirty-two beauties (laksapa)*; if he leave his home (that is embrace religious life), continued they, let him despise the dignity of royalty in seeking the doctrine; he will infallibly become Buddha, and receive the title of *universal guide*.†

The book entitled *Long (Agama)* speaks only of the *king of the Golden Wheel*, owner of the treasures above enumerated; but according to the *Kiu che lan*, (apparently a portion of the Abhidharma) there are four kings decorated with the sign of the wheel:

1st. The *king of the Iron Wheel*. He appears in the time when the age of man, after having reached its term of extreme brevity (10 years), returns by successive augmentations to 20,000 years. He reigns only over his single southern continent, or Jambudwípa. If any one resist his beneficent influence, the king displays his power, compels submission, and establishes anew the observance of the ten good ways.

2d. The *king of the Copper Wheel*, will appear when the duration of life is 40,000 years. He rules two continents, the eastern, or *Fe in thaï*, and the

* *Sieou hing pen khi king*, quoted in the *San tsang fa sou*, B. XXX. p. 11.
† *Foe pen hing tsy king*, Book V. p. 2.

southern, or Jambudwípa. He conducts himself as the former, and by his power and virtue, converts all those who have strayed from the good way.

3d. The *king of the Silver Wheel.* He makes his appearance when the life of man extends to 60,000 years. He governs three continents, to wit, those above named, and the western, or *Kiu ye ni.* If amongst the kingdoms there be any who resist his influence, he subjugates them and re-establishes by force the observance of virtue.

4th. The *king of the Golden Wheel.* Governs the four continents, as we have seen above.—R.

The explanation here and formerly (see Chap. V. note 6) given of the significance of wheels as emblematic of temporal and spiritual dominion, will readily account for the frequent occurrence of this symbol upon ancient Buddhist coins, of which many have been figured in the Journ. As. Soc. Vol. IV., and elsewhere. In Vol. XVI. of the same work, p. 748, Capt. J. D. Cunningham has given a sketch from the sculptures at Bhilsa of a man kneeling in adoration before a wheel supported upon a pillar, and most likely typifying the Bauddha faith, or perhaps Buddha himself, who is designated *Chakkawatti* in Pali books. (See Mahawanso, Glossary).

The religious as well as temporal meanings attached to the wheel are common, however, to the Hindu as well as the Bauddha faith. Thus Menu (Chap. XII. Sloka 124) compares transmigration,—that fundamental and undisputed dogma of all Indian theology—to the wheel of a car: and in the *Vishnu Purana* we read,—" The mark of Vishnu's discus is visible on the hand of one who is born to be a universal emperor, one whose power is invincible even by the gods." (*Wilson's Translation,* p. 101). In a note to this passage Professor Wilson gives the following explanation of the term Chakravertti; " one who abides in, or rules over an extensive territory called a Chakra."—J. W. L.

(13) *The seven precious things.* (See above, Chap. XIII. note 4.)

(14) The *king of the Gods, Fan.* Twenty years have elapsed since I first explained this Chinese word.* The Missionaries never interpreted *Fan,* which Deguignes always vaguely renders *Indian,* and to which he had apparently attached the signification of *prayers.* The word Fan, then, is in Chinese the equivalent of *Brahma,* and is further used to designate the Sanscrit language and character, as well as books written in that language. Its true etymology is for the first time indicated in my observations on the memoirs of Deguignes. It was obtained from a unique passage in a Buddhist work; for this word is never employed but in its abridged form, which renders it not easily recognisable. *Fan* is the contraction of *Fan lan ma,*

* *Nouv. Jour. As. tom.* VII. p. 298.

the transcription of *Brahma*. The meaning of the word is *exempt from desire, or pure*.

Brahma is, in the Buddhist system, the first of the twenty gods having functions to exercise and protection to bestow on other beings. He has the title of king. His person and his soul are alike replete with perfect majesty and purity, untainted with any imperfection. He is a strict observer of the precepts, illuminated and qualified to govern the band of secondary Brahmas. It is he who in the *Fa houa king* is called the *Lord of the Savaloka*, the great Brahma, who governs the grand chiliocosm, that is the greatest of the three aggregations of universes, containing a thousand million of suns, of Sumerus, and quadruple continents such as we behold.*

In other arrangements of the Buddhist pantheon, Brahma is represented in a more or less elevated position. He occupies, either himself, or by his subjects and ministers, the three heavens of the first contemplation in the world of forms (*Rúpya vachara)* that is to say the seventh, the eight, and the ninth heaven in ascending mount Sumeru. In the seventh is the troop or army of Brahma (*Brahmaparipatyá*) ; the ministers of Brahma (*Brahma-purohita*) are in the eigth, and the ninth is the abode of the great Brahma (*Mahá brahmana*) himself. According to this account Brahma must be very far from being the supreme Lord of the *Grand Chiliocosm*, since the *little chiliocosm*, is enclosed by the heavens of the second contemplation with which it is connected, and this lesser chiliocosm, is comprised a thousand times under the heaven of the fourth contemplation, which covers the grand chiliocosm. The *Savaloka* has a meaning yet more vast, seeing that under this denomination are united all the parts of the three worlds, to wit, the world of desires, the eighteen heavens of the world of forms, belonging to the first, the second, the third, and the fourth contemplation ; and the world of beings without forms.

The Buddhists of Nepal, reckon thirteen heavens in the world of forms subject to Brahma,† the names of four of which expressly denote this dependence. A *sloka* from the Raja kanda, a modern work composed in Nepál from respectable authorities, would lead us to believe that Padma-páni (Avalokiteswara) produced Brahma to create, Vishnu to preserve, and Mahésa, to destroy. Another work, more ancient, asserts that the sun and the moon were produced from the eyes of Avalokiteswara, Mahádeva from his forehead, Brahma from the interval of his shoulders, Vishnu from his chest, Saraswati from his teeth, Váyu from his mouth, Príthvi from his feet, and Varuna

* *Thian chouan*, History of the Gods, cited in the *San tsang fa sou*, B. XLVI. p. 13.

† See Hodgson, *Trans. Roy. Asiat. Soc.* Vol. II. p. 233.

from his navel. After the creation of these divinities it is further stated that Avalokiteswara thus addressed them: "Be thou Brahma, Lord of *Satyaguna*, and create; and thou, Vishnu, be thou Lord of the *Rajaguna*, and preserve; and Mahesa, be thou Lord of the *Tamaguna*, and destroy. According to Sarvajna Mitrapada, an ascetic of Cashmere, the three Indian divinities were born under the same circumstances, but from the body of the supreme *Prajna* (divine thought).

We easily perceive that the origin here assigned to Brahma, belongs to the Brahmanico-Buddhic syncretism of Nepál, first explained to us by Mr. Hodgson. The Buddhists, whose works we have in Chinese, in no way admit the creative function of Brahma, and even quote the idea of such as one of the fallacies taught by the heretics.

Those who adhere to the doctrines of the Vedas maintain that the God Náráyan begot the four families (Bráhmans, Khsetriyas, Vaisyas, and Sudras); that from his navel was produced a great nymphæa, and that from this nymphæa was produced Brahma, surnamed the *Grand sire*, as being the great father of all beings. Brahma possessed the power of creating all beings, animate or inanimate. They hence deem this deity eternal, unique, the cause of all things, even of *Nirvána*, that is, of the absolute state in which nature is conceived to exist anterior to the formation of the universe, and of the birth of individuals as well as of the relations which link these to each other. We shall by and bye give further details concerning these heterodox opinions.

According to Buddhist cosmography, the gods of the band of Brahma inhabit the first heaven of the first contemplation in the world of forms, are 875 *dom pa*, or quadruple cubits, in height, and live one half of a revolution of the world; the ministers of Brahma in the heaven immediately above are 1000 *dom pa* high, and live three-fourths of a revolution; and the great Brahmas in the third heaven of the first contemplation are 1125 *dom pa* in stature, and live an entire revolution, that is to say, a period of 1,344,000,000 years, or according to another calculation, six times the entire cycle of the nine ages of man, which makes the number of years much more considerable,* and scarcely to be expressed in figures. Elsewhere the life of Brahma is stated at 60 smaller Kalpas, or 1,008,000,000 years.†

The Tibetans have rendered the name of Brahma in their tongue by the word *Thsangs pa*, the signification of which implies the notion of purity attached by Buddhists to the original word. The Tartars replace it by *Esroun*, which is apparently formed from *Isuren* (*Iswara*), and has been transferred from one of the persons of the *trimurti* to the other.—R.

* *Alphab. Tibet*, p. 471.
† *San tsang fa sou*, B. XVIII. p. 11.

(15) *A chowry.*—An instrument employed in Buddhist ceremonies and formed of a handle and a tuft of hair from a deer's or a bear's tail, or of red silk. That which contemplative ascetics hold in the hand is of a white color; a figure of it may be seen in the Japanese Encyclopedia, B. XIX. p. 12.—R.

(17) *A throng of Gods.*—The word *gods* is applied in Buddhism, to designate those beings superior to man who inhabit the elevated regions of the world of desire, as well as the world of forms and that of incorporeal beings: but this word must not be taken in the sense attached to it in western mythology. The gods of Buddhism are imperfect beings, limited alike in power and in the duration of their existence, amongst whom it is not merely possible for men to be re-born by the practice of virtue, but whom they may even surpass by attaining the quality of purified Intelligence (Buddha or Bodhisattwa), and thus emancipating themselves from the vicissitudes of birth in the three worlds. Their Sanscrit name is *Deva.* The Tibetans call them *Lah.* The Chinese, having no word in their language applicable to the idea of an incorporeal and divine being, designate them by that which signifies *heaven,—Thian.* After their example, the Mongols denominate them *Tagri,* and the Manchous *Abka,* both signifying the same thing.

The gods are distinguished into four classes; *The gods of the world,* or the kings who, though dwelling among men, are under celestial influence. The *gods by birth;* these are those beings who by the observance of the precepts and the practice of virtue, or by the exercise of contemplation, have merited rebirth amongst the gods of the three worlds; it is these that are spoken of on the present occasion. The *gods of purity,* or the men of the two *translations,* that is to say, the *Sravakas* and the *Pratyeka Buddhas* who by devoting themselves to the contemplation of vacuity (spirit), suppress the errors of sense and thought, and attain a high degree of purity. The *gods of justice* are the Bodhisattwas, who by the ten kinds of moral perfection have fulfilled the entire law of deliverance.* The eight classes of living beings superior to man are, beginning with the least exalted, the *Mahoragas,* or terrestrial dragons; the *Kinnaras,* or horned genii and musicians of Indra; the *Garudas,* golden-winged birds; the *Asuras;* the *Gandharvas,* other musicians of Indra; the *Yakshas;* the *Nágas* or dragons, and the *Devas* or gods. These last are celestial beings, who enjoy a high degree of felicity, whose bodies are pure and resplendent, and who deserve to be honored with unequalled veneration. They are the most elevated in the *five conditions,* (gods, men, the damned, *pretas,* and brutes) very superior (to man); very great, very respectable. They find in themselves the sources of their own

* *Ta chi tou lun,* B. XXII, and the *Book of the Nirvána,* XXI, quoted in the *San tsang fa sou,* B. XVI, p. 8 *v.*

happiness; nothing opposes their wishes. These are the recompensing advantages of the pure character of their former life. Their colour is described as white, indicating the purity of their actions; hence the metaphors applied to them connected with this color, and with the *west*, in which direction it is supposed to predominate.* Their number is very great; but they have for chiefs, Brahma, the Lord of the great chiliocosm, and Indra, prince of the thirty-two gods of Sumeru.†

Formerly there were reckoned but sixteen principal gods, of whom there were images, and of whom each had his peculiar influence and dominion. Subsequently, four were added; the *Sun*, because he dissipates darkness; the *Moon*, because she illumines the night; *So kiei*, king of the dragons, because he conceals the treasure of the law, (see note 27) and *Yan ma lo*, because he reigns in darkness. We must give some account of these gods of the Buddhic Pantheon according to Chinese mythography.

1st. The *king of the Gods*, *Fan* or *Fan lan ma*. (See note 14.)

2d. *The king of Heaven*, *Indra*. See Chap. IX, note 2.

3d. *Pi sha men*, or the *glorious*. This god is so called because the fame of his glory is spread abroad in all parts. He is the king of the gods of the north, dwelling half way up the mountain Sumeru, on the fourth story of this mountain, on the northern side, by the wall of crystal. He commands innumerable myriads of *Yakshas* or valorous genii, and the north is under his protection. The Mongols call him *Bisman tayri*.

4th. *Thi theou lai tho*, or *Thi to lo tho*, the *protector of the kingdoms*, or the *pacificator of the people*. This god, whose power is propitious towards terrestrial kingdoms, is king of the eastern part of the Heavens. He dwells half way up Sumeru, on the fourth stage, facing the east, by the wall of gold. He commands the *Gandharvas* or musicians of Indra, and the *Fudannas*, or demons who preside over fevers. The east is subject to his dominion, and for the people of those parts he obtains peace and repose. In Mongol, *Ortchilong tetkouktchi*.

5th. *Pi leou le cha*, or *Pi lieou li*, whose name signifies *greatness augmented*, to express how his power, his majesty, and his virtues increase and cause those of others to increase also. This god dwells in the same story of Sumeru, as the foregoing, but on the southern side, and by the sapphire wall (*Lieou li*). He commands the *Kheou phan tho* (*Kumbhanda ?*), and other genii and demons in number infinite. He presides over the south. The Mongols call him *Ulumtchi tareltou*.

6th. *Pi lieou po cha*, or *Pi lieou pho cha*, whose name is explained in

* *Yuan kio king lio sou chhao*, B. XXIII. p. 20 *verso*.

† *Fan i ming y*, B. II, quoted in the *San tsang fa sou*, B. XXIII. p. 13 *verso*.

two ways: *mixed language*, because he can speak in every tongue; *great eyes*, because his eyes are far greater than those of men. This god inhabits the same region as the foregoing, but on the west side of Sumeru, and by the silver wall. He commands the demons named *Pi she che* (*Visachas*) and innumerable troops of dragons and other demons. He protects the west. He is the *Sain bousou nidoutou* of the Mongols.

These four last named gods are called the gods of the Heaven. They are the ministry of Indra. They are also denominated the *protectors of the world*, in conformity with the part they are called upon to play.*

7th. *Kin kang mi tsi*, that is to say in Chinese,—'the god who holds in his hand the diamond mace' (*Vajra páni*) and who knows thoroughly all the actions and all the proceedings of the Tathágatas. There was in ancient times a king who had a thousand and two sons. The first thousand all attained the rank of Buddhas, and their every thought was directed to the perfection of the doctrine. But the two youngest acknowledged it not. One of them made this vow; "If my thousand brothers accomplish the law, may I become a demon to attack and annoy them!" The other on the contrary, sought to become a warrior that he might defend them. It was this last who became *Kin kang* or *Vajra páni*. He commands the five hundred *Ye sha* (Yakshas) and other genii, who are all great Bodhisattwas. He dwells with them on the summit of the most elevated mountains, and they are all protectors of the law of the thousand Buddhas of the Kalpa of sages, that is of the present age.

8th. *Ma i sheou lo* (*Maha Ishwara*) The *Great Lord*, or as some understand it, the *Majestic Intelligence.* Some give him three eyes, as being the most venerable Lord of the three worlds. The *Tou hing ki*, says on this subject:—"The god of the world of forms has three eyes and eight arms. He is mounted upon a white ox, and holds in his hands a white brush. He is endowed with great strength and majesty. He dwells in the place of the Bodhisattwas and can reckon the number of rain-drops that fall in a grand chiliocosm. He governs a grand chiliocosm, and there is none more worthy of honor in the three worlds.

9th. *The great General Sa chi*, or *Sa chi sieou ma.* This word signifies *silence, repose.* The collection of *Dharanis*, or formulæ, contains a passage in which it is stated that the mother of the demons had three sons; the first named *Weï she wen*, the second the *General Sa chi*, and the youngest *Mani pa tho;* and that these were adequate to protect all the beings in all the worlds of space; to remove all their errors and vices. They dwell on the

* *Fa hona wen kia*, B. II. quoted in the *San tsang fa sou*, B. XVI, p. 9 *verso.*

earth or in the air. Each of them has five hundred officers attached to him, and twenty-eight dependent orders of demons and genii. Wherever the sacred doctrine is promulgated, thither they hasten to protect its preachers, to guard them from evil, and keep them in peace. They favour them in the triple repose of the body, the mouth, and the spirit; causing all manner of sweet savours, and subtile emanations to penetrate the pores of their bodies; fair speech and eloquence to adorn their mouths; and activity, courage, and penetration to fortify their spirits. They cause those also who hear the law to receive the happiness that belongs to men and gods, and speedily to obtain *bodhi*. Such are the good offices they perform in rewarding virtue and punishing vice.

10th. *The Great Discerner*, so called because of his lofty intelligence and profound penetration. He dwells in the most precipitous parts of the mountains, or in caverns and the depth of the forests. In the places where he dwells, he has always the head high, a single foot, eight arms and a handsome figure. He holds a bow, arrows, a sword, a lance, a long club, and an iron wheel. Indra and the other gods hold him in honor and celebrate his praises. He is provided with a power of discernment which nothing can resist; and under all circumstances he protects the world; coming to the help of all beings and diffusing the doctrine of Buddha, without wearying, by reason of his intelligence and happy gifts. By the light he diffuses at religious meetings he is the most propitious of all the gods.

11th. The *God of Virtues*, or of *Merits*, so named in the book of the *Nirvána* and in the collection of the Dharanis; and in the *Kouang ming king* and *Sa chi pin*, called the *first in majesty, promoter of virtuous acts, great god of merits*. It is in him that the Tathágata *Kin shan chao ming (light of the golden mountain)* deposited the seeds of all the virtues which obtained for him all sorts of blessings. His figure and exterior are admirable. He diffuses virtue and happiness among all beings. He dwells in a magnificent garden called the 'Pavilion of gold.' He supplies those who proclaim the Law with all that is requisite for them, and delights in heaping upon them all the gifts of virtue and of knowledge.

12th. *The General, God of the Weï*, or *Weï to* (*Védas*). This last word signifies *discourses of science*. The *Ling weï yao lio* states that this god, named *Weï*, and surnamed *Khuen*, is one of the generals subject to the king of the gods of the south (*Pi leou le cha*,—see § 5). There are thus thirty-two generals under the orders of the four kings of the gods, and the present is the first of them. He is endowed with great intelligence, and early knew how to emancipate himself from the desires of the senses; he adopted a pure and bráhmanic *(fan hing)* conduct, and consecrated himself to virginity and deeds of sincerity. Instead of the pleasures of the gods, he received the instructions of Buddha. He defends religion from without and protects the three continents (*Jambudwípa, Vidéha, Goyeni*) to the great benefit of all living beings whom he converts and succours in crowds. Thus whenever a *Kia lan* (temple) is erected, his statue is there placed for adoration, in consideration of the glorious protection he affords to religion.

13th. The genius called *Earth of Solidity*. Solidity is the quality of that which is indestructible, of that which cannot be broken, as the diamond. The word *Earth* denotes that this genius has merits profitable to the world, and that he may be compared to the great earth which sustains all, producing trees, plants, grain, and all precious things. He keeps and protects all places where the doctrine is diffused; he bears upon his head the teachers of the Law, causing them to perceive the savour of a sweet dew, and augmenting the strength of their bodies. In the *Ti tsang king*, Foe says to the genius of the Earth; "All the lands of Jambudwípa receive protection from thee. All that the earth produces is furnished in abundance. Thou protectest the doctrine of Buddha. In the age, and out of the age, thy merits are equally great."

14th. *The genius of the Bodhi tree*, or *of Intelligence*, constantly watches the places where the Tathágatas accomplish the doctrine, and hence his name. He thus speaks of himself; "I think constantly of Buddha; I enjoy the sight of the *Honorable of the Age;* I vow never to separate from the sun of Buddha." He shows moreover his power and his attention in following him in his most minute and subtle acts; he protects all living beings and insures them corporeal benefits; and hence the sacred books are replete with his praises, and celebrate his immense deserts.

15th. *The Goddess mother of the demons.* This goddess had a thousand sons. The youngest, named *Aï nou*, whom she cherished most tenderly, was in the habit of devouring the children of men. Foe converted this Aï nou, and hid him under his pot. His mother sought him in heaven and among men, but in vain. She submitted herself (to Foe); and Foe removing the pot, restored her son. These thousand children became the kings of the demons, of whom they command several legions of ten thousand each. There are five hundred in heaven ever occupied in seducing and tormenting the gods: and five hundred in the world in a similar manner engaged in seducing the people. Foe gave (the mother of the demons) the five precepts to bring her back to the good law; she became *protapanna*, (see sequel) and dwells in the temples of Foe. Those who have no children address her to obtain them. Those who are sick pray to her and are restored to health. After she had received the precepts from Foe, she summoned her thousand sons, and induced them to submit as she had, and no longer to offend against either gods or men.

16th. *Ma li chi,* so called from a word that signifies, *flame of day* (*Yang yan*), because his body can neither be perceived nor laid hold of. This god ever precedes the sun and the moon. He protects the kingdoms and the people, and delivers them from the fury of war and other calamities. In the book of the great god *Ma li chi,* there is a phrase of great efficacy,—"*An! ma li chi so po ho* (*Om! marichi swáhá*); whoever possesses this formula is prepared for all; a supernatural power is assured him, and upon that he may rely.

17th. *The Son of the Gods who dwell in the palace of the Sun.* This god, whilst yet in the *bonds of cause* (i. e. in the world), practised charity, observed the precepts, cultivated virtue, and honoured Buddha. By these means he merited birth among the gods. His palace-walls are adorned with the most precious things, while five whirlwinds perpetually hurry it along without permitting it to halt a moment. It revolves circularly at one half the height of Sumeru, and enlightens the four continents. When it is midday in *Jambudwípa,* the sun* begins to set in *Vidéha* and to rise in *Goyeni,* whilst at *Uttarakuru* it is midnight. It is thus that one sun enlightens four continents, drives away night from them, dissipates darkness, and promotes the maturity of all things. This is the same god that is designated in the *Fa hoa king, Son of the Gods of Precious Light.*

18th. The *Son of the Gods of the Palace of the Moon.* The god so named obtained the same advantages as the preceding, by the practice of similar virtues. His palace is similarly adorned with precious things and wheeled around Sumeru, by five whirlwinds, so as to illumine the four continents. The full and the new moon occur in the following mode. At the commencement of the *white moon* (the apposition) the sun is before;—at that of the *black moon* (the conjunction), the sun is behind. According as the reflex of the sun is hidden, or apparent, it is new and full moon; this is what is named the sun's approach; and when the reflex of the sun is diminishing, then is the moon's disk on the wane. Now the moon's light pours sweet and secret influences upon all beings; she illumes the night. Her services succeed those rendered by the sun. This is the same god that is designated in the *Fa hoa king,* '*son of the gods of the brilliant moon.*'

19th. *So ko lo* (Ságora), that is to say the *salt sea* (ocean); a name translated also *king of the dragons.* He is the seventh of the hundred and seventy-seven kings of the dragons who dwell in the salt sea. He is the only one now mentioned, because of his having attained the rank of the

* *Vocab. pentagl.* sect. XI.

most exalted Bodhisattwas, and dwelling in the ten earths,* that is to say, having passed through the ten degrees that lead the saints to this kind of perfection. He shows himself under the figure of a dragon, and makes his abode in the salt sea. When rain is about to fall it is he that beforehand spreads out the clouds and watches that it be equally distributed. He follows the assemblies of Foe, protects his law and his people, and thus himself acquires great merit. His palace, adorned with the seven precious things, differs in no respect from that of the gods.

20th. *Yan ma lo,* whose name signifies '*double king,*' or according to others, '*unique king ;*' double king, because this king and his younger sister are sovereigns of hell ; unique king, because he has sole charge of that which concerns men, whilst his younger sister has the care of what appertains to women. His name is also translated as *that which allays strife,* because he puts an end to the disputations of sinners. It is maintained that a Bodhisattwa assumed this form for the benefit of living beings. The *Ching fa nian king* contains a *gatha* addressed to men, by *Yan man lo,* in these terms : "You have received the body of a man, but you cultivate not the doctrine ; this is as it were to enter a treasury and to come out empty handed ! What avails to utter cries for the pains you endure, when you but suffer the recompense of your own acts ?" The Book of Kings says : "The king *Yan* (*yan ma lo*) will in future times become Buddha, and will be called *Phou wang jou laï,* the Tathágata *Universal King.* So excellent will be the effect of the transformation of this Bodhisattwa."* His present name is *Yan ma,* or *Ye ma,* a transcription of the Sanscrit *Yama.* This deity is named in Tibetan *gChin otche,* in Mandchou *Ilmoun khan,* and in Mongol *Erlik khakan.*

Besides the twenty gods here enumerated, there are many others who have no mythological part to play, or who simply occupy sundry celestial mansions. Such are the thirty-two gods, the companions of Indra, who dwell with him on the summit of Sumeru, and from whom the region they occupy is denominated *Trayastrinsha,* or the *heaven of the thirty-three.* These are thirty-three personages who having combined together in performing good works, merited regeneration in this place. They occupy as many palaces, disposed by eights, at each of the four angles of Sumeru ; and the Lord of Heaven, Indra, has his in the centre. The names of these gods of *Trayastrinsha* are unknown ; but Indra was their chief at the time of the former Buddha.

They name also *Ye ma,* in Sanscrit *Yáma* (not the *Yama* of Hell) and in Tibetan *Thab bral, he who is remote from war,*' or in 'Chinese, *happy*

* *San tsang fa sou,* B. XLVI. p. 13.

time,' because he incessantly sings and plays) a god, who by the observance of charity and the precepts, attained to excellence even beyond that of the thirty-three.* He was rewarded by translation to the third heaven of the world of desires. Then come the gods of *Tushita* or the '*heaven of sufficient knowledge,*' and the other heavens ascending up to those of the Bráhmas, and of the great king Brahma, the first born at the beginning of every kalpa, and the first to die at the end. Lastly, the name of *gods* is bestowed on all the beings who inhabit the other heavenly mansions, which added to those of which I have already spoken, amount to twenty-eight. The Tibetans minutely detail their stature, the duration of their lives, and other circumstances concerning them ; but the Chinese are much less particular.†

However superior the gods may be to other human passions, there is one from which they are by no means entirely exempt ; those at least, of the inferior mansions. Those who inhabit the two terrestrial mansions on the flanks and summit of Sumeru, that is the kings of the cardinal points and the *thirty-three*, are not strangers to the distinction of sex, and cohabit "*in the manner of the age.*" The gods of Yáma propagate by mere embrace ; those of Tushita by touching the hands. Those of the heaven of '*the joy of conversion*' have such limited desires that they confine themselves to the interchange of smiles. Lastly, the gods of the sixth heaven, '*where they convert others*, experience scarce any feeling of concupiscence ; mutual looks are the only expressions of desire that they direct to each other, and this is sufficient for their propagation.‡

In the world of forms the eighteen heavenly mansions are likewise inhabited by gods of different ranks. At the '*first contemplation*' are the Brahmas, or the people of the Brahmas, subjects of the great king Brahma pure, free from stain and desire ; the ministers of Brahma, or his companions ; the great king Brahma, also called *Sikhi.*§ Purity is the attribute of these three classes of gods. At the '*second contemplation*' there are also three heavens, the inhabitants of which are characterised by *light*, feeble in the first, immense in the second, and occupying the place of voice in the third. The classes of gods of the '*third contemplation*' enjoy, in similar degrees, a purity of thought which procures them happiness that is heavenly, ineffable, immense, universal. All these gods inhabit space, and rest upon the clouds. Higher up we come to the gods of the '*fourth contemplation,*' separated into nine different heavens. The lowest of these is

* *In kia sse ti lun.*

† Giorgi, *Alpab. Tibetanem*, p. 483.

‡ *San tsang fa sou*, B. XXII. p. 22.

§ *Thian faï sse kiao i tsy chu ;* a work not belonging to the Sacred Collection, but quoted in the *San tsang fa sou*, B. XXII. p. 22.

termed '*cloudless*,' because the gods who inhabit it have no need of the support which clouds lend to the inferior gods. The heaven immediately above is that of '*happy life*.' Next in ascending comes that of '*great rewards*;' that of '*no reflection*,' i. e. where the gods during the whole term of their lives are exempt from the labour of thought; that of '*no fatigue*,' where the gods have attained the limits of thought; pure intelligences without support, without locality, free, exempt from trouble; that of the gods who see admirably all the worlds diffused through space; that of the gods to whom all is present and manifest, without obstacle or restriction; and lastly *Aghanishta*, or the heaven of those gods who have attained the extreme limit of the tenuity of matter. An attempt has been made, as will be readily seen, to graduate the perfections of these eighteen classes of gods, by heaping on them ideas of purity, of light, of penetration, of repose, and of subtlety; but with very imperfect success; for there are many repetitions and incoherencies in this classification, in which moreover various authors differ. Some place the heaven of the supreme lord *Maheswara vasanam*, above *Aghanishta*.*

In the world of immaterial beings there are again four classes of gods; those who, wearied with the bonds of corporeal substance, reside in vacuity, or the immaterial; those who have no place (*substratum*) save knowledge, since even void is too gross for them; the gods who have no place; and last of all, those gods, at the head of immaterial beings, who have the attributes neither of the non-thinking gods without locality, nor those appertaining to the gods of whom knowledge is the sole locality;† a definition too absurd for me to seek to clear it up in this place. It must be borne in mind that the foregoing long classification includes neither Bodhisattwas or Buddhas, whose moral and intellectual perfections are infinitely above those of all the gods of the various orders.

The duration of the lives of the gods is proportioned to their rank in the mythological hierarchy here expounded. An Indra, king of the gods of Sumeru, lives 36,000,000 years. A great king Brahma equals in longevity a grand revolution of the world, 1,344,000,000 years. A god of the '*fourth contemplation*' (*exempt from thought*) sees five hundred such revolutions; and an inhabitant of the last heaven of the incorporeal world, eighty thousand of them. Father Horace and Deshanterayes have published these various degrees of longevity, upon which any further remark is unnecessary. We must not however suppose that this long duration of life is regarded as a

* *Vocab. pentagl.* §. LIII. p. 9.
† *San tsang fa sou* B. XLVII. p. 26.

privelege to which no drawback or privation is attached; for, by way of example, the god who passes five hundred revolutions of the world '*without thought*,' is in his inaction, like one imprisoned in ice, and is during this period deprived of the advantage of seeing Buddhas, and of hearing religion preached; hence many heretics, who have practised virtue, are reborn in this condition.*

As the gods are subject to the vicissitude of birth and death like other beings, although extending through these immense periods, so there are signs of decay which announce to them as more or less near the approach of their end. They cease to delight in joyous songs, and the shining light of their bodies becomes feeble or extinct. In their ordinary state a perfumed oil, similar to that of the lotus, protects their chest from the contact of water; but as their glory declines, water begins to moisten their skin, and they are no longer dry on emerging from the bath; and whereas nothing formerly staid their steps or retarded the execution of their wishes, they now experience obstructions and embarrassments. Their sight, which extended without obstacle through a *grand chiliocosm*, is enfeebled and begins to wink. These are the five *lesser signs* of the decay of their faculties; there are five great ones which indicate the approach of death. The gods are ordinarily clad in a light robe weighing six *chu* (the *chu* is equal to ten grains of millet), and hence they are named *chu yi;* this robe is always spruce and brilliant with the lustre of newness; but when their happiness is on the wane and their lives about to end, their robes soil of themselves; and this is one of the great symptoms of decay among the gods. They wear on their heads coronals of flowers, or precious stones, feathers and ornaments of various kinds; these flowers wither and dry up. Their bodies formed of so pure and subtle a matter, begin to allow transpiration and humours to escape. The perfumes of inexpressible sweetness which they exhaled, are now changed to fetid vapors. They themselves cease to delight in their ordained abode in spite of all the pleasures accumulated there.

There are five acts, or rules of conduct, which obtain for man the privelege of regeneration among the gods; and all living beings may practise these acts; 1st. To have a compassionate heart, to kill no living being, to take pity on all, and procure them rest: 2d. To follow wisdom, to abstain from taking the goods of others, to perform alms, to avoid avarice, to help the needy: 3d. To be pure, to be guiltless of sensuality, to keep the precepts, to fast: 4th. To be sincere, to deceive no one, to avoid the four sins of the mouth (lying, affected language, duplicity, calumny), to flatter none: 5th. A

* *Wei mo so shoue king*, chapter I. *Pa nan*, or the Eight Unfortunate Circumstances, quoted in *San tsang fa sou*, B. XXII. p. 24.

man who honors the good law and walks firmly in the brahmanical way, drinks no liquors which intoxicate and disturb the understanding.*

There are five signs which indicate that a man is about to be born among the gods: 1st. A vivid light surrounds his body, and as this is naked, the soul thus reflects, "*Provided that the other gods witness not my nudity.*" But at the same moment he appears to others clad, though in reality naked. 2d. He conceives extraordinary thoughts by discovering the things that are in heaven; and on perceiving in the woods and the celestial gardens things which he had never before seen, he looks at them and examines them on all sides. 3d. He is struck with confusion at the appearance of the heavenly damsels, and dares not at the sight of their beauty look them in the face. 4th. He is tempted to approach the other gods whom he sees; he ponders, he doubts, he hesitates what he should do. 5th. When he would raise himself in space, fears overcome him; he rises not high; he removes not far; he coasts along the walls, or supports himself upon the earth.†—R.

(18) *The king A yeou*: Asoka; see Chap. X. note 3.

(19) *Six toises*, about sixty English feet.

(20) *Thirty cubits.*—The measure spoken of is the *Cheou* or cubit. Its length is variously estimated. Sometimes at two *chhi*, (0.610 met.) Sometimes at one *chhi* and two *tsun* (0.4575 met.) Four *cheou* make one *koung* (bow) and three hundred *koung* make one *li*. According to this calculation the *li* would be 549 or even 732 metres.—R.

[The French metre is equal to 39.37 English inches, as determined by Kater.—J. W. L.]

(21) *Heterodox philosophers.*—Such are frequently spoken of in Buddhist books, and we must in general understand them to be bráhmans, though sometimes it may be that other oriental sects also are alluded to under this denomination. Their discussions with the Samaneans are frequently alluded to in narratives of the lives of Sákya Muni and his successors. The narratives of Soung yan and Hiuan thsang establish the advantage the bráhmans had obtained over their ancestors in the 6th and 7th centuries, and the corresponding decline of Buddhism in the central, western, and northern regions of Hindustan. We shall make no reference here to the doctrines of the heretics except inasmuch as they relate to the earlier times of Buddhism.

There are reckoned six principal heresiarchs, whose depraved hearts, preverse views, and mistaken judgment, disaffected to the true doctrine,

* *Pian i chang che tseu so wen king*, B. XXII. p. 18. *verso.*

† *Ching fa nian chou king*, B. XXXIX, quoted in the San tsang fa sou, B. XXII. p. 19.

brought forth error. The commencement of all these heresies is referred to *Kia pi lo* (the yellow, in Sanscrit *Kapila*); but they are divided into branches, and their propagation gave rise to six principal ones :

1st. ***Fou lan na kia she.*** *Fou lan na*, was the title of this heresiarch, the translation of which is not given. *Kia she* (Kásyapa) was the name of his mother, and became that of the family. The heresy of this man consisted in the repudiation of all law; he recognised neither prince nor subject; father nor son; honesty of heart, nor filial piety. He called it *form* and *void* (*ether*). *Form*, according to this heretic, breaks down whatever is in the world of desires; *Void*, whatever is in the world of forms. Void is therefore the supreme fact, the being above all beings.

2d. *Mo kia li kin she li.* *Mo kia li* (in Sanscrit, *non videns rationem*) is the title of this man. *Kiu she li*, the meaning of which is not given, is the name of his mother. He falsely inferred that the evil and the good experienced by living beings, arose, not from anterior acts, but of themselves. This opinion of the spontaneity of things is an error which excludes the succession of causes.

3d. *Shan che ye pi lo chi.* *Shan che ye* (Sanjaya) signifies *recta victoria*, and is the title of this heretic. *Pi lo chi* (*Vaïrayi*), *non agens*,—is the name of his mother. His heresy consists in thinking that it is not necessary to seek the doctrine (*bodhi*) in the sacred books, as the same will be obtained of itself when the number of Kalpas of birth and death have been exhausted. He thought also that after eighty thousand Kalpas the doctrine would be obtained naturally.

4th. *A khi to hiue she khin pho lo.* *A khi to hiue she*, was the title of this heresiarch, the explanation of which is not given. His surname, *Khin pho lo* (*Kambala*) signifies '*coarse garments*.' His error consisted in supposing that destiny might be controlled,—that happiness might be obtained, for example, independently of causes in an anterior existence; that the doctrine consisted in wearing coarse garments, tearing out the hair, exposing the nostrils to smoke, and the body to heat on five sides (the four sides of the body, and having fire besides on the head); in submitting in short to all manner of mortifications, in the hope that having in the present life experienced all sorts of suffering, eternal happiness would be obtained in a future existence.

5th. *Kia lo kieou tho kia chin yan.* *Kia lo kieou tho*, the title of this heretic, signifies '*Chest of ox*.' *Kia chin yan*, '*Shaven hair*,' was his family name. His error, not well defined, consists in asserting, that of the laws, some are accessible to the understanding, and others are not so.

6th. *Ni kian tho jo thi tseu.* *Ni kian tho* signifies '*exempt from bonds*,' and is a very common title of heretics. He derived from his mother the name of *Jo thi*, the signification of which is not known. This heretic asserted that crimes and virtues, happiness and misery, were fixed by fate; that as subject to these we cannot avoid them; and that the practice of the doctrine can in no wise assist us. In this notion his heresy consisted.*

The ideas adopted by the heretics on certain points of the law, are called *views*, that is, particular ways of seeing,—hypotheses,—enunciated opinions. They take, in various doctrines, false things for true ones, and verities for errors; they entangle men with explanations, and seduce them from right reason. There are seven *views* of this kind. The first consists in speaking ill of the law, in attacking it without proof, in treating as erroneous the sentiment of retribution for good or evil acts, and the doctrine of the origin of the six senses and the six sensible qualities; to refer them, for instance, to the god Bráhma or to atoms. The second is the '*view of me*,' which makes the party a sort of lord and master, existing of his own power, and constituting *me* (egotism or individuality), in ignorance that *person* is nothing more than the vain and transient union of the five *skandha*.† The '*view of perpetual duration*,' contemns the fluctuation of the person and the body, as also the doctrine that all external beings, whoever they be, are, without exception, subject to destruction, and *return to extinction*. Those who admit the '*view of termination*' know not that the laws (of nature) are naturally spiritual, eternal, indestructible; they erroneously deem them subject to a term, and falsely conclude that after death the body is not subject to re-birth. The fifth *view* is called *præceptorum furtum*, or *visionis captio*: it consists in despising the veritable precepts laid down by the Tathágatas, and in following other wicked precepts by which men distinguish and separate themselves from others to advance therein: as for example, where one persuades himself that he had been in a former existence, an ox or a dog, and restricts himself to feed on grass or impure objects; this is called following the '*precept of the ox or dog*.' In truth, small merit is acquired thus, although some persuade themselves that it is sufficient. They thus lead a disorderly life, and neglect the observance of the true concatenation of things. By the sixth *view*, called *fructuum furtum*, despising the same concatenation, as well as the *fruits* which are rightly expected from actions, they turn excellent resolutions into a blamable conduct, and strive to obtain the merit of mortification by exposing themselves naked to the

* *Tho lo ni tsy king; Collection of the Dharanis. Fan y ming i*, quoted in the *San tsang fa sou*, Book XXVII. p. 11.
† *Vocab. pentagl.* sect. XXXIII.

rigors of cold or to the heat of fire and of the sun, (named the *five heats*) in covering themselves with ashes, and sleeping upon thorny plants; and the trifling merit derived from these acts, they exaggerate by a false persuasion that there is none superior. Lastly, the seventh *view*, called that '*of doubt*,' consists in hesitating among all these opinions, whether of individuality, or non-individuality; eternal duration, or non-eternal duration; without the power of making up the mind to either of these classes of ideas.*

We are elsewhere assured that heterodox opinions do not exceed four in number; but the *views* are announced in an almost enigmatic manner. The partisans of the system of numbers (*sankhya*) admit only *unum* amongst causes and effects, and not *diversum*. Those of the opposite system see nothing among these but *diversum*. Those of the *Le so pho* (Rishabna) admit equally *unum* and *diversum*.† In the absence of elucidations, it is difficult to say whether logic or cosmogony is here referred to.

The heretics are equally divided upon the identity of *ego* and the five (*Skandha*): some think that *ego* and the five (*Skandha*) equally exist; others that neither do. Others again, to escape the preceding errors, believe that *ego* and the five *Skandha* both do and do not exist, thus falling into a manifest contradiction. The last, to avoid this contradiction, assert by a kind of play of words, that *ego* and the five *Skandha* are neither existent nor non-existent,‡ a difficulty which orthodox Buddhism can alone explain away. The heretics again deny the duration of *ego*; some think that the *ego* of preceding generations is the same as that of the present one, without interruption, and so fall into the error of perpetuity. Others think that the *ego* of now began in the present generation and not in foregoing ones; they therefore believe it not eternal, and so fall into the hypothesis of interruption. Others think that *ego* is eternal and that the body is not so; but in this way the body is set aside, and is no part of *ego*. This therefore is an erroneous notion. Lastly, others have remarked that the body being compound (*diversum*) is not eternal; and that *ego* not being compound, cannot be eternal. But in this manner also, there can be no *ego* without the body.§

In several legends concerning Sákya Muni, some controversies are mentioned which that personage and his disciples held with the partisans of ninety-five sects: but we learn that this number was reduced to eleven, whose doctrines, books and discipline were diffused throughout the east. They are pointed out as follows: 1st. The sectaries of the doctrine of

* *San tsang fa sou*, B. XXX. p. 2, v.
† *Ibidem*, XVII. p. 26, verso.
‡ Idem, B. XVIII.
§ Ibid.

numbers (*Sankhya*) ; so called either because they discourse in the first place of numbers, or because ratiocination begets (proceeds by) number ; or because they treat of numbers and make these their study. They teach that darkness begets intelligence, and that, up to spiritual *ego*, there are twenty-five principles or realities ; 1st, obscurity, or primordial nature, (natura per se ;) 2d. The principle of knowledge or intelligence (*Buddha*) ; 3d. The thought of *ego* (conscience) ; 4th, 5th, 6th, 7th, 8th, the five subtile things, or colour, sound, odour, savour, and tactility. 9th, 10th, 11th, 12th, 13th, the five great (beings), earth, water, fire, air, and ether ; 14th, 15th, 16th 17th, 18th, the five roots of knowledge, the eye, the ear, the nose, the tongue, and the body ; 19, 20, 21, 22, 23, the five roots of action, the mouth, the hand, the foot, the fundament, the urethra ; 24, the co-disposing root of the heart, or *mens*, composed of five elements and completing with ten preceding the eleven roots ; 25, the spiritual *ego*, or the knowledge that has its seat in the eighth viscus. The heretics believe that the spiritual *ego* is able to beget the laws, that it is eternal, indestructible, and that it is the *nirvána*.*

The discovery of these twenty-five principles is ascribed to *Kia pi lo* (*Kapila* or the Tawny). Those who adopt his opinions, devote themselves to contemplation ; they pretend to possess divine intelligence, and to be able to come to the knowledge of what has happened during eighty thousand Kalpas. As for what happened before these Kalpas, they know nothing about it, and hence name it *obscurity*, whence arises nature, then understanding, then the intellectual *ego*, the supreme principle. They arrange these 25 principles under nine divisions ; but in reality they make the first twenty-four principles originate from the twenty-fifth, the spiritual *ego*, which they consider the Lord, ever intelligent and enlightened, eternal, indestructible, embracing and including all the laws, by consequence unique, the cause of all beings, and of *nirvána* itself.

2d. The sectaries of the *Wei chi* (Vaishesika), a Sanscrit word signifying '*without superior*,' '*without victor*.' This man appeared in the world 800 years before Buddha. The people of his time hid themselves during the daytime in the mountains and marshes to avoid noise and distractions. At night they saw and heard well, and came forth to beg. In this they resembled the owls, and were hence named the *owl-hermits*. *Weï chi* had the five faculties (see above p. 125); he composed ten times ten thousand verses in testimony of *bodhi*, and then joyously entered *nirvána*. He put forward the *six generative words :* 1st. Substance, which is the body of the laws (of nature) upon which quality and action are supported ; 2d. Virtue, or quality ; 3d. Action, use, or employment. 4th. The *great being*, that is

* *San tsang fa sou*, B. XLVII. p. 26.

what is common to substance, quality and action, or these three predicaments considered in their unity. 5th. The *common* and the *different;* as for example, the earth considered with reference to earth,—this is the common; with reference to water, this is the *different;* and so on with water, fire, air, &c. 6th. Union or aggregation; by which is understood the union of all the laws (of nature). For exemplification,—a bird is flying in space; suddenly he arrives at the branch of a tree; he stops there. It is the same of the laws (of nature) in the union of which stability consists.

3d. Sectaries who cover themselves with ashes (Vibhúti); these imagine that the sixth god of the world of desires, *Iswara,* created all things.

4th. The sectaries of the Vedas imagine that Náráyana, (he whose strength is comparable to a lock by reason of the strong articulation of his members) created the four families; that from his mouth were created the Bráhmans, from his arms the Kshetriyas, from his thighs the Vaisyas and from his feet the Shudras.

5th. The partisans of the *An chha* (*Anda,* egg, *Hiranya garbha* of Indian mythology); these admit a first principle, or end of the past. They believe that in the beginning of the world there were vast waters. Then was produced the great *An chha,* which had the form of a fowl's egg. It divided into two parts or sections; the upper produced the heaven; the lower, the earth. Betwixt these was produced a god, Brahma, who had the power of creating all beings without exception, animate and inanimate. They consider Brahma as the lord and creator. By another error they believe him immortal.*

6th. The sectaries who admit of *time,* that is to say, who believe that beings are born of time, remark that plants, trees and other vegetables have one time for the production of flowers, another for that of fruits; that there is a time to make use of them; that sometimes there is an expansion, sometimes a contraction, so that a branch of a tree is at one time covered with flowers, at another it is dried up. They hence infer that time exists, although it be a thing invisible and infinitely subtle.

7th. The sectaries who recognise in *space* the principle of all things. Space or extension doth, according to them, beget all things,—men, the heaven and the earth; and after their extinction, these return to original *space.*

8th. The *Lou kia ye* (Laokika), so called from a word signifying '*conformable with the age,*' believe that form, thought, and other laws (of nature) are infinitely subtle principles; and that these are produced from the four great beings (the elements); that the subtle may beget the gross; and

* *San tsang fa sou,* B. XVII. p. 26, verso.

that the grosser beings of the universe are perishable, but that subtile causes are indestructible.

9th. The sectaries, '*strong of mouth*,' are those who admit *ether* as the principle of all things; they believe that ether begets air; that air begets fire; fire, heat; heat, water; water, ice; which solidified becomes earth. The earth begets five diverse sorts of grain; these produce life, which when destroyed, is reduced to ether.

10th. The sect of those who believe that happiness or misery follows the actions of men; and that there are punishment and reward suitable to the actions performed during life. If any one observe the precepts and practise virtue, the sufferings of the soul and body which he undergoes, efface anterior acts; and when these are destroyed, sufferings also cease and *nirvána* is attained. Anterior acts are therefore, according to these sectaries, the universal cause.

11th. The sectaries who admit of *no cause*, but maintain that every thing happens of itself; who believe that beings are neither *yiu* nor *youan*, that is, neither dependent *à parte priori*, nor linked *à parte posteriori*; that all is produced and destroyed of its own spontaneity.* We have seen (note 14) that nine different opinions upon the origin and production of the world have been declared heterodox by the Buddhists. The heretics, say they, understand not that the laws of nature have had no beginning and will have no end. When causes and effects are combined and concatenated, they erroneously call this *birth*; when causes and effects are disunited and isolated, they falsely denominate this *extinction*. Birth and extinction follow destiny (are its effects), and are not in truth the realities of nature. But, following their peculiar caprices, some have thought that that which produces birth is a distinct creature, who had the power to form the world and all beings. There are, as respects this matter, nine '*false views*' (erroneous hypotheses); 1st. There are heretics who believe that all beings are born of *time*; as trees have a time to bear flowers, and a time not to bear them. Time therefore exercises an action; it expands and it contracts. It causes the branch of a tree, according to the season, to clothe itself with leaves, or to wither. Time, although so subtle and imperceptible a substance, manifests its existence by its action upon flowers, fruits, and other objects of the same kind. Time therefore is to be taken as an eternal being, the sole cause of all beings, even of *nirvána*. 2d. The partisans of *space* suppose that the four parts of space, namely, the east, the west, the north and the south, are able to produce men, the heaven, and the earth; and that after extinction, all these return to *space*; ether, the universe, all, is *space*. Space is that by which men and all beings live and die; nothing is independent of

* *San tsang fa sou*, B. XLIII. p. 24.

space. Space must be taken therefore for an eternal being, &c. 3d. *Atoms*, that is the most attenuated particles of dust, have been held by the partisans of *Lou kia ye* (' conformable with the age') as begetting form, thought, and the other laws. They say that the most subtle particles of the four great (beings), that is the elements, are eternal, and capable of engendering the grosser beings; that although their form be exceedingly subtle, the *substance* or *matter* still exists; and that while the grosser substances of the world are changeable, their cause, exceedingly subtle, is unchangeable; they hence maintain that these subtle elements are the unique, eternal being, &c. 4th. *Ether* or *empty space*, is considered by the sectaries designated *strong of mouth* (*ore fortes*) as the cause of all beings; for they say, of ether is begotten air; of air, fire; of fire, heat; of heat, water; of water, ice; of indurated ice, earth; of earth, the five kinds of grain; of these, life; and life, on its termination, returns to empty space. In the opinion of these therefore, ether is the eternal, unique being, &c. 5th. The sectaries who *conform to the age* admit the *seed* of the elements, that is of earth, water, fire, and air, as being sufficient to cause all things; they believe that all the beings in the universe are born of the four elements, and on their destruction, return to these. For example, in the body (literally *the root of the body*), the solid part corresponds with earth; the humid part, with water; the warmth, with fire; the mobile part (or mobility), with air. From this we may infer that the body, and all beings, differ in no respect from the four elements. Thus the *seed* of the four elements is, according to these sectaries, the unique, eternal being, &c. 6th. The *spiritual I*, or that which heretics call the *knowledge of the eighth viscus*. *Kia pi lo* and his sectaries teach, as we have already seen, that the principle of the twenty-five realities, or the obscure principle, produces intelligence; that of intelligence is born the thought of *I*; that the thought of *I* begets color, sound, smell, taste, and touch, or the five atoms; that of the five atoms are born the five elements, earth, water, fire, air, and ether; that of the five elements are born the eleven *roots*, the eye, the nose, the tongue, the body, the *mens*, the hand, the foot, the mouth, the intestinal orifice, and the urethra, which, with the spiritual *I*, make twenty-five principles, the first twenty four of which are born of the spiritual *I*, and depend upon it as upon a master. They look upon this spiritual *I* as eternal, intelligent, enlightened, and quiescent. In it reside eternity and indestructibility; it includes and embraces all the laws (of nature). They accordingly regard it as unique being, &c. 7th. The partisans of the Vedas recognise the *excellent vanquisher*, or *Náráyana, the most excellent and the most victorious of the Gods*, he who begot the four families or castes. From his navel issued a great lotus, and of this lotus was born the god Brahma, who possessed the power of creating all things. The *victorious god* is, according to this system, superior to Brahma, and it is he who is regarded by these sectaries as the unique, eternal being, &c. 8th. The worshippers of the *Lord* (*Ishwara*), or the governor of the three thousand worlds, residing in the heaven called *Aghanishtá*. These sectaries rub themselves over with ashes, as do also the bráhmans in general, who regard this god as the cause of all things. They attribute to him four virtues (guna); substance, or substantial reality, ubiquity, eternity, and the power of creating all the laws (of nature). They assert also that this god has three bodies; the *body of the law*, signifying that his substance is eternal, universally diffused, and co-extensive with empty space, and having the power of creating all things; the *body that disposes*, because superior to forms; the *body of transformations*, because he converts in the six conditions all the beings whose form he assumes. 9th. The partizans of Mahá Brahma.*

Nine other points are enumerated upon which the heretics are at fault in regard to form, relation, cause, effect, sight, nature, concatenation (destiny), action, conduct; and which have been expounded by the Tathagatas to the very intelligent Bodhisattwa in the congregation of Lanka, to spare all subsequent ages the danger of mistake on this subject. There are twenty kinds of error respecting the nature of *nirvána*: 1st. The death of the body when it is destroyed, and when respiration ceases and goes out like a lamp, is so called. 2d. Those who deem *space* to be the prime being, name the destruction and return of the universe to its origin, *nirvána*. 3d. Those who believe *air* to produce, prolong, and destroy life, and to give birth to all things, called the air *nirvánâ*. 4th. The heretical followers of the *Vedas* believe, as we have seen, that a lotus arose from the navel of Náráyana, from which sprung the prince and father of the gods, Brahma, who gave birth to all beings, animate and inanimate, which issued from his mouth; as also all the great lands, the theatre of happiness, virtue, and the precepts, where are presented in offering flowers and plants, and victims such as hogs, sheep, asses, horses, &c. Birth in such lands is called by them *nirvána*. 5th. The heretics of *I she na*, and their different offsets, assert that the venerable master *I she na* is invisible, and fills all space; and that he can of what is invisible and formless, constitute all beings, animate and in animate, and all things without exception. They call him therefore *nirvána*. 6th. The heretics that go about naked think that the clear and distinct perception of all things in their different modes of being is *nirvána*. 7th. The partisans of *Pi shi* assert that the union or combination of the earth, water, fire,

* *Houa yan king, Souï sou yan i chhao*, quoted in the *San tsang fa sou*, B. XXXV. p. 3.

air, and ether, of atoms and other beings, begets the world and all beings intelligent or unintelligent; that when there is no union, there is then dispersion; and that this dispersion is *nirvána.* 8th. The heretics who mortify the body name thus the end of that body and of the happiness it might enjoy. 9th. Those who place themselves in dependence upon woman, believe that the supreme lord, *Ma i sheou lo* (*Mahá Ishwara*), made a woman of whom were born gods, men, dragons, birds, as well as all the beings produced from eggs, serpents, scorpions, flies, &c. And that he who understands this is in *nirvána.* 10th. The sectaries who give themselves up to bodily mortifications (*tapasví*), think that sins and happiness have an end; and that virtue has one also; and that this is *nirvána.* 11th. The sectaries named of the *pure eye,* believe that passions have their limit; they attach themselves therefore to prudence (*prajna*), which is their *nirvána.* 12th. The sectaries of *Ma tho lo* believe that their master, *Náráyana,* hath said: "It is I who made all things; I am the being of all beings; I created all worlds. All animate and inanimate beings are born of me; and when they return *to another place* (*paratra*), that is called *nirváná.*" 13th. The partisans of *Ni kian tseu* say that there were born in the first place a male and a female, and that from the union of these are produced all things, animate and inanimate; and when the latter separate and return on their destruction *to another place,* that is *nirvána.* 14th. The sectaries of *Seng kia* (Sánkhya) admit the twenty-five principles as being the cause of nature and of all beings, and they call this *nirváná.* 15th. The sectaries of *Ma i sheou lo* (*Mahá Ishwara*) say that it was in truth Brahma who produced Náráyana, who is the cause. That which they call *Brahma* and *Náráyana* are sovereign gods and lords, the cause of birth and of extinction; all things are born of the lord, and are extinguished of the lord, who is therefore *nirvána.* 16th. Those sectaries who admit of no cause, say that it is neither cause nor effect that produced all beings; that there is neither pure cause nor impure cause; that the thorns of a prickly plant and the colours of the peacock are the work of no one, but exist of themselves unbegotten of any cause. 17th. The partisans of *time* say that time ripens all the elements, forms all beings, and disperses them. It is said in the books of these heretics that though struck with a hundred arrows if your time has not come, you cannot die; but if your time have come, contact with the slightest plant will destroy you forthwith. All things are produced by time, matured by time, and extinguished by time. 18th. The sectaries of *water* believe that water is the principle of all things; that it formed the heaven and the earth, and all beings, animate and inanimate; that it can make and destroy; and they call it *nirvána.* 19th. The partisans of the *ether* system think ether the cause and first principle of all things; that of ether is born air, and then other elements in succession, as already mentioned. The earth begets all kinds of seeds and medicinal herbs after their kinds, amongst which are grains conducive to life, which after being nourished, returns at last to ether. 20th. The sectaries who believe in the *An chha* (*Anda*) think that there were originally no sun, no moon, no stars, no earth, no ether. There was but a vast water. The great *An chha* was there produced of the form of a hen's egg, of the colour of gold; when it arrived at maturity, it separated in two parts, between which Brahma was born, as seen above. When animate or inanimate beings are dissipated and lost *in the other place*, this is called *nirvána.**

Independently of the erroneous opinions which they profess on points of doctrine, there are observances which the heretics deem requisite to assure them real merit. Six kinds of mortification are reckoned among the heretics: 1st. They refuse to eat and drink, and endure for a long time hunger and thirst, vainly persuading themselves that they thus acquire a title to reward. 2d. They plunge into very cold streams. 3d. They burn themselves on different parts of their bodies, or breathe burning vapors by the nostrils. 4th. They remain perpetually seated, naked, and exposed to cold and heat. 5th. They select cemeteries and funeral groves for their dwelling-places, and bind themselves to perpetual silence. 6th. Some pretend that in anterior existences they were oxen or dogs, and observe therefore what are called the *precepts of the ox or dog*, that is, they browse on the grass, and drink foul water in the hope of re-birth in heaven.†

There are five kinds of doubts to which heretics are prone, named *the five cut thoughts* (cogitationum præcisiones). 1st. They doubt about Foe, and reason thus; "Is Foe great? is he *Fou lau na*, or every other that is great?" Which amounts to blasphemy and the destruction of the good principles (roots) of the thoughts. These heretics believe that all the laws have no existence, like vacuity, and are subject neither to birth nor extinction. 2d. They doubt about the law, and inquire whether the law of Foe or that of the Védas be the better? the Védas (*weï tho*), the title of which signifies *discourses of science*, are compositions replete with the false science of the heretics. 3d. They have doubts concerning the *Seng* (Sanga), not knowing whether the disciples of Foe or those of *Fou lan ma* deserve the preference. Hence they believe not in the Three Precious (Ones), *Buddha, Dharma* and *Sanga*, and this is elsewhere declared to be an unpardonable sin; stupid and

* *Thi pho phou sa*; *Shy leng kia king*; *Weï tao siao ching*; *Ni phan king*; quoted in the *San tsang fa sou*, B. XLVI. p. 20.

† *San tsang fa sou*, B. XXVII. p. 12. verso.

ignorant men who in their perversity believe not in the three precious ones, and who are without rectitude and filial piety, but who abound in the elements of all crimes which expose them to retributions, are at their death as certain to fall into the evil conditions (see above), as the shadow is certain to follow the substance. This is one of those crimes from which there is no delivery, with however much desire it may be attempted. 4th. They doubt the precepts; instead of having perfect confidence in the precepts, they ask themselves if it were not more useful to adhere to the practice called that of '*the hen and the dog*,' which consists in supporting one's-self on a single leg like a hen, or of feeding upon foul aliment like a dog; or in other austerities which require the renunciation of good manners. 5th. They doubt the truth of the Precepts, that is they hesitate betwixt the Precepts of Foe and those of Fou lan na.*

According to the account of Seng chao, master of the law, the heretics multiplied eight hundred years after Foe entered nirvána; they established violent sects and wicked doctrines; repressed truth, and disturbed sound judgment. It was then that *Deva Bodhisattwa*, disciple of *Loung shou (Naga króchuna)* composed the work entitled *Pe lun*, (the hundred discourses) defending truth and closing the road to error.†

Long as the foregoing note may appear, the reader will not deem it too much so when he considers that in showing us what the Buddhists held to be heterodox opinions, it places us in a better condition to decide upon what they held to be orthodoxy. It is a round-about but certain way of fundamentally understanding a doctrine to contrast the latter with all that its partisans hold to be erroneous in other creeds. Lastly, amongst all passages in Chinese authors relative to what the Buddhists denominate heresies, I have met with none that was particularly applicable to the fire worshippers of Persia, of whom it would appear that certain legends written in Mongolian make mention under the name of *Tarsa*.—R.

(22) *A loud roar.*—This prodigy is very famous, and is apparently alluded to in a book which I have found several times quoted under the title of *Fa fang kouang sse tseu heou king*, that is to say, apparently the Sanscrit words *Maha vaïpulya Sinhanádanádi*. There was a Bodhisattwa whose name, *Sinhanádanádi*, '*roaring of the lion*,' appears to refer to a similar circumstance.—R.

(23) *Divine sustenance;*—an ascetic phrase, signifying apparently contemplation, or meditation; applied to the most sublime perfections of the understanding.—R.

* *Chhing chy lun*, quoted in the *San tsang fa sou*, B. XXIV. p. 9. verso.
† *San tsang fa sou*, Chapter of the *San lun*, *or three discourses*, B. IX. p. 15. verso.

(24) *The men of the age ;*—a designation used to distinguish ordinary men from the saints of different ranks who have delivered themselves from corporeal bonds, and assured themselves against human infirmities.—R.

(25) *His hair and his nails.*—Compare the account of Hiuoan thsang, in his description of *Ayodya*, of *Sou lou kin na*, and of *Kiu pi shouang na.* The hair, nails, and teeth of the Buddhas, Bodhisattwas, and other saints, are the relics most ordinarily spoken of, and over which *sthupas* were erected.—R.

(26) *The three Foes of the past times ;*—that is, Karkuchanda, Kanaka Muni, and Kasyapa.—R.

(27) *Shy kia wen*, or *Shy kia muni*,—the *anchoret*, or *ornament of the house of Sákya ;* for Sákya is the family, and not the personal name of the last Buddha, and is used in the latter sense by way of abbreviation only.

There was a very ancient Buddha of the name of *Sákya* in the time called *the three asankya*, when our Buddha began the period of his existence, was then named *Fa kouang ming*, 'the very luminous.' This application of the same name to two or more personages has been but little attended to. Thus we have two Amitabhas, two Sákya Muni's, two Avalokiteswaras, &c.—R.

(28) *A dragon.*—The Chinese word Loung corresponds with the Indian term *Naga.* The idea of a fabulous being analogous to reptiles, but endowed with the faculty of flight, is much more ancient in China than the Buddhist religion. It would be curious to ascertain if this idea had not been taken from India from the highest antiquity, and whether *Loung* is not a corruption of the Sanscrit *Nága.* The reference here is not to the part that dragons play in the national mythology of the Chinese, but to that assigned them in the fables of the Buddhists.

There are eight classes of intelligent beings to whom the doctrines bequeathed by the Buddhas may be profitable, and may secure ultimate deliverance: these are the eight classes who are represented as attending in crowds (like the shrubs of a thicket), upon the preachings and the assemblies of the saints of the *three translations*, that is to say, of the Sravakas the Nidána Buddhas, and the Bodhisattwas : 1st, the gods (*Devas*) ; 2d, the dragons (*Loung, Naga*) ; 3d. the *Ye cha* (*Yakshas*) ; 4th, the *Kan tha pho* (*Gandharvas*) ; 5th, the *A sieou lo* (*Asuras*) ; 6th, the *Kia leou lo* (*Garuras*) ; 7th, the *Kin na lo* (*Kinnaras*) ; 8th, the *Ma heou lo kia* (*Mahoragus*).

I shall have occasion in the sequel of these notes to recur to the different classes of genii ; at present I shall restrict myself to the consideration of the Nagas, who, as we see, occupy a place amongst beings superior to man and endowed with reason. They are, say the Buddhists, intelligent animals. In the '*Book of the Peacock*' (*Khoung tsio king*), the '*Book of Great Clouds*'

(*Ta yun king*), and other sacred works, we find the dragons named by their titles, and their kings designated as protectors of the law of Buddha.* There are in the sea, one hundred and seventy-seven kings of the dragons. The seventh is named *So kie lo*, 'the salt sea' (Ságara); he is the nineteenth of the twenty gods, and is the most powerful dragon-king. It is he who when the Bodhisattwas reside in the ten earths (or grades of unification) appears with his dragon-body above the ocean. When it rains, it is he who spreads (over the skies) the thick clouds so as to ensure the most advantageous rain for all. He constantly attends the assemblies of Buddha; defends the law, protects the people, and thus acquires for himself great merits. His palace is adorned with the seven precious things, and presents the same magnificence as those of the gods. It is in this palace that the dragons compiled the work called *Hia pen king*, or '*the Last Volume*,' from the discourses of Manjusri and Ananda; and it is there that the Bodhisattwa, *Nága kochuna* saw it when he penetrated the palace of the dragons. This book was divided into three parts, or volumes; the superior, the mean, and the inferior. The inferior contained a hundred thousand gáthás, distributed into forty-eight classes. *Nága kochuna* retained them in his memory, and published them to the world. There, too, are preserved books of marvellous extent, seeing that one among them contains as many *gáthás* as there are atoms in ten great chiliocosms, and as many sections as there are atoms in the four mundane continents.†

Dragons are produced in four different ways; from an egg, from the womb, from humidity, and by transformation, according as they dwell to the east, the south, the west, or the north of the tree *Cha she ma li* (herd of deer). Their palaces are adorned with the seven precious things. They enjoy, as do other creatures superior to man, the faculty of transformation, saving on five particular occasions, when it is not permitted them to conceal their form; namely, at their birth, at their death, at the time of their merriment, when they are angry, and when asleep. It is narrated on this subject that at the time when Buddha was with the Sangas in the garden *Ky kou tou*, there was a king of the dragons of the sea, who, endued with human form, came and asked to embrace religious life. The Bhikshus, ignorant that they were dealing with a dragon, received him according to his request. The dragon-monk withdrew to yield himself up to contemplation; but the dragons are of a dull stupid disposition; he became drowsy, and having lost the faculty of disguising himself, his body entirely filled the apartment.

* *Fan y ming i*, B. II. Chapt. '*of the eight classes.*'

† *Houa yan king sou*, or History of the Gods, quoted in the *San tsang fa sou*, B. XLVI. p. 10 *v*.

The Bhikshus who dwelt with him, having returned to the house, were seized with terror on beholding him. They uttered loud cries to summon their companions, and thus awakened the dragon, who resumed the figure of a bhikshu, and sat with his legs crossed in the attitude of meditation. The disappearance of the dragon, and the restoration of the monk renewed the terror of the assembly, which immediately reported the affair to Buddha. "This is not," said he, "a man, but a king of the dragons." He then summoned him, preached the law in his behalf, directed his return to the palace of the dragons, and forbade the bhikshus ever to admit a dragon to monastic life. This gave Buddha occasion to explain the five circumstances appertaining to the destiny of this class of beings.* The dragons are the kings of scaly animals and of those called insects. They can conceal themselves, or shine with a brilliant light, and assume a larger or a smaller stature; but they are subject to three scourges which torment their existence. They dread the scorching winds and burning sands, which consume their skin and flesh and occasion them the most lively pain in their bones. They are liable to fall in the midst of tempests, which occasion them to lose the ornaments which embellish their garments, and strip them naked, circumstances infinitely annoying to them. Lastly, they dread that, while they are disporting the *Garuda*, enter the palace and carry away the newly born dragons, upon which he feeds.

We shall see in the course of this narative many fabulous adventures, in which dragons of either sex figure;—and shall then take occasion to recur to the subject.—R.

(29) *Fifty Yojans:*—about 2 to 300 miles.

(30) *Limit of fire;*—in the text *Ho king.* The great distance here indicated, if it is not erroneous, carries us to the northern boundaries of India, or even to Tibet, in the direction of the sources of the Ganges.

There is doubtless in the name of the evil genius, '*Boundary of fire,*' an allusion to some legend that has hitherto escaped our research, and perhaps some tradition of a volcanic eruption; or it may refer to thermal springs such as are found in the Himalaya. Father d'Andrada, speaking of the element of fire, repeats a fable referring to a hot spring in the same countries. A country named *Agníya* is mentioned in the enumeration of the northern countries of India. *Agni*† *déva*, or the god of fire, residing at *Agnipura*, is reckoned among the divinities of Nepal.‡

(31) *Sang kia lan.*—Buddhist temple; see Chap. III. note 5.

* *San tsang fa sou*, B. XXIII. p. 23.
† *Markandeya Purana*, quoted by Ward, *view of the Hist. of the Hindus*, Vol. II. p. 11.
‡ *Asiatic Researches*, Vol. XVI. p. 166, note 37.

(32) *Py chi foe.*—We have already seen thus named a class of saints who occupy a high rank in the Buddhist hierarchy. The Sanscrit expression is ***Pratyeka Buddha***; the Páli, *Pacheka Buddha*; the Mongolian ***Pradiyaboud.*** M. Schmidt has not recognised this last form, but has satisfied himself with transcribing the word without tracing its origin. It is apparently from the Pali form, *pacheka*, that the Chinese have transcribed the word ***Py chi***; but this presents a difficulty: the translators assert that the ***fan*** word entire, is ***Py chi kia lo***, which would give a form wholly unknown in Sanscrit, ***Pratyekara***, and does not correspond with the analysis made by the Chinese of the Sanscrit word. However it be, when the authors of the Chinese translations, instead of confining themselves to the transcription of the word, endeavour to give its meaning, they render it in three different ways, which lead to the supposition of some equivoque in the Sanscrit radical. They assert that ***Py chi foe*** signifies *Yuan kio*, 'complete intelligence;' ***Yuan kio***, 'intelligence produced by destiny' (or the concatenation of causes) and ***Tou kio***, 'isolated, or distinct intelligence.' This triple translation must arise from some equivocal meaning in Sanscrit: the last is the only one which completely coincides with the well known sense of ***Pratyeka.***

However this be, the place occupied by the Pratyeka Buddhas in the hierarchy of saints is fixed with precision in Buddhist works. There are five ***fruits*** which set those who have gathered them on the way to the supreme *Bodhi*; and names are given to the various degrees of perfection indicated by these five fruits. The lowest of these is that of the ***Srotápanna***, who has still 80,000 kalpas to pass ere he be completely emancipated from the influence of error and passion. Above these, are in the ascending scale, the *Sakridágamí*, the *Anágámi*, and the ***Arhan.*** Above these are the *Pratyeka-Buddhas*, who have gathered the fifth fruit. These have for ever renounced the errors of the three worlds, lusts, anger, hatred, and ignorance; and when they shall have passed through 10,000 Kalpas, will obtain the first degree, above which is none other.* Buddha himself has said; "A hundred wicked men are not worth one virtuous one; a thousand virtuous men are not worth one observer of the five precepts;† ten thousand observers of the five precepts are not worth one ***Sakridágámí***; ten million Sakridágámís, are not worth one *Anágámí*; one hundred millions of Anágámís are not worth one *Arhan*; a thousand millions of Arhans, are not worth one *Pratyeka Buddha.*" But he adds, "Ten thousand millions of Pratyeka Buddhas are not equal to one of the Buddhas of the three times, that is the past, the present, and the future; and a hundred times ten

* *Book of the great Nirvána*, quoted in the *San tsang fa sou*, B. XXII. p. 3 v.
† See XVI. n. 20.

thousand millions of Buddhas are not equal to the being freed from thought, locality, action, and manifestation."

The *Yuan kio*, by the contemplation of the twelve *Yuan* (*Nidánas*) emancipates himself from *ego* and the other errors; knows and comprehends the true *void* (spiritual substance) and the nature of *Nirvána*. He is thus carried beyond the girdle of the three worlds; it is his *Yána* or medium of translation into nirvána; and as the *Yuan* (the twelve degrees of individual destiny) have place in him, he is on this account named *Yuan kio*,—which appears to mean *Nidana-Buddha*.

The *Tou kio* make their appearance in ages destitute of Buddhas. They are solitary and devoted to the contemplation of things and their vicissitudes; and being without master, it is of their own understanding that they attain the comprehension of the veritable void; hence their name *Tou kio* ('isolated intelligence'), apparently Pratyeka-Buddha. Men who have attained this rank can effect their own salvation only; they are not permitted to experience those grand emotions of compassion which are of service to all living beings without exception, and which are peculiar to the Bodhisattwas. Such are the bounds to which the Tou kio are restricted, and by which they are disabled from becoming Buddhas (immediately).*

The Tou *kio* and the *Yuan kio* are mentioned concurrently in the same passage,† which seems to prove that the Buddhists of China at least, have established some distinction betwixt the Nidána-Buddhas and the Pratyeka-Buddhas, a distinction not altogether justified in the passage itself.

There are two kinds of *Tou kio*; those who form *classes* or *herds*; that is to say, who after the manner of deer, take up with their own kind, and look back to see if any follow them; they are named in Sanscrit *Varggachári*. The others think of nought but their own salvation, indulging no thought about that of other men. They are compared to an animal with but one horn (*Khi lin* in Chinese), and are named in consequence *Khadgavisánákalpa*, 'Pratyekas resembling a unicorn.'‡

The contemplation of the twelve *Nidánas*, which forms the occupation of the Yuan kio, is a subject much more difficult to clear up. It would be interesting to determine how the succession of these twelve causes and effects leads the spirit to lay hold upon the 'veritable void,' or spiritual substance; but I can find on this subject but one passage, and that conceived in almost enigmatic terms. The Yuan kio sees that *Avidya* (ignorance) attains to *Járámaranam* (old age and death) and that thus are produced the

* *San tsang fa sou*, B. XX. p. 25.
† *Leng yan king*, B. VI. quoted in *San tsang fa sou*.
‡ *Sy hiuan ki*, quoted in the *San tsang fa sou*, B. XLVIII. pass.

twelve *Nidánas.* He then sees that the extinction of *Avidya* conducts to the extinction of *Járámaranam*, and he thus comprehends that there is neither birth nor death, or he comprehends that which is not subject to birth or death, that is to say, spiritual nature.* The perfection to which the Yuan kio attain, their exemption from the vicissitudes of life and death, and their faculty of becoming men or gods, render them worthy of adoration, and they are therefore among the eight classes of beings in honor of whom towers are erected. These eight classes are the Buddhas, Bodhisattwas, Arhans, Anágámís, Sakridágámis, Srotápannas, and the Chakravartí kings. (M. Remusat seems to have omitted the Pratyeka Buddhas.—J. W. L.)

From the foregoing explanations the word *Buddha* which enters into the term *Pratyeka Buddha*, cannot mislead us as to the true position of these personages, who are very far from being classed amongst 'absolute intelligences.' It was therefore a grievous error of M. Schmidt, when he said that "Buddhist books make a great difference among the various Buddhas, not merely with reference to their sanctity, but to their activity in the salvation of living beings;" and then comprised in this class the Sravakas and the Pratyeka Buddhas.† This confusion is by no means cleared away by the distinctions which follow; and others, we shall see, have yet to be established between the Buddhas and Pratyekas, separated in the hierarchy of saints by the Bodhisattwas, who are infinitely above the latter, though still far inferior to the former.—R.

(33) *The spot of the nihouan.*—The place where the Pratyeka-Buddha, of whom he spoke, entered nirvána, that is to say died.—R.

(34) *Where he dried his clothes.*—Compare Chap. VIII. note 7.

CHAPTER XVIII.

Town of Ki jao i.—River Heng.—Forest of Ho li.

Fa hian halted at the temple[1] of the dragon and remained there some time. His sojourn ended, he turned towards the south-east; and having travelled seven *yeou yan,* he came to the town of *Ki jao i.*[2] This town touches the river *Heng.*[3] There are two *Seng kia lan* entirely devoted to the study of the *less translation.*

* *Fa houa king,* B. II. Chapter '*on comparisons drawn from plants.*'
† *Ueber einige Grundlehren des Buddhaismus.*

To the west of this town, about six or seven *li*, and on the northern bank of the river *Heng*, is a place where Foe preached in behalf of his disciples. Tradition says that in this place he discoursed upon instability[4] and upon pain ;[5] upon the comparison of the body to a bubble of water,[6] and upon some other similar subjects. In this place they have erected a tower, which subsists still.

Crossing the *Heng*, and proceeding southward three *yeou yan*, you come to a forest named *Ho li*. Foe there preached the law. They have erected tours wherever he passed, or walked, or sat.

NOTES.

(1) *The temple :*—in Chinese, *Tsing she*, 'pure or holy house.' This name is given to the *Seng kia lan*, because *those who restrain their thoughts*, that is the Samaneans, dwell in them. There are five *Tsing she* more celebrated than all others, of which mention will be made in the subseqent chapters, when the word itself will be further considered.—R.

(2) *Ki jao i.*—This name, which the Chinese do not interpret, is identical with that of *Ku jo keï che* in the narrative of Hiuan thsang.—R.

It is the transcription of the Sanscrit name of the town of Kanouj, or rather कन्याकुब्ज, *Kanyakubja*, which signifies the "hunch-backed girl." This etymology refers to a legend according to which the hundred daughters of the king *Kusanabha*, who reigned there, were rendered hunch-backed because they would not submit to his lawless desires. Kanyakubja is the same town which Ptolemy* calls Κανογιζα, and which in our times bears the name of Kanouj. It is situated on the right bank of the Ganges, in Lat. N. 27° 4′ and Long. E. 79.5°. The name of this town is sometimes written Kanarji in the Sanscrit books of the middle ages. The Chinese Buddhist works translate Kanyakubja by *Khiu niu chhing*, or 'the town of *hunch-backed damsels.*' In this town, say they, there was formerly the '*hermit of the great tree ;*' he cursed ninety-nine women, who became in the same instant hunch-backed ; hence the name. Foe descended here from the heaven *Tao li* (Trayastrinsha), where he had preached the law, on which account a tower was erected in the place, the fifth among the great towers of Buddha.—Kl.

* B. VII. ch. 2.

(3) *The river Heng.*—We have seen, (Chap. VII. 2) that the Chinese name the Ganges *Heng* or *Heng kiá*, and that the Sanscrit etymon of which these words are the transcript, signifies according to them '*come from the heavenly mansion*,' because this river flowed from an elevated place, that is, from the summit of the Snowy Mountains. We need not repeat here what has been said on the subject of the sources of the Ganges. There is a nymph who presides over this river and bears its name : she had no nose and yet distinguished smells very well. This peculiarity is quoted to prove that when any great organ of sense is wanting, the rest may supply its place. Thus *Anarodha* is mentioned, as having been deprived of his eyes, yet seeing none the less whatever exists in a triple chiliocosm as readily as you may distinguish a fruit placed in your hand ; also the Naga *Pa nan tho* (Vananda), who heard without the aid of ears ; *Kiao fan pa the* (Kavanpate), who ruminated like an ox and ceased not to discern flavours ; of the genius of empty space (Sunyatá) who, though without body, was sensible to external bodies ; and of Máha Kásyapa, who had no necessity for *mens* to understand all the laws of the universe.*—R.

(4) *Instability.*—In the text the *non-duration*, the *non-eternity ;* in Sanscrit *anidyam ;* one of the fundamental conditions of relative existence ; or in Buddhist parlance, one of the four realities acknowledged by Sákya Muni. This subject will be treated in the notes to Chapter XXII.—R.

(5) *Pain.*—One of the four realities recognised by Sákya ; in Sanscrit *dukham.*

(6) *A bubble of water.*—Sákya affirmed that the human body, formed by the union of the five elements, possessed no more stability than a bubble. But this observation was made by him in his promenades around the town of Kapilavistu. He apparently resumes this subject, as well as the two preceding ones, in his sermons preached near the town of Kanouj.—R.

* *Leng yan king*, cited in *San tsang fa sou*, B, XXVIII.

CHAPTER XIX.

Kingdom of Sa chi.

Thence proceeding ten *yeou yan* towards the south-west, you come to the great kingdom of *Sha chi*. On issuing from the town of *Sha chi* by the southern gate, you find to the east of the road the place where Foe bit a branch of the nettle-tree, and planted it in the earth. This branch put forth and grew to the height of seven feet, and never after increased or diminished. The heretical bráhmans, excited by envy and jealousy, cut it, or tore it up, to cast it away; but it always sprang up again in the same place as before.

There are also in this place four stations of Foe, where they erected towers which are extant to this day.

NOTES.

(1) *Ten yeou yan*;—about fourteen leagues.—R.

(2) *The great kingdom of Sha chi*.—According to the route of Fa hian, this kingdom must be placed on the Goomty, in the territory of Lucknow.—Kl.

There is a difficulty in this part of Fa hian's route which can be explained away only on the supposition of a misprint in the French edition or an error in the original Chinese. Ten *yojanas* to the *south-west* would be a retrograde movement on the part of our pilgrim; and would moreover be incompatible with his subsequent course. Professor Wilson,* has suggested Cawnpore, lying south-east of Kanouj, as the probable position of *Sha chi*, and has traced our pilgrim's route accordingly on his sketch-map. But, as we see in Chapter XX, the next journey of eight yojanas *south* from *Sha chi* brings our pilgrim to *She weï* (*Srávasti*) in the kingdom of *Kiu sa lo* (*Kósala*, Oude); and hence I make no doubt we should read *north-east* in the text, instead of *south-west*. Still the difficulties are by no means solved by this explanation; for if, as we shall see presently, *She weï* was somewhere in the neighbourhood Fyzabad or Oude, we must suppose some error in the estimation of the distance passed by our traveller, or make the *yojana* of unusual length to suit the present occasion. Unfortunately the itinerary of Hiouan thsang throws no light upon the subject.—J. W. L.

* *J. R. A. S.* vol. V. p. 122.

CHAPTER XX.

Kingdom of Kiu sa lo. Town of She wei. Temple of Chi houan. Town of Tou wei.

Thence proceeding south to the distance of eight *yeou yan*,[1] you arrive at the kingdom of *Kiu sa lo*,[2] and the town of She wei.[3] The population of this town is very inconsiderable; they only reckon about two hundred families (or houses.) It is there that the king *Pho sse no*[4] resided. They are there extremely attached to the Law; and within the enclosure of the temple, at the spot where was the wall of the old man *Siu tha's*[5] well; at the spot where the wicked genius *Yng kiue*[6] obtained the doctrine; and at the spot of the *pan ni houan*,[7] where the body was burnt, men of after ages have built towers, which remain to this day. The heretical bráhmans[8] of the town, excited by feelings of jealousy, desired to destroy these; but the heavens thundered and the lightning flashed, so that they could not approach to overturn them.

On issuing from the town by the southern gate, at twelve hundred paces to the east of the road, you find the temple which the patriarch *Siu tha* caused to be erected. The gate of this temple faces the east. There are two pavilions[9] and two stone pillars. On the pillar to the left side is executed the figure of a wheel;[10] on that to the right side is placed that of an ox. The reservoirs are filled with the purest water, and the groves are formed of bushy trees; the rarest flowers grow there in abundance and charm the sight by their lively hues. There, too, is the temple called *Chi houan*.[11]

Foe having ascended to the heaven *Tao li*,[12] remained there ninety days preaching the law in favour of his mother. The king *Pho sse no* experienced a vivid desire to behold Foe again. He accordingly caused the head of an ox to be carved of sandal wood, by way of representing an image of Foe, and placed it in the spot where Foe sat. When on his return Foe entered the temple, the statue rose and approached to meet him. Foe said, "Return, and be seated; after my *pan ni houan* thou shalt be the model for imitation by the four classes."[13] The statue returned and sat down. It was the first of all the statues of Foe, and that which men of subsequent times have copied. Then Foe transported himself into a small temple constructed on the south side, different from that of the statue, and situated at twenty paces distance.

The temple of *Chi houan* had originally seven stories. The kings and the people of various countries were full of veneration for this place and came hither to celebrate the festivals. Canopies and streamers were hung up, flowers were scattered, perfumes burnt. Lanterns supplied the place of day, and even in daytime were never extinguished. A rat having taken into its mouth the wick of one of these lanterns, set fire to the flags and the drapery of the pavilions; and the seven stories of the temple were utterly consumed. The kings and the people experienced profound sorrow at this event. They thought that the image of sandal wood had been burnt; but five or six days after, on opening the little eastern temple,[14] they suddenly beheld the ancient image! They reconstructed the temple, and when they had completed the second story, they installed[15] the statue in its former place.

On arriving at the temple of *Chi houan*, Fa hian and Tao ching reflected that in this place the *Honorable of the Age* had passed twenty-five years[16] in austerities! By their side was a multitude of people animated with the same thoughts, who had traversed many regions, some to return to their own country, others to experience the instability of life.[17] That day on seeing the place where Foe no longer was,[18] their hearts experienced a lively emotion. Other ecclesiastics addressing Fa hian and Tao ching, "From what country come you?" they asked. "We have come from the land of *Han*," replied the former. The ecclesiastics then replied, and sighing, observed, "How marvellous!

that men from the extremity of the world are enabled to come in search of the law even to this place!" Then they spoke amongst themselves, "We other masters and *Ho shang*,"[19] said they, "since we succeeded each other, have never before seen the priests of Han[20] come hither."

To the north-west of the temple, distant four *li*, there is a thicket called the *Wood of the Recovered Eyes*. In former times there were five hundred blind persons, who, coming to the temple, sojourned in this place. Foe preached the law in their behalf, and they all recovered their sight. These blind men, transported with joy, planted their staves in the ground and performed an act of devotion, turning their faces aside. Their staves took root and grew. The people of that age out of respect, dared not cut them, and they formed this grove, called for this reason the *Wood of the Recovered Eyes*. The clergy of the temple of *Chi houan* frequently repair after meals to sit in this grove and abandon themselves to meditation.

To the north-east of the temple of *Chi houan*, at the distance of six or seven *li*, the mother of *Pi she khiu*[21] caused a temple to be built, and invited Foe and the ascetics thither. This place is in strict dependence upon the temple of *Chi houan*. The town has two gates, one facing the east, the other the north. There is the garden that the patriarch *Siu tha* caused to be made after having paid money to buy it.[22] The temple is situated in the midst, on the very spot where Foe stayed, and for a long time preached the Law for the salvation of man. At the places where he passed, or where he sat, every where they have erected towers, and all these places have appropriate names; such as that where *Sun to li* accused Foe of murder.[23]

On coming out of the temple of *Chi houan* by the eastern portal, and proceeding northerly, at the distance of seventy paces to the west of the road you come to the place where Foe formerly disputed with the adherents of ninety-six heretical sects.[24] The kings of the country, the grandees, the magistrates, and the people, were all heaped up like clouds, and listening intently. At this moment a heretical girl named *Chen che mo na,* urged by a feeling of jealousy, gathered up her garments in suchwise over her belly as to make her appear pregnant, and in the presence of the whole assembly, she reproached Foe with having infringed the Law.[25] Then the king of the gods, *Shy,* having transformed himself into a white rat, came and gnawed the cincture she had around her loins; so that the garments fell to the earth; the earth opened, and this woman fell living into hell! *Thiao tha,*[26] who with his venemous nails sought to tear Foe, fell likewise living into hell! These places were known and marked by men of subsequent times. In the place where the dispute (with the heretics) took place, they have raised a temple. This temple is about six toises[27] high; within it is a statue of Foe seated.

To the east of the road is a chapel[28] of the gods appertaining to the heretics, and named *Covered by the Shadow.* It is in front of the chapel built upon the site of the dispute, and the two chapels are thus opposite to each other on either side of the road. This last is also about six toises high. Here is the reason why it is called *Covered by the Shadow:* When the sun is in the west the temple of the *Honorable of the Age*[29] covers with its shadow the temple of the gods belonging to the heretics; but when the sun is in the east, the shadow of the latter temple deflects to the north and never falls on the temple of Foe. The heretics had a custom of sending people to watch the chapel of their gods, to sweep it, water it, burn perfumes, and light the lanterns for the performance of their worship; but the next morning all the lanterns were found transported to the temple of Foe. The bráhmans,[30] full of resentment said, "The *Sha men* take our lanterns to use them in the worship they perform to Foe; why do we not resist them?" The bráhmans then set themselves to watch by night; but they saw the gods and the genii whom they worshipped themselves carry away the lanterns, thrice encircle the temple, worship Foe, and suddenly disappear. The bráhmans thus learnt to appreciate the greatness of Foe, and abandoning their families, entered upon religion.

Tradition relates that at a time not remote from this event, there were around the temple of *Chi houan* ninety-eight *Seng kia lan*, all provided with apartments for the ecclesiastics, and which were empty in but one place. In the Kingdom of the Middle[31] there are ninety-six kinds of sectaries who all recognise the present world,[32] every sect has its disciples, who are numerous; they beg their subsistence, but they carry no beggar's pot.[33] They seek happiness, moreover, in waste places, and in the highways, and establish in those situations houses for the supply of travellers with shelter, beds, and wherewithal to eat and drink. Men who have embraced religious life lodge there equally going and coming: but the time during which they are thus harboured is not the same (as in the monasteries). *Thiao tha* has also sectaries who still subsist; these honor the three Foes of the past time;[34] *Shy kia wen foe*[35] alone they honor not.

To the south-west of the town of She weï, at the distance of four *li*, the king *Lieou li*[36] endeavoured to attack the kingdom of *She i*.[37] The *Honorable of the Age* placed himself on the road, and at the place where he stood they have erected a tower.

At fifty *li* west of the town you come to a little town named *Tou wei*;[38] it is the birth-place of the Foe *Kia she*.[39] At the place where the father and son held an interview,[40] as also at the place of the *pan ni houan*,[41] towers have been erected. In like manner they have raised a great tower for the *She li*[42] of the entire body of the *Joulaï*[43] *Kia she*.

NOTES.

(1) *Eight yeou yons*—about 11 leagues and a fifth.—R.

(2) *Kiu sa lo*.—This kingdom, called by the same name by Hiuan thsang, is easily recognised as Kósala, or Oude, one of the most celebrated countries in primitive Buddhism. It is both important and easy to determine its position, which will enable us to fix preceding stations, and establish a solid basis for the subsequent march of our pilgrims through a country which it is extremely interesting to recognise. The map of India found in the great Japanese Encyclopedia,* and reproduced in French by M. Klaproth (see

* B. LXIV. p. 13.

plate) gives separately the two names *Kiao so lo* and *She weï*, making them thus two distinct kingdoms, betwixt which is placed *Kia pi lo*. Now, Fa hian re-unites *Kiu sa lo* and *She weï* into one kingdom, making *She weï* the capital of *Kiu sa lo*. As he had travelled through the country his testimony is entitled to higher credit than that of the unknown geographer who compiled the materials for the map just mentioned. *Kiu sa lo* is the Kosala of Sanscrit books, the celebrated kingdom of Ráma, whose capital was *Ayodhya*. The position of this country is therefore one of those best ascertained in the itinerary of Shy fa hian, since it results from an incontestible synonyme and coincides with both the foregoing and the subsequent march of the traveller, that is to say from Mathurá and Kanouj to Patna. We might suppose that the name Kósala extended to other countries of India seeing that in the Chinese map *Kiao sa lo* is placed to the west of Benares, south of Kusambi and Mathurá, and stated to be a kingdom six thousand *li* in circumference. Further still, a country named *Kiu tse lo*,—(apparently a transcription of the same Sanscrit word Kósala) may be seen to the north-west of *Ou che yan na* (Ujjain). It is this country that Hiuan thsang places in western India, and the capital of which he names *Pi lo ma lo*. It must be Guzerat.

Ma touan lin quotes a history of *Kiu sse lo*,—*Kiu sse lo chouan*, composed anonymously; but he gives no details on the subject.

A difficulty attending this identity of *Kósala* and *She weï* (admitted by Fa hian and rejected by Hiuan thsang) will be discussed in the next note.—R.

(3) *She weï*.—The name of this town is translated by *Fung te*, 'abundant or flourishing virtue,' and also by *Wen we*, 'celebrated productions;' because this town excels all others on the reputation of its production. Hiuan thsang assures us that the name of this town is corrupted, and that it should be pronounced *Shy lo fa sy ti* (Srávasti).

The town of She weï was commended for four properties worthy of remark. It contained all kinds of riches and precious things, so that no other kingdom could compare with it. The five kinds of desires (corresponding to the five senses) were there more vivid than elsewhere. No other country presented such abundance. Nowhere were the people in a better condition to study the doctrine and obtain final deliverance.*

But what is remarkable, Hiuan thsang describes Kósala and Sravasti separately, while Fa hian makes the latter the capital city of the former. Hiuan thsang after leaving Pi so kia reached Sravasti, and passed thence to Kapilavastu. It was later, after having traversed Kalinga, that he came to Kósala, whence he reached the country of *Andhra*, which corresponds

* *Fan y ming i*, B. III. Art. kingdom.

with modern Telinga. It is thus easy to see that the name Kósala was applied in the time of Hiuan thsang to a part of India which Fa hian never visited and of which he does not speak. The details too given in the *Si iu chi*, regarding this country, have no correspondence whatever with those given by the author of the *Foe koue ki*. They refer exclusively to the preaching of the thirteenth patriarch Nága Koshuna, principally in the southern countries of India, eight hundred years after Sákya. On the other hand, the scenes in the life of Sákya which Fa hian places in Kósala and She weï, (for with him these names are synonymous,) are those of which Hiuan thsang indicates *Shy lo fa sy ti* as the site. The latter country is therefore the Kósala of the *Foe koue ki*. But it is allowable to suppose that the memory of the powerful empire the foundation of which the Bráhmanical writers ascribe to Ráma, was perpetuated in other regions of India, and especially in that of which the name Kósala is preserved in the *Si iu chi*.—R.

(4) *Pho sse no.*—This name is uniformly given in Buddhist works to the prince of Kósala who was contemporary with Sákya. It is translated 'victorious or triumphant army.' Hiuan thsang declares it to be corrupted, and restores it to *Po lo si na chi to*, translating it in the same manner. The Sanscrit form is Prasenájit. This prince shortly after ascending the throne, sought in marriage from the king of Kapila, a princess of the race of *Shy choung*, or *Shákya suta*. A female slave of Ma ha nan having given birth to a daughter of exquisite beauty, the latter was sent to the king Prasenájit, who had by her a son named *Lieou li*, of whom we shall speak by and bye. Ma ha nan was the son of king *Hou fan*, and cousin of Sákya.

Sanang Setsen names the prince who in the time of Buddha reigned over Kósala in the town of *Vaisáli*, *Saltchan* in Mongol, and says that he was the son of the king *Arighona Œkuktchi*. I suspect there is some error in this recital, at least as regards the town of Vaisáli, which could not at that time have been included in the kingdom of Kósala. The translator of Sanang offers no elucidation of any part of the text of his author which refers to the history of ancient India, but confines himself to transcribing without explaining the names of Indian princes translated into Mongol.—R.

(5) *Siu tha.*—This name is also corrupted according to Hiuan thsang, who restores its orthography, *Sou tha to*, and translates it by '*well giving*;' it must be the Sanscrit *Sudátá*. The title of *Chang che* given him, designates indifferently superiority of age or of rank: he is therefore the *aged*, the *patriarch*, the *chief*, the *great*. Thus Sudátá was in reality one of the grandees or ministers of Prasenájit. Pious and enlighted, knowing both how to amass wealth and how to expend it; generous towards and helpful to the needy, to orphans, and lonely men, he deservedly obtained the fair

surname of Ky kou tou (largitor erga orphanos et derelictos). It was he who erected to Buddha the temple of *Chi houan*, of which mention will be made lower down, and which obtained for that spot the name of *Ky kou tou youan*, 'the garden of the benefactor of orphans.' Hiuan thsang saw the ruins of this minister's palace in the 7th century.—R.

(6) *The wicked genius Yng kiue*,—elsewhere named *Yng kiu ma lo*, a word signifying, 'he who exhibits dresses, or ornaments.' Another malignant being who was the scourge of the kingdom and town of *Shy lo fa sy ti* (Srávasti) is indicated by the same name. He killed people and carried off their caps and heads to bedeck himself with. Hiuan thsang repeats a legend respecting this malignant spirit, found in the *Si iu chi*, chapter on *Shy lo fa sy ti*.—R.

(7) *Pan ni houan*:—the death of eminent personages in Buddhism.—R.

(8) Or it may be translated "the western pavilion with two stone pillars."—R.

(9) *Bráhmanical heretics*:—those attached to the Bráhmanical worship and the doctrines of the Vedas.—R.

(10) *A wheel*.—The wheel is a familiar emblem of the Buddhists, expressive of the successive passage of the soul in the circle of various forms of existence; the power of the Chakravartti kings over the whole habitable earth; and the preaching of the Buddhas, as well as the good effects of the prayers and invocations repeated with the help of a chaplet. In the absence of explanation we cannot determine the meaning of the wheel placed on the summit of a pillar, as at the temple of Jétá.—R.

(11) *The temple of Chi houan*.—This is one of the most celebrated edifices of Buddhism; its name is changed by Fa hian, but other Samanean writers spell it *Chi tho*, and explain it to mean 'victory.' Hiuan thsang, who affects great accuracy in the transcription of names, declares that *Chi tho* is also corrupt, and writes the word *Chi to*, or *Shi to*. He confirms also the interpretation of his predecessors, so that we may infer with certainty that this temple was called in Sanscrit जेता, Jeta, that is, to 'the temple of the victorious, or the triumphant.' The Chinese further add to this name the word *lin*, a forest; which is the exact equivalent of the Sanscrit Jetavana, जेतावण, so frequently occurring in Singalese books. It appears that this name of 'victorious' was that of the heir apparent to the kingdom, to whom belonged the garden in which the temple was erected; and as Sudátá defrayed the cost of its erection, the edifice and the surrounding ground were called indifferently the 'temple of Jeta,' and the 'garden of the benefactor of orphans.'*

* See note 5.

The temple of Jeta is one of the eight named *Ling tha*, 'divine towers,' or 'towers of the spirits.' The seven others were that in the garden of *Loung mi ni*, or *Lan pi ni*, in the town of Kapila; that which was built upon the banks of the *Ni lian* in Magadha; that of the deer-park near Benares; that of Kanouj; that of Raja Griha; that of the '*Beautiful town*;' and lastly that of the town of Kushina. There is a book bearing the title of *Pa ta lig tha ming hao king*, or 'the sacred book of the names and titles of the eight great divine towers.' According to this book, if any one by great faith and the impulsion of a well directed heart, build a tower or a temple and there establish the ceremonies and worship, he will obtain rebirth among the gods. There are upon this earth and in the heavens a great number of towers that have been erected for the *Sarira* of Buddha. But the eight towers here spoken of were erected on the sites where the Tathágata '*descended in birth*,' and where he accomplished many important acts of his terrestrial career.

We shall see in the sequel of Fa hian's narrative, how much importance he attached to a visit to the temple of Jeta, one of the most celebrated of those existing at that time. Many passages in the sacred books are supposed to have been revealed by Buddha while he was in the town of Srávasti (She weï) and in the temple of Jeta.—R.

Srávasti, as we learn from the analysis of the several portions *Kah-gyur*, by the late Csoma de Körös, was one of the principal scenes of Sákyas ministration; and a fuller examination of that voluminous work would doubtless supply all the particulars so briefly hinted at in the present chapter by Fa hian. The circumstance of the erection of a large religious establishment in a grove called the *Princes Grove* (*Jeta vanam*) by a rich householder of Srávasti (*Mnyan yod, Tib.*) is mentioned in the *Lalita vistara*. Thither the founder invited Sákya, who with his disciples passed twenty-three years and propounded the greater part of the *Sutras* in that place. See de Körös's various notices of the *Kah-gyur* in the twentieth Vol. of the *Asiatic researches*.—J. W. L.

(12) *The heaven of Tao li*; i. e. *Trayastrinsha*.*

(13) *The four classes*.—In the text *Sse pou*, elsewhere called *Sse weï*, the four herds, that is to say, 1st, The *Pi khieou* (Bhikshu), those mendicants or monks who profess to obtain their sustenance by alms. They *beg above*, to sustain their intellectual life, and *below*, to support their visible body. 2d, The *Bhikshuni* or female mendicants. 3d, The *Yeou pho so* (Upasika). This word signifies *pure*, and signifies that those who bear it

* Chap. XVII. note 2.

remain in their homes, that is lead a lay life, observe the five precepts and maintain a pure character. The name is also explained to mean 'men who approximate duty,' to express that in accomplishing the precepts they prepare themselves to receive the law of the Buddhas. 4th. *Yeou pho i* (Upayi) pure lay women.*—R.

(14) *The little eastern temple.*—I adopt here the reading of the *Pian i tian*, that of the *Foe koue ki* being faulty in this place.—R.

(15) *Installed the statue.*—A lacuna in the text is here supplied from the *Pian i tian.*—R.

(16) *Twenty-five years.*—This period of twenty-five years of proofs is indicated nowhere but in this place. Sákya passed five years in the deserts before attaining absolute perfection. He became Buddha, in his thirtieth year, and lived afterwards forty-nine occupied in preaching his doctrine. Probably some period of penance in an anterior existence when Bodhisattwa is here referred to.—R.

We learn from a preceding note that according to the *Lalita vistara* Sákya dwelt twenty-three years at Srávasti. It may be to this residence that Fa hian alludes, with a slight error regarding its duration.—J. W. L.

(17) *The instability of life.*—In Sanscrit *anityam.* It is one of the conditions of relative existence that it cannot last, but is subject to change. This expression is somewhat pompous to be employed on so simple a reflexion. Perhaps it is borrowed from some passage in the sacred books.—R.

(18) *Where Foe no longer was*;—a phrase of much energy in the text, and literally, '*Seeing the place void of Foe.*'—R.

(19) *Ho shang.*—This expression, much used in China, has never been properly explained. The ordinary dictionaries render it '*priest of Foe, bonze.*' It is foreign to the Chinese language and belongs to that of Khoten, in which it represents the Sanscrit word *Upasika (Yeou pho se, Yeou pho shy kia, Ou pho so kia)*. The Chinese intrepret it as *fortes, robore nati, in vi viventes*; also as *purissimi doctores*, and *officio proximi*; which is further explained by saying that these are men who by their purity approach the state necessary for the reception of the doctrine of Foe. It is elsewhere rendered by *magistri doctrinâ donati*, or *magistri doctrinæ proximi. Upásika* means simply '*faithful*' in a religious sense, and is the general name of the Buddhists of Ceylon and Pegu. But this word more particularly designates the laics, as we have seen above, note 13. To what has been said about the four Buddhist classes I will add that *seven* are also distinguished, called the '*Seven multitudes*' (*Thsy choung*). Of these seven, five are considered to belong to the monastic order, or, as it is expressed in Buddhist works, to have *left their homes*, and two are described as *remaining*

* *Fan y ming i*, B. VII. Art. 'of disciples.'

at home, that is to say, leading a lay life. The following is what I have found touching this classification:

1st. The *Pi kheou*, or mendicants; also named *Pi tsou* from an allusion to a Himálayan plant which in five respects resembles religious mendicants: it is soft and flexible, marking thus the simplicity of their exterior, and of their language indicating submission and humility; it is creeping, and extends on all sides, emblematic of their unceasing labours for the salvation of man; its perfume diffuses itself far, just as the odour of the doctrine is spread abroad by the example of these men; it has curative properties, typifying the power of mendicants to subdue vice and passion; it turns not aside from the sun's rays, thus imaging their conduct in keeping their eyes ever fixed upon the sun of Buddha.

2d. The *Pi kheou ni*, or *Pi tsou ni*, female mendicants. These, according to the *Ta chi lun*, have a vast number of duties to perform, for which they possess less aptitude than the *Pi khheou*, and hence are placed next after them.

3d. The *Sha mi*, or *Shy li mo li lo kia*, whose name expresses their abstinence from the affections which sully the age, and that they *love* and succour all living creatures. As they are but beginning to enter upon the law of Foe, they still possess many affections of which it is necessary that they should divest themselves to the end that they abstain from evil and do that which is right.

4th. The *Sha mi ni* or *Shy li mo li kia*, '*a diligent and painstaking woman;*' to indicate the subtile attention and efforts of women exercising the law of Foe.

5th. The *Shy cha ma na*, or women studying the law. The *Hing sse chhao* says, "The *Shy cha ni* have three studies to pursue: 1st. The principles, or bases (of the law), that is the prohibitions to kill, to steal, to commit impurities, and to lie. 2d. The six laws, which forbid polluting the thought, the body, the touch; stealing the smallest sum (quatre deniers) from any one, taking the life of living creatures, committing petty deceptions, eating at forbidden hours, and drinking wine. 3d. They study the practice and thus come to understand the principles which great *Ni* (female ascetics) ought to observe.

6th. The *Yeou pho se*, formerly *Ou pho so kia* (Upasika) see above.

7th. The *Yeou pho i*, or 'very pure women.'

It will be seen from all these passages that far from designating the bonzes or priests of Foe, the word *Ho shang* in the language of Khoten, and its equivalent Upasika, is properly applied to lay Buddhists, who observe the precepts of religion and lead a regular and blameless life. This title exactly corresponds with that of *Vajra A'chárya* found by Mr. Hodgson in the Buddhist books of Nepal.—R.

(20) *Priests of Han*,—that is Chinese ascetics.—R.

(21) *The mother of Pi she khiu.*—Hiuan thsang very briefly alludes to the invitation addressed to Buddha by the mother of *Pi she khiu*, but adds no particulars.—R.

(23) Of *murder*.—This accusation belongs to what Buddhists call the *nine tribulations of Foe.* "Foe narrated that formerly in the town of *Pho lo naï* (Benares) there were a comedian named *Thsing yan*, and an abandoned woman named *Lou siang*. *Thsing yan* invited this woman to go out of the town with him in a car. Arrived at a garden planted with trees, they were diverting themselves together, while a *Py chi foe* was in the same place performing acts of piety and studying the doctrine. Thsing yan awaited till the *Py chi foe* had proceeded to the town to beg his meal, when he killed *Lou siang* and buried her in the tent of the Py chi foe. He accused the Py chi foe. When the latter was brought to the place of punishment, Thsing yan beholding him, was touched with remorse and said, 'For what I have done, I should be punished.' He confessed his crime and was put to death by the king. This *Thsing yan*, said Foe, was myself, and *Lou siang* was *Sun to li.* In consequence of this crime I have undergone infinite suffering during an infinite number of thousands of years, and even now that I am become Buddha, there remain sufferings for me in consequence of the unjust accusation borne against me by *Sun to li.*"*—Kl.

(24) *Ninty-six heretical sects.*—The *San tsang fa sou* reckons but ninety-five† and reduces them yet further to eleven principle ones. (See Chapter XVII. note 20.)

(25) *Having infringed the law.*—Hiuan thsang repeats this adventure with slight variations of detail. The bráhman damsel who accused Foe of having sinned with her was named *Chin chha*, *Chin sha*, or *Chen she*.* Foe afterwards explained to his disciples how he became exposed to this calumny. "In very ancient times," said he, "there was a Buddha named *Tsin shing Jou laï*, (the very victorious Tathágatá). In the religious assembly gathered around him, there were two Bhikshus, one named *Wou shing* ('without victory') and the other *Chhang houan* ('ever joyous'). There was at that time in the city of Benares a grandee named *Ta aï*, ('great love') whose wife was named *Shen houan* ('fair deceiver'). The two mendicants frequented this house where they received abundant alms. *Wou shing*, who had burst the bonds of the world, never relaxed in the religious duties of his condition; but *Chhang houan* on the other hand, still detained in error and

* *San tsang fa sou*, B. XXXIII. p. 22. † B. XLIII. p. 24.

(wordly) deeds, could not resist giving way to negligence in his religious exercises. Thence arose within him a feeling of envy which induced him to spread a false report that the intercourse between *Wou shing* and *Shen houan* was dictated by more tender considerations than those of the law and of religion. Now, continued Foe, the *Chang houan* of that time was no other than myself; and this *Shen houan*, of whom I speak, was identical with *Chin chha*. The calumny which I spread abroad regarding Wou shing justly subjected me to various kinds of punishment; and even now that I am arrived at Buddhahood, there yet remains for me this suffering to endure. At the moment when I was preaching the law in behalf of heretics, in the presence of mendicants, and kings, and subjects, a damsel came suddenly before me, having a pot suspended before her belly, and interrupted me with these opprobrious terms: "Samanean," said she, "why do you not look to the business of your own house, rather than discourse thus on that of other people? thou thinkest of thine own case alone, and troublest not thyself about my sorrows: thou that wert with me in time agone, and madest me pregnant. I must a month hence have butter for my child; see to procuring it!" At these words all the assembly hung their heads and remained silent. But *Shy thi houan ni* (Indra) having transformed himself into a rat, passed under the garments of the damsel, and gnawing the string which suspended the pot, caused it to fall to the ground to the great satisfaction of the assembly."*

Hiuan thsang beheld the pit through which this calumniatrix fell living into hell.† This is another example of the eight tribulations to which Sákya Muni, even after attaining the rank of Buddha, was subjected in expiation of the sins committed in former existences, and for which notwithstanding punishments prolonged during myriads of ages, he was still subject to a remnant of penance. Sákya Muni expounded these tribulations to his followers with the view of animating them in the practice of good deeds, since even a Tathágata, after having accomplished the doctrine, extinguished all the ills to which the condition of man is subject, and acquired ten thousand kinds of happiness,—could not divest himself of certain sins committed in foregoing Kalpas.—R.

(26) *Thio thá*, or, according to more regular orthography, *Thi pho tha tou*, or *Thi pho tha tho*, (Devadatta), a Sanscrit word the explanation of which is given, in two ways; 'celestial warmth, or the gift of the gods.' This last interpretation, given by Hiuan thsang, is the only true one. The same author makes this personage the son of the king *Hou fan* (Amitodana.)

* *Ta chi tou lin*, B. IX. and *Hing khi hing king*, quoted in *San tsang fa sou*, B. XXXIII. p. 25.

† *Pian i tian*, B. LXXV.

Other writers, who do not appear well informed, make him to be the son of the king *Pe fan* (Dhotodana). In either case Devadatta was the cousin german of Sákya Muni. On all hands it is agreed that he was the most inveterate enemy of the founder of this religion. Several notices of his implacable hatred may be found in these relations. Hiuan thsang narrates in detail the adventure here spoken of, and in which Devadatta having rubbed his nails with a poisonous substance came from afar with the intention of causing the death of Buddha, while feigning to pay him homage.—R.

(27) *Six toises.*—About 60 feet.

(28) *A chapel of the gods.*—It is not easy to find appropriate equivalents for the terms employed by the Chinese, to designate the buildings consecrated to their worship according to their scope, importance, and destination. The temple of Jeta, of which so magnificent an account has been given, is named *Tsing she.* According to the *Shy kia pou,** a *Tsing she* is a spot where those who had mastered their thoughts (the Buddhas) halted. The word signifies the 'abode of subtlety.' Five principle edifices of this denomination are reckoned: 1st. The *temple of the benefactor of orphans*, built by Sudata, on the site of the garden of the prince of Jeta, and otherwise named the *Temple of Jeta.* 2d. *The temple of the Vulture Mountain*; of which more will be spoken hereafter. 3d. *The temple of the river of Apes*, which will also be again noticed in subsequent chapters. 4th. *The temple of the tree An lo*, offered to Buddha by a woman of that name. 5th. The *Temple of the Bambu garden* in the mountain *Khi che khiu*, otherwise named the garden of *Kia lan tho.* Fa hian gives the same name to many other less celebrated temples constructed in places where Buddha had sojourned.

But the word which our author here makes use of to designate a Brahmanical temple is *Sse*, to which he unites the word *thian*,—*thian sse*, 'temple of the gods,' to designate the *dévas*, objects of Brahmanical worship, but reduced in the Samanean system to a very subordinate position—in Sanscrit *Devâlaya.* Hiuan thsang always employs the word in the same sense.—R.

(29) *The Honorable of the Age.*—Sans. *Lokajyesta.*—R.

(30) *The Bráhmans.*—There is frequent mention of the bráhmans in the legendary accounts of the earlier times of Buddhism. A very ancient work, the *Ma teng kia king*, speaks of the four castes in the following terms: "They falsely suppose that we (the family of Buddha) are born of Brahma, and give us on this account the surname of 'children of Brahma.' The bráhmans pretend that they were born from the mouth of Brahma; the *Sha ti li*, (Kshatryas) from his navel; the *Pi she*, (Vaisyas) from his arms; and

* '*Genealogy of Sákya*,' quoted in the *San tsang fa sou*, B. XXXVI. p. 5. v.

the *Sheou tho*, (Sudras) from his feet. On this account they look upon themselves as first in rank, but are truly not so. The word ***Pho lo men*** (Brahmana) signifies *'one that walketh in purity.'* Some are laics, others embrace religious life; and succeed each other from generation to generation, making their business the study of the doctrine. They call themselves the offshoots of Brahma; their name comes from their keeping the doctrine, and preserving purity. The name, *Sha ti li* signifies ***Lords of the fields***; they are in truth the possessors of the great countries of the world, and are of regal race. The *Pi she*, or *Tei she*, are the merchants; and the ***Sheou ho***, or *Shou tho lo*, are the labourers."

We see from the history of the Buddhist patriarchs, that the distinction of castes in no way interfered with the selection of the chiefs of religion. Sákya Muni was a Kshatrya; Maha Kasyapa, his successor, was a bráhman; ***Shang na ho sieou***, the third patriarch, who was invested with this dignity only eighty years after the nirvána of Buddha, was a Vaisya; and his successor, ***Yeou pho khieou to***, who succeeded forty-four years later, was a Sudra.* Thus in conformity with the doctrines of Buddhism, moral merit alone was kept in view in selecting those to whom the transmission of the doctrine was committed, without any reference to the distinction of caste.

The word bráhman is not used in decidedly ill part in Buddhist works unless conjoined with the epithet *Waï tao*, heretic, heterodox; but accusations of jealously and ill-will against this caste are very common, and such will be found occasionally in the sequel of Shy fa hian's narrative.—R.

(31) ***The Kingdom of the Middle.***—Central India, or ***Madhya désa***, comprising the countries of Mathura, Kósala, Kapila, Magadha, &c.—R.

(32) ***The present world.***—This phrase appears to signify that the heretics restrict themselves to speaking of the duties of men in the present life without connecting it, by the doctrine of metempsychosis, with anterior periods of existence which must have been passed through.—R.

(33) ***No begging pot.***—This is an essential distinction of Buddhist mendicants, with whom the begging pot is an indispensible attribute. (See chap. XII—note 8.)—R.

(34) ***The three Foes of the past time.***—The first three Buddhas of the present age, called the 'Kalpa of the wise:' namely, ***Keou leou sun*** (Krakuchchanda), ***Keou na han mou ni*** (Kanaka Muni) and ***Kia she*** (Kásyapa). These will be spoken of in detail hereafter. The times of their respective appearance may be seen in the table I have given, Journal des Savans for 1831, p. 723.—R.

* See the great Encyclopedia *San thsai thou hoeï*, edited by *Dr. Wang khi.* Section *on the affairs of men*, B. IX. p. 4, v.

(35) *Shy kia wen :* Sákya Muni.—It is curious to note this indication of a sect among the Buddhists who acknowledged the Buddhas of anterior ages, but rejected the Buddha of the present, the sole real type after whom, according to general belief, these imaginary personages were created by an afterthought, and referred to mythological times. It would be extremely interesting to learn what were the religious opinions of Dévadatta, the cousin, rival, and persecutor of Sákya. This passage is of importance as it seems to favour the opinion that the dogma of the plurality of Buddhas, and of their successive manifestations, was concurrent with the foundation of Buddhism itself.—R.

(36) *The king Leou li.*—This is the transcription of a Sanscrit word which signifies a transparent stone of a blue colour, and is extended to mean glass. Hiuan thsang names this prince *Py lon tse kia*, and mentions another corrupt orthograply, *Py lieou li.* When Prasenajit ascended the throne of Kósala, he asked in marriage a princess of the country of Kapila and of the race of Sákya (Shy choung, *Sákyæ semen.*) One of the slaves of Mahánanda, son of Amitodana, and cousin of Sákya Muni, had a daughter of perfect beauty. She was offered to Prasenajit, who married her, and had by her a son, the prince Lieou li. At the age of 18 this prince proceeded with the Brahmachari Hao khou to the house of Mahánanda. There had been erected in the kingdom of Kapila a hall of conference to which the Tathágatha was invited to receive the homage of his sectaries. The prince Lieou li having entered his hall, ascended the Lion-throne (Singhásana). On beholding this the children of Sákya were transported with rage. "This son of a slave," they exclaimed, "dares to enter and be seated here!" He then went out and said to the brahmachari *Hao khou :* "The children of Sákya have mortally affronted me: remind me of this insult when I ascend the throne!" And so when afterwards the prince Lieou li became king, Hao khou reminded him of this matter. Lieou li collected together his troops and proceeded to attack the children of Sákya. Sákya Muni took part in this event which threatened the tribe from which he sprung. I here transcribe the explanation of it to his disciples; it is a further example of those *destinies* to which men are subject in expiation of sins committed in anterior existences, and from which Buddha himself was not exempt, as we have already seen. The following are the words used by Sákya in explaining to the Bhikshus the causes of the adventure of Lieou li with the children of Sákya. "Very anciently," said he, "there was near the town of *Lo youe*, a village inhabited by fishermen; a famine occurred, and as there was on one side of the village a tank abounding in fish, the people went thither to catch these for food. Among the fish there was one named *fou* ('ball of wheat'), the

other *to shi* (babbler, slanderer), who conceived resentment (against the fishermen). At the same time a little boy who was amusing himself on the edge of the tank watching the frisking of the fish, took a stick and struck them on the head. Well, the inhabitants of the town of *Lo youe* are now the children of Sákya; the fish *fou*, is the king *Lieou li*; the fish *to shi* is the Brahmachari Hao khou; and the little boy, myself. See by what train of events the destiny of the king Lieou li has caused the destruction of the race of Sákya."*—R.

(37) *The kingdom of She i.*—The sequel of the narrative shows that the country here spoken of is that inhabited by the children of Sákya, that is, by the tribe to which the founder of the Buddhic religion belonged, himself surnamed *Sákya Muni*, 'the ascetic of the race of Sákya,' *Sákya Sinha*, 'the Lion of Sákya,' &c.: for we must not forget that *Sákya* is the name of a race, and not of a man, although we habitually use it to designate this Buddha, son of Suddhodana. The denomination *She i* here given to the kingdom of the children of Sákya must be one of those applied to Kapila; but its etymology is hitherto unknown.—R.

(38) *Tou wei.*—I know not the Sanscrit form of this name, but the following note will show that it was not in the country of Kósala that the Buddha Kásyapa was supposed to have been born.—R.

(39) *Foe kia she,*—that is, Kásyapa Buddha. This name Kásyapa, borrowed from bráhman antiquity, is applied by the Samaneans to one of their Buddhas, who immediately preceded Sákya Muni; it is interpreted '*imbibing light*,' also, '*tortoise*.' The first explanation is but a play on the words, Kásyapa being in fact translatable '*Splendorem bibens vel absorbens*;' because the brilliant light which emanated from his body eclipsed all other lights. It is rendered by the Mongols *Gerel sakitchi* (Schmidt). Many legends and mythological particulars are narrated of the life of the Buddha Kásyapa. According to the '*Chronological series of the predecessors of Buddha*,* the third Buddha, Kásyapa, appeared in the ninth little Kalpa, of the present age, in the time of the decrease, when the life of man was reduced to twenty thousand years; that is to say, nearly two million years ago. According to the '*long Agama*,'† he was of the race of bráhmans, of the family of Kásyapa. His father's name was *Fan te* ('*virtue of Brahma*,' *Brahma sila?*), his mother's *Tsaï chu* (opulent). He dwelt in the city of Benares, and seated beneath a *nyagrodha (ficus indica)*, he preached the law to an assembly of which he converted twenty thousand men. The two

* *San tsang fa sou*, B. XXXIII. p. 24. v.
† *Foe tsou toung ki*, quoted in the *San tsang fa sou*, B. XVIII. p. 12.
‡ Quoted in the *Shin i tian*, B. LXXVII.

spirits that assisted him (*genii pedes*) were *Thi she* and *Pho lo pho* ; he who assembled his troops was *Shen fan tseu.* I am unable to explain the meaning of the terms *genii pedes*, *exercitum colligere* ; there are similar ones in each of the notices of the six Buddhas anterior to Sákya Muni.

According to the book entitled 'Procedures of the Tathágatas,'* if the formulæ are properly repeated, Kásyapa Buddha maintains himself in space, and extends his protection to all living beings, assuring them against all sickness, all misfortune, and the influence of evil spirits. Here are the formulæ to which I add their restored Sanscrit forms.

1. Nan wou Foe tho ye.	Namo Buddháya.
2. Nan wou Tha my ye.	Namo Dharmáya.
3. Nan wou Seng kia ye.	Namo Sangáya.
4. Nan wou Kia she pho Tho kia to ye na.	Namo Kásyapáya.
5. An !	Om !
6. Ho lo, ho lo, ho lo, ho lo.	Hara, hara, hara.
7. Ho, ho, ho.	Ho, ho, ho.
8. Nan wou Kia she pho ye.	Namo Kásyapáya.
9. A lo han ti.	Arhate.
10. San miao San foe tho ye.	Samyaksambuddhaya.
11. Sy chu ho shi.	
12. Ma to lo po tho.	
13. Sou pho ho.	Swáhá.

When the Buddha had finished the revelation of these formulæ, he addressed the bodhisattwa Akásagarbha and said : "Excellent young man ! these formulæ have been recited by Buddhas in number equal to thirty-three times the grains of the sands of the Ganges : thou shouldst collect them and recite them, practising good works. Oh Akásagarbha ! if there be any virtuous man or virtuous woman who by day and night, and in the three times, shall repeat these formulæ, he shall behold the Buddhas in a dream, and be delivered from all the impediments arising from the acts of his life."

The invocation of Kásyapa given in the '*Praises of the Seven Buddhas*,' is conceived in the following terms : "I adore Kásyapa, the lord of the world, the most excellent and most eminent sage, born in Benares, of a family of Brahmans reverenced by princes ; the life of his illustrious body endured twenty thousand years, and the waters of the three worlds were dried up by the lamp of that divine wisdom which he acquired beneath the *nyagrodha* tree." We may observe that this Sanscrit passage, agreeing in some particulars with the Chinese version of the *long Agama*, is contrary to

* Quoted in the *Shin i tian*, B. LXXVII.

the direct testimony of Shy fa hian, who makes the birth-place of Kásyapa far from Benares, in the northern part of the district of Oude.

The book entitled *Jou kouan foe san mi king*, says that the body of Kásyapa was sixteen toises high, and the glory round his head twenty yojanas. According to another work (the *Fa yuan chu lin*), the Buddha Kásyapa having preached upon the sacred books, in one assembly twenty thousand bhikshus obtained the dignity of Arhan.

The *King te chouan teng lou* reckons Kásyapa Buddha as the third Honorable of the Kalpa of sages, that is the third Buddha of the present age.—R.

(40) *An interview.*—This must be a consecrated phrase, for it is again found lower down on the occasion of the Buddha Krakuchchanda. As Sákya Muni had an interview with his father Suddhodana, an attempt has no doubt been made to imitate this particular of his life and reproduce it in that of the pretended predecessors of the historical Buddha.—R.

(42) *She li;*—the Sanscrit word Sárira, translated by the Chinese, the '*bones of the body*.'—R.

(43) *The Jou laï,* that is the Tathágata, he whose advent has actually happened, according to the meaning of the Chinese and Tartar terms which answer to the Sanscrit word; and more exactly according to the analysis of this last, and to the Buddhic doctrine, the '*thus gone*,' who has definitely quitted relative to enter upon absolute existence, or nirvána. It is translated in Tibetan *De bjin gshegs pa*, in Manchou *Mekou dzikhe*, in Mongol *Tagoutsilan iraksan*. It is the first of the ten honorable names assigned to the Buddhas. It is understood in three different senses according as it is applied to the three states of the Buddha (the three bodies), to his state of law (Dharmakáya), to his glorious manifestation in the world of ideas (Sambhogakáya), and to his bodily transformation (Nirmánakáya). A Buddha is *Tathágatha* in the second sense, because the first principle, the essence of things, is *similitude, identity* (with intelligence, an idea conceived by it) and he has come to assimilate to perfect intelligence.* He is *Tathágata* in the third sense, inasmuch as borne along by the real nature of *Similitude* (identity of intelligent nature), he has *come* to the state of perfect intelligence.†—R.

The word *Tathágata* in Sanscrit means the same as *De bjin* in Tibetan; '*he who has gone in the manner of his predecessors*.'—Kl.

For a further elucidation of the meaning of the word *Tathágata*, the reader may consult Mr. Hodgson's article, *European Speculations on Buddhism*, *J. A. S.* vol. 3, p. 384, from which I quote the following passage.

* *Chouan fa lun lun.*
† *Ching chi lun.*

"The word *tathágata* is reduced to its elements and explained in three ways ; —1st, *thus gone*, which means gone in such a manner that he (the *tathágata*) will never appear again ; births having been closed by the attainment of perfection. 2nd, *thus got or obtained*, which is to say, (cessation of births) obtained, degree by degree, in the manner described in the Bauddha Scriptures, and by observance of the precepts therein laid down. 3d, *thus gone*, that is, gone as it (birth) came—the pyrrhonic interpretation of those who hold that doubt is the end, as it is the beginning, of wisdom ; and that *that* which causes birth causes likewise the ultimate cessation of them, whether that 'final close' be conscious immortality, or virtual nothingness. Thus the epithet *tathágata*, so far from meaning *come* (avenu), and implying incarnation, signifies the direct contrary, or 'gone for ever', and announces the impossibility of incarnation; and this according to all schools, sceptical, theistic, and atheistic."

To this I may add the interpretation of the word as given by Wilson in his dictionary :—" तथागत, A *Gina* or *Buddha* ; तथा, thus (what really is), and गत, known, obtained."—J. W. L.

CHAPTER XXI.

Town of Na pi kia.—Birth-place of Keou leou thsin foe and of Keou na han meou ni foe.

Proceeding twelve *yeou yan* south-east of the town of *She wei*, you come to a city named *Na pi kia*.[1] It is the birth-place of *Keou leou thsin foe*.[2] There also are *Seng kia lan* in the places where the father and the son held an interview,[3] and on the site of the *pan ni houan* are erected towers.

Proceeding thence less than a *yeou yan* towards the south, you come to a city which is the spot where *Keou na han meou ni foe*[4] received birth. There too have they erected towers on the spot where the father and the son held an interview, and on that of the *pan ni houan*.

NOTES.

(1) *Na pi kia.*—This place is unknown.—R.

Wilson in discussing the position of *Na pi kia*, observes that with reference to the succeeding as well as the preceding route, it should be to the north of Gorakhpur: but as our pilgrim journeyed in a *south-easterly* direction from *She weï* (Fyzabad, or Oude), it seems more probable that Na pi kia lay to the south of that town. Nor will this supposition be at all inconsistent with the subsequent course of Fa hian to *Kapilavastu, Lan mo,* &c., as we shall see further on.—J. W. L.

(2) *Kieou leou thsin foe.*—The name of one of the Buddhas anterior to Sákya Muni. It is sometimes spelt *Keou leou sun,*—a corruption of the Sanscrit Krakuchchanda,—and is interpreted '*that which should be interrupted or suppressed;*' referring to vices and passions which should be so annihilated that no trace of them may remain. The Mongols render the name *Ortchilang i ebdektchi.* This Buddha was born in the ninth kalpa of the present cycle, when the life of man was reduced to sixty thousand years, and therefore five million nine hundred and ninety-two thousand eight hundred years ago.* The book entitled 'the Long Agama,' brings him down to the time when men lived only forty thousand years, that is, two millions of years nearer us. According to the same work he was a bráhman of the family of Kásyapa; his father was named *Li te,* and his mother *Shen chi.* He dwelt in the town *An ho* ('peace and concord'), and preached the law seated under a tree *Shi li sha* (*sirísha, acacia sirisa*), and in a single assembly effected the salvation of forty thousand men. His 'spiritual supports' were *Sa ni* and *Pi leou;* his guardian, the supreme conqueror *Shen kio tsen* (Son of Good Intelligence).

The book of the 'Proceedings of the Tathágatas' teaches that when good use is made of the prayers and formulas, the Buddha Krakuchchanda retains himself in space, extending his protection to all living creatures, expelling sickness and all manner of evil, as also demons. To this end the following formula is repeated: (I omit this as it is nearly identical with the foregoing, p. 181, the word Krakuchchanda being substituted for Kásyapa.—J. W. L.)

Then said the Buddha Krakuchchanda to the Bodhisattwa Akásagarbha: "Excellent youth! these *dháranís* (invocations) are such as the Krakuchchanda Buddhas, having the same name (as I), in number equal to the sands of the Ganges, as also the Buddhas of the three times, have taught, and of

* *Fau y ming i*, Book I.

which they have proclaimed the efficacy. If men keep these divine formulas, they may be able, even in the last kalpa of future time, to establish firmly the worship of the three precious (ones), and give birth to the veritable faith. As for the bhikshus, the bhikshunis, the upasikas, the upayis, who shall constantly recite and observe them, they shall expel from their visible bodies all kinds of maladies and ailings."

This is the invocation of Krakuchchanda as given in the *Sapta Buddha Stotra:* "I adore Krakuchchanda, Lord of the Munis, the unequalled Sugata, the source of perfection, born at Kshemavati of a family of bráhmans reverenced by the kings: the life of this treasure of excellence was forty thousand years; and he obtained at the foot of the *Sirísha* tree the state of Jainendra with the arms of the knowledge which annihilates the three worlds."—R.

(4) *Keou na han meou ni Foe,*—otherwise *Ka na hia meou ni,* or *Kiu na han meou ni,* in Sanscrit *Kanaka Muni.* The word is interpreted '*golden quietude;*' *Kanaka* signifying gold, and marking the external lustre of the personage; and *Muni* the absence in secluded life of all obstacle to repose.* Others translate the word '*Golden Anchorite,*' because this Buddha had a body of the colour of gold.† The Mongols name him *Altan chidaktchi.*‡ He was born in the world at the time when human life was reduced to forty thousand years, that is to say, three millions seven hundred and fourteen thousand one hundred years ago. This personage was a bráhman of the family of Kásyapa; his father was named *Ta te* (great virtue) and his mother *Shen shing* (very victorious). He lived in the town of *Very-pure,* and under the tree called *Ou tsan pho lo men* (*Udambara, ficus glomerata*) held an assembly where he preached this law and converted thirty thousand men. His 'spiritual supports,'§ were *Shu phan na* and *Yo to leou,* his guardian was '*guide of the multitude, son of tranquil concord.*' Of the meaning of these mystical expressions I am ignorant.

According to the book of the 'Procedures of the Tathágatas,' when the formulas are properly recited, Kanaka Muni Buddha sustains himself in space. He extends his protection to all living creatures, expels all maladies, and drives away all evil spirits. It is with this purpose that he delivered the following invocations. (Nearly identical with those given in poge 181, *Kia na kia menou* being substituted for *Kia she pho.*—J. W. L.)

After having finished the utterance of these invocations, the Buddha

* *Fan y ming i,* quoted in the *San tsang fa sou,* B. XXVIII. p. 10.
† *Ta chi tou lun,* quoted as above.
‡ Schmidt, Notes sur Sanang Setsen, p. 306.
§ See note 39, Chap. XX.

Kanaka Muni addressed the Bodhisattwa Akásagarbha and said; "Excellent young man! if a man or a woman endowed with virtue incessantly repeat these *dharani* (invocations) and observe them, all maladies shall be removed and cured."

The *Sapta Buddha Stotra*,* contains the following invocation to Kanaka Muni: "I adore Kanaka Muni, sage and legislator, freed from the blindness of mundane illusions, who was born in the city of *Sobhanavati*, of a race of bráhmans honored by kings. His resplendent person existed thirty thousand years. Generous as the mountain of precious stones, he obtained Buddhahood under the tree *udumbara*."

The *Jou kouan foe san mi king* assures us that the height of Kanaka Muni, was twenty-five yojanas, and that of his aureola thirty; and that the light emanating from his body extended forty yojanas.

Krakuchchanda, Kanaka Muni, and Kásyapa, are denominated the Buddhas of the past time. They are the first three of the thousand Buddhas, who are to appear in the present Kalpa, called the *Kalpa of sages;* Sákya Muni is the fourth. Or, uniting with these the three Buddhas who appeared in the preceding ages, Vipasyi, Sikhi, and Viswabhu, there are seven personages of this rank habitually named together as the seven Buddhas; but no sufficient reason has been given for this association of the last three Buddhas of the anterior with the first four of the present Kalpa. Mr. Schmidt, thinks that "the first three are not named in Buddhic works;" ("indess findet man in Buddhaischen Büchern die drei ersten nicht genannt.")† An error which arises from this, that in books which have no reference to any but the present age, they begin the series of Buddhas with the first of that Kalpa, Krakuchchanda, without ascending to an anterior period. But the very work which this savant has translated negatives his own observation; for Sanang Setsen mentions *Sikhi* and *Viswabhu*.

Mr. Hodgson thinks that we cannot doubt the historical existence of the six Buddhas anterior to Sákya Muni;‡ while Mr. Wilson on the other hand thinks their real existence very questionable.§ To judge this matter merely from the fabulous accounts of them that have reached us, there need be no doubt upon the subject. Another point well worthy of consideration is the succession of the four Buddhas and their distribution in the four yugas. "It is well worthy of remark," says Mr. Hodgson, "that according to the most authentic ancient scriptures, the succession of the seven Bud-

* Asiat. Res. Vol. XVI. p. 454.
† Notes on Sanang Setsen, p. 306.
‡ As. Res. XVI. p. 445.
§ Ibid. p. 455.

dhas fills the entire duration of time: the two first being referred to the *Satya yuga;* the next two to the *trita;* the succeeding to the *dwápara:* Sákya and the future Buddha being Lords of the present age." This is a Bráhmanical notion inoculated upon Buddhism by the inhabitants of Nepal, and not to be found in original works, where the succession of Buddhas is exhibited in a very different manner. Without repeating here what I have said elsewhere, the following table will recall the principal features of this fantastic chronology, which appears subject to no variation among Buddhist nations.

Kalpa of Wonders. 1000 Buddhas.	997 Anonymous Buddhas. Vipasyi, 998th Buddha. Sikhi, 999th do. Viswabhu, 1000th and last Buddha of that age.
Kalpa of sages (the present age). 1000 Buddhas.	Krakuchchanda, 1st Buddha of this period. Kanaka Muni, 2d do. Kásyapa, 3d do. Sákya Muni, 4th do. Maitreya, 5th (future). 995 future Buddhas.

—R.

The following observations on this highly curious and important subject by the late Honorable Mr. Turnour are so à propos, that no apology is necessary for their introduction in this place. "It is an important point connected with the Buddhistical creed, says Mr. Turnour, which (as far as I am aware) has not been noticed by any other writer, that the ancient history, as well as the scheme of the religious Buddhists, are both represented to have been exclusively developed by revelation. Between the manifestation of one Buddha and the advent of his successor two periods are represented to intervene—the first is called the Buddhantaro or Buddhot-pádo, being the interval between the manifestation of one Buddha and the epoch when his religion becomes extinct. The age in which we now live is the Buddhot-pádo of Gotamo. His religion was destined to endure 5000 years, of which 2380 have now passed away (A. D. 1837) since his death, and 2620 are yet to come. The second is the Abuddhot-pádo, or the term between the epochs when the religion revealed by one Buddha becomes extinct and another Buddho appears, and revives, by revelation, the doctrines of the Buddhistical faith. It would not be practicable, within the limits which I must here prescribe for myself, to enter into an elucidation of the prepos-terous term assigned to an Abuddhótpádo, or to describe the changes which the creation is stated to undergo during that term. Suffice it to say, that during that period, not only does the religion of each preceding Buddha become extinct, but the recollection and record of all preceding events are also lost. These subjects are explained in various portions of the Pitakattaya, but in too great detail to admit of my quoting those passages in this place.

By this fortunate fiction, a limitation has been prescribed to the mystification in which the Buddhistical creed has involved all the historical data contained in its literature, anterior to the advent of Gotamo, while in the Hindu literature there appears to be no such limitation; inasmuch as Professor Wilson in his analysis of the Puránas, from which (excepting the Raja Tarningini) the Hindu historical data are chiefly obtained, proves that those works are, comparatively, of modern date. The distinguishing characteristics, then, between the Hindu and Buddhistical historical data appear to consist in these particulars;—that the mystification of Hindu data is protracted to a period so modern that no part of them is authentic, in reference to chronology; and that their fabulous character is exposed by every gleam of light thrown on Asiatic history, by the histories of other countries, and more especially by the writers who flourished, respectively, at the periods of, and shortly after, the Macedonian and Mahomedan conquests; while the mystification of the Buddhistical data ceased a century at least prior to B. C. 588, when prince Siddhato attained Buddhahood, in the character of Gótamo Buddho. According to the Buddhistical creed, therefore, all remote historical data, whether sacred or profane, anterior to Gótama's advent, are based on his revelation. They are involved in absurdity as unbounded as the mystification in which Hindu literature is enveloped."

A firm belief in the predecessors of Buddha must have been general at a very early period; and it is not a little curious to observe that at the time of Fa hian's transit, the heretical followers of Devadatta "honored the three Foes of the past time," that is, Krakuchchanda, Kanaka Muni, and Kasyapa; but placed no faith in Sákya Sinh, to whose impostures alone these owed their mythological existence.—J. W. L.

CHAPTER XXII.

Town of Kei 'wei lo 'wei.—The King's Field.—Birth of Foe.

Thence proceeding easterly one *yeou yan*[1] you come to the town of *Kei 'wei lo 'wei.*[2] In this town there are neither king nor people; it is literally a vast solitude. There are only ecclesiastics, and some tens of houses of inhabitants. This is the site of the ancient palace of the king *Pe tsing,*[3] and it is here that they made a representation of the Prince and mother, taken at the moment when the Prince seated on a white elephant entered the womb of the latter.[4]

At the place where the Prince issued from the town by the eastern gate; at that where, at the sight of a sick man,[5] he caused his chariot to turn and retraced his way; everywhere they have erected towers. At the place where *A i*[6] contemplated the Prince; at that where *Nan tho* and others struck the elephant; in that where they drew the bow,[7] the arrow of which proceeding to the south-west entered the ground at the distance of thirty *li,* and cause a spring of water to issue (arranged by men of aftertimes in the form of wells from which drinking water is supplied to travellers); at that where Foe, after having obtained the doctrine,[8] came back to visit the king his father; at that where the five hundred sons of the *Shákyas*[9] embraced monastic life and paid homage to *Yeou pho li;*[10] at the place where the earth trembled in six ways;[11] at the place where Foe preached in favour of the gods, the kings of whom so guarded the gates thereof that the king his father could not approach the assembly; at the place where *Ta 'aï tao* gave a *Seng kia li*[12] in alms to Foe, who was seated facing the east under a *Ni keou liu*[13] tree, which exists still; in the place where the king *Lieou li* destroyed the family of the Shákyas,[14] which had first attained the rank of *Siu tho wan;*[15]

(in all those places) they have erected towers which still remain.

To the north-east of the town, at the distance of several *li*, is the Royal Field. Here is the place where the Prince, under a tree, watched the labourers.[16] To the east of the town fifty *li* is the Royal Garden;[17] this garden bears the name of *Lun ming*. The *Lady*[18] having entered the tank to bathe, came out therefrom by the northern gate; she proceeded twenty steps, took in her hand the branch of a tree, and turning to the east give birth to the Prince. Fallen to the ground, the Prince made seven steps. Two kings of the dragons washed his body.[19] On the site of this ablution they have made a well; and it is at this well, as also at the tank where the washing took place, that the ecclesiastics are in the habit of drawing the water they drink. There are, for all the Foes, four places determined from all eternity; the first is that where they accomplish the doctrine;[20] the second, that where they turn the wheel of the law; the third, where they preach the law,[21] where they hold discussions, and subdue the heretics;[22] the fourth where they re-descend from the heaven of *Tao li*,[23] whither they ascend to preach the law in favor of their mother.[24] The other places are those of sundry manifestations called forth by circumstances. The kingdom of *Kia 'weï lo 'wei* is a great solitude; the people are scattered, and white elephants and lions are to be apprehended on the roads, so that one may not travel there without precaution.

Travelling five *yeou yan* towards the east from the place where Foe was born, you come to the kingdom of *Lan mo*.

NOTES.

(1) *One yojana.*—About one league and a third.

(2) *Kia 'weï lo 'weï.*—It must certainly be by an error of the press that the third syllable of this name has been suppressed in the *Wen hian thoung khao*, where we read *Kia weï 'weï*; a fault recurring elsewhere. The Mongols write *Kabilik*, and the author of the *Tarikh khatayeh*, كيا پيلا وى *Kiápílaví*. The greater number of Chinese Buddhist writers render it *Kia pi lo*; some by mistake interpreting the word *beneficent*; others, more exactly, *tawny*.

The signification of the word *Kapilavastu* cannot be a matter of doubt, since we possess the Tibetan translation སེར་ སྐྱའི་གཞི *Ser s'kyaï g'ji* (the deep yellow soil) or སེར་སྐྱའི་གྲོང་ *Ser s'kyaï g'hrong* (the town of the deep yellow). *Ser s'kyaï* signifies *deep yellow* or tawny, *kapila* in Sanscrit. It was also the name of the celebrated hermit कपिल *Kapila,* who gave the founders of the kingdom of *Kapila* the ground upon which they erected their town, as will be seen in note 9 of this chapter. The author who spells this word most correctly is Hiuan thsang ; he renders it *Kie pi lo fa sa tou,** the exact transcription of *Kapilavastu,* or *Kapilavatthu* of Páli works. The Burmese write the word *Kapilavat ;* the Siamese *Kabinlawathou* or *Kabilapat ;* the Singhalese, *Kimboulvat ;* and the Nepalese *Kapilapúr.*

The kingdom of Kapila is mentioned by *Ma touan lin* under the name of *Ka pi li.* In the article *India,* he says: " In the 5th of the years *Yuan kia,* in the reign of the emperor Wen ti of the Soung (428 A. D.), *Yu ai,* king of *Kia pi li* in Thian chu, sent an ambassy to the emperor. It conveyed a letter and presents consisting of diamond rings, bridle-rings of gold, and rare animals, amongst which were a red and a white parroquet. Under the emperor *Ming ti* of the same dynasty, the second of the years *Thaï chi* (A. D. 466) *Kia pi li* again sent an ambassador to China bearing tribute."†

The *Ly taï ki szu* also mentions an embassy from the king of *Kia pi li* in the year 428 of our era, adding that the letter to the emperor was conceived altogether in the style of the sermons of Buddha.‡

The editors of the great geographical collection entitled *Pian i tian,* speaking of *Kie pi lo fa sou tou,* say that the name was formerly written erroneously *Kia pi lo weï,* and that this country was situated on the frontier of Mid-India ; but they appear to have remained in doubt whether the *Kia weï lo 'weï* of Fa hian, and the *Kie pi lo fa sou tou* of Hiuan thsang, were identical ; so that after having inserted in its appropriate place the quotation from the *Foe koue ki* referring to the former name, they have referred elsewhere the chapter of the *Si yu chi,* applicable to the second. But then they have omitted to transcribe this chapter ; an omission most unfortunate for us, as we are thus deprived of sundry points of comparison of the utmost importance for the elucidation of the portion of Fa hian's narrative at present before us.

* *Pian i tian.* B. LXXV.

† See *Wen hian thoung khao,* B. CCCXXXVIII. p. 15. and *Pian i tian,* B. LXVII. art. 5, Notice of the kingdom of Kia pi li, p. 1 ; taken from the History of the *I* and *Man.*

‡ *Ly taï ki szu,* B. XLVI. p. 350.

I believe that I was the first to point out the error of the common opinion that Sákya Muni was born in *Magadha*, or South Behar. In a note which I appended to the French translation of Mr. Wilson's '*Notice of three Buddhist works*,' inserted in the Nouveau Journal Asiatique for 1831, p. 103, I observed, "It is not very easy to indicate with precision the site of *Kapilavastu*, or *Kapilapur*. According to Chinese accounts, it would appear that this town was situated in the north of India, in the country of Ayodhia or Oude. * * * All our ideas of the country of Sákya Sinha lead us to search for it further to the north, in the country at present named *Oude*, and anciently *Ayodhya*."

According to the *Kah gyur*, or great collection of Buddhist works translated into Tibetan, the town of *Kapila* or *Kapilávastu*, was situated in Kósala, or the Oude of our times. At the time of Sákya's birth the greater part of central India was subject to the kings of *Magadha*, and for this reason the country of Kósala in which Kapila was situated, was considered as belonging to Magadha, to which it was probably tributary. At all events, Magadha was the scene of the earliest labours of Sákya Muni, and there is less wonder that many Buddhists have referred the birth of their legislator to Magadha also.*

The Tibetans assert that Kapila was near to Mount Kailas, (a denomination which must here extend to the whole Himálayan chain) and upon the river *Bhágírathí*, which is the upper Ganges, or on the *Rohini*, which is not to be confounded with that known at present by the same name, one of the affluents of the Gandak. Kapila must moreover be close to the frontier of Nepal, since according to Buddhist legends, when the Sákyas were expelled from their own country, they retired to the former place. The Chinese chronology of the Buddhist patriarchs places it indeed to the south-west of Nepal,† and according to another Buddhist narrative the country of Benares, was situated to the south of that of *Kia 'weï lo weï*;‡ *Kia pi lo* is placed in the Chinese map of Hindostan, given in the Japanese Encyclopedia, to the north of Benares, and the kingdom of *A yu tho* (Ayodhya) of *Kiao changmi* and *Kiao sa lo* (Kósala). Thus, as far as we can gather from a map confusedly compiled from the notions of Chinese travellers, Kapila should be north of Benares, north-east of that part of the province of Oude which constituted the kingdom of Ráma; and thus far its position is confirmed by the narrative of Fa hian. From Kanouj our author travelled south-east to reach Kósala; he pursued the same direction, then that of east to arrive at

* *J. A. S.* Vol. I. p. 7.
† Japan. Encyclop *han*. B. LXIV. p. 27.
‡ *Yuan kian houi*, B. CCXVI. p. 6.

Kapila. According to this indication and that of the *Kah ghyur* quoted above, this town should be situated on the banks of the river Rohini, or Rohein, which flows from the mountains of Nepal, unites with the Mahánada, and falls into the Rapti below the present town of Goruckpore. Thus we may consider the birth-place of Buddha as a well ascertained point.

In his *Essay on Buddhism*, Mr. Hodgson says that Kapilavastu was situated near to *Gangá Ságar*. The following particulars regarding the latter name are from Wilson's Dictionary: "सागर the ocean. To bathe the bones of Sagara's 60,000 sons, the Ganges is said to have been led by Bhagíratha, his great-greatgrandson, to the ocean, at a place now called Gangá Ságar." —Kl. (The story is given at length in the *Vishnu Purána*, Wilson's translation. p. 377—379.—J. W. L.)

The exact position of Kapilavastu is one of the desiderata in the geography of ancient India, which may possibly yet be ascertained by local enquiries, assisted by the route of our pilgrim, and the incidental notices to be found in Tibetan and Pali books. According to the *Dul-va*, it was situated near *Kailas*, on the *Bhágirathí*, or as elsewhere stated, on the *Rohini* river.* Professor Wilson in his account of the Foe kue ki, observes, 'that Kapilavastu must have been situated to the eastward, somewhere near the hills separating Nepal from Gorakhpur, it being described as situated on the Rohini, a mountain stream which is one of the feeders of the Rapti. The Itineraries of Fa hian and Hiouan thsang show that the position was accurately described, and that Kapila or Kapilavastu, the birth-place of Sákya, was situated north of Gorakhpur, near where the branches of the Rapti issue from the hills."†

This does not appear to me so clear however. That portion of Hiouan thsang's Itinerary referring to Kapilavastu is unfortunately omitted in the copy of the *Pian i tian* accessible to the learned French editors; and if we trace Fa hian's course from *She weï* or Fyzabad, we shall find that the direction is south-easterly; which, making every allowance for the loose and general way in which the bearings are enunciated, would bring us to the south, and certainly not to the north, of Gorakhpur. This would place Kapilavastu on the banks of the Gogra, or even on the Ganges. That it was situated on the bank of a navigable stream, we have the authority of the Rájávali, whatever that be worth.‡ In the same work we have the following tradition of the foundation of that city, which would lead us to infer

* See Wilson, Abstract of the *Dul-va*, *J. A. S.* Vol. I. p. 7.
† *J. R. A. S.* Vol. V. p. 124.
‡ Upham, *Sacred and Hist. books of Ceylon*, Vol. II. p. 177.

that its site was north of and not very far from Benares. "Upon hearing this, all the following people left the country and accompanied the four princes; viz. the daughter of the said king with their attendants and property, 1000 ministers, bráhmins, rich men, and several thousands of merchants; and on the first day the whole company proceeded on their march as far as a mile, on the second day they marched eight miles, and on the third day they marched twelve miles, pursuing their march in the wilderness, and on one side of the city called Bareness (Benares); and there the princes took council, and spoke amongst themselves, saying, "if we take a town not belonging to us by force, it will greatly tarnish our fame," and so they determined to build a new town. One of the said princes remained there with the multitude to clear the wilderness, and when the others went through the wilderness in search of a good place to make a town, they found a hermit called Capilawastoo, at the foot of a bogaha tree, in front of a lake, which hermit had devoted himself to piety and religion. He asked the princes what they inquired for? and the princes related to him that which they searched for; then the hermit advised them to place their city where his own hermitage stood, and also he gave them encouragement by reciting to them a good account of the said ground, saying, that when the foxes happened to run after the hares, as soon as the hares came to that hermitage they used to turn about and run after the foxes, and in like manner the does after the tigers, &c.; likewise, that any person or persons who should live in this place would always be in great favour with the gods and brahmas, and also be able to vanquish their enemies in time of war; therefore that this ground would be the most proper for their purpose; and also the hermit requested the princes, after they made the city, to call it by his own name, Capilawastoo; then according to the advice given by the hermit, the four princes built the city, and gave it the name of Capilawastoo pura."

In the extracts from the *Atthakathá*, called the *Maduratthawilásini*, on the Buddhawanso, given by the Honorable Mr. Turnour in the *Journal Asiatic Society*, Vol. VII. p. 791, we read that Sákya at the requisition of his relatives and disciples, proceeded from *Rajagahan* on a visit to *Kapilawatthu*, and that by travelling at the rate of one yojana daily he reached the latter city in two months; thus making the distance sixty yojanas. Mr. Turnour estimates the yojana at sixteen English miles; but this is manifestly an excessive valuation. Judging from the distances given by our pilgrim in Magadha, the *yojana* of that part of his route could not greatly exceed 4 miles (see Capt. Kittoe, *On the route of Fa hian through Behar*, *J. A. S.* Vol. XVI. p. 954,) while in other parts of his itinerary the yojana must represent double that distance, or even more. If we take 4 miles as the average equivalent of the yojana in Magadha, the distance of Kapilavastu from Rajagriha will be about 240; and deducting one-fifth or one-sixth for the sinuosities of the route, we shall have the direct distance 190 or 200 miles. This would coincide well enough with Fa hian's account, and make the site of Kapilavastu on the Gogra south or south-west of Gorakhpur: a position which will be further confirmed by tracing our pilgrim's course retrogressively from *Phi she li*. See my note on the locality of that town, Chap. XXV. when the present subject will be resumed.—J. W. L.

(3) *The king Pe tsing.*—This was the name of Sákya Muni's father; it signifies in Chinese *white and pure.* He is sometimes named *Tsing fan wang*, or '*the king who eats pure food.*' It is the translation of the Sanscrit *Sudhódana.*

I subjoin the genealogy of the house of Sákya Muni. The Chinese and Páli names are in italics, the latter preceded by a P; the Tibetan and Mongol are in roman letters, the latter being [illegible].

Ta shen seng wang.
|
I szu mo wang.
|
Yeou lo tho wang.
|
Khiu lo wang.
|
Ni feou lo wang.
|
Szu tsu kie wang.
(P. *Sinhahána Kabáná.*
Sengghe h'ghram.
M. Oghadjetou arsalan).

Tsing fan wang. (P. *Suddhódana*, Zas d,zzang ma, M. Arighon ideghetou.)	*Pe fan wang.* P. *Suklodana*, Tas d,kur, M. Tsagha ideghetou.)	*Hou fan wang.* P. *Amitódana*, Bre'wo zas, M. Tangsouk ideghetou.)	*Kan lou fan wang.* P. *Dhótódana*, b,Douah r,'tsi zas, M. Rachiyan ideghetou.
Si tha to — *Nan tho*	*Thiao ta.* — *Anan*	*Ma ha nan* — *A na liu.*	*Pho so* — *Pa thi.*

Si tha to, in Sanscrit Siddhárta, is the prince who, having obtained the rank of Buddha, was called Sákya Muni. The Chinese portion of the above table is taken chiefly from the *Loui shou san thsaï thou hoeï*, B. IX. p. 2. —Kl.

(4) *In the womb of his Mother.*—When Sákya Muni, yet a Bodhisattwa

in the heaven Tushita, was about to become incarnate in the womb of his mother *Mahá máyá,* spouse of the king Suddhódana, he mounted a white elephant with six tusks and entered the body of his mother in the form of a five coloured pencil of light. This white elephant bears the name *Arajavartan,* that is to say, the *spotless way.*—Kl.

In addition to the Chinese illustration of the incarnation of Sákya Muni copied from the original, I give one taken from a fine piece of Hindu sculpture in the Asiatic Society's museum, to show the difference of style adopted by the artists of these two nations in handling the same subject.—J. W. L.

(5) *At the sight of a sick man.*—According to the great Japanese Encyclopedia and other legends which I have had it in my power to consult, it was in issuing not by the eastern, but by the southern gate, that *Sy tha,* (in Sanscrit *Siddha,* or *Sarvártha Siddha,* 'he who produces salvation') fell in with the sick man. The legend of the life of Sákya Muni, while he was yet a Bodhisattwa, states the same thing.

Siddha, while yet in his paternal home, was ever sad and thoughtful. To divert his attention, his father married him to the princess *Kieou i* (Kachá-ná) daughter of *Shun kio* (Suva buddha) king of *Siu pho foe* (Suprabuddha). This alliance, however, did not restore tranquillity to the soul of his son. He was married to other wives of exquisite beauty; one named '*All praise*' (Sarvastuti) and the other, '*Ever joyous,*' (Sadánandá). These three wives of Siddha had each twenty thousand damsels in their service, all beautifuly formed, and lovely as the nymphs of heaven. The king, his father, addressing *Kieou i* and the others, said to them; "The prince hath now sixty thousand women to entertain him with their music and to tend upon him; is he happy and joyous?" They answered him; "The prince is from morn till eve occupied with subtle studies and the doctrine; he dreams neither of desire nor of joy." The king, downcast at this news, summoned his ministers to consult anew. He stated to them how the pains he had taken in behalf of the prince were thrown away; that neither wealth nor beauty could attract him from his pursuits; no pleasure delighted him. "Is this then what *A i* hath said?" he added. The Ministers replied; "Since sixty thousand damsels and all the pleasures of the world delight him not, let him travel to study government, and divert his thoughts from the doctrine." Thereupon the king commanded that the prince should travel to observe. The prince said to himself—"I have been long secluded in the midst of my palace, and I long to go abroad and inform myself of that which occupies my thoughts." The king issued a mandate throughout his kingdom, that wherever the prince should go, the roads and the streets should be swept and watered, that perfumes should be burnt, and tapestries and flags and canopies hung up. The order was executed; all was purified and adorned. The prince, attended by a thousand chariots and a thousand horsemen, went forth from the town by the eastern gate. Then a god of the class of Sutras, named *Nan thi ho lo*, to confirm the prince the choice of a religious career, and to help him in emancipating himself from desires inflamed like three poisonous fires in the ten parts, showered down the water of the law to extinguish these empoisoned flames. He accordingly transformed himself into an aged man, and sat down by the roadside; his head white; his teeth fallen away; his skin flaccid and his face wrinkled; his flesh dried up; his back bent; the articulations of his frame prominent; the eyes watery; his nostrils running; his breathing short and difficult; his skin darkened; his head and hands trembling; his frame and members emaciated and shaky; deformed and naked, he exhibited himself set up in this place. The prince asked, "Who is this man?" "He is an old man," replied the attendants. "And what is an *old* man?" again asked the prince. "It is one who hath lived many years, whose organs are worn out, whose form is changed, whose colour hath faded, whose respiration is feeble, whose strength is exhausted. He no longer digests what he eats. His joints become worn out; if he would lie down or sit, he cannot do so without the assistance of others. His eyes are dim, his ears dull. In turning round, he forgets all. If he speak, it is to complain or mourn. This is what we call an old man!" The distressed prince replied: "If man, by being born in the world, is thus exposed to the wretchedness of old age, none but fools would desire to be so! What satisfaction is there in it? Beings that are born in springtime, dry up and wither in autumn and winter! Old age comes like a lightning-flash; what is there that should attach us to the body?" And he uttered the following *gatha*; "By old age the colour becomes faded and loses its freshness, the skin relaxes, and the back becomes bent; death approaches and haunts us. In old age the body changes and may be compared to an old chariot. The law can expel this bitterness. Our whole strength should be applied to study the means of subjecting our desires. When the days and the nights are ended, we should be diligent and resolute. Instability is the reality of the world. If every faculty be not applied to it, we fall into darkness. Study must light the lamp of the spirit; let us of ourselves choose and follow knowledge and avoid every uncleanness. Contract no impurity. Take the torch, and examine the world and the doctrine." The prince then turned his chariot and went back. His sorrow increased yet more; and the pain he experienced in thinking that all without exception are subject to this grevious misfortune, deprived him of every happiness. The king asked of the attendants wherefore the prince who had but just issued for an excursion had so quickly returned? They answered, that on the road he had fallen in with an aged man, the sight of whom so afflicted him, that not being able to enjoy any pleasure, he returned to the palace, and distressed himself with the thought of longevity.

"Shortly after he would again go forth. The king caused publish throughout the kingdom that the prince would again go abroad, and forbade that any foul or indecent object should be found on the roads. The prince then ascended his chariot and issued by the south gate of the town. The god counterfeited a sick man and stood by the way-side. His body was emaciated and his belly swollen up. His skin yellow and fevered. He coughed and groaned. He had pains in all his joints. From his nine orifices issued a bloody liquid. His eyes distinguished no colours. His ears heard no sounds. His breathing was short. His hands and feet struggled with empty space. He called his father and his mother, and clung grievously to his wife and his son. The prince demanded, Who is this?" The attendants replied, "It is a sick man." The prince again asked, "And what is a *sick* man?" "Man, they replied, is formed of the four elements, earth, water, fire, and air. Every element hath a hundred and one maladies that follow each other successively. When the four hundred and four maladies are produced together, an extreme cold, an extreme heat, an extreme hunger, an extreme satiety, an extreme thirst, and extreme quenching are experienced; all times being disturbed, the vicissitude of sleeping and waking is lost; and it is thus that he hath got this sickness." The prince sighed, and said: "I am in the richest and most prosperous condition, such as the world honors. Meat and drink abound for my mouth. I can yield myself up to my caprices, and when no longer able to exercise my understanding upon myself, I shall fall sick too. What difference will there then be betwixt this man and me?" He then pronounced this gáthá: "How frail a thing is the body! It is formed of four elements and hath nine impure and disgusting orifices. It is subject to the torments of old age and sickness; even when born again among the gods it is subject to instability. Born among men, it is scourged with diseases. I regard the body as a drop of rain! What satisfaction is there in the world?" Then the prince returned to his palace, pondering how without exception all are subject to grievous misfortune. The king enquired of the attendants how the prince felt himself during the promenade? They replied that having fallen in with a sick man, the sight would long deprive the prince of all happiness.

"Shortly afterwards, he would go forth again. The king issued an edict to the effect that when the prince should go abroad, the ground should be cleared and no impurity should come near his route. He issued by the western gate of the town. The god transformed himself in a corpse which they were carrying out of the town. The relatives of the deceased followed the vehicle sobbing and weeping, complaining to heaven of their loss and eternal separation. The prince asked, "What is this?" They replied, "It is a corpse." The former again asked, "And what is that?" The attendants replied, "It is the end. The soul hath departed. The four elements are now about to dissipate. The sensitive soul and the spirit, being no longer in equilibrium, the air passes away and entirely ceases, the fire is extinguished, and the body becomes cold. Air having departed first, and afterwards fire, the soul and the understanding disappear. The members elongate and stiffen. There is nothing more to recognise. At the end of ten days the flesh decays, the blood flows, the belly swells, putrifies, and becomes fetid; there is nothing there to take. The body is filled with worms which devour it. The nerves and the veins are destroyed by putrefaction; the articulations are disjointed and the bones dispersed. The skull goes one way, the spine, the ribs, the arms, the legs, the feet and hands, each another. The birds that fly, the beasts that walk, assemble to devour them. Gods, dragons, demons, genii, emperors and kings, people, the poor, the rich, the noble, the plebeian,—none are exempt from this calamity." The prince gave a long sigh, and said in verse, "When I contemplate old age, sickness and death, I groan over human life and its instability! It is even so in my own person. This body is a perishable thing; but the soul hath no form. Under the false semblance of death, it is re-born! Its crimes and its good works are not dispersed. It is not a single generation that comprises its beginning or its end. Its duration is prolonged by ignorance and lust. It is thence that it obtains grief and joy. Though the body die, the soul perisheth not. It is not ether, it is not in the sea, it entereth not into mountains and rocks. There is no place in the world where there is exemption from death." Thereupon the prince turned his chariot and proceeded back to the palace, pondering sadly how all living beings are subject to old age, sickness, and death. He was so distressed that he eat none. The king enquired if the prince had been cheerful during his excursion. They answered that he fell in with a funeral and hath laid up sadness for several years.

A little while, and again he desired to go abroad, and his beautiful chariot issued by the northern gate. The god again transformed himself and became a Samanean. He had the costume of the law, carried a begging-pot, and walked afoot, considering carefully and not casting his looks aside. The prince enquired, "Who is that man?" They answered, "A Samanean." "And what is a Samanean?" "Samaneans are those who practice the doctrine and quit their houses, their wives, and their children. They renounce all tender desires; they suppress the six affections; they observe the precepts, and by quietude, having attained simplicity of heart, extinguish all impurity. He that practises simplicity of heart, is denominated *Arhan*. The *Arhan* is the true man. Sounds and colors cannot soil him. Rank cannot prevail with him. He is immovable as the earth. He is delivered from affliction and pain. Living or dead, he is master of himself." The prince exclaimed, "How excellent! there is no happiness like this!" He then pronounced a *Gátha*, signifying, "Oh grief! he who possesses this life of affliction is subject to the pains of old age, of sickness, and of death. The soul returns to the road of sin and experiences all manner of painful agitations. Nevertheless it may extinguish all evils; birth, old age, sickness, and death are driven away; enter no more upon the circle of the affections and obtain eternal salvation by extinction." Thereupon the prince caused his chariot to be turned, and went back so sad that he was unable to eat. The king enquired of his attendants, "The Prince hath been once more abroad; are his spirits more cheerful?" The attendants answered—"On the road he met a Samanean, who has redoubled his sadness and his contemplative disposition. He thinks neither of meat nor of drink." At this the king became violently enraged, and raising his hands, smote himself. He renewed the interdiction against studying the doctrine, and commanded that if the prince again went abroad, every one of evil augury whom he should fall in with should be punished or put to death. He then convoked his ministers, and commanded them to deliberate on the best means of preventing the prince from going forth in quest of the doctrine."* These then are what the Buddhists call the *four realities* recognised by Sákya Muni, when issuing from the gates of the town; namely, *old age, sickness, death,* and the final *dissolution* of the *atoms of the body*.—Kl.

(6) *In the places where A i.*—The *Tao szu*, called by Chinese authors *A i*, is in Sanscrit तपस्वी, *tapasvi*, or the ascetic who leads an austere life. It is under this name that there is mention of his visit to the infant Buddha in a very curious inscription in the Magah language, found in a cave near Chittagong.†

A i, or Tapasvi Muni, is, according to Georgi, called *Trang srong tsien po* ('the great man who acts according to the doctrine') in Tibetan works. (This aged hermit is described in a legend which is scarce worth repetition here, as having recognised the birth of Buddha by super natural signs, and

* *Shin i tian*, B. LXX.
† *As. Researches*, II. p. 383.

proceeded by flight from a distant solitude to the Royal palace. He there beholds the child, and described all the bodily perfections which were supposed to have distinguished the Buddha. The legend is extracted from the *Shin i tian*, B. LXXVIII. pp. 17—19 *v*.—J. W. L.

(7) *Drew the bow.*—The Japanese Chronology places this event in the year Kouei hai, which is the 60th of the XXXVth cycle, or 1018 B C.

On the occasion of the marriage of *Siddhárta* with the princess *Kieou i*, the king *Pe tsing* directed *Yeou tho* to intimate to the prince that he must publicly exhibit his rare talents. " *Yeou tho* having received this order, proceeded to intimate to the prince that the king wishing to have immediate proof of the prince's knowledge of the rites and of music, he must forthwith proceed to the theatre. The prince then proceeded with *Yeou tho* (*Udá*), *Nan tho* (Nanda,) *Thia tho* (Dévadatta), *A nan* (Ananda), and others to the number of 500, having in their hands all the necessary utensils for the rites, instruments of music, and the requisites for the practice of archery. As they were about to issue from the town, there stood an elephant before the gate. The powerful Thiao thá happened to be in advance, and seeing the elephant on the road, struck him a blow with his fist, so that the elephant fell down stone dead in an instant. Nan tho immediately drew him aside out of the way. The prince, who followed, asked of his attendants " Who has killed this elephant without an object ?" They replied " Thiao thá killed him." " Who drew him aside ?" " Nan tho." The Bodhisattwa, endowed with a compassionate heart, dragged the elephant and raised him up outside the town. The elephant was raised from death and restored to life as before. Thiao thá having arrived at the theatre attacked the athletes ; not one of these could resist him. All the most famous wrestlers were overthrown and put to shame. The king enquired of his attendants, " Who is this conqueror ?" They replied, *Thiao thá.* The king then said to Nan tho, " Thou and Thiao thâ must wrestle together." Nan tho having received the command, closed with Thiao thá and handled him so that he became quite insensible. He recovered by degrees on being sprinkled with water. The king again asked who was the conqueror, and was informed that Nan tho was he. The king then commanded Nan tho to wrestle with the prince ; but Nan tho replied, " My elder brother is like mount Sumeru, and I but a grain of mustard seed ; I am not his match," and withdrew, excusing himself. Next came the trial of archery. First an iron target was placed at the distance of 10 li, and so on to seven targets. The shafts of the most renowned archers went no further than the first target. Thiao tha having drawn, shot beyond it and reached the second. Nan tho surpassed this, and pierced through the third. The other archers being unable to shoot so far, the prince broke all the bows of those who had shot before him; not one was equal to his strength. The king then said to his attendants, "My ancestors possessed a bow which is now in the temple of the gods; go, bring it." They went to fetch the bow, which required two men to carry. No man in that assembly could lift it. When the prince shot with it, the twang of the string was heard forty *li*. The bent bow hurled the shaft so as to pass through the seven targets. He shot again, and the arrow having passed the targets pierced the earth and caused a spring of water to gush forth. At the third shot he pierced the seven targets and reached the mountains of the iron girdle. The whole assembly wondered at this unheard of prodigy. All who had come to partake in the sports were overcome, and returned confounded. There was still the *King of Strong Men*, who came last of all. His strength was extreme: nothing in the whole world could surpass his courage and ferocity. He pretended that Thiao tha and Nan tho were no matches for him, and that he would only measure his strength with the prince. All who had been conquered longed for some one to avenge them: they leapt for joy, and said to the King of Strong Men, "Prince, as your strength is incomparable in the world, come and prove it, and bear off the victory." Themselves, highly delighted, followed to assist in his engagement with the prince. Thiao thá and Nan tho animated the courage of the latter, and would themselves have first combatted the King of Strong Men, but they said, "This is not human strength; it is that of the demon of death. If thou triumph not, Oh prince, what disgrace will be yours!" The king learning this, deemed the prince too young, and from habitual sadness, too delicate. All who came to assist at the fight, spoke of the moment as come when the prince was to be vanquished. The King of Strong Men stamped the earth with his foot, and boldly raised his arms and stretched forward his hands. He advanced to seize the prince; but in that instance the latter caught him and threw him to the ground. The earth trembled. The entire assembly dispersed, more confounded than before, and suddenly disappeared. The prince having thus obtained complete victory, the bells were rung, the drums beaten, and amidst vocal and instrumental music he mounted his horse and returned to the palace."*—R.

(8) *Where Foe obtained the doctrine.*—The Japanese chronology, entitled *Wa kan kwo to fen nen yakf oun—no tsou* places this event in the year *Koueï weï*, which is the 20th of the XXVII. cycle, corresponding with the 4th of the reign of Mou wang of the dynasty of the Chou, and 998 B. C. Buddha was then in his twenty-ninth year. The Mongol history of *Sanang*

* *Shin i tian*, B. LXXVII. pp. 21—23. v.

Selsen states that "in the year *Ping* of the *Ape*, Buddha attained his twenty-ninth year, and being before the truly holy tower, he, of his own free will embraced the ecclesiastic condition."*

The *Fa yuan chu lin* says ; "The place where the Tathágata (Jou laï) obtained the doctrine, is in the kingdom of *Mo kie tho* (Magadha) under a *Phou thi* tree (*Bodhi, Bauhinia scandens*), where a tower has been erected.—Kl.

(9) *Five hundred sons of the Sákyas.*—शाक्य, Sákya, is the name of that tribe or family of Sákya Muni, belonging to the Kshatria caste. According to Buddhist traditions, this race descends from *Ikswaku*, a prince of the solar line and founder of the royal race of Ayodhya, or Oude. The name however does not appear in the genealogical lists of Hindus, as that either of a tribe or of a people. M. Ksoma de Körös has given the following extract on this subject from the 26th Vol. of that division of the *Káh ghyur* named m*Do*.† "They accordingly met, and elected one for their master and proprietor of their lands, and for the arbitrator of their controversies, saying to him ; "Come, animal being, punish from among us those that are to be punished, and reward those with a gift that merit to be remunerated ; from all the products of our lands we will pay you a certain rate, accordingly to a rule." Afterwards on both sides, they did accordingly. Since he was carried (or honoured) by a great multitude of animal beings, he was called མང་པོས་བཀུར་བ *Mang-pos* b*kur-va ;* Sanscrit, *Mahá Sammata*, "Honoured by many."

Gautamas ! At the time of *Mahá Sammata*, man was called by this name, "Animal being."

[The following five leaves (from 171—175) are occupied with an enumeration of the descendants of MAHA SAMMATA down to KARNA (རྣ་བ་ཅན) at *Potala* (གྲུ་འཛིན *Gru-hdsin*‡ the harbour.) He had two sons, GOTAMA and BHARADHWAJA (T. r*Na-va-chan.*) The former took the religious character, but *Gotama* being afterwards accused of the murder of a harlot, was unjustly impaled at *Potala*, and the latter succeeded to his father. He dying without issue, the two sons of GOTAMA inherit, who were born in a præter-natural manner ; from the circumstances of their birth, they and their descendants are called by several names ; as, ཡན་ལག་སྐྱེས *Yan-lag-s,kyes ;* (S. Angirasa.) ཉི་མའི་གཉེན; *Nyi-mahignyen*, (S. Surya Vánsa,) Gautama, གཽ་ཏམ ; བུ་རམ་ཤིང་པ *Bu-ram shing-pa*, (S. Iskhwaku.) One of the

* *Geschichte der ost Mongolen*, p. 13.
† *J. A. S.* Vol. II. p. 389.
‡ The ancient *Potala*, or the modern *Tatta*, at the mouth of the Indus.

two brothers dies without issue, the other reigns under the name of IKSHWAKU.

" To him succeeds his son, whose descendants (one hundred) afterwards successively reign at *Potala* (གྲུ་འཛིན) *Gru-hdsin*. The last of whom was བུ་རམ་ཤིང་པ འཕགས་སྐྱེས་པོ : Ikshwaku Virudhaka, (or Vidéhaka.) He has four sons, སྐར་མདའ་གདོང, ལག་རྣ, གླང་པོ་ཆེའཉལ, and རྐང་གདུ-བ་ཅན. After the death of his first wife, he marries again. He obtains the daughter of a king, under the condition that he shall give the throne to the son that shall be born of that princess. By the contrivance of the chief officers, to make room for the young prince to succession, the king orders the expulsion of his four sons.

" They taking their own sisters with them, and accompanied by a great multitude, leave *Potala* (གྲུ་འཛིན), go towards the Himalaya, and reaching the bank of the *Bhagirathi* river (སྐལ་ལྡན་ཤིང་རྟ) settle there, not far from the hermitage of CAPILA the *Rishi* (དྲང་སྲོང་སེར་སྐྱའི་སྐྱི་གནས), and live in huts made of the branches of trees. They live there on hunting; and sometimes they visit the hermitage of CAPILA the Rishi. He observing them to look very ill, asks them why they were so pale. They tell him how much they suffer on account of their restraint or continence. He advises them to leave their own uterine sisters, and to take themselves (to wife) such as are not born of the same mother with them. O great Rishi! said the princes, is it convenient for us to do this? Yes, Sirs, answered the Rishi, banished princes may act in this way. Therefore, taking for a rule the advice of the Rishi, they do accordingly, and cohabit with their non-uterine sisters, and have many children by them. The noise of them being inconvenient to the Rishi in his meditation, he wishes to change his habitation. But they beg him to remain in his own place, and to design for them any other ground. He therefore marks them out the place where they should build a town: since the ground was given to them by CAPILA, they called the new city *Capilavastu*. They multiply there exceedingly. The gods seeing their great number, show them another place for their settlement. They build there a town, and call it by the name of ལྷས་བསྟན *Lhas-bstan*, (shown by a god.)

" Remembering the cause of their banishment, they make it a law, that no one of them hereafter shall marry a second wife of the same tribe, but that he shall be contented with one wife.

" At *Potala* (གྲུའཛིན) the king IKSHWAKU VIRUDHAKA, recollecting that he had four sons, asks his officers, what has become of them. They tell him, how for some offence His Majesty had expelled them, and how they had settled in the neighbourhood of the *Himálaya*, and that they have taken their own sisters for their wives, and have been much multiplied. The king, being much surprised on hearing this, exclaims several times: *Shákya! Shákya!* Is it possible! Is it possible! (or O daring! O daring!) ཕོད་པ *phod-pa*, and this is the origin of the *Shákya* name.

"After the death of IKSHWAKU VIRUDHAKA, བུ་རམ་ཤིང་པ་འཕགས་སྐྱེ-སཔོ at *Potala*, succeeds his younger son རྒྱལ་སྲིད་དགའ, *rgyal-srid dgha*, (he that desires to reign). On his dying without children, the banished princes successively inherit. The three first have no issue; the son of སྣང་གཙུབ་ཅན སཁྲིམ the fourth prince, is, *Gnag*-*hjog*, གནས་འཇོག. His son is ས་ཁྲིམ His descendants to the number of 55,000 have reigned at *Capilavástu*. [An enumeration of the princes who reigned at *Potala* after IKSHWAKU follows, which is indentical with the list in Sanskrit authorities; the names being translated into Tibetan according to their literal meaning; as for *Mahá Sammata*, *Mang pos* b*kur-va*, greatly honoured, &c."]

"Here ends the narration of MONGALYANA. SHA'KYA approves and recommends it to the priests."

We are indebted to M. E. Burnouf, for the subjoined extract from the Mahávansa, or History of the great family, a work of more than twelve thousand slokas, in the Páli language. It contains a history of the royal family from which Sákya sprung,—an exposition of his doctrine and worship,—and a list of such Indian and Ceylonese sovereigns as have most effectually contributed to propagate the religion of which he is the recognised head. This passage is in perfect conformity with the extract from the *Káh ghyur* given above, and with the genealogy of Sákya Muni as detailed in Chinese works.

(I here substitute Mr. Turnour's English version, for that given in Latin by M. Burnouf.—J. W. L.)

"There were eighty-two thousand sovereigns, the sons and lineal descendants of king Sihassaro,—the last of these was Jayaseno. These were celebrated in the capital of Kapillawatthu, as Sákya kings.

The great king, Sihahanu was the son of Jayaséno. The daughter of Jayaséno was named Yasódará. In the city of Dewadaho there was a Sákya ruler named Dewadaho. Unto him two children, Anjano and Kachchána, were born. This Kachchána became the queen of king Sihahanu.

To the Sákya Anjano the aforesaid Yasódará became queen. To Anjano two daughters were born, Máyá and Pajápati; and two sons of the Sákya race, Dandapáni and Suppabuddho.

To Sehahanu five sons and two daughters were born,—Suddhódano, Dhotodano, Sukkódana, (Ghattitódano) and Amitódano; Amita and Pamita; those five, these two. To the Sákya Suppabuddho, Amita became queen. Subhaddakachchána and Dewadatta were her offspring.

Máyá and Pajápati both equally became the consorts of Suddhódano. OUR VANQUISHER was the son of the Maharaja Suddhódano and Máyá. Thus the great divine sage was, in a direct line, descended from the Maha Sammabo race, the pinnacle of all royal dynasties."*

(10) *A Yeou pho li,*—(*Upali* in Sanscrit.) It signifies '*superior head,*' and according to others, '*he who is at hand and preserves.*' It is the name of the ninth of the ten great disciples of Foe. While the latter was prince Yeou pho li was entirely devoted to his person, and had special charge of his affairs. After embracing monastic life, he observed the precepts and was a model to all. On that account he is called '*the first observer of the precepts.*'—Kl.

(11) *Trembled in six ways.*—Reference is here made to the great earthquake which happened at the birth of Foe, and which was felt in all the *Kshamas* of the three thousand grand chiliocosms. The Buddhists admits six moments in an earthquake: the beginning of the motion, the augmentation of its intensity, the overflowing of the waters, the true quaking, the noise it occasions, and the vibration which follows.†

The Buddhists assert that there are eight causes of earthquakes:

1st. They are produced by water, fire and air. According to the sacred books, Jambudwíp is 21,000 yojanas in length from north to south; from east to west 7,000; and its thickness 68,000 yojanas. Beneath the earth to the depth of 40,000 yojanas is water; beneath the water fire to the depth of 87,000 yojanas. Beneath the fire there is a bed of air, or wind, 68,000 yojanas thick. Beneath this air, there is a wheel of steel in the centre of which are the *sarira* (reliques) of all the past Buddhas. If there be a great wind, it agitates the fire; the fire, the water; and the water communicates the motion to the earth. And this is the earthquake occasioned by water, fire, and air.

2d. Earthquakes are occasioned by the entrance of the Bodhisattwas into the wombs of their mothers. When the Bodhisattwas, about to be incarnate to become Buddhas, descend from the heaven *Tushita*, and proceed to occupy supernaturally the wombs of their mothers, there happen great earthquakes.

* *Mahawanso*, transtated by Turnour, p. 9.
† *Houa yan king fa sou*, quoted in *San tsang fa sou*, B. XXVII. p. 24.

3d. Earthquakes happen when Bodhisattwas issue from the wombs of their mothers.

4th. Earthquakes happen when Bodhisattwas accomplish the law. The Bodhisattwas having quitted their homes to embrace monastic life, and having studied reason, become that pure intelligence without superior, named a *Buddha being*; the earth then quakes with great violence.

5th. When the Buddhas enter nirvána, there are also great earthquakes.

6th. There are earthquakes when the *bhikshus* or religious mendicants desire to avail themselves of their supernatural faculties. The sacred books state that there are bhikshus endowed with great supernatural powers, and able to effect different kinds of metamorphoses. They can divide a single body into a hundred thousand others, and can again reduce these to a single one; fly through space without obstruction from hill or rock; plunge into water; and penetrate the earth. In all such cases there are great earthquakes.

7th. The earth also quakes when the gods quit their primitive form and become masters of heaven (*Thian chu*). The sacred books state that there are gods who have great supernatural and infinite virtue. When their life is ended they are reborn elsewhere, and by the virtue and power of Buddha, they quit their previous form and become Indra (*Ti shy*) or Brahma (*Fan cha*).

8th. When there is a famine, or a great war about to happen; for then the life of living beings, or their happiness must end; since they fight and expose themselves to the sword.*—Kl.

(12) *The alms of a seng kia li.*—*Seng kia li*, in Sanscrit Sangháti, is the mantle or cowl of Buddhist ascetics. (See page 93, note 10.)

(13) *Ni keou liu*; the Chinese transcription of the Sanscrit न्यग्रोध, *Nyagródha*, ficus indica.—Kl.

(14) *Destroyed the family of Sákyas.**—See note 36, Chap. XX.

(15) *The rank of Siú tho wan*, in Sanscrit स्रोतापन्न, Srótápanna: it is the name of the first class of the Srávakas, or hearers of Buddha. It means, according to the Chinese, "those who are secured against the current (of the flux of worldly beings)." It is however translated in Tibetan r,*Ghioun dhou joughs bha* (those who enter every where).—Kl.

(16) *Watched the labourers.*—When the prince Siddharta was returning from his promenades towards the four gates of the town, "one of his father's ministers proposed to show him the operations of agriculture, to divert his mind from the thoughts of the doctrine. All manner of agricultural imple-

* *Thseng y A han king*, quoted in the *San tsang fa sou*, B. XLI. p. 26.

ments were provided, ploughs, and whatever else was requisite; and the attendants, accompanied by inferior officers, proceeded to a field and began to work. The prince sat under a *Jambu* tree and watched them. In digging the soil they turned up some worms. The god *Nan thi ho lo*, by a novel metamorphosis, caused the ox who went along raising the sod, to make them fall back again; a crow came to peck and eat them up. The God further made a toad appear, that sought out and swallowed them; then a serpent with tortuous folds came from a hole and devoured the toad. A peacock stooped in his flight and pecked the serpent; a falcon next seized and devoured the peacock; finally a vulture fell upon the falcon and eat it up. The Bodhisattwa seeing all these beings mutually devouring each other, felt his compassionate heart moved, and under the tree where he was seated, attained the first degree of contemplation. The sun was shining in full splendor; the tree curved its branches to shadow the person of the Bodhisattwa. The king, pondering how in his palace the prince had never yet experienced any sorrow, enquired of his attendants how he was? "He is even now, replied they, under the tree *Jambu*, his whole heart fixed in contemplation." "I will immediately see him," returned the king; "my thoughts are troubled; for if he yields himself up to contemplation, how different will that be to his sojourn in the palace!" The king called for his beautiful chariot, and proceeded to the prince. In approaching the latter, whose body was resplendent with divine lustre, he beheld him protected by the curved branches of the tree. He alighted from his horse, saluted him, and returned with his suite. He had not yet reached the gates of the city when innumerable thousands having presented perfumes, the astrologers proclaimed the praises of the being whose life must have been immense. The king enquired the cause of these acclamations; the Brahmacharís responded, "To-morrow, oh great king, at the rising of the sun, the seven precious things will be delivered to you. Good fortune and felicity will make you the holy king!" At this moment the prince returned to the palace, ever exclusively occupied with thoughts of the doctrine and its purity, which required him to abandon lay life and retire to the woods and mountains, there to search deeply into subtle things and to practise contemplation."—Kl.*

(17) *Bears the name of Lun ming.*—In Chinese Buddhist works the name of the garden is transcribed *Lung mi ni* and *Lan pi ni*. It is explained by *Kiaï tho chhu*, i. e. 'the place existent of itself without obstacle or hindrance.' I find the same term explained also *Pho lo thi mou chha*, in Sanscrit पराधिमोच, *Parádhi móksha*, that is to say, '*extreme eternal*

* *Chian i tian*, B. LXXVII. p. 28.

beatitude.' Kiaï thö properly signifies 'to help any one to avoid misfortune.' This garden is also called *Weï ni.* See p.—Kl.

(18) *The Lady.*—In Chinese *Fou jin;* the title generally given to the mother of Buddha.—Kl.

(19) *Two kings of the dragons washed his body.*—The following legend gives an account of the delivery of Mahá Máyá and the birth of Sákya Muni.

"Mahá Máyá went forth to walk: she passed through multitudes of people and seated herself beneath a tree. (This was an *Asoka, Jonesia asoka.*) The flowers began to blow and a brilliant star appeared. The *Lady* supporting herself by a branch of the tree brought forth the child from her right side. At birth the child fell to the ground and walked seven steps; then stopt, and raising its hand, "In the heaven and below the heaven," said he, "there is none honorable but I. All is bitterness in the three worlds, and it is I that shall sweeten this bitterness."

At this moment the heavens and the earth trembled violently, and all the Kshmas in the three great chiliocosms were illuminated by a brilliant light. Indra, Brahma, the four kings of heaven, with all their suite and their subject gods, the dragons, the genii, the Yakshas, the Gandharvas, the Asuras, came together to encircle and protect the new-born. Two brother-kings of the dragons, one named *Kia lo*, the other *You kia lo*, caused a shower of water to fall on him, warm on the left side and cool on the right. Indra and Brahma held a celestial robe in which they wrapped him. The heavens showered down odoriferous flowers; the sound of musical instruments was heard; and every variety of perfume was shed in profusion, filling the surrounding space.

The *Lady*, holding the prince in her arms, ascended a chariot drawn by dragons and ornamented with streamers and drapery; and accompanied by musicians returned to the palace. On hearing of the birth of the prince the king evinced great tokens of satisfaction (literally, he leapt for joy), and went forth to meet him followed by a great company of magistrates, subjects, brahmacharís, officers, grandees, ministers and soldiers. As soon as the horses of the king touched the ground with their feet, five hundred treasures displayed themselves, and an ocean of good deeds was produced to the infinite advantage of the age. The assemblage having arrived, the brahmacharís and the astrologers gave vent to their acclamations, and with one accord hailed the prince by the name of *Si tha* (*Siddha*, blessed). When the king beheld Indra, Brahma, the four kings of heavens, all the gods, the dragons and the genii occupying the entire space, his heart was struck with reverence, and without being sensible of it, he dismounted from his horse and paid homage to the prince. They had not yet returned to the gate of the city, and there was by the wayside the temple of a genius whom all the world adored. The brahmacharís and the astrologers with one voice proposed that the prince should be carried to do homage to the statue of that genius. They took him in their arms and bore him to the temple; but all the genii immediately prostrated themselves before him. Then the bramahcharís and the astrologers pronounced the prince to be a genius, a being truly excellent, since he exercised such authority over the gods and genii. Every one therefore gave him the title of god of gods (Dévátidéva). All then returned to the palace.

The gods caused thirty-two signs or presages of this event to appear. 1st. The earth shook with a great earthquake. 2d. The roads and the streets were made clean of themselves, and foul places exhaled perfumes. 3d. Withered trees within the boundaries of the kingdom were covered with leaves and flowers. 4th. Gardens spontaneously produced rare flowers and delicious fruits. 5th. Dry lands produced great lotuses equal in size to the wheels of a chariot. 6th. Treasures buried in the earth spontaneously displayed themselves. 7th. The precious stones and other rarities of these treasures shone with extraordinary brilliancy. 8th. Vestments and bed-clothing locked up in boxes were drawn forth, and displayed. 9th. Streams and water-courses acquired a higher degree of limpidity and transparence. 10th. The wind ceased, clouds and fogs dispersed, and the sky became pure and serene. 11th. The sky on all sides shed an odoriferous dew. 12th. The divine pearl of the full moon was suspended in the hall of the palace. 13th. The wax tapers of the palace were no longer required. 14th. The sun, moon, stars, and planets stood still. 15th. Shooting stars appeared and assisted at the birth of the prince. 16th. The gods and Brahma extended a precious canopy above the palace. 17th. The genii of the eight parts of the world came presenting precious things. 18th. A hundred kinds of heavenly and savoury meats offered themselves spontaneously (to the prince). 19th. Ten thousand precious vases were found suspended and filled with a sweet dew. 20th. The gods and the genii conducted the chariot of the dew with the seven precious things. 21st. Five hundred white elephants, spontaneously caught in the nets, were found in front of the palace. 22nd. Five hundred white lions issued from the snowy mountains, and appeared bound at the gate of the town. 23rd. The nymphs of heaven appeared upon the shoulders of the musicians. 24th. The daughters of the kings of the dragons encircled the palace. 25th. Ten thousand celestial virgins appeared on the walls of the palace holding chowries of peacocks' tails in their hands. 26th. Heavenly virgins holding in their hand urns filled with perfumes ranged themselves in space. 27th. Celestial musicians descended and began together a harmonious concert. 28th. The torments of hell were suspended. 29th. Venemous insects hid themselves, and birds of happy omen sang, flapping their wings. 30th. Sweetness and gentleness in a moment replaced the harsh and savage sentiments of fishermen and hunters. 31st. All the pregnant women in the kingdom gave birth to boys. The deaf, the blind, the dumb, the paralytic, the leprous, men in short affected with all kinds of maladies, were radically cured. 32nd. The anchorites of the woods came forth, and, bowing down, offered adoration.*

An inscription in the Magah language engraved on a silver plate found in a cave near Chittagong, and published in the second Vol. of the Asiatic Researches, gives an account of the birth of Buddha in nearly the same terms.

In the various Buddhist works written in Chinese, and recounting the birth of Foe, which I have had an opportunity of referring to, his first words are variously reported; according to the *Ni pun king*, he said, "Amongst gods and men, and asuras, I am the most venerable." A great Buddhist collection published in China under the dynasty of the Ming, and of which I possess some fragments, gives a representation of his birth and baptism, and makes him say, "In heaven and under heaven, I am the sole venerable one." The *Shy kia pon* reports these words otherwise :—"Among all gods and all men, I am the most venerable and the most exalted." Lastly, the *Foe siang thou weï*, of which the latest edition was published in Japan, 1796, gives these words : "Within the four cardinal points, the zenith and the nadir, I alone am most venerable."

The pseudo-*Abdallah Beidhawi* makes him say :

مرا خدای فرستاده تا پیغمبر باشم تا وقت دیگر پیغمبر بیایند

"God hath sent me as a prophet until other prophets shall come."—Kl.

(20) *Where they accomplished the doctrine*, that is to say, where from Bodhisattwa they became Buddha Tathágata, or accomplished. As for the Buddha Sákya Muni, he attained this dignity in a garden in the kingdom of *Ma kia tho* (Magadha) upon the bank of the river *Ni lian*, (Chinese authors confess their ignorance of the meaning of this name). The saint was seated under two *Po thi* trees *(ficus religiosa)* and there became *pure Intelligence*. In this place is erected the second of the eight holy towers.†

* *Shin i tian*, B. LXXVII. p. 15—17.

† *Pă ta ling thă king*, quoted in the *San tsang fa sau*, B. XXXIII. p. 5. v.

The river *Ni lian* whose banks were for six years the theatre of austerities to which Sákya Muni while yet a Bodhisattwa submitted in order to attain Buddhahood, is called in the itinerary of Hiuan thsang *Ni lian chen* and *Ni lian chen na*, (*Pian i tian*, B. LV. 25), and in Mongol works, Niranjara, *Nirandzara.* These are all transcriptions of the Sanskrit term नीलाञ्चन, *Nilanchana*, (in Pali *Niranjanam*), which signifies *sulphate of copper*, also *lightning*. It is the name of a considerable torrent, which flows from the south-west, and which uniting with another, named the Mohana, forms the Phulgo. As the Phulgo, named Amanat in our maps, has a longer course than the Mohana, it may be regarded as the upper portion of the Phulgo. Its source lies in the wooded hills of the district of Torí in the province of Ramghur, in about 23-40 N. L.

(21) *To turn the wheel of the Law.*—This is an allegorial expression implying that a Buddha has begun to preach the doctrine. The *Fa yuan chu lin* says,—"The place where the Tathágata turned the wheel of the law is not well determined. According to some it was in the retreat of silence; according to others in the Deer-Park (near to, and north-east of Benares); or in the heavens and other places."—Kl.

(22) *Where they overthrew the heretics.*—We have already expounded (Ch. XVII. note 21), the doctrines of heterodox philosophers in the times of Sákya Muni. It was at Benares that the latter sustained the greater part of discussions with these doctors, who, named *Ters* in the Buddhist books of the Mongols, were the sworn enemies of the doctrine of Buddha. At the time of Sákya's reformation, the sectaries of Siva felt themselves too weak to combat it; but the uncle of Sákya, placing himself at the head of the *Ters*, adopted their creed and sought to introduce it in the courts of the petty princes of India. Hoping to overthrow Sákya Muni, he summoned the six principal doctors of the *Ters* to oppose his nephew, at a great banquet at which all the princes were assembled: but they all grounded before his supreme understanding. The fifteen kings who were present upon this occasion, met together every day from the first to the fifteenth of the first month; and the six doctors of the *Ters* strove at these meetings to vanquish Buddha by the instrumentality of magic. Unmoved by fear, the latter triumphed over them in a most glorious manner, by the force of his reasoning, and his divine and supernatural power; so that at the end of the fifteen days, the leader of his adversaries was constrained to prostrate himself before him and worship him. All those present rose up, and followed the example. By this last victory his fame and his doctrine were diffused throughout India; and in memory of the event his followers still celebrate the first fifteen days of each year.—Kl.

(23) *To ascend to the Heaven, Tao li.* (See ch. XVII. note 2.)

(24) *To preach the Law in behalf of his mother.* (See chap. XVII. note 3, and chap. XX.)

The Mongol historian, Sanang Setsen, thus narrates how Sákya preached on behalf of his mother: "Six days after the birth of the prince royal *Khamouk tousayi butaghektchi* (in Sanskrit, Sarvártha Siddha, he "who effects the salvation of all,") his mother Mahá Máyá entered nirvána. He obtained in the year *Ting* of the tiger, the rank of Buddha; and six years after in the year *Ting* of the ram, looking one day with the eyes of divine inspiration, he beheld his mother Mahá Máyá under a new incarnation in the region of the thirty-two *tegrí*. Immediately he raised himself thither to guide her in the way of divine sanctity, and remained there ninety days preaching to her the law."—Kl.

CHAPTER XXIII.

Kingdom of Lan mo.—The Dragon's tank.—Adventure of the King A yu with the king of the dragons.—Elephants performing the service prescribed by the Law.

Leaving the place where Foe was born, and proceeding easterly five *yeou yans*,[1] you come to a kingdom called *Lan mo*.[2] The king of this country having obtained a fragment of the *she li*[3] of Foe, built a tower called the *tower of Lan mo*.[4] By the side of this tower there is a tank, and in the tank a dragon who continually watches the tower. When the king *A yu*[5] went forth from the age, he wished to break the eight towers to make eighty-four thousand others. He had already broken down seven towers and was coming with the same purpose to this, when the dragon appeared, and conducting king *A yu* to his palace, showed him the things used in the celebration of worship. Then said he to the king, "If by thy oblations thou canst excell this, thou mayst destroy (the tower), and I shall not prevent thee." The king A yu acknowledged that the objects appertaining to the celebration were not those of the age, and returned.

In this sterile and solitary place there are no men to sweep and to water; but you may there see continually herds of elephants which take water in their trunks to water the ground, and which, collecting all sorts of flowers and perfumes, perform the service of the tower. There were *Tao sse*[6] from various countries who had come to perform their devotions at this tower. They met the elephants, and overcome with terror, concealed themselves among the trees whence they witnessed the elephants performing the duty according to the Law. The *Tao sse* were greatly affected to observe how, though there was no one to attend to the service of the tower, it was nevertheless kept watered and swept. The *Tao sse* thereupon abandoned their grand precepts, and returning became *Sha mi.* Of themselves they plucked up the grass and the trees, levelled the ground, and kept the place neat and clean. They exerted themselves to convert the king and induce him to found an establishment of ecclesiastics, as well as to erect a temple. There is at present there a habitation of ecclesiastics. This happened not long ago, and tradition has transmitted it to the present time. There are always *Sha mi* who administer at the temple.

Proceeding thence easterly three *yeou yan,*[7] you come to the place where the prince sent away his chariot and quitted his white horse.[8] Here too have they built a tower.

NOTES.

(1) *Five yeou yans*, about six and a half French leagues.

(2) *A kingdom named Lan mo.*—Hiuan thsang, who in the first part of the seventh century visited this country, calls it *Lan mo*, writing the latter syllable with a different character from that employed by Fa hian. He also found it desert, and gives nearly the same account of it as our traveller. We must seek for *Lan mo* somewhere to the north or north-east of the present town of Gorakhpore, and to the south of the hills which separate Nepal from the kingdom of Oude. The latter is celebrated as the country of *Rama*, of whose name *Lan mo* may possibly be the Chinese transcription; nevertheless the two towns named Rampúr, situated near where the Gunduk enters Bengal from Nepal, appear to me too remote from the *Rohein* or *Rahini* to be taken for the *Lan mo* of Fa hian.—Kl.

Lan mo appears to me identical with the Ramagamo of the Pali Annals and the Mahawanso. It was one of the eight cities or kingdoms among which the reliques of Sákya were distributed; and was the only one of these, as will be seen from the subjoined extracts, from which these reliques were not removed by Asoka; circumstances which precisely correspond with the details alluded to by Fa hian. After narrating the particulars of the partition of Buddha's reliques, the Annals proceed; "The reliques of the Eye (Buddho) consist of eight *donani*; seven *donani* are objects of worship in *Jambudwípa*, and one *donan* of the reliques of the supreme personage the Nagas worship in *Rámagámo*." Again—"the *Ramagamian Kosaliyans* built a *thupa* at *Rámagámo* over the corporeal relics of Bhagawán and celebrated a festival." The mention of the Nagas worshipping these relics at Rámagámo is another circumstance confirming this identification.

In the Mahawanso we read: "The pre-eminent priest, the then Maha-Kassapo, being endowed with the foresight of divination, in order that he might be prepared for the extensive requisition which would be made at a future period by the monarch Dhammásóko for relics, (by application) to king Ajátasattu, caused a great enshrinement of relics to be celebrated with every sacred solomnity, in the neighbourhood of Rájagaha; and he transferred the other seven donas of relics (thither); but being cognizant of the wish of the divine teacher (Buddho), he did not remove the dona deposited at Rámagámo.

"The monarch Dhammásóko seeing this great shrine of relics, resolved on the distribution of the eighth dona also. When the day had been fixed for enshrining these relics in the great thupa (at Pupphapura, removing them from Rámagámo), on that occasion the sanctified ministers of religion prohibited Dhammásóko. The said thupa which stood at Rámagámo on the bank of the Ganges, by the action of the current (in fulfilment of Buddha's prediction) was destroyed. The casket containing the relic being drifted into the ocean, stationed itself on the point where the stream (of the Ganges) spread in two opposite directions on encountering the ocean, on a bed of gems dazzling by the brilliancy of their rays, &c."

From the foregoing I have little doubt of the identity of Rámagámo and Lan mo, and that instead of looking for the site of the latter to the north of Goruckpore, as Professor Wilson suggests, that it must be referred to the banks, not indeed of the Ganges (a name frequently applied to any large stream) but perhaps of the Gogra, or some other affluent of the Ganges. I may add that *Rammo* is mentioned in the Pali Annals as the name of one of the palaces of Sákya before his adoption of ascetic life.—J. W. L.

(3) *A fragment of the she li.—She li* is the Sanscrit word *sárira*, which properly signifies *corporeal*, and hence the reliques of Buddha and other holy personages. The Mongols transcribe the word *Sarie*. As the bodies of the Buddhas, when these appear in the three worlds, belong only in appearance to *sansara* or matter, their material remains, form no portion of their immaterial and eternal essence. According to a passage of the *Maháyána suvarna prabhása* (in Mongol *Altan gerel*), translated by M. Schmidt, *Routchiraketon*, desirous of being instructed upon this point, thus addressed *Sákya Muni;* "Most gloriously accomplished one! if according to what the four preceding Buddhas have taught, the most gloriously accomplished one hath already attained nirvána before a sárira be left in the world, why say then the Sutras, 'when Buddha enters nirvána the sárira which he leaves in the world are venerated by gods and men with remembrance and religious confidence? by the veneration and ardent devotion with which men and gods have regarded the sárira of former Buddhas, inconceivable merits have been acquired. How does this quadrate with the assertion that these are not veritable reliques? Would the most gloriously accomplished Buddha deign to explain this contradiction, and unfold the truth of this matter?" The most gloriously accomplished one then replied to Routchiraketon and the others present, saying, "The doctrine that the most gloriously accomplished in entering nirvána leave *sárira* to the world, must be taken as provisionary (that is, intended for those who are not as yet enlightened); for, oh son of illustrious descent! the Bodhisattwas Mahásattwas teach that the truly Samaneans and the completely accomplished Buddhas become already indubitably and perfectly nirvána by the ten following qualities, &c." Hence we infer from these words of Sákya Muni that the sanctity of the sárira was intended only for the people.—Kl.

(4) *The tower of Lan mo.*—This tower is not comprised among the eight divine towers spoken of in note 11, Chap. XX.—Kl.

(5) *When the king A yu.*— This is *Asoka*, king of Magadha, great grandson of Bimbására, and grandson of Ajátasatru, in the eight year of whose reign Siddhárta became Buddha. Asoka flourished a hundred years subsequent to the nirvána of Sákya. The Japanese chronological work, *Wa kan kwo to fen nen yakf oun-no tsou* fixes the construction of the 84,000 towers built by *A yu* king of India (*Zen Zik*), in the year of the XXXI cycle corresponding with 833 B. C.

The kings of Magadha had waged long wars against those of *Anga*, a country situated near Bauglepore on the lower Ganges. A short time before the birth of Sákya Muni, the kings of Magadha became tributary to those, and continued so till the reign of Mahá Padma (*Padma chenbo*, in

Tibetan, "the great lotus"). Bimbasára or Vimbasára, son of Mahá Padma, succeeded the latter, and bore the surname of *Srenika*. It was he who encouraged his father to resist the payment of tribute. In the war that followed he killed the king of Anga and added his country to that of his own family. At the time of the birth of Sákya he resided at Rajagriha.*

The Mongol history of Sanang Setsen contains the following list of the predecessors of Asoka, king of Magadha; but their names appear to be translated from the Sanscrit. To recognise them I have given the translation of their names, as it was by this means that I arrived at the original.

Yekè Linkhoa (the Great Lotus). This is the *Mahá Padma pati Nanda*, or Nanda the master of the great lotus, of the Bhágavat Purána, and the *Padma tchenbo* of Tibetan books.

Tsoktsas djirouken (the Exalted Heart). He was contemporary with Sákya Muni and resided at Váránasi (*Benares*). This prince is omitted in the list of the Bhágavat Purána. According to Hindu authors *Nanda*, the Great Lotus, was killed by the Brahman *Chanakya*, who placed *Chandragupta*, of the Maurya family, upon the throne. Tibetan books from which extracts are given by M. Csoma de Körös, make *Bimbasára* or *Vimbasára* succeed his father Padma Tchenbo (the Great Lotus).

Erdeni Sarà (the Precious Moon). This is *Chandragupta*, the moon-protected, the Chandagutto of the Maháwansa.

Margisiri amogolangá oniledouktchi (*Márgasira*, 'who conducts himself calmly'). The Bhágavata names this King *Várisára* ('aqueous essence'), and the Maháwanso *Bindhusáro* ('essence of the drop of water'). The Chinese call him *Phing sha* and *Pin po so lo*, which is their transcription of Bimbasára.

Arsalan (the Lion). This King is the Ajátasatru of Sanscrit books. In the eighth year of his reign Siddhárta became Buddha. Ajátasatru reigned thirty-two years.

Arban terghetou (the ten-seated). This I take to be the Dasaratha (ten chariots) of the Bhágavata. This book makes him second successor of Asoka, and not his predecessor.

Ghasalang Oughei Nomunkhaghan (the king of the law who is without sorrow). This is Asoka (in Chinese *A yu*) who reigned one hundred and ten years after the Nirvána of Sákya Muni. Hiuan thsang transcribes his name *A shou kia*.†—Kl.

Professor Wilson (Ariana Antiqua, p. 322) seems disposed to identify the *A yu* of the Chinese with the *Azes* of the Bactrian coins. He remarks that the name in Arianian letters is *Aya-sa*, that the *y* in this case was

* *J. A. S.* Vol. 1, p. 2. † *Pian i tian*, B. LXV, p. 11.

probably pronounced as *j* (a change which does occur in some Indian dialects), and that *Aja* is a genuine Hindu name. "The Buddhists, says Professor Wilson, indeed seem to identify him (*A yu*) with Asoka, grandson of Chandragupta, who lived, therefore, in the third century B. C., and of whom it is fabled that he erected eighty thousand monumental towers in various parts of India. *This* was certainly not the Azes of the coins, but there may have been some confusion either in the traditions picked up by the Chinese, or in the manner in which they have been transferred to European languages." It seems to me extremely improbable that a mistake of this kind regarding so famous a prince as Asoka could be made by a Buddhist priest in the age of Fa hian, when possibly the very name of Azes had ceased to be remembered. The more correct transcription of the name by Hiouan thsang removes all doubt upon the identity of *A yu, Wou yu*, or *A shou kia* with Asoka.

The phrase "went forth from the age" (sortit du siècle) I take to mean, "abandoned heretical opinions and adopted Buddhism."—J. W. L.

(6) *There were Tao sse.* It is very remarkable that in the course of his narrative, Fa hian should so often speak of the Tao szu who in his time existed not merely in central Asia, but also in India. It would from this appear that the doctrines of that philosophical school were already diffused throughout the countries situated to the west and the south-west of China. We have already seen (Chap. XXII. Note 6,) that the Tao szu *A i* arrived at Kapila at the birth of Sákya Muni and drew his horoscope. The *Tao szu* are named in Tibetan བོན་བོ་ *bon bo and* གཡུང་དྲུང་པ *young dhroung pa* (Sectaries of the mystical cross, in Sanscrit *swastika*). Their doctrine named བོན་གྱི་ཆོས་ *Bon ghü tsiös*, was the ancient religion of Tibet, which prevailed until the general introduction of Buddhism in the 9th century. It still has a number of professors in *Khamyul* or Lower Tibet. They have several works expounding their doctrines, called by the Mongols *Bom bo ün nom.* གཤེན་རབས་ *Chen ræbs* was their founder.

(8) *Sent away his chariot and quitted the white horse.*—In the Maga inscription quoted above, it is said, "Sákya quitted his palace having with him but one servant and a horse; he crossed the Ganges and arrived at Balu Kálí, where, after having commanded his servant to leave him and to lead away his horse, he laid aside his armour." This circumstance of Buddha having crossed the Ganges to arrive at that place, is contradicted by the Chinese translations of Buddhist works. Buddha arrived there from the palace of his father situated in the town of Kapila, and did not proceed till afterwards to the kingdom of Magadha which lay south of the Ganges. The

place called *Balu Káli* in this inscription is named *A nou mo* in Chinese Buddhist works; in Pali, *Anumanam.*

The following is the legend that preserves this passage in the life of the Bodhisattwa: "Siddhárta having attained his nineteenth year on the 7th day of the 4th moon, made a vow to leave his home; and the following night a brilliant star appeared and all the gods in space exhorted the prince to issue forth. At the same time *Kieou i* had five dreams which caused her to waken in great alarm. The prince enquiring the cause of her terror, she replied: "I have seen in a dream mount Sumeru topple down; the full moon fall to the earth; the light of my jewels to be suddenly quenched; the knot of my hair to be loosened; and some one that offered me violence! This is what has alarmed me and caused me to awaken." The Bodhisattwa reflected that these five dreams referred to himself, and on the point of issuing from the palace he said to *Kieou i*, "Sumeru shall not fall; the moon shall continue to lighten us; the brilliancy of your pearls shall not be extinguished; the knot of your hair shall not be loosened; nor shall any offer you violence. Sleep in peace and disturb not yourself on these grounds." The gods then intimated to the prince that he must depart: but fearing that he would loiter or be detained, they summoned *On sou man* (the spirit of satiety) to enter the palace. Whilst all the inmates were asleep, *Nan ti ho lo* transformed all the chambers of the palace into tombs and *Kieou i* and the rest into corpses whose bones were scattered, whose skulls where carried to various places, whose entrails were putrid and green and fetid, and whose blood was extravasated and mingled with pus. The prince beholding the halls of the palace converted into tombs, and amongst these, birds of prey and foxes and wolves, birds that fly and beasts that walk; seeing that all existence is but illusion, change, dream, talk; seeing how all returns to inanity, to which one must be mad to become attached, summoned his squire, and directed him forthwith to saddle his horse. The squire observed that the day had not yet dawned, "Wherefore such haste to saddle the horse?" The prince replied to the squire by this Gáthá: "I take delight in the world no longer, squire; detain me not! Let me fulfil my primal vow and emancipate myself from the sorrows of the three worlds." Then went the squire to saddle the steed; but the steed, prancing, prevented his approach. He returned to the prince and said, "The horse cannot now be saddled." The Bodhisattwa went thither himself and gently patting the horse with his hand repeated these verses: "Thou hast long been in life and in death; now thy labours are about to cease. *Kian the* (the horse's name), only bear me away, and when I have obtained the law, I shall not forget thee." Then was the horse saddled. *Kian the* reflected within himself, 'I have but to strike the ground with my hoofs to cause a noise which shall reach those without.' But four spirits restrained his feet so as to prevent them reaching the ground. Then would the horse neigh that his voice might be heard afar; but the gods so dispersed the sound that it was lost in space. The prince then mounted his horse, and proceeded on his journey. Having reached the gate of the town, the gods, the dragons, the genii, Indra, Brahma, and the four kings of heaven assembled to guide him to the wilderness. The guardian spirit of the gates appeared, and prostrating himself before him, said, "The kingdom of *Kia 'weï lo 'weï* is the most flourishing and happy in the world; why quit it?" The son of the king replied with this *gáthá:* "Birth and death are of long continuance: the soul travels the five paths. If my primal vows are fulfilled, I shall open the gates of *nirvána.*" The gates of the town then opened spontaneously; he issued, and went away like one flying.

He proceeded under the eyes of the gods for the distance of four hundred and eighty *li*, and arrived at the kingdom of *A nou mo.* There the prince alighted from his horse, threw off his precious vestures, his ornaments, and his tiara, and placing them upon *Kian the*, "Take back, he said to his attendant, take back my horse to the palace, and thank on my part the great king and his officers." "I would follow thee, exclaimed *Kian the*, to furnish thee with what may be requisite. I can not return alone; for if thou leavest thy horse and goest into the mountains, many shall be the wild animals found there, tigers, and wolves, and lions. Who beside shall provide thee with food and drink, with water and boiled meat, and whatever is necessary for repose? How shalt thou procure all there? I must follow, I must accompany thee." *Kian the* then made a long genuflexion; the tears flowed from his eyes; he kissed the feet (of the prince). He no longer drank; he no longer cropped the grass; he wept, he groaned, he hesitated tō leave the prince. The latter addressed him a new *gáthá*; "The body, said he, is subject to disease. The vital energies weakened by old age sink into decrepitude and death. The quick and the dead cannot avoid separation. Wherein then consists the happiness of the world?" Deeply afflicted, and weeping, *Kian the* then did homage at the princes feet; and forming his resolution, that gentle steed returned. He had not reached the royal town when at the distance of forty *li* he uttered a dolorons groan. The sound echoed through the kingdom, and every one exclained, "The prince returns to maintain the state." The people poured forth to meet him; but they beheld the horse, led by the groom, returning empty! *Kieou i*, on seeing this, hastened from the palace to embrace the horse, weeping and lamenting her misfortune. The king witnessing the distress of *Kieou i* and of the five officers of the interior, restrained himself and said, "My son consults his true nature." But all the people of the kingdom, having beheld the sorrow of the king and of *Kieou i*, experienced the most lively sympathy. *Kieou i* dwelt on the thought of her loss night and day. The king having summoned his officers said to them, "My eldest son has left me to dwell among the mountains; let five of you by turns proceed and protect him, watching with the utmost care whatever may come to pass."*

The Chinese and Japanese chronology *Wa kan kwo to fen nen gakf oun no tsou*, places the flight of Siddhárta from his paternal house in the year *Y hai*, the 12th of the XXVIIIth cycle: that is in the year 1006 before our era.—Kl.

CHAPTER XXIV.

The Tower of the Charcoal.—Town of Kiu i na kie.—River Hi lian.

Thence proceeding four *yeou yan* to the eastward, you come to the *Tower of the Charcoal.*[1] There is there also a *seng kia lan.*

Going thence again to the east the distance of twelve *yeou yan*, you come to the town of *Kiu i na kie.*[2] It is to the north of this town betwixt two trees[3] on the bank of the river *Hi lian*[4] that the *Illustrious of the Age*, his face turned to the north, entered *ni houan.*[5] There, where *Siu po*[6] long after obtained the law, and where they adored for seven days[7] in his golden coffin the *Illustrious of the Age;* there where *the hero that bears the diamond sceptre*[8] let go the golden pestle, and where the eight kings divided the *she li;*[9] in all these places they established *seng kia lan*, which exist to this day.

In this town the population is scattered and not numerous. There are but ecclesiastics and families of the commonalty.

Thence proceeding south-west the distance of twenty *yeou yan*, you see the spot where all the *Li chhe*[10] wished to follow Foe

* *Pian i tian*, B. LXV. p. 11.
† *Chian i tian*, B. LXXVII. p. 28.

when he entered *ni houan*, but were not permited by him; the place where they detained Foe and would not let him go; that where Foe prepared a very deep ditch that could not be crossed; the place where Foe inferred a happy omen from his begging pot;[11] and that where he sent back his family to raise a stone pillar upon which there was an inscription.[12]

NOTES.

(1) *The Tower of the Charcoal.*—According to the narrative of Hiouan thsang, this tower was more than thirty *chang* or Chinese toises high. It was situated in a forest of Indian fig-trees and covered the spot where the body of Foe was burnt, and where the earth was intermingled with ashes and charcoal. In the *kia lan* attached to this tower the thrones of the four preceding Buddhas were to be seen.—Kl.

The tower here spoken of is mentioned in the *Lalita Vistára*, where after describing the cremation of the Buddha and the distribution of his reliques among eight different tribes, the narrative proceeds to state that the urn or vessel in which the relics were first deposited was afterwards given to the bráhman who acted as mediator between the different parties. "He took with him this vessel to his own city, called the city of Baívotáng Nyámpá, and built a chaitya, and paid all sorts of respects to the relics of Chomdándás, and in honor of them established a great festival. Afterwards a young bráhman called *Nyagrodha*, requested the champions of *Kusha* that they would cede to him the *ashes* or *coals* of the fire on which the dead body of Chomdándás was burned. Having obtained his request, he built in the village of *Nyagrodha* trees a Chaitya called that *of the Coals;* and paying all sorts of reverence and worship to them, he established a great festival in honor of them. There were now in *Jambudwípa* ten Chaityas of the relics of Chomdándás; eight were styled those of the remains of *his body;* one that of the *Urn* or *Vessel* and one that of *the Coals*."* We have no mention in Fa hian of the tower of the Urn. The bráhman who erected the tower over the Urn is called Dónó in the Páli annals; and the village of the *Tower of the Coals*, *Pipphalawano*.—J. W. L.

(2) The town of *Kiu i na kie.*—Hiuan thsang transcribes more correctly the name of this town *Kiu shi na kie lo*, (कुशिनगर, *Kusinagara*), which signifies the '*town of the grass kusa*' (*Poa cynosuroides*). This accords perfectly with the Tibetan translation. r*Tsa mtchogh grong*, "the town

* Csoma de Körös, *As Res.* XX. 316, 317.

of the excellent plant." M. Csoma de Körös, who quotes the latter as the name employed in the *Kahgyur*, places the town in question in the district of Kamrup in Assam ;* but the narratives of Fa hian and Hiouan thsang will not admit of a locality so far east. Kusinagar must have been situated on the eastern bank of the river Gunduk. Wherever it may have been, it cannot have been far from the kingdom of Magadha.—Kl.

The scene of Sákya's apotheosis is erroneously placed in Assam by Tibetan authors. Professor Wilson has with much plausibility suggested *Kusia*, on the road betwixt Bettiah and Gorakhpúr, as the modern representative of the ancient town ; an identification countenanced by the existence of certain evidently Buddhist remains in its neighbourhood, as well as by the correspondence of its position with the Chinese narrative. The remains are thus described by M. Liston :†—" Should a traveller happen to encamp at Kusia, a village situated about 5 kos from the Chapra boundary of the Gorakhpur district, and on the road joining the two stations, it may so happen that his eye may alight on a pyramidal-looking mound of bricks about half a mile S. W. of the Terai, over which spreads a magnificent banyan tree. Should he be of an inquisitive turn, his natural enquiries will be, what is it, and who has the fame of being its builder ? He will be informed that it once belonged to *Mata kuanr ;* a somewhat less ruined brick pyramid with other brick mounds about three quarters of a mile to the west of the object that first caught his observation, will probably be pointed out as Mata Kuanr's fort ; and if it should be observed that our traveller's curiosity is thus excited, he will be told that Mata Kuanr himself lies petrified at but a short distance from his former abode. A walk of about a couple of furlongs from the ruins called the fort, will bring our traveller to the side of a colossal alto-relievo of very respectable execution, surrounded by much carved work, many of the figures of which are well designed and cut, though others of them are of an exaggerated and outré character ; but the features of almost all of the images, as well as those of the principal idol, have been destroyed with an unsparing hand, and with a care worthy of a better cause." The author then proceeds to describe these mutilated sculptures and the local worship still paid to them ; and adds, " Tradition relates that *Mata Kuanr*, on the arrival of a Musalmán army to attack his fort, feeling unable to cope with the force arrayed against him, caused his family and dependents to descend into a well, and he himself having become a stone, lay down on the mouth of it to conceal it from his enemy, and ensure that no disgrace should befal the objects of his affection." Prinsep, to whom drawings of these objects were sent, pronounced them decidedly Buddhist, one being a statue of Sákya ; and conjectured

* *J. A. S.* Vol. I. p. 5. † *J. A. S.* Vol. VI. p. 477.

that Mata Kuṇar was a corruption of *Mrita Kumára*, "the defunct Kumára." Wilson restores however the popular reading, 'the dead prince,' and applies the expression to the prince and prophet Sákya Sinha. But this ascription can hardly be admitted, as the term *prince* is never applied to Sákya after his entrance upon religious life; and when used, the expression is, I believe, rajaputra, and not kuṇar. I incline to think the story of the Musalmán foray may have some historical foundation, and that with the usual addition of accessory fable, it superseded the older legends which these remains embodied. The site and the legend are well worthy of a more particular examination with particular reference to their surmised connection with that last scene in the life of Sákya. In the meantime our decision upon this identification must be suspended, as there are difficulties attending it which are not very easily explained. For instance, Hiouan thsang, as will be seen in note 4, states that Kusinagara was on the eastern side of the Gandak, while the modern Kusia lies many miles to the west of that river. I am not without hopes that this point will be cleared up by the researches of my friend Capt. Kittoe, who in a letter just received mentions the discovery of the ruins of an extensive town to the north of Bettiah, consisting of mounds, &c. and a *pillar with an inscription*. There are ruins also near the Gandak. These may be the site of Kusinagara, although the *name* may have migrated, as not unfrequently happens, to another locality.—J. W. L.

(3) *Betwixt two trees.*—In Chinese *So lo*, in Sanscrit *Sála* (*Shorea robusta*).—Kl.

(4) *The River Hi lian.*—*Hi lian* appears to me undoubtedly the Sanscrit word हिरण्य *hiranya*, gold. In ancient Buddhic works written in Chinese, this river is called *Shi lai na fa ti*, स्वर्णवती, *Swarnavati*, explained to mean, *having gold*. Hiuan Thsang indeed names this river *A chi to fa ti*, which he explains 'unparalleled in the world,' and assures us that the ancient orthography of the name, *A li lo pho ti*, is faulty. It is, as I have said, above the Gandak. In the *Fo siang thou 'weï*, which is a collection of images relative to Buddhism, published in Japan, this river is called *Pho ti ho*.—Kl.

Is the *Hi lian* of our pilgrim the *Erannoboas* of the Greeks? The identification of this river has occasioned much discussion among the learned, as forming for a long time the principal element in determining the position of Pálibothrá. We have now however so much better data for deciding the latter point that the former has become of comparatively little consequence, and the problem is reversed, namely to identify the river from the well ascertained position of the town.

Sir W. Jones was the first to suggest the identity of the Són and the Erannoboas, chiefly I believe from the epithet *Hiranyabáhu* being applied to the former river in Sanscrit books. The same hypothesis was adopted by Wilford and others. The principal difficulty attending this edentification is the distance of the Són from Pálibothrá which according to Megasthenes, as quoted by Arrian was situated near the confluence of that stream with the Ganges: *μεγίστην δὲ πόλιν 'Ινδοισιν εἶναι Παλίμβοθρα καλεομένην εν τῆ Πρασίων γῆ, ἵνα αἱ σύμβολαί είσι τοῦ τε 'Ερανvoβόα ποταμοῦ και του Γάγγεω.* This objection has been combatted with learning and ingenuity by Mr. Ravenscroft, who in an able article in the Journal of the Asiatic Society Vol. XIV. p. 137, endeavours to prove that a former bed of the Són ran nearer to Patna than the present course of that river. It would exceed the space I can afford to enter at length upon this question; but the reader will find Mr. R.'s interesting paper well worthy of perusal. He concludes from a careful investigation of the neighbouring country that the Són, or one of its principal branches disembogued at Bákipur, a few miles west of Patna, and thus in some measure removes the difficulty arising from present course of that river. Mr. R.'s reasoning would be sufficiently satisfactory were it not for the name given by our pilgrim to the Gandak (*Hi lian*, the Chinese transcription of *Hiranya*), and that given in Páli Buddhistical works, *Hirannawattiya*, which seem to give this river equal claims, *etymologically*, to be identified with the Erannoboas, while its position is unexceptionable. This conjecture is not new however; for I find on referring to Schmieder's edition of Arrian published in the last century, that Mannert had suggested the same identification: non procul a Patnis ruinæ veteris urbis repertæ sunt cui nomen *Patelputer*, vel *Pateliputra*, et hæc quidem urbs Palimbothra (Palibothra, Palibotra) veterum esse videtur, * * * Hoc solum obstat, ab Arriano Erannoboam vocari *magnum fluvium*, qui ibi non invenitur; sed errorem in Arriano esse arbitratur Mannert, vel esse intelligendum *fluvium Ganduk*," &c. After all the question is more curious than important, and no fact of any consequence is dependent upon its solution.—J. W. L.

The scene of Sákya Muni's death is thus described by Hiuan thsang: at the distance of three or four *li* to the north-west of the town (*Kiu shi na. kie lo*) you cross the river *A chi to fa ti.* Near the western bank there is a forest of *so lo* trees. These trees are a species of *hoû;* their bark is of a greenish white, and their leaves are very glossy. Four very fine ones are to be seen planted together on the spot where the *Jou laï* (Tathágatha) died. In a great chapel erected in that place is a representation of the nirvána of the Jou laï. His face is turned to the north and hath the appearance of one slumbering. Near by is a tower built by the king *A yu* (Asoka). The foundations are injured, but the tower still stands about two hundred Chinese toises high. Before the tower is a pillar of stone erected in commemoration of the death of the *Jou laï*, on which is inscribed the recital, thus, "Buddha, aged eighty years, entered nirvána at midnight the 15th day of the moon of Bysákh (*Fei she khiu*);" that is the 15th day of the third month. There are some authors who say that Buddha entered nirvána at midnight on the 8th day of the moon of Kártika (*Kia la ti kia*) which would be the 8th day of the ninth moon. As for the year of his nirvána, accounts differ. Some make it 1200 years ago, others more than 1300, others again more than 1500. There are some too that assure us that this event occurred about 900 years ago, and that one thousand are not yet fulfilled since."* Hiuan thsang wrote about the year 640 A. D. These calculations therefore place this event in 560, 660, 860, and even 360 B. C.

The Chinese legend given by Deshauterayes, gives the following account of the death of Foe: "Foe being seventy-nine years of age, after conversing with his disciples and the assembly as one delivering his testament, laid down on his right side, his back turned towards the east, his face to the west, his head towards the north, and his feet to the south, and became extinct. At the same moment many miracles occurred; the sun and the moon lost their light; the inhabitants of the heavens groaned and exclaimed; "Oh grievous event! by what fatality hath the sun of wisdom become extinct! Must all indeed lose their good and true parent, and the heavens be deprived of the object of their veneration!" The whole assembly was melted in tears. The body of Foe was placed upon a litter, but when they were about to carry it to the pile, they were unable to lift it, when one amongst them called out in the attitude of prayer, "O Foe! thou dost equalise (or identify) all things, admitting no distinction among them; thou makest equally happy both men and the denizens of heaven." When he had thus spoken the litter rising high of its own accord, entered the town of *Kiu shi* by the western gate and issued by the eastern; again entered by the southern and re-issued by the northern gate. It then made seven times the circuit of the town, the voice of Foe being audible from the litter. All of the inhabitants gathered at the funeral ceremony, all in tears; and a week having thus passed they carried the body of Foe on a magnificent litter, washed it with perfumed water, and wrapped in rich coverings; then replacing it on its original litter, they poured upon it perfumed oils. A lofty pile was prepared of odoriferous wood, upon which the litter was deposited; fire was applied to the pile, but it suddenly became extinguished. At this prodigy the whole assembly wept bitterly, and awaited till some holy personage should come to finish the

* *Pian i tian*, B. LXXV. p. 1 *v.* and 2.

ceremony. As soon as such had arrived, the litter opened spontaneously and disclosed the feet of Foe encircled with a thousand rays. Again they applied the torches to the pile; but still the fire took not. That holy personage then explained that the litter could not be consumed by the fire of the three worlds, and hence, a fortiori, not by material fire. He had scarcely spoken when the pure fire of fixed contemplation (*San mei;* in Sanscrit *Samádhi*) issuing from the chest of Foe through the midst of the litter, inflamed the pile, which at the end of seven days was wholly consumed. The fire being extinguished, the litter appeared entire without even the calico and the rich coverings with which the body was enveloped being in any degree injured."

Dr. Siebold has published in his *Archives du Japan*, a reduced copy of a celebrated image representing the nirvána of Foe, preserved in the temple of Too fuk si (Toung fou szu) at Miyaho. It was executed by the celebrated Japanese painter, *Teo den tsou.* Sákya Muni is there represented in his ecclesiastical dress, placed upon a catafalque, betwixt the two holy trees, with his head reclined upon a lotus flower. He is surrounded by a numerous group of men and animals, among whom a general sadness pervails; grief is expressed in all their countenances. The apostles and disciples surround most immediately the bier of their master, and are recognised by their shaven heads. The Bodhisattwas have the forms and figures of women, and the gods appear with their ordinary attributes.—Kl.

As the learned French commentators have supplied so few particulars of Sákya's death and cremation, no doubt from the want of the original sources of information since made available, the insertion of these in the present place may add interest to this part of our pilgrim's narrative and be not unwelcome to such of my readers as have not the requisite works of reference at hand. Full details of thes events are preserved in the body of Buddhist scripture, and particularly in the *Lalita Vistara*, of which M. Csoma de Körös has given an abstract in the *Asiatic Researches*, Vol. XX; but the most interesting account is that taken by the Honourable Mr. Turnour from the *Parinibbánansuttan* of the *Maháwaggo* in the *Dighanikayo* of the *Suttapitako*, from which principally I draw the following particulars.

The illness which eventually terminated the carrier of Sákya overtook him while holding *wasso* at *Belugamako*, a village near Vaisali. The narrative proceeds to state that he still retained the full possession of his mental faculties, and summoned around him his disciples, bearing up under the trial with fortitude and maintaining his opinions and professions in regard to the transitory nature of the matters of this life. From this sickness (which appears to have been a diarrhœa) he partially recovers however; is able to sit up in his pulpit and to preach upon a variety of subjects in the chaityas of Vaisali. He there explains that it is in the power of any Buddha by his four miraculous attributes, to prolong his existence indefinitely if duly entreated there to while sojourning in certain holy places which he names, amongst which is the chaitya at Vaisali. Máro (death) interposes his influence and prevents Ananda from comprehending the exposition made by the Buddha, though twice repeated. Ananda retires disconcerted and seats himself at the foot of a tree. He had hardly departed when the impious Máro approaches Buddha and entreats him to realize his *parínibbánán* then. Buddha replies that his *parinibbánán* will take place in three months, and announces his resignation of all connection with this transitory state of existence in the following hymn: "Having voluntarily overcome his desire for this life, the Muni has vouchsafed to relinquish all that is transitory, connected either with his human or his divine essence, casting his existence from him, like a victorious combatant who divests himself of armour." On his uttering this announcement the earth quakes, and Ananda hastens to Buddha to learn the cause of the phenomenon. The latter explains the causes of earthquakes, (as already detailed in a foregoing note) and informs Ananda of the interview he had with Máro formerly, as well as on that day. The *Suttan* then proceeds:

"On this explanation being afforded, the venerable Anando thus addressed Bhagawa: "Lord Bhagawa, vouchsafe to live a *kappo*: for the welfare of multitudes, for the happiness of multitudes, out of compassion for the world, and for the welfare and happiness of the *déwá* as well as men: O Sugato, live for a *kappo*." "Enough Anando, importune not Tathágato. Anando, the time is now past for making this entreaty of Tathágato. Anando, however, made the same entreaty a second and a third time; (and Buddho said) Anando, dost thou believe in the Buddhohood of Tathágato?" "Yes, lord." "Then, Anando, why dost thou now even to a third time afflict Tathágato with unavailing importunity?" "Lord, from thyself have I heard, and by thyself have I been taught, saying: Anando, to whomsoever is fully vouchsafed the sanctification of the four *Idhipádá* should he desire it, he may live a *kappo*, or any part of a *kappo*; and unto Tathágato also is vouchsafed those four *Idhipádá*." "Dost thou, Anando, believe therein?" "Yes, lord." "Then, Anando, in that case, the neglect and the fault is thine—for it occurred not to thee, when that revelation was made by Tathágato, in the most solemn and public manner (at the *Chepála chétiyo*), to comprehend the same, and to implore of Tathágato, saying: Bhagawá, vouchsafe to live for a *kappo*, for the welfare of multitudes, for the happiness of the *déwá* as well as men: O, Sagato, live for a *kappo*. What dost thou now, Anando, still importune Tathágato? Tathágato has rejected thy prayer twice: could he grant it on the third application? In this matter, Anando, most assuredly, both the neglect and the fault is thine."

Buddho then reminds Anando of the various places, all which he names, where he had made this revelation to him before, and finally tells him that having announced that he is to die in three months that destiny cannot be altered. They next repair to the *Kuṭágara* edifice, and Buddho delivers a solemn charge to the priesthood, which he concludes with these words:

"Bhikkhus, I am now addressing you (for the last time): transitory things are perishable; without procrastination, qualify yourselves (for *nibbánan*). At no distant period unto Tathágato *parinibbánan* will be vouchsafed. Within three months from this day, by death Tathágato will realize *nibbánan*.

"Thus spoke Bhagawá, and having so delivered himself, the divine teacher of happy advent again spoke saying: My age has attained the fullest maturity: the remnant of my existence is short: I shall depart, separating (myself) from you, and having earned the salvation of my own (*attá*) soul. Bhikkhus, unremittingly embuing your minds with faith, lead the life of the righteous; and keeping your thoughts under entire subjection, carefully watch over the aspirations of your minds. Whoever steadfastly adheres to the tenets of this *dhammo*, escaping the eternity of transmigration, will achieve the extinction of misery."

Next day Buddha enters Vaisali, and discourses on sundry subjects. Thence he proceeds to Bhágaṇagaron and delivers to the priesthood his discourses, called *Padésa Suttani*, in which he inculcates moderation upon his audience and the propriety of examining dispassionately and with reference to his *winéyo* and *sutto* (*vinaya*, *sutra*) any new doctrine set forth, and to adopt or reject it accordingly.

He then visits *Páwá*, tarrying in the *Ambawano* or mango grove, belonging to a goldsmith called Chundo who waits on Buddho, and invites him, as the *Wésáli* courtesan had done, to a repast the next day at his house in the city of *Páwá*. On reaching the goldsmith's house Buddho thus addressed him: Chundo, if any pork is to be dressed by thee, with it only serve me: serve to the priests from any other food or provision thou mayest have prepared. Chundo having replied: Lord, be it so: Bhagawá again calls him, and says, Chundo, if any of the pork prepared by thee should be left, bury it in a hole—for Chundo, I see not any one in this universe, though inhabited by dewos, maros and brahmos, with their hosts of ascetics, brahmans, dewos and men, excepting Tathágato, who would digest it, if he ate the same. Chundo accordingly buries the remnants of the pork.

Having gratified, edified, and comforted his host, Buddha departs for

Kusinara, the destined spot of his *parinirvana*; an event fast approaching from the predicted effects of the pork. Having reached the *Uppawattana* grove of *sála* trees on the further bank of the Hirannawattiya river, in a very debilitated state, he desires Ananda to prepare his bed between the *Sála* trees, on which he lays himself down (like a lion, says the *Lalita Vistara*) with his head turned to the north. Flowers are spontaneously showered down by the trees upon him; and the air is filled with hosts of *dévas* making the air ring with celestial music, and scattering flowers and incense. Buddha points out these supernatural recognitions of his Buddhahood, and enjoins upon Ananda the stedfast observance of *dharma* as equally acceptable to him. Sundry injunctions are given by Buddha to his followers; and amongst others that his body should be burnt with all the honors of a *Chakkawatti* Rája, which he thus describes: "They wind a new cloth round the corpse; having wound it with a new cloth, they enclose it in a layer of floss cotton; having encased it in a layer of floss cotton, they bind that with another new cloth. Having in this manner enclosed a *Chakkawatti* rája's corpse, in five hundred double layers (of cotton and cloth) and deposited it in a metal* oil-chaldron, and covered it with another similar vessel, and having formed a funeral pile with every description of fragrant combustibles, they consume the body of a *Chakkawatti* rája; and for a *Chakkawatti* rája they build the *thupo* at a spot where four principal roads meet. It is in this manner, Anando, they treat the corpse of a *Chakkawatti* rája. Whatever the form observed in regard to the corpse of a *Chakkawatti* rája may be, it is proper, Anando, that the same form should be observed in regard to the corpse of Tathágato."

Ananda then entreats the Buddha that he would not realize his parinirvana at Kusinara, which was an insignificant and *branch* town, but at one of the chief cities, *Champá*, *Rájagahán*, *Sáwatthi*, *Sáhétán*, *Kósambi*, or *Báránasi*. Buddha forbids the mention of such a proposition, and directs him to summon the Malla princes of Kusinara to witness the *parinirvana* of the Tathágato to be realized in the last watch of that night. These being assembled and introduced, "Bhagawá then thus addressed the beloved Anando: Anando, can there be, or has there been any precept of mine, not imparted unto thee by Satthá (the divine teacher)? No, Satthá there can have been none. If there be none such, Anando, be it understood that whatever *dhammo* or *winéyo* may have been propounded or established by me for thee, the same, after my demise, is to stand in the stead of the divine teacher unto thee. Anando, although the bhikkhus are now in the habit of addressing each other (indiscriminately) with the appellation *áwuso*, after my death this practice must

* The *Aṭṭhakatha* requires this word to be rendered gold.

no longer prevail among you. By a senior bhikkhu, a junior bhikkhu ought to be addressed by the appellation *áwuso*,* preceded either by his family or personal name. By a junior bhikkhu an elder bhikkhu ought to be addressed *bhanté* (lord), or *áyasmá* (venerable). Let no well-disposed priesthood reject any of my precepts, whether they be trivial or important. Anando, after my death, let the *brahmadando* penalty be awarded to the bhikkhu Chhunno.

"Lord, what is the *Brahmadando?* Anando, whatever any bhikkhu may have desired, that Chhunno has been advocating: it is not proper that he should be spoken to, exhorted by, or communed with, by the bhikkhus.

"Bhagawá then thus addressed the bhikkhus: Bhikkhus, should there ever unto any one bhikkhu be any doubt or incomprehensibility as regards either *Buddho, Dhammo, Sangho, Maggo*,† or *Patipadá*, inquire (at once): do not reproach yourselves hereafter saying, although Satthá was personally present to us, we lost the opportunity of making our inquiry personally of him. On being thus addressed the bhikkhus remained silent. Bhagawá simi-larly exhorted them a second and a third time; and the bhikkhus still re-mained silent.

"Bhagawá again exhorted them saying: Bhikkhus, if it be out of profound reverence for the Satthá that ye abstain from inquiring directly from him;—bhikkhus, let one confiding priest make the inquiry through another in whom he confides. Even on being thus conjured the bhikkhus remained silent.

"Thereupon the venerable Anando thus addressed Bhagawá: Lord, this is miraculous: Lord, this is wonderful: I place implicit confidence in this congregation of bhikkhus: not even unto one bhikkhu is there any doubt or incomprehensibility in regard either to *Buddho, Dhammo, Sangho, Maggo* or *Patipadá.* Anando, it is thy faith that impels thee to make this declaration: the omniscience of Tathágato is in the same manner conscious, that not even unto one bhikkhu is there any doubt or incomprehensibility in regard to *Buddho, Dhammo, Sangho, Maggo* or *Patipadá.* Anando, among these five hundred bhikkhus, even the last one, has attained the *Sotápanno*,—the grace that rescues him from hell, and the sanctification that realizes arahathood.

"Bhagawá then addressed the bhikkhus saying: Bhikkhus, I am exhorting you (for the last time), transitory things are perishable: without procras-

* This term implies perfect equality, and as in the order of ordination one bhikkhu must be senior to another, an appellation implying equality applied by a junior to a senior *Upasampadá* is disrespectful and irreverent.

† *Maggo* is the road that leads to *nibbánán*, and *patipadá* is the life of righte-ousness that ought to be observed on that road.

tination qualify yourselves (for nibbánáu). These were the last words of Tathágato.

"Bhagawá then became absorbed in the first *Jhánán-samápati*; passing from the first *Jhánán* he became absorbed in the second *Jhánán*; passing from the second *Jhánán*, he became absorbed in the third *Jhánán*; passing from the third *Jhánán*, he became absorbed in the fourth *Jhánán*; passing from the fourth *Jhánán*, he became absorbed in the *ákásánáncháyatánan*; passing from the *ákásánancháyatánan*, he became absorbed in the *winnánancháyatánan*; passing from the *winnánancháyatánan*, he became absorbed in the *akincháunnáyatánan*; passing from the *akincháunnáyatánan*, he became absorbed in the *néwasannánasannáyatánan*, and passing from the *néwasannánasanannáyatánan*, he became absorbed in the *sannawédayitanirodhan*.

"The venerable Anando then thus inquired of the venerable Anurudho: Lord, has Bhagawá expired? No, *áwuso* Anando, Bhagawá has not expired: he is absorbed in the *wédayitanirodhan*.

"From this *wédayitanirodhan*, Buddho step by step descends again to the first *jhánan*, and again rises to the fourth *jhánan*. In the transition between the fourth and fifth *jhánan*, Bhagawá expired.

We may omit the effects produced on the celestial and terrestrial beings by this event; and pass on to the cremation of the body. Anando having announced the death of Buddha to the Kusinarians and called upon them to perform their allotted duties, the "*Mallians*, the *Mallian* youths, the *Mallian* damsels, and *Mallian* wives—afflicted, disconsolate, and oppressed with grief,—some wept with dishevelled hair, some bewailed with uplifted arms—some dropt as if felled, and others reeled to and fro, exclaiming: Too soon has Bhagawá died: too soon has Sugato died: too soon has the *Eye* closed on the world.

"Thereupon the *Kusinárian Mallions* issued this command to their men: collect then in *Kusinára* garlands of flowers, and procure every description of musical instruments. Accordingly the *Kusinárian Mallians*, taking with them garlands of flowers, every description of musical instruments, and five hundred pairs of cloths—wherever the *Upawattano sálá* grove of the *Mallians* might be, there they approached the corpse of Bhagawá. Having approached the corpse of Bhagawá—with dancing and vocal and instrumental music, and with odoriferous garlands,—performing the prescribed offices, and rendering (every mark of) reverence, respect and submission, they employed themselves that day in suspending cloth-draperies, and erecting tented pavilions.

"This thought then occurred to the *Kusinárian Mallians*:—The time is altogether insufficient to burn the corpse of Bhagawá to-day: we will perform the cremation of Bhagawá to-morrow. The *Kusinárian Mallians*, with dancing, and vocal and instrumental music, and odoriferous flowers performed the prescribed offices to the corpse of Bhagawá, reverently, respectfully and submissively; suspending cloth draperies and erecting tented pavilions, and in this manner they passed the second day also. They in like manner occupied themselves, the third, the fourth, the fifth and the sixth day.

"Then on the seventh day this thought occurred to the *Kusinárian Mallians*:—Having, unto the corpse of Bhagawá,—with dancing and vocal and instrumental music, and with sweet-scented flowers,—performed the prescribed offices, with reverence, respect and submission; taking it out of the southern gate to the southward of the city,—and by the suburb (keeping to) the outside to the southward of the city, we will perform the cremation of the body of Bhagawá.

"Instantly eight *Mallian* chieftains, bathing from head (to foot), and clothing themselves in new raiment, said, we will bear the corpse of Bhagawá. They, however, failed in their effort to lift it. The *Kusinarian Mallians* then thus inquired of the venerable Anurudho: Lord Anurudho, whence, and from what cause, is it that these eight *Mallian* chieftains, who purified from head (to foot), and clad in new raiment, said: we will bear the corpse of Bhagawá—have found themselves unequal to the effort of raising it?—*Wásetthians*, your intentions and the intentions of the *déwatá* are different. What, then, lord, is the intention of the *déwatá? Wásetthians*, your intention is this: we will carry the corpse of Bhagawá with dancing, and vocal and instrumental music, and decorated with sweet-scented garlands, performing every requisite office reverently, respectfully, and submissively, through the southern gate to the southward of the city, and through the outskirts, keeping to the suburb on the southward of the town, will perform the cremation of Bhagawá. But *Wásetthians*, the intention of the *déwatá* is this: we, with celestial dance as well as heavenly vocal and instrumental music, decorated with odoriferous garlands, carrying the body of Bhagawá—performing every prescribed office thereto, reverently, respectfully and submissively—through the northern gate to the northward of the city, and entering the town by the northern gate, and by the central gate, conveying it into the middle of the city, and departing out of the eastern gate to the eastward of the town, there, in the coronation hall, (*Makutabandhanán*) of the *Mallians*, we will perform the cremation of the body of Bhagawá. Lord, whatever be the intention of the *déwatá*, be it acceded to.

"Instantly, every place in *Kusinárá* which was a receptacle of dirt, filth and rubbish became covered knee-deep with the celestial flower *mandárá*—

and the *déwatá* as well as the *Kusinárian Mallians*, carrying the corpse of Bhagawá, with celestial and human dance, as well as vocal and instrumental music, and with odoriferous garlands, performing every requisite office, with reverence, respect and submission; and conveying it through the northern gate to the northward of the city, and entering through the middle gate to the centre of the town,* and departing through the eastern gate to the eastward of the town, deposited the corpse of Bhagawá there in the coronation hall of the *Mallains*.

"The *Kusinarian Mallians* then thus inquired of the venerable Anando: How, lord Anando, should we dispose of the corpse of Bhagawá? *Wasetthians*, it is proper that it should be treated in the same manner that the corpse of a *Chakkawattí* rája is treated. And in what manner, lord Anando, should the corpse of a *Chakkawattí* rája be treated?

"Anando here repeats the explanation that he himself had received from Buddho.

"Thereupon the *Kusinarain Mallians* gave this order to their people: Fellows, collect for us *Mallains* some floss cotton; and then the *Kusianain Mallians* wound the corpse of Bhagawá with a new cloth; having wound it with a new cloth, they covered it with a layer of floss cotton; having covered it with a layer of floss cotton, they again wound it with a new cloth; and in this manner having wound the body of Bhagawá with the five hundred pairs of cloths (which they had brought), and deposited it in a metal oil-vessel, covering it with another metal oil-vessel, they placed the body of Bhagawá on the funeral pile.

"At that time the venerable Kassapo was on his road from *Páwá* to *Kusinárá*, attended by a great priestly retinue, consisting of five hundred bhikkhus: and while the said venerable Mahákassapo was seated at the foot of a tree, having digressed from the road, a certain individual, who was on his way from *Kusinárá* to *Páwá*, passed, having in his possession some *mandárá* flowers. The venerable Mahákassapo observed him as he was journeying on, at a distance; and having recognized him, he thus accosted him: *Awuso*, art thou acquainted with our Satthá? Yes, *Awuso*, I was acquainted with him: the said ascetic Gótamó died seven days ago, and it is from that spot that these *mandárá* flowers were obtained by me. Thereupon among the bhikkhus who were there (with Mahákassapo), some who had not attained the sanctification of arahathood, wept with uplifted arms,—some dropt as

* The *Atthakathá* notices that while the corpse was in the city, the princess Mallaká, the widow of Bandhulo, the late *Mallian* commander-in-chief, invested the corpse with her late husband's official insignia called *mahálatá*, which jewels had remained unused from the time of his death.

if felled, and others reeled about saying ; Too soon has Bhagawá died : too soon has Sugato died—too soon has the *Eye* been closed on the world. But bhikkhus who had attained arahathood, collectedly and composedly submitted themselves, saying : Transitory things are perishable : how can we in this world obtain it (permanency).

" In that congregation, there was at that time one Subhaddho,* who had been ordained in his old age. The said Subhaddho who had been ordained in his dotage, thus addressed those bhikkhus : *Awuso*, enough ! weep not ; bewail not ; we are happily rid of that ascetic, (under whom) we were kept in subjection (by being told), this is permissible unto you—that is not permissible unto you—now, whatever we may desire, that we can do ; and that which we do not desire, that we can leave undone.

" Thereupon the venerable Mahákassapo thus addressed the bhikkhus : Enough *Awuso*, weep not, bewail not ; why ! has it not been emphatically declared by Bhagawá himself, saying : even amidest every community of happy and contented persons, various destructive and changeable issues come to pass ? *Awuso*, how can we in this world realize it (permanency). It is not merely by saying of any thing that is born or otherwise produced, which by its perishable nature is transitory, most assuredly it perishes not,—that it will come to pass.

" At this instant (at *Kusinárá*, four *Mallian* chieftains, having purified themselves from head (to foot), and clothed themselves in new raiment, said :—We will apply the torch to the funeral pile† of Bhagawá—but were not able to ignite it. Thereupon the *Kusinárá Mallians* thus inquired of the venerable Anurudho : Lord Anurudho, whence, and from what cause, is it, that these four *Mallian* chieftains who are purified from head (to foot), and arrayed in new garments, and who have said : we will set fire to the funeral pile of Bhagawá, have not been able to ignite it ? Because, *Wasetthians*, the intention of ths *déwatá* is different. Lord, what then is the wish of the *déwatá ? Wásetthians*, the venerable Mahákassapo, attended by a great sacerdotal retinue, consisting of five hundred bhikkhus, is now on his way from *Páwá* to *Kusinárá*, and as long as Mahákassapo shall not have bowed down, with uplifted hands, at the feet of Bhagawá, so long will the funeral pile of Bhagawá resist ignition. Lord, whatever be the design of the *déwatá*, be it complied with.

" Thereafter, wherever the coronation hall of the *Mallians* might be in *Kusinárá*, thither the venerable Mahákassapo repaired to the funeral pile of

* His history is given at some length, in different portions of the *Atthakathá*—he had been a barber in the village *Atumá*.

† The funeral pile was composed of sandal-wood, and was 120 cubits high.

Bhagawá. On arriving there, so adjusting his robes as to leave one shoulder bare, and with clasped hands having performed the ***padakkhinán***, perambulation, three times, round the pile, he opened (the pile) at the feet; and reverentially bowed down his head at the feet of Bhagawá. The aforesaid five hundred priests, also, adjusting their robes so as to leave one shoulder bare, and with clasped hands, having performed the ***padakkhinán***, perambulation, thrice round the pile, likewise, reverentially bowed down at the feet of Bhagawá. While the venerable Mahákassapo and these five hundred bhikkhus were in the act of bowing down in adoration, the funeral pile of Bhagawá spontaneously ignited.

"It thus came to pass in regard to the corpse of the Bhagawá who was consumed by fire: neither his surface skin, nor his flesh, nor his nerves, nor his muscles deposited any ashes or soot; none (of those parts) of his corpse remained (unconsumed). In the same manner that neither butter nor oil, which is consumed by fire, leaves either ashes or soot—so it came to pass in regard to the corpse of the Bhagawá who was consumed—neither his surface skin, nor his under skin, nor his flesh, nor his nerves, nor his muscles left any residuary ashes or soot: none (of those substances) of his corporeal remains was left unconsumed. All the cloths, composing the five hundred pairs of cloths, were consumed. At the instant that the internal and external parts of the corpse of Bhagawá were absorbed, streams of water pouring down from the skies, caused (the flames of) Bhagawá's funeral pile to be extinguished: the flame was thus extinguished by the down pour on the top of the funeral pile of Bhagawá. The *Kusináran Mallians* also helped to extinguish the funeral pile by sprinkling every kind of scented water.

"The *Kusinárian Mallians* then forming a trelice work with lances, and fencing the place round with their bows (transferred) the remains of Bhagawá to the assembly hall* (within the town); and for seven days, with dancing and vocal and instrumental music, and with garlands of fragrant flowers, rendered every mark of respect, reverence, devotion and submission.

"The *Mágadha* rája Ajátasattu, the *Wédéhian* descendant, heard that Bhagawá had attained *parinibbánán* at *Kusinárá;* thereupon the said *Mágadha* monarch Ajátasattu, the *Wédéhian*, sent an embassy unto the *Kusinarian Mallians*, with this message: Bhagawá was a kattiyo; and I am also a kattiyo. I am likewise worthy of possessing a portion of the corporeal remains of Bhagawá. I will also erect a *thúpo* over the remains of Bhagawá, and celebrate a festival.

* The *Atthakathá* gives a detailed account of the procession which transferred the bones of Buddho, still contained in the metal vessel in which he was burnt, from the coronation hall to the house of assembly.

"The *Lichchhawi* of *Wésáli*, as being also of the kattiyo race: the *Sákya* dynasty of *Kapilawatthupura*, as the relations of Buddho; the *Balayo* of *Allakappá*, as of the kattiyo tribe; the kattiya dynasty of *Ramagámo*, as of the kattiyo tribe; the brahmans of *Wátthadípo*, as being of the brahman tribe; the *Mallians* of *Páwá*, as being of the kattiyo tribe;—all lay claim to a portion of the relics of Bhagawá in precisely the same terms as the message sent by Ajátasattu.

"On being thus addressed, the *Mallians* of *Kusinárá* thus replied to the assembly of emissaries: Bhagawá died within our territory: we will not give you any portion of his corporeal relics. On this answer being delivered,* the brahman *Dónó* thus spoke to the assembly of emissaries: Beloved, listen to this one observation I am about to address to you: Our Buddho was of a most pacific character: it is improper to raise a contest at the moment of the corporeal dissolution of so excellent a being. Beloved, let all of us, willingly, cordially and unanimously, divide the relics into eight portions: many nations are converted unto the *Eye* (Buddho)—let *thupá* therefore be extensively built in different regions. They answered: Well, brahman, do then thyself carefully divide the relics of Bhagawá into eight equal portions. Replying; be it so, beloved;—the brahman *Dónó* according to the request of that assembly, carefully dividing the relics of Bhagawá into eight equal portions, thus addressed that concourse of emissaries: My friends, give me this *kumbhán*, (the vessel with which the relics were measured,) and I will erect a *thúpo* to that *kumbhán*:† and they gave that *kumbhán* to the brahman *Dónó*.

"The *Mórians* of *Pipphaliwano* heard that Bhagawá had died at *Kusinárá*; and thereupon the *Mórians* of *Pipphaliwano* sent an embassy to the *Mallians* of *Kusinárá*, saying: Bhagawá was a kattiyo; we are kattiyá, and are also worthy of a portion of the corporeal relics of Bhagawá: we will erect a *thúpo* over the relics of Bhagawá, and celebrate a festival. They answered: there is no portion of the relics of Bhagawá left: the relics of Bhagawá have been divided: take from hence the charcoal of the funeral pile; and they accordingly did take away charcoal.

"The *Mágadha* monarch Ajátasattu, the *Wédéhian*, built a *thúpo* at *Rájagahan* over the relics of Bhagawá, and celebrated a festival. The *Wésálian Lichchhawi* built a *thúpo* at *Wésáli* over the relics of Bhagawá, and cele-

* The uninjured bones were the following; the four canine teeth—the two collar bones—the frontal bone, with a long hair growing on it, which gave to that relic the appellation of the *renhísa* or hair relic. The rest of the bones were partially injured by the fire. The smallest atoms were reduced to the size of mustard seed; the middling atoms were of the size of half a grain of rice; and the larger atoms were of the size of half a grain of *mugga* seed.

† A measure containing 4 *álhákán*.

brated a festival. The *Sákyans* resident at *Kapilawatthu* erected a *thúpo* at *Kapilawatthu* over the relics of Bhagawá and celebrated a festival. The *Allakappa Balayans* built a *thúpo* at *Allakappo* over the relics of Bhagawá and celebrated a festival. The *Rámagamian Kósalíyans* built a *thúpo* at *Rámagámo* over the corporeal relics of Bhagawá, and celebrated a festival. The *Wétthadipian* brahmans built a *thúpo* at *Wétthadipo* over the corporeal relics of Bhagawá, and celebrated a festival. The *Páwéyan Mallians* built a *thúpo* at *Páwá* over the relics of Bhagawá, and celebrated a festival The *Kusinárian Mallians* built a *thúpo* at *Kusinárá* over the corporeal relics of Bhagawá, and celebrated a festival. The brahman *Dónó* built a *thúpo* for the *kumbhán:* and the *Pipphalawarian Morians* built a *thúpo* at *Pipphalawano* over the charcoal, and celebrated a festival. Thus there were eight *thúpo* over the corporeal relics; a ninth over the *kumbhán*, and a tenth over the charcoal. This is the origin of this matter, (the erection of *thúpos.*)—J. W. L.

(9) *There were Siu po.*—This name is also written *Siu pho tho lo.* Hiuan thsang renders it *Sou po tho lo* (in Sanscrit सुभद्र, *Subhadra*), and translates in Chinese *Shen hian*, that is, '*the good sage.*' He was a master of these bráhmans, and attained the age of one hundred and twenty years. He was contemporary with Anan and the other disciples of Sákya Muni whose doctrine he adopted.—Kl.

(11) *The hero of the diamond sceptre.*—That is to say, the Bodhisattwa, *Vajrapáni*, so called because he holds in his hand a kind of sceptre of diamond, or a thunderbolt.

The name of this Bodhisattwa is translated in Tibetan *Phyough na rdor rdzie*, or *Lagh na rdo rdzie;* that is, ' he who holds in his hand the diamond sceptre.' The Mongols often disfigure the name, writing it Vtchir bani, which they pronounce *Olchir bani*. Pallas and Georgi have given a figure of this divinity.

Hiuan thsang has given the same Bodhisattwa the title of 'the hero of the hidden trace of the genius of the diamond sceptre.' When he saw that Foe was about to die, he exclaimed in grief, " The *Ju laï* is about to leave us to enter the great nirvána; he will no longer improve, he will no longer protect us. The poisoned shaft hath entered deep, the flame of sorrow riseth up!" He then threw down his diamond sceptre, (the golden pestle of Fa hian) and in despair rolled himself in the dust; then rising up full of grief and compassion he exclaimed, " In the vast ocean of birth and of death who shall be our boat and our oar? In the darkness of a long night, who shall be our lamp and our match?"*

* *Pian i tian*, B. LXXVII. art. 7. p. 3–4.

Vajrapáni is the second of the five *Dhyani*, or celestial *Bodhisattwas*.—Kl.

(12) *Where the eight kings divided his she li.*—In the second part of the *Ni pan king* we read, that when Sákya Muni had accomplished his *Chha phi* (cremation) in the village of *Kiu shi*, all the neighbouring states raised armies to contend for his *sarira*, or reliques. There was then a bráhman who divided these reliques into eight parts, in order that the eight kingdoms might each erect a tower in honor of them.

1st. The Champions of the town of *Kiu shi* had a portion of the *sarira*; they erected a tower in the midst of their country and there made offerings.

2d. The Laity (in Sanscrit *Upásika*, in Chinese *Ly seng*) of the kingdom of *Pho kian lo pho*, obtained a part of these reliques, with which they returned to their country and there erected a tower in veneration of them.

3d. The *Kiu leou lo* of the kingdom of the *Szu kia na pho*, the same.

4th. The Kshatryas of the kingdom of *A le che*, the same.

5th. The Bráhmans of the kingdom of *Phi neou*, the same.

6th. The Li chhe of the kingdom of *Phi li* (*Phi she li*), the same.

7th. The Sákyas of the kingdom of *Che lo kia lo*, the same.

8th. The king *A che shi* of the kingdom of *Mo kia tho*, the same.*—Kl.

(14) *Where the Li chhe wished to follow Foe.*—Mr. Abel Remusat had translated this passage, "At the place where the Chu chhe li wished to follow Foe in his pan ni houan;" but the inhabitants of the town of *Phi she li* (Vaisáli) are here spoken of. These formed a republic, and called themselves in Sanscrit *Lichchiwi*,—*Li chhe*, in the Chinese transcription. The same expression is likewise found in the *Ni pan king*, *Heou fen*, where this division of the reliques is spoken of. The name of Vaisáli is abridged *Phi li*; "And all the *Lichchiwi* of that town had their share of the reliques, as well as the laics of *Kiu chi*, the *Chha ti li* (Kshatriyas) of *A le che*, and the *Pho lo men* (bráhmans) of *Phi neou*.—Kl.

(15) *Foe inferred a happy omen from his pot.*—In the 'Abridgment of the doctrine of Buddha Gautama,' written in Singalese and published by Mr. Upham, we read; "He (Buddha) was seated near the river *Niranjara* where he divided the rice into forty-nine balls, which he ate. He then threw the golden pot into the stream, reflecting that if it should float against the current, he should ultimately attain Buddhahood. The miracle indeed occurred, and he proceeded onwards with renewed ardour."—Kl.

(16) To detail all these events in the life of Sákya Muni would require that we should have access to his complete biography, which is not available in Paris.—Kl.

* *Ni pan king Heou fen*, quoted in the *San tsang fa sou*, B. XXXI. p. 4, 5.

Several pillars have been discovered in this neighbourhood. Mr. Hodgson has figured and described* that at Mathia betwixt Bettiah and the Gandak. Another exists at Radhia in the same district, and a third near Bakra on the high road to Hajipore. None of these however is the pillar described by our pilgrim and Hiouan thsang, as they were all erected by Asoka and are inscribed with an edict of that prince: unless, indeed, we suppose with Professor Wilson that Hiouan thsang saw that of Mathia, but was misinformed as to the purport of the inscription; a supposition which does not appear to me very probable. The pillar alluded to in the text has, therefore, yet to be discovered.—J. W. L.

CHAPTER XXV.

Kingdom of Phi she li.—Tower of half of the body of A nan.—Garden of the woman An pho lo.—Place where Foe entered nirvána.—Tower of the bows and deposited arms.—A nan entreateth not Foe to remain in the world.—Collection of the acts and the precepts of Foe.

Thence proceeding five *yeou yan*[1] to the east, you come to the kingdom of *Phi she li.*[2] Here are a great forest and a chapel of two stories; it was one of the stations of Foe, and here you see the *Tower of half of the body of A nan.*[3] There lived formerly in this town a woman named *An pho lo,*[4] who erected a tower to Foe; and still to the south of the town, distant three *li*, and westward of the road, you see the garden which this woman gave to Foe, and which is one of the stations of the latter.[5] When Foe was on the eve of entering *ni houan*, he with his disciples issued from the town of *Phi she li* by the western gate, and turning round to the right,[6] and casting his eyes upon the town of *Phi she li*, he prophesied to his disciples, saying, "It is here that the last of my acts will take place."[7] Men of after times have there erected a tower.

Three *li* to the north-west of the town there is a tower named that of *the bows and deposited arms.* What gave rise to the name is

* *Pian i tian*, B. LXIV. art. 9. p. 3.

this: It happened that on the bank of the river *Heng*,[8] one of the inferior wives of the king was delivered of a ball of flesh. The principal wife of the king observed, "That which thou hast brought into the world is a sign of evil augury." They put it into a wooden coffer, and cast it into the river *Heng;* the coffer followed the course of the stream. There was a king, who looking about observed the coffer on the surface of the water; he opened it, and beheld a thousand little children extremely well formed. The king took them and brought them up. Afterwards, becoming great, they waxed strong and valiant, and none whom they attacked could withstand them, but were obliged to succumb. They came to attack the kingdom of the king their father. The latter was terrified. The inferior wife asked him the cause of his dejection. He answered, "The king of such a country has a thousand sons exceedingly valiant, and without their equals; they are coming to attack my kingdom, and this is the cause of my sadness." The young woman replied, "Grieve not, but construct a lofty pavilion to the eastward of the town; and when the enemies come, you shall place me on the pavilion, and I undertake to resist them." The king did as she said; and when the enemies were come, the young woman, placed in the pavilion, thus addressed them; "You are my children," said she; "why come you thus to rebel and to make war upon us?" "Who art thou," replied the enemies, "who callest thyself our mother?" Then the young woman replied, "If you believe me not, stretch towards me your mouths!" Then pressing with her hands her two breasts, she caused to issue from each five hundred jets of milk, which fell into the mouths of her thousand sons. These enemies acknowledging then that she was their mother, deposited their bows and their arms, and the two kings, in consideration of this event, obtained each the dignity of *Py chi foe*.[9] The two towers of these *Py chi foe* exist to this day. *The Honorable Ones of after Ages* who have accomplished the law, have declared to their disciples that it was here that the *bows and the arms were deposited;* men of subsequent times having learnt this, erected a tower in this place, and hence its name. The thousand children are the thousand Foes of the *Epoch of the Sages.*[10] Foe finding himself at the tower of the *bows and deposited arms*, warned *A nan*, saying to him, "In three months hence I must enter *ni houan*." The king of the demons disturbed A nan and prevented him from entreating Foe to remain in the age.[11]

At three or four *li* from this place there is a tower. A hundred years after Foe had entered *ni houan* a mendicant of *Pi she li* collected all his acts and every thing referring to the ten forbidden things of the law, accompanying them with the very words of Foe. It is thus that at a more recent period, a convocation of arhans and mendicants, who maintained the precepts and were all doctors, seven hundred ecclesiastics in all, examined anew the treasure of the Laws.[12] Subsequent people have erected a tower at this place, which still exists.

NOTES.

(1) *Five yeou yans.*—Twenty or five and twenty miles.

(2) The kingdom of *Phi she li.* This is the Chinese transcription of the name of the formerly famous town of *Vaisáli*, वैशालि ; in Pali *Vesáli* and *Vesaliya puri;* in Tibetan ཡངས་པ་ཅན་ *Yangs ba djian.* The Mongols have preserved the Sanscrit name *Vaisáli balghasoun*, 'the town of Vaisali.' It is celebrated as the residence of Sákya Muni and the scene of his preaching. He came thither on the invitation of the *Lichchivis*, the iuhabitants of Vaisali, who had a republican Government, and were very wealthy. *Hiuan thsang* visited Vaisáli ; he transcribes the name *Fei she li*, and says that the country appertains to Mid-India. He makes it 5000 li in circumference, and says that the soil is fertile, producing fruits, flowers, and grasses. It produces many *An mou lo* and *Meou che* fruits. The country is rich, the temperature pleasant and subject to few vicissitudes. The manners of the people are gentle ; and the people themselves content with their happy circumstances. As to their creed, it is a medley of the false and true. More than a hundred *Kia lan* (monasteries) are in ruins. There remain but three or five, in which there are but very few religious disciples ; these have about ten chapels, live mingled with the heretics, and appear in fact scarcely different from them. The town of *Feï she li* is at present fallen to ruin.

The ancient walls are 60 to 70 *li* in circumference, and the fort (*Koung chhing*, town of the palace) 4 or 5. It is no longer inhabited.*—Kl.

The site of *Phi she li* (the *Vaisali* of the Hindus, the *Wesali* of Páli books, and the *Yangs pa chan* of the Tibetans) is easily identified from the narrative of our traveller. It will be seen that this city was four yojanas distant from the Ganges and on the eastern bank of the Gandak. Precisely in this locality, betwixt the towns of Sinhiya and Bakra are to be found large mounds, brick rubbish, and other unmistakeable evidence of the former existence of a large city on the spot. These have been described in the *Journal of Asiatic Society*, Vol. IV. p. 128 by Mr. J. Stephenson, who also mentions the remarkable pillar alluded to in a former note. "This superb monument is the only remains of former grandeur that has escaped the ravages of time, owing to the solidity of its structure. The smooth polished shaft is an immense solid block of small grained reddish coloured sandstone, surmounted by a singular and beautiful sculptured capital, on which rests a square tabular block, supporting a well sculptured lion in a sitting posture of the same material. This pillar seems to have no pedestal, though from the soft and alluvial nature of the ground on which it stands, it is reasonable to suppose that it must have sunk and buried itself deep in the soil. * * * * The numerous magnificent (though old) tanks amounting to about 50 in number large and small, strengthen the general opinion that this place is the site of a large city, at a remote period inhabited by a numerous and civilized wealthy people." I think there need be little doubt that this was the site of *Vaisali*, so long supposed to be Allahabad, and one of the most famous of Sákya's stations, or places of sojourn and religious instruction. It is well worthy of a more thorough investigation. It was from these ruins that the first statue of Buddha with the celebrated inscription "*Ye dharma hetu prabhava*," &c. was found.

Starting from Phi she li as a well ascertained point and retracing our pilgrim's steps according to his own distance, and bearings, we shall have his route from *She wei* and the approximate positions of *Kapilavastu*, *Lan mo*, and *Kivi i* confirmed. The length of his yojana in Magadha will be found however not greatly to exceed 4 miles as will be further proved by his distances in south Behar. On the subject of the length of the yojana, the following observations by Wilford are not inapposite. After quoting Pliny's account of the distance of Pálibothrá from the confluence of the Jumna and the Ganges, he remarks "that Megasthenes says the high ways in India were measured, and that at the end of a *certain Indian measure* (which is not named but is said to be equal to *ten stadia*) there was a *cip-*

* *Pian i tian*, B. LXIV. art. 9. p. 3.

pus or sort of *column* erected. No *Indian* measure answers to this but the bráhmaní or astronomical *Kos* of *four* to a *yojana*. This is the Hindu statute *Kos,* and equal to 1·227 British miles. It is used to this day by astronomers and by the inhabitants of the Punjab, hence it is very often called the *Punjabí Kos:* thus the distance from Lahor to Multán is reckoned to this day 145 *Punjabí*, or 90 *common Kos.* "*Asiatic Researches*, Vol. V. p. 274. It is not a little remarkable that the length of the *yojana* in the north-west of India as determined by Capt. Alex. Cunningham, from our pilgrim's distances, namely within a fraction of 7 miles, bears precisely the same proportion to the Magadhi *yojana*, determined from the same source, as the Punjabí does to the common Kros. The learned Colebrooke* makes the *Standard Kros* equal to 2¼ English miles nearly, and the computed *Kros* half that, or 1⅛th.—J. W. L.

(3) *One half the body of A nan.*—We shall see in the next chapter how the *sarira* of *A nan* were disposed of.—Kl.

(4) *A woman named An pho lo.*—Hiuan thsang writes this name *An mou lo.*—Kl.

Professor Wilson conjectures this holy woman to be the *Ahalyá* of the Hindus, who lived at Vaisali at the time of Rama's visit; but I make no doubt she is the *Ambapáli* of the Pali Buddhistical Annals, and the *Amra-skyong-ma* of the *Kah-gyur*, described in the latter work as a celebrated harlot of *Yangs-pa-chan (Vaisali).* The story of her amours with Vimbasára is given in the *Dul-va;* where also she is described as entertaining Sákya with great splendour in her grove or garden near Vaisali. As the whole circumstance is interesting from the light it throws upon ancient Indian manners, I shall give it in detail as narrated in the Páli annals. "The courtesan *Ambapáli* having heard that Bhagawán had arrived at Wésáli and was sojourning in her garden *Ambapáliwano*, equipping a superb vehicle for herself, and magnificent conveyances (for her suite), setting out from Wésáli, proceeded to the garden, using those conveyances as far as they could be used; and the rest of the way, descending from the vehicle, she proceeded on foot, and waited on Bhagawán. Having approached and bowed down to him, she took her seat on one side of him. Bhagawán then addressed the courtesan *Ambapáli*, who was thus seated by his side, a discourse upon *dhammo.* He confirmed her faith, comforted her, and made her steadfastly confide (therein). She who had been thus confirmed in her faith, comforted, and made steadfastly to confide (therein), addressed Bhagawán, saying; Lord Bhagawán! vouchsafe to accept the repast I shall prepare for thee, as well as thy disciples, to-morrow. Bhagawán, by his silence

* *As. Res.* vol. V. p. 105.

consented to accept the same. The courtesan *Ambapáli* thereby understanding that the invitation was accepted by Buddho, rising from her seat, and performing the *padakkhinan* (walking respectfully round him) thrice, departed." On her return, continues the translator, she meets the rulers of Wésáli, repairing to *Ambapaliwano*, gorgeously apparelled, and in superb equipages. Her suite compel them to make way for her, and she declines acceding to their entreaty to resign to them the honor of entertaining Buddha the next day; and Bhagawán himself, though solicited by these chiefs, adheres to his promise made to the courtesan. He attends accordingly, and he and his disciples are served by her own hands. After the repast, she takes her seat again beside him, and implores him to accept the *Ambapáli* garden as an offering to himself and his disciples. The offering is accepted; and he preaches another sermon at her house.

There seems to have been no derogation to his dignity in being entertained by persons of Ambapáli's calling and character; for Sákya appears on other occasions to have been similarly favoured by the Thais or Aspasia of the town in which he happened to sojourn.

Mr. Turnour quotes a passage from the *Tika* of the Mahavanso, which would lead us to enfer that there was an office, called *Chief of the Courtesans*, instituted at Wésáli. "Upon a certain occasion, the Lichchawi rajas consulted together, and came to the resolution, that it would be prejudicial to their capital, if they did not keep up the office of "Naggarasóbhini tharantaran," (chief of courtesans, or of the beauties of the town). Under this impression they appointed to that office a lady of unexceptionable rank. One of these rajas receiving her into his own palace, &c."—There is mention made in M. de Cörös' analysis of the *Mdo* of a pious woman named *Nagara avalambika*, who presented a lamp to Sákya; no further details are given regarding her in the short abstract of M. de C., but we might infer from her name that she is another example of a similar official.

The classical reader will not fail to recall many passages, particularly in the dramatic literature of the ancients, which indicate an analogous condition of society in Greece and Rome. On this subject Professor Wilson makes the following interesting remarks: "The defective education of the virtuous portion of the sex and their consequent uninteresting character, held out an inducement to the unprincipled members both of Greek and Hindu society, to rear a class of females, who should supply those wants which rendered home cheerless. And should give to men hetæra, or female friends, and associates in intellectual as well as in animal enjoyments. A courtesan of this class inspired no abhorrence; she was brought up from her infancy to the life she professed, which she graced by her accomplishments, and not unfrequently dignified by her virtues. Her disregard of social restraint was not the voluntary breach of moral, social, or religious precepts ; it was the business of her education to minister to pleasure, and in the imperfect system of the Greeks, she committed little or no trespass against the institutes of the national creed, or the manners of society. The Hindu principles were more rigid, and not only was want of chastity in a female a capital breach of social and religious obligations, but the association of men with professed wantons was equal violation of decorum, and, involving a departure from the purity of caste, was considered a virtual degradation from rank in society ; in practice however, greater latitude seemed to have been observed, and in the Mrichchkati, a bráhman, a man of family and repute, incurs apparently no discredit from his love for a courtesan ; a still more curious feature is, that his passion for such an object seems to excite no sensation in his family nor uneasiness in his wife ; and the nurse presents his child to his mistress, as to its mother ; and his wife besides interchanging civility (a little coldly, perhaps, but not compulsively) finishes by calling her sister, and acquiescing therefore in her legal union with her lord. It must be acknowledged that the poet has managed his story with great dexterity, and the interest with which he has invested his heroine prevents manners so revolting to our notions, from being obtrusively offensive. No art was necessary, in the estimation of a Hindu writer, to provide his hero with a wife or two, more or less ; and the acquisition of an additional bride is the ordinary catastrophe of the lighter dramas." It requires no very intimate acquaintance with Hindu manners to trace the influence of this loose morality in the present day.—J. W. L.

(5) *One of the stations of Foe*, i. e. one of the places where he had preached the law to his disciples.—Kl.

(6) *Turning round to the right.*—The expression here employed by our learned pilgrim has perhaps more significance than at first appears. According to a whimsical notion of Buddhists, all Buddhas, as well as Chakkravartti rájahs, are peculiarly formed in the neck, having a single bone instead of the usual cervical vertebræ. Hence they are unable to look aside without turning the entire body after the manner of elephants. On this account, the farewell look here spoken of by Fa hian, is elsewhere denominated the "*Elephant-look at Vaisalí.*" In the Pali Buddhistical Annals we are told that when Sákya wished, on the night of his escape from his father's palace, to cast a farewell glance at Kapilavastu, the spot on which his horse stood, turned half round, "like a potter's wheel," doubtless in consideration of the inflexibility of neck of which we now speak.—J. W. L.

(7) There seems to have been some doubt about the exact meaning of this sentence in the original. M. Remusat, translates it, "This is the place to which I shall return a long time hence." The version in the text is by M. Klaproth.

(8) *The river Heng.*—The Chinese transcription of Ganga—the Ganges. Hiuan thsang writes it *Khing kia.*—Kl.

(9) The rank of *Py chi foe,*—i. e. Pratyeka Buddha. (See Chap. XIII. note 13.)—Kl.

(10) *The epoch of Sages.*—In Chinese, *Hian kie;* in Sanscrit भद्रकल्प, *Bhadrakalpa,* 'the era of virtuous sages.' According to the cosmogony of the Buddhists, the mundane systems succeed each in perpetual renewals and destructions, having their origin at the second Dhyána, in the kalpa or *epoch of the foundation.* The successive formation of the various regions of the world occupies an *intermediate kalpa,* or the twentieth part of the *kalpa of the foundation.* It is only on the completion of all these formations from the regions of the gods to the surface of the earth, and as far as mount Sumeru, that they become peopled by beings who proceed from the third region of the second Dhyána, which is also the most elevated. This population continues during nineteen intermediate kalpas, till the origin of the infernal regions and the time when the life of man is reduced from innumerable years to 80,000. Then begins the second period, which is the *kalpa of habitation* or of *stability.* During this kalpa, a thousand Buddhas must appear to renew by turns the Buddhic doctrine, and for this reason it is designated the *Bhadrakalpa,* or *kalpa of virtuous sages.* The first intermediate kalpa lasts till the age of man is reduced from 80,000 years to 10; then follows the second intermediate kalpa, in which the age of man reascends to 80,000 years; and so for seventeen such revolutions, which then complete the great kalpa.

The kalpa in which we live is the *Bhadrakalpa,* or *kalpa* of the virtuous sages. A list of all the thousand Buddhas of this kalpa, who have already appeared, has been printed in China, in Sanscrit, Tibetan, Mandchu, Mongolian, and Chinese. A similar list may be found in the Mahayana Sutra, *Bhadrakalpángya,* which has been translated into Mongol. Mr. J. J. Schmidt, has extracted from these two works the list of the thousand Buddhas in Sanscrit. (Ueber Die Tausend Buddhas, read at the Academy of St. Petersburgh, 10 Oct. 1832).—Kl.

(11) *To remain in the age.*—Hiuan thsang thus reports this event according to the legend. "Hard by the garden of *Au mou lo,* there is a tower erected in the place where Foe announced his Nirvána. Foe being here, said to *A nan,* "He that has fathomed the primal cause of the four species

of supernatural properties (in Sanscrit ऋद्धि) may remain an entire Kalpa in the world. Now I have accomplished this age; how much longer should I remain in the world?" Thrice did he repeat the question; but A nan answered not, for the heavenly Mara had darkened his understanding. A nan then rose from his seat and proceeded to the forest to meditate in silence. The prince of the Máras then approached Foe, and said; "The *Ju lai* hath been long in the world! He hath converted and saved as many as there be grains of sand in the dust. Now the Buddha hath attained such advanced age as makes it well for him to enter nirvána." The Venerable of the Age then took a little earth, and placing it on the nail of his finger, asked the Mára, "Is there more earth on all the terrestrial surface than on my finger?" The Mára replied, "There is more earth on the terrestrial surface." Then said Buddha: "The number of beings whom I have converted and saved, is as the little earth upon my finger; while the unconverted are as the mass of the whole earth. Nevertheless, in three months hence I shall enter nirvána." The prince of the Máras having heard this went away satisfied, and withdrew to his ordinary abode.

A nan being in the forest dreamt that he beheld a great tree, whose wide spread branches, were covered with a beautiful thick foliage, offering a pleasant shade. Suddenly a frightful storm arose, uprooted that tree, and scattered it in fragments. A nan then thought, "Is the Venerable of the Age about to enter Nirvána? My heart fears it!" He then went and enquired of Foe, who answered, "Already have I warned thee of it, but thou wert darkened by the Mára. The king of the Máras hath but now left me, and to him have I promised soon to enter nirvána. Behold the purport of thy dream."*

The मार, *Mára*, in Chinese *Mo*, in Tibetan བདུད *dhoud*, in Mongol *Simnou* or *Shimnou*, in Mandchu *Ari*, are powerful demons, who dwell in the heaven *Paraniritavas avartitá* ('that exercises a power over the metamorphoses produced by others'). This heaven is placed immediately below that of the first Dhyána; and is the fourth above the Trayastrinsa, or thirty-three inhabited by Indra and the genii, subject to his authority. The Máras reign over all the six heavens of the world of desires. The chief of the Máras is named Mára in Sanscrit, and *Mo wang* in Chinese. He is the *Kama* or god of pleasure of the Hindus. The Máras are the redoubted enemies of Buddha and his doctrine, which principally aimed at the conquest of sensuality by every possible effort, and they employ a variety of pernicious means to prevent mankind from following that doctrine. To this end they assume human forms, and appear in the world as heretic phi-

* *Pian i tian*, B. LXVI. art. 9. p. 5.

losophers, seducers, and tyrants. Sákya Muni himself suffered greatly from their persecution, and his uncle Devadatta, who sought to counteract him in every way, is regarded as an emanation of the Máras. The life of the king of these demons is equal to about ten thousand millions of years; for one thousand six hundred of these make one day of his life, and he lives eighteen thousand of such years. He bears the title of the 'All powerful Happy One.' In spite of all their opposition to Buddha and his doctrine, the Máras are not after all his true enemies; and in acting as they do, they but augment the glory and excellence of his doctrine.—Kl.

(12) *Examined anew the treasure of the Laws.*—According to the Mongolian History of Sanang Setsen, the first compilation of the sayings and doctrines of Buddha was made in the time of *Margasira*, (Bimbasárá) king of Magadha. At that era, the three chiefs of the clergy, Ananda, Chikhola Akchi, Kasyapa, and five hundred Arhans, assembled together at *Vimala-jana-i in koundí*, and collected the sayings of Buddha relative to the primary principles of his doctrine, the four great truths.

A hundred and ten years after that of the nirvána, when *Ghasalang oughei nom-un khaghan* (Asoka) was master of the gifts of religion, seven hundred Arhans assembled in the great town of Vaisáli, and under the presidence of the monk *Tegölden amourliksan*, collected his saying relative to the principal mean of the doctrine, the nullity of all existence. This king included in the collection of the words and images of the Glorious One, a vast number of objects fitted for spiritual edification.

Three hundred years after that, following the Nirvána of Sákya Muni, when Kanika, king of *Gatchu* (or *Gatchi*) was master of the gifts of religion, it happened that an emanation of *Siumou* (Mára), named Máha deva, became a devotee in the convent of *Jalandhara*, in the kingdom of *Gatchiin Kunasana*, and mixed up unnatural transformations (*Riddhi Khoubilghan*) with religion. For this reason five hundred Bodhisattwas, five hundred Arhans, five hundred Pandits, assembled under the presidence of *Vishnu mitra*, and collected Buddha's dicta concerning the ultimate principle of the doctrine, which was their final completion. This last collection consists principally of the *Dharanis* or formulæ of conjuration, &c.

The Shaster *Chirkola kereglekchi*, translated into Mongol; and quoted in the notes of M. Schmidt, contains the following notice of the dicta and doctrines of Buddha: "The first collection was made in the summer of the year following that in which Buddha entered nirvána, at the head of the river *Routá*, where Ananda and five hundred Arhans collected his first sayings. The collection of intermediate sayings was made one hundred and ten years after the Nirvána, when *Ghasalang oughei Nom-un khan*, of the kingdom of Aghodoughar, was master of religion. It was made by ***Amourliksan***, and seven hundred other Arhans, who collected the intermediate words of Buddha.

"Three hundred years after the entry of Buddha upon nirvána, at the time when Kanika was master of the gifts of religion, five hundred Bodhisattwas and five hundred Arhans, assembled under the presidence of *Vishnumitra* in the convent of Jalandri, in the kingdom of Keshmeri (Kashmír) and collected the last words of Buddha. At this epoch all the sayings of Buddha were collected in books, and they adopted as his true and infallible doctrine fonr great sections which contain eighteen subdivisions. The first great section is composed of seven, the second of three, the third also of three, and the fourth of five of these sub-divisions."

The three compilers of these books after the death of Buddha were *Ananda, Upali* and *Kasyapa*. "A nan, says the *Fou fa thsang yu yuan king*, signifies *jubilation* in Sanscrit. He was the son of the king *Hou fan wang*. He was born on the very day that Buddha attained the supreme degree of intelligence. As on this occasion the whole kingdom was in a state of joyousness, A nan received this name. He followed Buddha, embraced the life of an anchorite, and obtained the rank of Arhan. He is the first among those '*who had heard much*,' and was therefore in the better position to compile the treasure of the law. After the death of the Tathágata, he and Manjusri convoked a great assembly in the '*iron-girt mountain*' and other places where they collected the treasure of the *Sutras*. *Upali*, signifies in Sanscrit, '*born by metamorphosis*;' but the word is also explained to mean '*superior head*,' because it was he who best received the precepts; and as he best understood events, he assembled, after the death of the Tathágata, five hundred pious persons in the *cavern of the Pi pho lo* (the tree of *Pho ti*) and with them compiled the *Vinayas*. Kasyápa signifies in Sanscrit 'imbibed splendor.' It is said that his body was shining and resplendent, and had the property of reflecting other objects. After the death of the Tathágata, he convoked a great assembly in the cavern of *Pi pho lo*, and in other places where he compiled the *Abhidharmas*.* Hiuan thsang states that the sages engaged in preparing the compilation called *San tsang*, or the Three Treasures, collected at first a hundred thousand *Slokas*, or double verses of the *Sutras* of Sákya Muni, then a hundred thousand *Slokas* of the *Vinayas*, and lastly a hundred thousand *Slokas* of the *Abhidharmas*; in all three hundred thousand Slokas, containing six million six hundred thousand words.†—Kl.

* *San tsang fa sou*, B. XI. p. 7.
† *Pian i tian*, B. LIII. p. 10.

CHAPTER XXVI.

Confluence of the five rivers.—Nirvána of A nan.—His death in the middle of the river.

At the distance of four *yeou yan*[1] you come to the *Confluence of the five rivers.*[2] *A nan,* proceeding from the kingdom *Mo kie* towards *Phi she li,*[3] with the intention of entering *ni houan* the gods informed the king *A che shi*[4] of the circumstance. The latter, full of diligence, marched after him at the head of all his troops and arrived on the banks of the river.[5] All the *Li chhe* of *Phi she li* having learnt the arrival of *A nan,* came also to the interview. All having arrived at the river, *A nan* reflected and considered, that if he should proceed in advance *A che shi* would await him ; if he should retrace his steps he would have the *Li chhe* following his footsteps. In his indignation he burnt himself in the middle of the stream ; the flame of the *san meï*[6] consumed his body and he entered *ni houan.* His body was divided into two parts, and one part was carried to each side of the river, so that the two kings[7] had each a half of the *she li* of his body. They returned with these and erected towers.[8]

NOTES.

(1) *Four yeou yans.*—about, 6 miles.

(2) *The confluence of the five rivers.*—Fa hian crossed the *Hi lian* or Gandákí before arriving at *Phi she li,* or *Vaisáli,* as that town was situated several *li* to the east of the river. From Vaïsáli he followed the left bank of the Gandákí to its confluence with the Ganges near the present town of Hajypore, and north of Patna. Several rivers fall into the Ganges betwixt this place and the Sone, so that it is probable the neighbourhood bore in former times the name of the *five rivers.*—Kl.

(3) *From Mo kie towards Phi she li.*—A nan came from the kingdom of Magadha, situated on the south of the Ganges, and crossed that river on his

way to Vaïsálí, to enter nirvána, most probably at the same place where Buddha had departed the world.—Kl.

(4) *Informed the king A che shi.*—This, or rather *A cha shi*, is the transcription of a Sanscrit word which signifies, according to the last section of the *Ni phan king*, '*he who begets not hatred,*' or '*who makes not enemies.*' Hiuan thsang writes the name of this prince *A tou to she tou lou*, and asserts that the ancient orthography, *A che shi*, is corrupt and abridged. The Sanscrit word is अजातशत्रु (he who begets not hatred). He was a king of Magadha, who reigned about 868 years before our era; for it is to that year that Chinese and Japanese Chronology refers the death of A nan or Ananda, namely, in the 30th of the XXXth sexagenary cycle, and the 11th of king *Li wang* of China. Ananda must have lived therefore 130 years, as he was born in the year when Sákya Muni obtained Buddhahood, that is 998 of our era.—Kl.

It is impossible in the present state of our knowledge to account satisfactorily for the great discrepancy between the chronology of the Chinese, and Trans-Himalayan Buddhists and that of the Burmese, Singhalese and Siamese; but it is not difficult to show that the former furnishes sufficient materials for its own complete refutation. In the first place; all authorities concur in referring the death of Sákya, to the reign of *Ajatasatru.* Now according to the chronology of the *Váyu* and *Matsya Puránas*, this prince flourished about 243, or according to the *Vishnu Purána* (in which the reigns of the Saisunága princes are made to average 36 years), about 280 years before *Chandragupta;* and as the latter was a contemporary of Seleucus Nicator, who reigned from 310 to 305 B. C., we have but to add three centuries to the above numbers to determine approximately the era of Sákya's death. If we adopt the chronology of the *Váyu* and *Matsya*, the result will very closely coincide with the Burmese and Ceylonese date of that event, namely 544 B. C. In the second place, the northern authorities aver that the second revision of the scriptures took place 110 years after the death of Sákya, in the reign of Asoka. But the well ascertained era of this prince (about the middle of the third century before Christ) is violently inconsistent with Chinese and Tibetan chronologies, which fix the Nirvána respectively in 949 and 882 B. C. On the whole the balance of evidence and probability is greatly in favour of the Burmese and Singhalese determination of this epoch; and I think there need be no hesitation in affirming that Sákya flourished towards the close of the seventh and in the earlier part of the sixth century before Christ. The events spoken of in the text must have occurred towards the close of the sixth century.—J. W. L.

(5) *On the banks of the river;*—the Ganges par excellence.

(6) *The flame of his san meï.*—The bodies of the Buddhas, Bodhisattwas, and other sanctified personages are, according to the Buddhist notions, held to be incombustible by natural fire, being consumable only by that of समाधि Samádhi, transcribed in Chinese *San meï;* that is to say, the fire of profound religious meditation, which issues from the body of the defunct, and consumes it, in order to reproduce it in all the beauty with which it was adorned in life.*—Kl.

(7) *The two kings.*—It would appear that though the inhabitants of Vaisálí had a republican government, they had nevertheless a king. The two kings of our text are *A che shi* of Magadha, and the chief, whoever he was, of the *Li chhe*, or Lichchawí of Vaisálí.—Kl.

(8) *And built towers.*—One of these towers, containing a moiety of the reliques of Ananda, has already been mentioned as belonging to the town of Vaisálí.—Kl.

CHAPTER XXVII.

Kingdom of Mo kie thi.—Town of Pa lian fou.—Mount Khi che kiu.—Mountain raised by the Genii.—Anniversary festival of the birth of Foe.—Hospitals.—Print of the foot of Foe.—Inscription.—Town of Ni li.

Crossing the river and proceeding southward one *yeou yan,*[1] you arrive at the kingdom of *Mo kie thi,*[2] and the town of *Pa lian fou.*[3] This was the capital of king *A yu.* The palaces of the king within the town have walls, the stones of which were put together by the genii. The sculptures and the carved work which adorn the windows, are such as cannot be equalled in the present age; they still exist.

The younger brother of the king *A yu,*[4] having obtained the doctrinal degree of Arhan, dwelt constantly in the mountains *Khi che kiu,*[5] where he delighted himself in leisure and repose. The king, who revered him, beseeched him to come and perform divine worship in his palace; but the prince, pleased with his tranquil abode among the mountains, refused to accept the invi-

* See Chap. XXIV. note 4, p. 227.

tation. The king then said to his younger brother: "Only accept my invitation and I shall cause a mountain to be raised for you in the midst of the town." The king caused meat and drink to be brought, and called the genii, and said to them :—"Accept, all of you, my invitation for to-morrow; but you must not seat yourselves at table till each hath made me a present." Next day all the genii brought, each one, a large stone four or five paces square. When the assembly was over, he charged the genii to construct a great mountain of stone, and to erect at the foot of the mountain with five great square stones, a stone-house, three *chang* long, two wide, and about 1 chang high. There was then a bráhman of the *Great Translation*, named *Lo thaï szu pho mi*, who dwelt in that town; he was enlightened and full of wisdom; there was nothing that he did not fundamentally understand; he maintained himself in perfect purity. The king conferred upon him all manner of honours, obeyed him as a master, and when he went to consult him, dared not to sit in his presence. The king in token of his respect and regard, took him by the hand; but after he had done so, the bráhman immediately washed himself. For more than fifty years the eyes of the kingdom and its confidence were placed upon this single man. He extended and spread abroad the Law of Foe, so that the heretics could not resist its prevalence.

The body of the ecclesiastics founded very lofty and very beautiful *Mo ho yan Sen kia lan*[6] near the towers of king *A yu*. There are also temples of the *Less Translation*, inhabited by altogether six or seven hundred ecclesiastics. There are also to be seen colleges admirably built in a severe and majestic style. *Sha men* of lofty virtue, from the four quarters of the globe, and students in quest of instruction in philosophy, all repair to these temples. The masters of the sons of Brahmans are called also *Wen chu szu li*.[7] In this country, the *Sha men* of exalted virtue are of the *Great Translation*; the *Pi kheiou* follow their example and obey them; and those that dwell in the *seng kia lan* are all of the Kingdom of the Middle.[8]

The towns and cities of this kingdom are great; the people rich, fond of discussion, but compassionate and just in all their dealings. Every year in celebration of the eighth day of the moon *Mao*,[9] they prepare four-wheeled cars on which they erect bamboo stages, supported by spears, so that they form a pillar two *chang* high, having the appearance of a tower. They cover it with a carpet of white felt, upon which they place the images of all the celestial divinities, which they decorate with gold and silver and coloured glass. Above they spread an awning of embroidered work; at the four corners are little chapels, having each a Buddha seated, with Boddhisattwas standing beside him. There may be about twenty cars, all differing from each other in their ornament and importance. On this day all the streets are thronged with the assembled population. Theatrical representations are exhibited, gymnastic sports, and concerts of music. The bráhmans come to visit Foe; the Buddhas arrive in the town according to their order, and halt at the resting places. At nightfall they every where light lanterns in the places where they perform gymnastic sports, and where concerts are given in honor of the fête. People repair thither from all the provinces, and the delegates whom the chiefs of the kingdoms maintain in the town, have each established there a *Medicine-house of happiness and virtue.*[10] The poor, the orphans, the lame, in short all the sick of the provinces repair to these houses, where they receive all that is necessary for their wants. Physicians examine their complaints; they are supplied with meat and drink according to expedience, and medicines are administered to them. Every thing contributes to soothe them: those that are cured go away of themselves. The king *A yu*, having destroyed seven towers, erected eighty-four thousand others. The great tower which he first erected is about three *li* south of the town. Before this town is the print of the feet of Foe;[11] they have there erected a temple, the gate of which is turned to the tower, and faces the north. To the south of the tower there is a pillar about four or five *chang* in circumference, and at least three *chang* high; upon this pillar is an inscription to this effect:—"The king *A yu* gave *Yan feou thi* to the priesthood of the four parts; he redeemed it from them with silver; and this three times." At three or four hundred paces to the north of this tower, the king *A yu* formerly built the town *Ni li.*[12] In the centre there is a pillar of stone, also three *chang* high, upon the summit of which is placed a lion. Upon this pillar is an inscription which rehearses the foundation of the town of *Ni li*, the reason for building it, and the year, the day, and the month.

NOTES.

(1) *The space of one yeou yan.*—About 4 miles.

(2) *The kingdom of Mo kie thi.*—The name of this kingdom is transcribed by other Chinese authors, *Mo kia tho*, and *Mo kie tho;* it is *Magadha*, or South Behar, situated south of the Ganges. Fa hian is the first Chinese author who makes mention of this kingdom, which in A. D. 647, sent an embassy to the emperor *Taï tsoung* of the dynasty of the *Thang.* According to the account of western countries annexed to the history of this dynasty, it appertained to Mid-India, and was a hundred thousand *li* in circumference. The soil is fertile and produces different kinds of grain, amongst others a variety of rice, called the '*rice of great folks.*' The king resides in the town of *Kiu che kie lo pou lo*, called also *Kiu sou mo pho lo*, and town of *Po to li tsu*, which extends on the north as far as the river *King kia* (Ganges).

The memoir upon the western countries under the great Thang dynasty also calls it the kingdom of *Mo kie tho*, and gives it likewise one hundred thousand *li* in circuit. It adds that there were few large towns, but many villages and hamlets. The emperor *Kao tsoung* of the same dynasty, who reigned betwixt A. D. 650 and 683, dispatched as ambassador to the kingdom of Magadha *Wang yuan thse*, who erected a monument with an inscription in the temple *Mo ho phou thi.* At a later period the emperor *Te tsoung* (780-804) presented a bell with an inscription to the temple of *Na lan tho.* This is the last mention of Magadha in Chinese history.*

According to the last section of the *Ni phan king*, *Mo kia tho*, or Magadha, signifies in Sanscrit '*excess of goodness.*'—Kl.

* *Pian i tian*, B. LXV. p. 8 *verso.*

The *Na lan tho* mentioned in the foregoing note is the *Nálanda* of the Pali Buddhistical annals, situated at one yojana distant from Rajágriha. See note 6, Chap. XXVIII.—J. W. L.

(3) *The town of Pa lian fou,*—the ancient transcription of Palibothra, so celebrated in classical history. Hiuan thsang names it *Pho ta li tsu chhing*, that is to say, the town of the Son of the (tree) Pho ta li. We shall see lower down the origin of this name, which in Sanscrit (पाटलिपुत्र Pátaliputra) has the same signification. The Chinese translate the latter part of the name *putra, son*, by the character *tsu*, having the same meaning. They do the like in other cases; for instance, they express the name *Sáriputra* (in Pali, *Sáriputtó*) the son of the Sáras or Sári, by *She li tsu*, as well as *She li fou*, in which latter case the *fou* represents the Sanscrit *putra*, or Pali *putto*, as in the case of *Pa lian fou* of Fa hian; for in the common dialect the syllable *fou* is pronounced *fout*.

As for this transcription *Pa lian fou*, it coincides remarkably with the Παλίμβοθρα of Arrian and Stephen of Byzance, whilst the true Sanscrit orthography, *Pátaliputra*, which has no nasal after the syllable *li*, corresponds better with the Παλίβόθρα of Ptolemy and Strabo. The illustrious Rennell has already sufficiently shown (Mem. of a Map of Hind. p. 49) that this town, which Arrian calls the greatest in India, and places in the country of the Prasii, at the embouchure of the Erranoboas into the Ganges, was situated in the neighbourhood of Patna, below the confluence of the Sone with that river. The Sone indeed bears the appellation, हिरण्यबाहु *Hiranyabáhu* (golden arm), and हिरण्यवाह *Hiranyabáha* (rolling gold): and one of these two names has been changed by the Greeks into *Erranoboas*.

The name Pátaliputra given to this town, signifies the '*Son of the tree Pátali.*' The following extract (640 A. D.) from the '*Memoir regarding western countries under the Thang*,' thus accounts for the origin of the name.

"To the south of the river *Khing kia* (Ganges) is the ancient town; it is seventy *li* in circumference; its site is vacant and covered with jungle: neither foundations nor ruins are to be seen. Formerly, when the age of man still consisted of innumerable years, it bore the name of *Kiu sou mo phou lo*, that is, 'the city of the palace of odorous flowers,' (in Sanscrit, कुसुमपुर Kusumapura, 'flowery town.') The Royal palace was filled with flowers, and hence its name. When the age of man was no more than a thousand years, it was called *Pho to li tsu*, town of the Son of Pho to li, and not as formerly written, *Pa lian fou*. There was then a bráhman endowed with lofty faculties and immense knowledge. The number of his disciples amounted to a thousand, whom he instructed in all things relating to the sciences. His disciples, going forth one day to promenade, observed one of their companions dejected and sorrowful; they asked him what afflicted him. He replied: 'The most perfect beauty and strength, so much admired, are impeded in their progress; the arts acquired in so many years and months, are not perfected; this is that which afflicts my heart.' The other disciples rallied him with pleasantry; 'Come, he talks of soon having a son; we must have him married. Let us therefore name two amongst us who shall be the father and mother of the youth, and two who shall be the father and mother of the maiden." They went to some distance, sat under the tree Po to li (पाटलि) and called it the *tree of the husband of the maiden.* They gathered ripe fruits, drew limpid water, and prepared every thing for the nuptial ceremony. He who represented the father of the damsel being satisfied that the time was auspicious for the union, took up a flowering branch and presented it to the disciple, saying, 'The moment is propitious for your nuptials; be happy and separate no more.' These words filled the heart of the youth with joy. Towards evening, when all were about to return home, he, absorbed in amorous contemplation, would remain behind. The other disciples said to him. "What we have been doing, is a bit of mere pleasantry; come away with us; the woods are full of savage animals that will tear you to pieces.' But the young man left them, and walked towards the tree. When night had spread out her shades, a strange light illumined the plain; the ropes of a beautiful pavilion, adorned with curtains, were stretched out, and every thing properly arranged. Suddenly a venerable old man, resting upon a staff, made his appearance, as also an old woman leading a young damsel. These two personages received him graciously; the way was filled with people, all gaily decked, and singing, and playing musical instruments. The old man showed him the young maiden and said 'Behold your newly espoused!' Feast and song and music and rejoicing were kept up for seven days. Meanwhile the other disciples, fearing that their companion had been torn by wild beasts, went in search of him. When they saw him they entreated him to return; but he refused and followed not. Sometime afterwards, he came of his own accord to the town to visit his parents, and narrated to them what had happened. All who heard the tale were astonished. He conducted his friends to the forest, showed them the tree covered with flowers, and a great train of servants and slaves and horses coming and going. The old man approached to receive them, and entertained them with a dinner accompanied with music. Lastly, after that the master of the house had shown them every fitting attention, these friends returned to the town, and told of what they had seen wherever they went. At the end of a year a son was born (to the disciple), who then said to his wife, 'I would now return to my home; grieve not at my departure; and prevent it not; I will come back and abide with you.' His wife imparted what she had heard to the old white-headed man, to whom the disciple then said, 'In order that man should live happily, it is necessary that he should dwell in an inhabited place. Let houses therefore be constructed and think of nought else.' All the servants set forthwith to work and completed the task in a few days. This was '*the ancient town of oderiferous flowers*,' which received of this son, and because it was constructed by the genii, was called '*the town of the Son of the Pho to li.*"*

Although the notions received from Sanscrit works by Col. Wilford with the assistance of his pandits are not altogether free from suspicion, I must not omit to state here what he says of Pátaliputra, and the signification of the name. *Kushumapura* was, according to the Bráhmánda, built by the king *Udasi*, grandfather of Maha Bali (called also *Nanda*, and *Maha padma*). Kusumapura signifies the *City of flowers*, and was likewise called the city of the Lotus, *Padmavatí*. According to tradition its ancient site was at *Phulwari*, the name of which, in the spoken dialects, has the same signification as Kusumapura. The Ganges having altered its course, this town was gradually removed to Phulwari, or the present Patna, also called Pátaliputra, after the son of one form of *Dévi*, who took the name of *Pátalí dévi*, the slender goddess. Her son was named *Pátalíputra*, and the town *Pátalíputra pura*. This etymology of Col. Wilford's is untenable however, as the name of the town is पाटलिपुत्र, and not पातलिपुत्र. In another memoir Wilford places Pátalíputra, or Kusumapura, ten leagues west-south-west of Patna,† in which he may be perfectly justified.—Kl.

The narratives of Fa hian and Hiuan thsang leave no room to doubt that Patna is the true position of Palibothra. Another account of the mythological origin of this town is given by Mr. Ravenshaw, in the Journal of the Asiatic Society for February 1845, to which I refer the reader.

The approximate date of the foundation of this town, or of its erection into the capital of the empire may, I think, be ascertained with tolerable certainty. In the first place *Pátaliputra* is no where mentioned (as far as I can ascertain) in the Buddha scriptures, although Sákya must have frequently passed in its neighbourhood, if not over its actual site, in his various journeys to and from betwixt Vaisali and Rájagriha. This negative evidence would be sufficient to establish the non-existence of this famous city in that age;

* *Pian i tian*, B. LXV. p. 9 v. and seq. † *Asiat. Res.* Vol. IX. p. 36, 37.

and is further confirmed by a passage in the Páli Buddhistical Annals from which we learn that two ministers of the king of Magadha (no doubt Ajátasatru) were engaged in the erection of a citadel at the village of Pátali, as a check upon the *Wajjians*, at the time when Sákya passed that way for the last time en route to Kusinagara. On that occasion he prophesied that *Pátali* would become a great city, and predicted its destruction by fire, by water, and by treachery. It would further appear that the inhabitants of this village suffered great hardship and extortion by being turned out of their houses for a fortnight or a month at a time, to accommodate the officers and messengers continually passing and repassing betwixt Vaisali and Rájagriha. To avoid these oppressions they built an *áwásathágaran*, or rest-house for the accommodation of travellers. All this quadrates well with Hindu accounts ; for in the *Váyu* (see Wilson, *Vishnu Purána*, p. 467,) *Udayaswa* the son of *Ajátasatru*, is stated to have built *Kusumapura*, or Pátaliputra, "on the southern angle of the Ganges." This might be about two centuries before the reign of Chandragupta, giving ample time for the city to attain the extent and magnificence ascribed to it by Megasthenes.

The condition of Pátaliputra in the seventh century, as described in the foregoing note, sufficiently accounts for the obliteration of all trace of that ancient city in the present day. Nevertheless, the surrounding neighbourhood seems well worthy the diligent investigation of the antiquarian.—J. W. L.

(4) *The younger brother of king A yu.*—Hiuan thsang says he was named *Mo hi yan tho lo*, that is, 'the great emperor,' and that he was born of the same mother, as *A yu* or *A soka*. *Mo hi yan tho lo* is the Sanscrit महेन्द्र, *Mahendra*, which signifies pretty nearly as given above,—'the greatly powerful,' 'the sovereign.'—Kl.

The sanctified character of this *Mahendra*, would lead us to infer that he is identical with the *Mahindo* of the *Mahavansa*, the celebrated apostle of Buddhism in Ceylon. But in that work he is stated to be the son, and not the brother, of Asoka, who it will be remembered, is said to have slain all his brothers, save one.—J. W. L.

(5) *In the hill Khi che kiu.*—This hill, situated in the kingdom of Magadha, and forming part of the chain which traverses South Behar from the Sone to Rajmahal, will be more fully described in Chapter XXIX. It is named *Ky ly tho lo kiu ta*, in the narrative of Hiuan thsang. This is the transcription of the Sanscrit गृध्रकूट *Gridhrakuta*, 'the Peak of the Vulture.' The Chinese translate the name *Tsieou fung ;* they call it also *Ling tsieou fung*, or 'Peak of the supernatural Vulture.' This is one of the places where Sákya Muni longest dwelt and preached. It bears at present the name of Giddore in our maps.—Kl.

(6) ***Ma ho yan Seng kia lan.***—Monasteries of those monks who studied the *great translation*.—Kl.

(7) ***Are also called Wen chu szu li.***—One of the Chinese transcriptions of Manjusrí, a Buddhist divinity already spoken of in Note 29, Chap. XVI. It is also an honorific title applied to the most learned bráhmans.—Kl.

(8) ***Are all of the kingdom of the middle***, that is, मध्यदेश, *Madhyadésa*, in Páli, Majjadésa, or Central India. Under this title is comprised the entire country between *Kurukshétra* on the north, *Allahabad* on the south, the *Himalayas* to the east, and the *Vindhya* mountains to the west; including therefore the present provinces of Allahabad, Agra, Delhi, Oude, Behar, &c.—Kl.

(9) *The eighth day of the moon Mao*—that is the fourth moon, the character *Mao* being the fourth of the ten signs of the cycle of twelve. It is the anniversary of the birthday of Sákya Muni, and is celebrated to this day amongst all Buddhists with the greatest solemnity. It is distinguished in the Court Almanac of Pekin, as 'the holy birthday of *Shy kia wen foe.*' The Mongols call it the 'moon of grace.' The Kalmuks celebrate this festival from the 8th to the 15th of the first month of summer, and consequently the fourth of the year, i. e. in the middle of the month of May.—Kl.

In my former note upon the Bauddha procession at *Yu thian* (see page 21,) I omitted to mention a very singular fact which strongly confirms my opinion that the modern procession of Jagannáth originates in the Buddhist practice described by Fa hian. It is this, that in the ordinary native pictures of the *Avataras* of Vishnu, the ninth *avatar*, বৌদ্ধ অবতার (*Bauddha avatár*), is represented by a figure of *Jagannáth* or the *Rath Játtrá.* I have failed to ascertain from pandits any explanation of this. In the *Vishnu purána*, Vishnu is represented as becoming incarnate in the person of Buddha, for purposes of illusion; a convenient artifice of the bráhmans to dispose of all difficulties attending the popularly admitted supernatural character of Sákya; but this does not explain the circumstance of Jagannáth being regarded as typifying the Bauddhávatár. The circumstance would seem to indicate an under current of popular tradition which had survived the changes of national religion and all the efforts of the priesthood to suppress it.

Since writing the note above alluded to, I have perused some admirable observations upon the intermixture of Buddhism with Hinduism by the Rev. Dr. Stevenson of Bombay, who upon grounds nearly similar, infers the Buddhist origin of the festival of Jagannáth.* In the same volume is a highly interesting paper by the same author upon a *Bauddha-Vaishnava* sect in the

* *See the Journal of the Royal Asiatic Society*, Vol. VII. pp. 7, 8.

Marhatta country, in Guzerat, Central India, and the Carnatic. These sectaries worship Vishnu under the name *Pandurang*, or *Vitthal*, whom they recognise as the ninth or Bauddha avatár, undertaken however, not for the purpose of deluding mankind, but for the more rational purpose of instructing them and leading them in the way of salvation. In their writings these sectaries speak slightingly of the Vedas, of the bráhmans, and of Hindu superstitions; while their own practices seem to be essentially Buddhist. Dr. Stevenson's paper well merits a careful perusal. The subject of Indian syncretisms has never yet been sufficiently studied; and until it be so we can not hope to attain to any adequate comprehension of the strange and heterogeneous character of Hindu superstition.—J. W. L.

(10) *Medicine-house of happiness and virtue.*—The *Medicine-houses* or hospitals here alluded to were very probably established in conformity with the commands of Asoka, the second of whose famous edicts, still extant upon the rocks of Dhauli and Girinar, is thus translated by the late James Prinsep: "Every where within the conquered provinces of rája Piyadasi, the beloved of the gods, as well as in the parts occupied by the faithful, such as *Chola*, *Pida*, *Satiyaputra*, and *Ketalaputra*, and even as far as *Tamba panni* (Ceylon),—and moreover within the dominions of Antiochus the Greek (of which Antiochus' generals are the rulers), every where the heaven-beloved rája Piyadasi's double system of medical aid is established; both medical aid for men, and medical aid for animals: together with medicaments of all sorts which are suitable for men and suitable for animals. And wherever there is not (such provision), in all such places they are to be prepared, and to be planted; both root drugs and herbs, wheresoever there is not (a provision of them), in all such places shall they be deposited and planted."

These incidental correspondences are of infinite value in confirming the narrative of our pilgrim, as well as for the sure light they throw upon ancient manners. The reader will no doubt be reminded by the foregoing edict of the singular institution at Surat, known by the name the *Banyan hospital*, too often described by European visitors to require further notice here. The circumstance did not escape the observation of Prinsep, who boldly, but not without plausibility, remarks "If proper inquiry were directed to this building, I dare say it would be discovered to be a living example (the only one that has braved twenty centuries), of the humane acts of Asoka, recorded at no great distance on a rock in Guzerat."—J. W. L.

(11) *The print of the feet of Foě.*—Hiuan thsang also saw and discribed these footprints. They were one foot eight inches long, and six inches broad. The prints of both feet exhibited the figure of a heel and ten toes.

They were surrounded with garlands and speckled fishes, which shone with great brilliancy in serene and clear weather. Formerly, he adds, when the Jou laï had resolved upon entering nirvána, and was upon the point of proceeding towards the north to the city of *Kiu shi na*, he looked back upon the kingdom of *Mo kie tho*, standing upon this stone, and said to A nan: "For a long time I leave the impress of these feet in the kingdom of Mo kie tho; for I am about to enter extinction." One hundred years after, the '*King without sorrow*,' Asoka, reigned, and caused a palace to be erected in this place. He became converted by the help of the *three precious ones*, and became a servant of the divinities, as did also the kings, his successors. He there established his abode, built there a town, and erected a monument over the footprints which are near the palace, and which he ever zealously revered. Subsequently the kings of other countries endeavoured actually to remove this stone: but however numerous the labourers they employed, they were wholly unable to effect their purpose. Not long ago (this is written in the first half of the 7th century) the king *She shang kia*, who persecuted and sought to abolish the law of Buddha, tried also to destroy this stone and its holy impressions; but as often as he effaced the latter they were renewed in their original condition. He then caused the stone to be thrown into the *Khing kia* (Ganges); but the stream of that river reconveyed it to its ancient site.*—Kl.

(12) *And this three times.*—Hiuan thsang, who visited these places about two hundred years subsequently, found the characters of this inscription nearly effaced. He states that its purport was 'The *king without sorrow*,' firm in the faith, thrice made a gift of *Jambudwípa* (India) to the priests of the law of Buddha, and thrice redeemed it with all his pearls and all his treasures.†—Kl.

It is remarkable that in none of the inscriptions of this prince yet discovered, is he mentioned by his historical name, *Asoka*, but by that of *Piyadasi*.—J. W. L.

(13) *The town of Ni li.*—I nowhere find other mention of this town, which must be the residence mentioned in note 11.—Kl.

* *Pian i tian*, B. LXV. p. 13. † *Ibid.*

CHAPTER XXVII.

Mountain of the Isolated Rock.—Hamlets of Na lo.—New town of the Royal Residence.—Ancient residence of the king Ping cha.—Garden of An pho lo.

Thence proceeding south-west, you reach, at the distance of nine *yeou yan*, the *little mountain of the isolated rock.*[1] On its summit is a stone building facing the south. Foe being seated there, the king of heaven, *Shy,*[2] caused the *khin*[3] to be struck by the celestial musicians, *Pan che,*[4] in honor of the Buddha. The Lord of Heaven, *Shy,* questioned him regarding the forty-two things,[5] drawing each with his finger upon the stone: the remains of these drawings still exist. In this place also there is a *seng kia lan.* Thence going towards the south-west one *yeou yan*, you come to the hamlets of *Na lo.*[6] It was here that *She li foe*[7] was born. *She li foe* having returned to this village, entered also *ni houan.* They there built a tower, which still exists.

Thence going to the west the distance of one *yeou yan*, you come to the *New Town of the Royal Residence.*[8] This new town was built by the king *A che shi.* In the midst there are two *seng kia lan.* On leaving by the western gate, you arrive, at the distance of three hundred paces, at a tower raised by king *A che shi*, when he obtained a portion of the reliques of Foe: it is lofty, grand, beautiful, and majestic.

Leaving the town on the southern side, and proceeding four *li* to the south, you enter a valley which leads to the *Five Hills.* These five hills form a girdle like the walls of a town; it is the *Ancient Town of the king Ping sha.*[9] From east to west it may extend five or six *li*, and from north to south, seven or eight. Here is, the place where *She li foe* and *Mou lian* first beheld *O pi*;[10] the place were *Ni kian tse* made a pit filled with fire, and served poisoned food to Foe;[11] and that where the black elephant of the king *A che shi*,[12] having drunk wine, sought to injure Foe.

At the north-east angle of the town, the ancients erected a chapel in the garden where *An pho lo*[13] invited Foe and twelve hundred and fifty of his disciples to do them honor; this chapel still exists.

The town is entirely desert and uninhabited.

NOTES.

(1) *The little hill of the isolated rock*;—in Chinese, *Siao kou shy shan.*—Hiuan thsang calls this mountain *Yn tho lo shi lo kiu ho*, that is, इन्द्रशिलगुहा, *Indrasilaguhá* ('the cavern of the rocks of Indra.') He states that it hath deep valleys abounding in flowers, woods, and bushy thickets; its summit crowned with two peaks rising strait up.*—Kl.

We have now come to a country so abundant in Buddhist remains that the very number of these makes it perplexing to determine our pilgrim's route. Capt. Kittoe supposes that the *seng kia lan* here referred to is Behar, near which is an isolated rock now surmounted by a Muhammadan shrine.† I believe that I am myself to blame for having led him into error upon this point, by omitting to send him, when engaged in these identifications, the corresponding portion of Hiuan thsang's itinerary, in which, as will be seen above, this hill is denominated *Yu tho lo she lo kin ho* (*Indrasilaguhá*), and placed contiguous to *Keou li kia*,—evidently *Giriyek*. This establishes the length of the yojana in Magadha to be just 4½ miles; a value which answers very well for the rest of our pilgrim's journey through that neighbourhood.—J. W. L.

(2) *The king of heaven, Shy*;—that is, शक्र, *Sakra* or *Indra*, called also शक्रराज, *Sakrarája*, or शक्रदेव, *Sakradéva*; a word corresponding with the Chinese, *Shy ti*, or *Shy thian ti.*—Kl.

(3) *Caused the khin to be struck.*—The khin is a species of horizontal lyre with seven strings.—Kl.

(4) *The Heavenly musicians Pan che.*—I nowhere find any elucidation of the term *Pan che.*—Kl.

(5) *The forty-two things.*—The original character signifies *affairs*, but as Indra drew them on the stone, I have translated the word *things*. Hiuan thsang is not more lucid upon this point: "To the south of the western peak (of Indrasilaguha), says he, there is a great stone edifice on a precipice; extensive, but not high. In olden times, when the Jou lai established his

* *Pian i tian*, B. LXV. p. 64.
† *J. A. S.* Vol. XVI. p. 954.

abode there, the emperor of Heaven, Shy (Indra) drew forty-two doubtful matters upon the stone, and beseeched Foe to explain them fully. These tracings of Indra remain to this day."* The *Szu shy eul chang king*, the first Buddhist work translated from the Sanscrit into Chinese, has its title from allusion to this circumstance.—Kl.

The book here alluded to would appear to contain the Dogmatics, or the Metaphysics of Buddhism. It consists of *forty-two Sutras*, or brief aphorisms, which are supposed to embody the whole doctrine of the *Honorable of the World*, the entire spirit of the Scripture and the Law. Buddha, according to the work in question, having attained the height of his mission, having finished his doctrine, and vanquished all his enemies, sat in deep silence, absorbed in meditation. His disciples surrounded him; he resolved their doubts and instructed them in the Law. He explains the duties, virtues, gifts of the priesthood; discusses the ten virtues and the ten vices of the body and the soul, the nature of good and of wicked people, together with the *cause of causes*, or the *cause of all effects*. The work is most probably apocryphal; or it may be an abridgment of the 21 volumes of the *Shér-phyin* (*Prajná Paramita*), or discourses which treat of the logic, psychology, and metaphysics of the Buddhists, and which are stated to have been delivered by Sákya 16 years after his attainment of Buddhahood, or in the 51st of his age, on the *Gridhrakuta* hill, near Rájagriha. Amongst his numerous auditory was Indra, as intimated by Fa hian; and these put a question several times to Sákya. He gives them no direct reply, but forms such propositions as lead them to the proper decision. See M. de Körös, *Analysis of the Sher-chin*, As. Res. Vol. XX. p. 399. Recurring to the Chinese work alluded to by M. Klaproth, it was translated into Chinese, according to M. Neumann, from the Sanscrit by *Kea ye mo tang* and *Chu fa lan*. The celebrated *Chu he* or *Chu fu tse* says, that in this work the doctrine of Buddha is explained in very easy intelligible language; but that, generally speaking, it contains only the idle and fruitless speculations of *Lao tsze* and *Chwang tsze*. M. Neumann, from whose *Catechism of the Shamans* (more correctly *Sha mi*) I gather these particulars, gives the following specimen of the work:—(Buddha loquitur) "My religion consists in thinking the inconceivable thought; my religion consists in going the impassable way; my religion consists in speaking the ineffable word; my religion consists in practising the impracticable practice:"—a sample which the reader will perhaps deem sufficient!—J. W. L.

(6) *The Hamlets of Na lo.*—Hiuan thsang calls this place *Kiu lo pi na kia*, and adds that it was the birthplace of the venerable *She li tsou.* He

* *Pian i tian*, B. LV. p, 64.

adds also, that when that personage entered nirvána, a tower was there erected over his ashes.*—Kl.

The hamlet here spoken of is the *Nalanda*, or *Nalada*, of the b*Kah*-h*Gyur* and the Páli Buddhistical Annals. In the latter it is stated to be one yojana distant from Rájagriha. It seems to have been a favorite resort of the learned in those times of high debate, a second Academia; and to have been sometimes bestowed by the king as a prize on the most successful disputant, or withdrawn from the actual possessor, in the case of defeat, for presentation to his victor. See de Körös, *Analysis of the Dul-va.* Sákya is ferquently mentioned in the scriptures as resorting to Nalada for the purpose of discussion or instruction.—J. W. L.

(7) *She li foe.*—She li foe (in Sanscrit, शारिपुत्र, Sariputra) is one of the most famous disciples of Buddha. He was the son of a very learned bráhman. His mother saw in a dream an extraordinary man holding in his hand a diamond mace, with which he demolished all the hills with the exception of one, before which he humbled himself. The father took this dream for a good omen, announcing a son of great wisdom, who should destroy all false doctrine in the world and be the disciple of *the man par excellence*,—Buddha.—Kl.

(8) *Entered nirvána.*—In a Mongolian work translated from the Sanscrit, and entitled *Uligerün dalaï*, (the Sea of Parables) we read; "When Sariputra learnt that Buddha was bent on entering nirvána, he experienced profound sorrow, and said to himself; 'It is soon indeed and contrary to all expectation that the Tathágata hath resolved upon entering nirvána: who after him will be the protector and shield of souls and of beings enveloped in darkness?" He then said to Buddha, "It is impossible for me to witness the nirvána of Buddha." Thrice be repeated these words, when Buddha replied; "If thou believest thy time come, then do thy will like all the *Khutukhtu* (in Sanscrit, *Nirmmánkáya, incarnations*) who enter the nirvána of tranquillity." Sariputra having heard these words of Buddha, arranged his dress; and having a hundred times walked round Buddha, he repeated a great number of verses in praise of him. He then embraced the feet of the latter, placed them thrice upon his head, and joining the palms of his hands, said, "I have been found worthy to approach the gloriously accomplished Buddha." He then worshipped Buddha, and proceeded with his servant, the priest *Yonti*, to Rájagriha, his native town. When arrived there, he said to *Yonti*, "Go into the town, into the suburbs, and to the palace of the king, and to the houses of the high functionaries and of such as give alms, and thus say to them: "The *Khutukhtu* Sariputra hath

* *Pian i tian*, p. 12.

resolved upon entering nirvána; come and prostrate yourselves before him." The priest *Yonti* executed the order of his master, went to the places indicated, and thus delivered his message: "The *Khutukhtu* Sariputra hath arrived here; if you would visit him, come without delay." When the king *Ajátasatru*, the dispensers of alms, the great dignitaries, the officers of the army, and the heads of families heard this announcement, they were all filled with sorrow, and with heavy hearts said, "Ah! what will become of us when the second head of the law, the leader of so many beings, the Khutukhtu Sariputra shall have entered nirvána!" Hurriedly they proceeded towards him, bowing down and saying, "Khutukhtu! if thou becomest nirvána, who shall be our protector, and that of so many other beings?" Sariputra then addressed them the following words: "Since all is perishable, the end of all is death. As ye, too, belong to this world of torment, ye too, will not remain long: death will come and terminate your career. But as you all, in consequence of meritorious works in a former existence, have had the happiness of being born in the world with Buddha, and that too in the human form, do you add other accumulative merits, and accomplish such works as shall save you from Sansára." When Sariputra had finished preaching thus to the bystanders the inexhaustible law, and had comforted their spirits with salutary medicaments, they bowed down before the Khutukhtu, and each returned to his home. After midnight, Sariputra sat in a perfectly erect position; gathered all the faculties of his soul; directed these upon one point, and entered the first *Dhyána*. Thence he entered the second; thence, the third; and from the third, the fourth. From the fourth he passed into the *Samádhi of the births of boundless celestial space;* then into the *Samádhi of the births of complete nihility*. From this Samádhi he entered that of '*neither thinking nor not thinking;*' then into that of *limitation;* and lastly into *Nirvána*.

"When Khourmousda, the king of the Gods, learnt of the nirvána of Sáriputra, he came with several hundreds of thousands in his suite, bearing flowers, perfumes, and other objects meet for sacrifice. They diffused themselves through the whole space of heaven; their tears fell like rain; they scattered their flowers so as to cover the earth, saying, "Oh! he whose wisdom was as the depth of the sea, who had passed through all the gates of knowledge, whose musical speech flowed sweetly as a running stream; who was perfect in the fulfilment of every duty, in self-contemplation, in all wisdom; the sublime chief of the doctrine, the excellent Khutukhtu Sáriputra hath too hastily entered nirvána. Who shall succeed the gloriously accomplished Buddha and Tathágata, to spread abroad the law?" All the inhabitants of the town and neighbourhood, as soon as they were apprised of the nirvána of Sáriputra, came bearing much oil, perfumes, flowers, and other things appropriate for sacrifice. They wept loudly with accents of woe and sorrow, placing upon the ground the objects fit for the sacrifices. Khourmousda, the prince of the gods, then commanded Vishwamitra to prepare a car of various precious materials for the body of Sáriputra. When the car was finished the corpse of Sáriputra, was placed thereon in a sitting position, and taken forth to a beautiful plain, all the while the Nágas, the Yakshas, the king, the commanders of the army, the officers and the whole people uttering cries of sorrow. There they raised a pile of chandana (sandal) wood. After moistening it with oil and butter, they place upon it the body of Sáriputra and applied fire. Then all bowed down and each went to his home. When the fire was completely extinguished, the priest Yonti collected from the ashes the *sárira* of his master and conveyed them as well as his pot and ecclesiastical dress, to Buddha. He placed these things at the feet of Buddha, announcing at the same time the death of his master. When Ananda learnt this from the lips of Yonti, he was much grieved and said to Buddha, "Oh Buddha! the first of our band has entered nirvána; to whom now shall we unbosom ourselves, and whom shall we regard as our protecting sun?" Buddha replied; "Ananda! although Sáriputra hath entered nirvána, neither the charge of your duties, nor samádhi, nor understanding, nor plenary redemption, nor the *prajna* of plenary redemption, nor the nature of occult properties hath become so; moreover, many generations ago Sáriputra once became nirvána, because he could not endure to see me enter upon nirvána."—Kl.

(8) *The new town of the royal Residence.*—That is the new राजगृह, Rájagriha; in Páli Rájagaha, 'or royal residence.' This name is transcribed in Chinese, *Lo yue khi.* Asoka left this town and transferred the seat of his government to Pátaliputra.—Kl.

M. Klaproth forgets that Pátaliputra was the seat of government in the time of Chandragupta, the grandfather of Asoka.

That indefatigable antiquary, Capt. M. Kittoe, undeterred by the inclemency of the season, paid a hurried visit to this interesting locality in July last, and has published the results of his investigations in the Journal of the Asiatic Society, Vol. XVI. pp. 953—970. His paper is of the highest interest, and leads me to hope that much more remains for him to discover should he be able to revisit the spot at a more propitious time of the year. Speaking of the modern (or perhaps I should say *less ancient*) Rájagriha, Capt. Kittoe observes,—"An immense embankment, called Assurein, still exists, as well as extensive mounds of bricks and rubbish; sufficient remains of the citadel to show its form, a parallelogram with numerous bastions;

but these appear to have been the work of later times. * * * About the distance westward mentioned by Fa hian, there exists a tumulus called the *Awa* or *Punzawa*, which is no doubt the tower where Buddha's relics were placed by A che shi. Buchanan describes this remarkable mound which want of leisure prevented me inspecting closely." If it be what Capt. Kittoe conjectures, indeed whatever it be, this mound seems well deserving of very particular examination.—J. W. L.

(9) *The ancient town of the king Ping sha :*—The ancient Rájagriha. Hiuan thsang writes this name *Kho lo che ky li hi ;* a corrupted orthography, but one under which Rájagriha is still concealed, for Hiuan thsang translates the word '*royal residence, or house.*' *Ping sha* is the transcription of Bimbására.—Kl.

"The appearance of this valley and the hills is very striking," says Capt. Kittoe ; "every peak has a name and a small Jain temple crowning it, this sect holding the whole neighbourhood sacred, which is very remarkable. * * It is fully two miles or 4 *li* to the site of the old town, which is now called *Hansu Tanr ;* this must have been a very large place when in its glory, and, as described, is skirted by hills, five of which are more conspicuous than the rest, and are called respectively, Ratná Giri, Bipla Giri, Baibhar Giri, Sóna Giri, and Udhaya Giri. To proceed ; first of all as to the chapel in the northern hill, on the left or west side of the pass is a chamber called Sone Bhundar, of precisely the same shape as those of Burabur. There are sockets to admit of timber roofing on the exterior of the cave, and there have been buildings extending to some distance in front. It would be interesting to clear the rubbish here. There are several short inscriptions and some of the shell shape ; one has some resemblance to the Chinese. There are no Páli letters ; but the cave has been sadly ill-used by a zemindar who tried to blow it up with powder many years ago, hoping to find hidden treasure, and a large piece of rock has been broken away at the very spot where we should have expected to find an inscription. * * * * To the south of this cave, (near the centre of the town ?) is a high tumulus, the site of a dagope, or chaitya, on which is a small Jain temple. From this elevated spot a good view is to be had of the valley and of the pass and plains beyond, looking over Rájagriha nearly due north ; to the east the valley grows narrower for a mile or so, and thence two valleys branch off, one leading to the Gidhona peak, so called from the vultures which perch and build there, the other to Tupobun, where there are hot wells. * * * * Leaving the tumulus and proceeding southward, the road winds at the foot of *Sóna Giri*, close to a low ledge of laterite, forming a terrace as even as if cut by masons ; this place is called Bheem Sen's Ukhara, or wrestling-place. The many indentations and cavities peculiar to such formations, are supposed by the ignorant to be marks left by the wrestlers. Continuing to the southward towards *Udhaya Giri*, the road is formed in the bare rock, in which occur many short inscriptions in the shell pattern, and other curious forms, but much worn and some overgrown with moss and rubbish. I deemed this to be great curiosities, and think that if a clearance were made, more (and perfect ones) would be discovered. About a quarter of a mile further is a tumulus overgrown with jungle, and near it the remains of some extensive buildings. This tumulus may be one of the towers mentioned by Fa hian." These researches are extremely interesting; but we must not be hasty in our identifications, as it is evident that much remains to be explored in this little trodden field. The caves in particular are deserving of the most minute investigation, for there can be little doubt that they are among the most ancient in India, perhaps taking precedence even of those of Burabur. The five hills surrounding Rájagriha are named in the Páli Annals* *Gijjhakuto*, *Isigili*, *Webharo*, *Wepullo*, and *Pandawo*. Among these we may easily recognise the Pali forms of *Báibhar Giri* and *Bipla Giri*, in *Webharo* and *Wepullo*. It will be remembered that the *Sattapani* cave was in the former (Webhara) hill, and that the hall of the first convocation was in front of that cave; which I make no doubt is the *Son Bhundar* cave described above. See my note 6 to Chapter XXX.—J. W. L.

(10) *Saw for the first time O pi.*—I take *O pi* to be the same personage as the bhikshu named by Hiuan thsang *A shy pho shi*, (अश्वजित्, Aswajit, "that goeth on horse back.") He narrates how Sáriputra met this devotee in the town of Rájagriha, and that it was he that instructed Sáriputra in the law.—Kl.

(11) *Served Foe with poisoned food.*—This event is thus recorded by Hiuan thsang: "At a short distance from the place where *She li foe* (Sáriputra) was instructed in the law, there is a deep and wide fosse along side of which is erected a tower. It is there that *Shy li khieou to* ('the handsome concealed,' in Sanscrit श्रीगुह्, *Sirgudha*) in order to injure Foe, dug a pit which he filled with fire, and served him with poisoned food. This *Shy li khieou to* was attached the creed of the heretics and was ever ready for mischief. He invited many to a banquet in his house, before the gate of which was a deep pit filled with fire and only covered over with decayed sticks upon which he had scattered some dry earth. Besides this, all the dishes were poisoned with different kinds of poison, so that such as escaped death in the fiery pit might fall victims to the food. The inhabitants of the

* *J. A. S.* Vol. VII. p. 996.

town knowing that Shy li khieou to indulged implacable hatred to the Honorable of the Age, urgently intreated the latter not to place himself in the way of danger. The Honorable of the Age replied ; " Be not uneasy ! the person of a Tathágata cannot be injured thus." He saluted them and set forth. At the instant of his setting foot on the threshold of the door, the pit of fire became changed into a limpid pool, clear as a mirror, and covered with the floating flowers of the lotus. When Shy li khieou to witnessed this he was downcast and sad ; nevertheless he said to his disciples, " By his art he has escaped the fiery pit ; but there still remain the poisoned meats." But the Honorable of the Age, after having partaken of these, expounded the admirable law. Shy li khieou to having listened to his discourse, solicited pardon, confessed his crimes, and amended his conduct.*—Kl.

(12) The black elephant of king *A che shi.*—Hiuan thsang does not accuse *A che shi* (Ajátasatru) of this sin ; but he states that Dévadatta being with this prince and his relatives and friends, let loose an elephant which he had intoxicated, in the hope of injuring the Tathágata ; but the latter merely made a signal with his hand, when immediately there came forth four lions before which the drunken elephant became quiet and humble.†

A Mongolian legend of the life of Buddha, which I have published, recounts this miracle in very nearly the same manner. " Dévadatta, uncle of Sákya Muni, exhibited his animosity anew by bringing to his neighbourhood a tame elephant which he had caused to drink a large quantity of palm-wine till his thrist was assuaged. He fixed to the accoutrements of this elephant two sharp swords, and let loose the intoxicated animal upon *Goodam* (Sákya Muni), believing that he would vent his rage against the hermit. But the latter merely raised the five fingers of his hand, when the elephant took him for a lion and became quiet."‡—Kl.

(13) *An pho lo.*—This is the same *An pho lo* of whom an account is given in note 4, Chap. XXV. According to the *Dul-va,* she bore a son to Bimbasára, named in Tibetan G*yhon-nu-*H*jigs-med,* or the " intrepid youth ;" a circumstance which sufficiently accounts for her possessing a fine garden at Rájagriha, as well as one at Vaisali.—J. W. L.

* *Pian i tian,* B. LXV. p. 48.
† *Pian i tian,* ibid.
‡ *Journal Asiatique,* T. IV. p. 22.

CHAPTER XXIX.

Peak of Khi che.—The demon Phi siun changes himself into a Vulture.—Terror of A nan.—Throne of the four Buddhas.—Stone thrown at Foe by Thiao tha.—Fa hian's sacrifice.

Entering the valley and going to the mountains above fifteen *li* to the south-east, you arrive at the Peak of *Khi che.*[1] Three *li* before reaching the summit of the mountain you come to a cavern situated amongst the rocks and facing the south. Foe was seated there in meditation. At thirty paces to the north-east there is a stone grot; *A nan* was sitting there in meditation. The demon of heaven, *Phi siun,*[2] transformed into a vulture, stopped before the grot and terrified *A nan.* Foe by his supernatural power, opened the rock, took *A nan* by the arm with his hand, and removed his fear. The trace of the bird, and the hole through which Foe protruded his hand exist still. It is from this circumstance that the hill is called the *Hill of the cave of the Vulture.* Before the cave is the place of the throne of the four Buddhas.[3] All the Arhans likewise, had each his cave where they sat to meditate. The number of these caves is several hundreds.

Foe, being in front of the stone house, was passing from the east to the west. *Thiao tha,* standing on the steep edge towards the north of the mountain, threw down a stone which wounded Foe on the toe :[4] this stone still exists. The hall in which Foe taught the doctrine is in ruins ; there are but the foundations of a brick wall remaining. The peaks of these hills are regular and majestic ; they are the loftiest of the five mountains.

Fa hian having purchased in the new town perfumes, flowers, and oil-lamps, hired two aged *Pi khieou* to conduct him to the grots and to the hill *Khi che.* After having made an oblation of the perfumes and the flowers, the lamps increased the brilliance. Grief and emotion affected him even to tears; he said, "Formerly, in this very place was Foe; here he taught the *Sheou leng yan: Fa hian*, unable to behold Foe in life, has but witnessed the traces of his sojourn. Still, it is something to have recited the *Sheou leng yan* before the cave, and dwelt there one night."

NOTES.

(1) *The Peak of Khi che*,—in Sanscrit *Gridhrakuta*, or the Peak of the Vulture. It is one of those hills situated about 25° N. Lat. at the sources of the Dahder and Banurah rivers. The origin of its name we learn from the legend given in the text by Fa hian. Other Buddhist writers affirm however that it receives its name from its resemblance to a vulture.* "The Tathágata, says Hiuan thsang, when he had attained the age of fifty years, dwelt much in this mountain and there preached the admirable law.—Kl.

The position of this hill is too well defined to be mistaken: it was fifteen *li* south-east from the valley leading from the new to the ancient Rájagriha. What was the length of the *li?* Fa hian, in the next chapter, states the distance of the *Bamboo gardens of Kia lan tho* from the north of the town to be three hundred paces; Hiuan thsang calls the same distance 1 *li*. Taking 300 paces to be equal to 250 yards, this would give 7 *li* to a mile. To test this; Hiuan thsang makes the distance of the Ganges in a north-east direction from *Keou li kia* (Giriyek) 220 or 230 *li*. The direct distance on Rennel's map is 30 miles, which gives pretty exactly the same value to the *li*, viz. of 7 to the mile. Ki chhe was therefore about 2⅐th miles S. E. from the entrance of the valley, and cannot be identical with *Guddeh dwar*, as supposed by Capt. Kittoe, that hill being by far too distant to correspond with our pilgrim's account, or with those of other authorities, which represent Gridhrakuta as one of the hills surrounding the "mountain-girt city" like a wall. It was very famous as the place where Sákya delivered his instructions on the *Prajná Páramitá*, which occupy 21 volumes of the Bauddha Scriptures. See my note 5. Chap. XXVIII.—J. W. L.

(2) *The demon of Heaven Phi siun*;—this is one of the names of Mára and signifies according to the *Shy kia phou*, 'the wicked;' in Sanscrit, पिशुन *Pisuna*.

* *Fan i ming y*, quoted in *San tsang fa sou*, B. XXIV. p. 20 v.

Hiuan thsang details this event in the following terms: "Before the stone dwelling of Buddha, is a flat stone; it is there that A nan experienced the dread of Mára. The venerable A nan being there absorbed in meditation, the king of the Máras took the form of a vulture; and during a dark night unillumined by the moon, he smote the rocks, stretched forth his wings, and uttered frightful cries to terrify the Venerable; who indeed was seized with unbounded fear. The Tathágata, through his omniscience, perceived this; and in a kindmanner stretched forth his hand, passed it through the rock, and laid it upon the head of A nan, saying graciously, 'Fear not, A nan! it is Mára thus transformed.' A nan took heart, and became calm. The marks of the bird are still visible upon the rock, and in the cleft the hole through which passed (the hand of Buddha.")*—Kl.

(3) *The place of the throne of the four Buddhas*,—that is to say, of Sákya Muni, Kasyapa, Kanaki Muni, and Krakuchchanda, who have already appeared in the Bhadra Kalpa, or present epoch of the world.—Kl.

(4) *A stone which wounded Foe on the toe.*—This event is the eighth of the nine tribulations to which Sákya Muni was subjected in expiation of faults committed in anterior existences. He thus himself explains the cause of this blow inflicted by Devadatta; "In former times there was in the town of *Lo yue khi* (Rájagriha) a grandee named *Siu than.* His family was opulent; he had a son named *Siu mo thi.* The father *Siu than*, having ended his days, *Siu mo thi*, who had a younger brother by a different mother, named *Siu ye she*, was unwilling to divide his property with the younger brother. One day he took this brother by the hand, and ascended with him to the summit of *Khi che khiu;* when arrived on the brink of the precipice he pushed him down and cast stones upon him, and thus killed the younger brother." Foe gave the following explanation to *She li foe;* "The grandee, named *Siu than*, was the king my father, *Pe thsing:* *Siu mo thi*, was myself; and *Siu ye she* was *Thi pho tha to* (Devadatta). It was in consequence of this my former act, that when walking on the edge of mount *Khi che khiu*, *Thi pho tha to* detached a stone from the precipice to throw at my head. The genius of the mountain diverted the stone, so that but a small corner of it touched the great toe of my foot, and caused blood to flow."†—Kl.

(6) *The Sheou leng yan*;—the title of a work containing the instructions of Sákya Muni. The *Ta chi lun* explains *Sheou leng yan* to signify in Sanscrit, "things which are difficult to distinguish from each other."—Kl.

* *Pian i tian*, B. LXV. p. 49 v.
† *San tsang fa sou*, B, XXXIV. p. 21.

CHAPTER XXX.

Bamboo gardens of Kia lan tho.—Shi mo she na, or the Cemetery.—Grot of Pin pho lo.—Stone-house of Chhe ti.—First collection of the sayings of Foe.—Cavern of Thiao thâ.—Black stone of Pi khieou.

He then issued from the old town to return to the new. Proceeding to the north three hundred paces, he saw to the west of the road the *Bamboo gardens of Kia lan tho*,[1] where was constructed a chapel, which remains to this day; ecclesiastics sweep and water it. To the north of the chapel, at the distance of two or three *li*, is the *Shi mo she na*. *Shi mo she na*, signifies in Chinese, the *Field of Tombs where they lay the dead.*[2] On crossing the southern mountain and proceeding westward three hundred paces, there is a stone building called the *Grot of Pin pho lo*.[3] Foe, after his meals, habitually sat in this place to meditate. Five or six *li* more westerly, to the north of the mountain and in a shady spot, there is a stone house named *Chhe ti*;[4] it is the place where, after the *ni houan* of Foe, five hundred Arhans arranged the collection of the sacred books. When these sacred books were published, they prepared three vacant thrones sumptuously adorned; *She li foe* was on the left, *Mou lian* on the right. Amongst those five hundred Arhans, one alone was wanting; it was *A nan*, who, when the *Great Kia se*[5] ascended the throne, was outside the gate without ability to enter.[6] They have erected in this place a tower, which exists to this day. Beyond the mountains there are other caves, where the Arhans sat and meditated; and of these there are a great number.

Issuing from the ancient town and descending three *li* towards the north-east, you come to the stone cavern of *Thiao tha*.[7] Fifty paces further there is a great square black stone. There was formerly a *Pi khieou,* who in passing up, pondered thus to himself: "This body is not lasting; it is subject to pain, void, and exposed to uncleanness." Considering the weariness and the vexation of his body, he drew his dagger, and was about to destroy himself: then he reflected anew, "*The Honorable of the Age* has established a law* that no one should destroy his own life." He reflected again; "Be it so," said he; "but I seek this day only to destroy three mortal foes!" and stabbed himself. When he began wounding himself, he became *Siu tho wan;* when he had half done, he became *A na han;* when he had completed all, he became *Arhan,* and truly entered into *ni houan.*

NOTES.

(1) *The Bamboo Garden of Kia lan tho.*—Hiuan thsang states that this garden was situated one *li* from the northern gate of the *Mountain city.* In his time there was a chapel built of bricks upon a stone foundation, the gate of which faced the west. It was a place where the Tathágata often dwelt and expounded the doctrine, performed miracles and led all beings to salvation. There was an image of the Tathágata and of many other Tathágatas. There was in former times a grandee in this town whose name was *Kia lan tho;* he was very rich and distributed his bounty to all the heretics in his '*Bamboo Garden.*' Having however seen the Tathágata and heard his doctrine, he purified himself by faith, and ceased to enjoy the intercourse of the band of heretics who dwelt in the '*Garden of Bamboos.*' Then, before the instructor of gods and men came to occupy the dwelling, the genii and demons, to reward Kia lan tho, expelled the heretics, saying, "The chief Kia lan tho, would raise a chapel to Buddha in the *Garden of Bamboos;* leave therefore, that you may avoid all mischief." The heretics, though greatly enraged, were obliged to digest their spleen, and left the garden. The chief erected his chapel, and when it was complete, himself came and entreated Tathágata to take possession of it.*—Kl.

This is the འོད་མའི་ཚལ་བྱ་ཀ་ལན་ཏ་ཀའི་གནས, (*hod-mahi-tshal bya-ka-lan-da-kahi. gnas*) of the Tibetan scriptures; in Sanscrit, *Venuvanam Kalandaká nivasa:* stated in the *Dulva* to have been presented to Sákya by Bimbasára. It is called *Wélúwano* in the Mahawansa; a corruption, I presume, of the Sanscrit name. It was here that Sákya converted Sárihibu, or Sáradwati, and Mongalyana.—J. W. L.

* *Pian i tian,* B. LXV. pp. 52, 53.

(2) *The field of tombs.*—The word *Shi mo she na* is the transcription of the Sanscrit श्मशान, signifying cemetery.—Kl.

(3) *The grot of Pin pho lo.*—None of the learned commentators on Fa hian proposes any restoration of this name. It is elsewhere written *Pi pho lo*, and appears to me very plainly the Chinese transcript of *Baibhara*, in Pali *Webharo*, the name of the hill in which was situated the Sattapanni cave. See note 9, Chap. XXVIII.—J. W. L.

(4) *A stone house named Chhe ti.*—Hiuan thsang does not give the name of this edifice, but states that it was situated five or six *li* to the south-west of the garden of Bamboos, on the northern side of the mountain, and in a great forest of bamboos. After the nirvána of the Tathágata, he adds, the venerable Mahá Kásyapa, with nine hundred and ninety-nine Arhans, there made the collection of the three treasures.*—Kl.

(5) *The great Kia she;* Mahá Kásyapa.—Kl.

(6) *Without ability to enter.*—The circumstance alluded to is thus detailed in the Mahavansa. After describing the erection of the hall of the first convocation in front of the Satapanni cave in the *Webhara* mountain, the narrative proceeds: "The king thus reported to the theros: 'Our task is performed.' Those theros then addressed Anando, the delight (of an audience). "Anando, to-morrow is the convocation; on account of thy still being under the dominion of human passions thy presence there is inadmissible: exert thyself without intermission, and attain the requisite qualification." The thero, who had been thus enjoined, having exerted a supernatural effort, and extricated himself from the dominion of human passions, attained the sanctification of "Arahat." On the second day of the second month of "Wasso," these disciples assembled in this splendid hall. Reserving for the thero Anando, the seat appropriated to him alone, the other sanctified priests took their places according to their seniority. While some of them were in the act of enquiring, "Where is the thero Anando?" in order that he might manifest to the (assembled) disciples that he had attained the sanctification of "Arahat,"—(at that instant) the said thero made his appearance, emerging from the earth, and passing through the air (without touching the floor); and took his seat in the pulpit specially reserved for him."

A much fuller and very amusing account of these particulars may be found in Mr. Turnour's examination of the Pali Buddhistical Annals; but this volume has already extended so much beyond the limits I originally prescribed, that I cannot afford space to insert it. The reader is referred to

* *Pian i tian*, B. LXV. p. 53 v.
Geschichte der Ost Mongolien, p. 312.

the *Journal of the Asiatic Society*, Vol. VI. pp. 510, 518. The scene of the first convocation I have, in a foregoing note (9, Chap. XXVIII.), attempted to identify; and I trust that Capt. Kittoe may again have an opportunity of bringing his great antiquarian zeal to bear upon that deeply interesting locality.—J. W. L.

(7) *The stone cavern of Thiao tha.* Thiao tha is the transcription, as we have already seen, of Dévadatta. Hiuan thsang places the great stone building in which this personage yielded himself up to meditation, at the distance of two or three *li* east of the northern gate of the mountain city to the left, in the shadow of the southern slope of the hill.

Dévadatta, who was during life the enemy and persecutor of Buddha, is generally regarded as an incarnation of Mára (the malificent spirit). Such incarnations tend only to exalt and to bring out in all their glory the Buddhas and their doctrine. A Mongolian work translated by M. Schmidt, says upon this subject, "Men whose spirits are darkened maintain and believe that Dévadatta was the antagonist, enemy, and persecutor of Buddha. If during the five hundred generations that Buddha Tathágata followed the path of a Bodhisattwa, the illustrious Bogda Dévadatta proved him with all manner of evil and contradiction; this was but to fortify the excellence and surpassing qualities of the Bodhisattwa. Thus unenlightened men commit sin when they hold and teach that Dévadatta was an enemy and persecutor of Buddha Tathágata, and by such discourse they give occasion to their own regeneration in the three abject conditions (those of brutes, demons, and denizens of hell). The accumulated virtues of the illustrious Bogda Dévadatta are immense; the services he hath rendered to many Buddhas extraordinary, and thus has he contributed to the germ of the root of meritorious works. He belongs moreover to those Mahásattwas, who have truly fathomed the means of salvation, and have approached the dignity of a Buddha Tathágata. Those therefore who regard him with hatred and aversion, cause thereby their own injury and their rebirth in the three abject conditions."—Kl.

(8) *A law.*—The law here alluded to is mentioned in the *Dulva* (Vol. V. p. 162 to 239); where, in consequence of several instances of suicide among the monks, out of grief and despair at the miseries of human life, Sákya prohibits discourses upon that subject. So that the practice of self-immolation ascribed by the Greek historians to the Buddhists, was, like that of going naked, a departure from orthodox principles.—J. W. L.

CHAPTER XXXI.

Town of Kia ye.—Place where Foe lived six years in austerities.—Place where he accomplished the Law.—He is exposed to the attacks of a demon.—Other holy places.—Four great towers in honor of Foe.

Proceeding thence four *yeou yan*[1] to the west, you come to the town of *Kia ye.*[2] This town is also completely desert. Continuing twenty *li* to the south, you come to the place where the *Phou sa* spent six years in mortifications :[3] the place is wooded. Thence three *li* to the west, you come to the place where Foe descended into the water to bathe ; the gods held branches of trees to cover him[4] at his exit from the tank. Two *li* further to the north you come to the place where the young women of retired families offered Foe rice and milk.[5] Thence two *li* to the north Foe, seated on a stone under a great tree, and looking to the east, eat the rice : the tree and the stone still exist. The stone may be six feet long and the same broad, and two feet high. In the *Kingdom of the Middle* the heat and the cold are so equal and temperate, that there are trees which live several thousand years, yea even ten thousand years.

Thence going half a *yeou yan* to the north-east you come to a stone grot ; the *Phou sa* having entered it, and having turned to the west, sat with his legs crossed and pondered in his heart : " In order that I should accomplish the law, it is necessary that I should have a divine testimonial." Immediately on the stone wall the shadow of Foe depicted itself : it appeared three feet high, and the weather was clear and brilliant. The heaven and the earth were much moved, and all the gods in space said ; " This is not the place where the Foes past and to come should accomplish the law. At the distance of a little more than half a *yeou yan* to the south-west, under the tree *Peï to*[6] is the place where all the Foes past and to come should accomplish the law."

The gods, having thus spoken, proceeded before him, sang, and showed him the way on withdrawing. The *Phou sa* rose, and when he was at the distance of thirty paces from the tree[1] a god gave him the *grass of happy omen* :[7] the *Phou sa* took it, and advanced fifteen paces further. Five hundred blue birds came and fluttered three times around him, and then flew away. The *Phou sa* advanced towards the tree *Pei to*, held out the grass of happy omen towards the east, and sat down. Then the *king of the demons* sent three beautiful girls,[8] who came from the north, to tempt him, and himself came with the same purpose. The *Phou sa* then struck the ground with his toes and the bands of the demon recoiled and dispersed themselves : the three girls were transformed into old women. During six years he imposed upon himself the greatest mortifications. In all these places people of subsequent times have built towers and prepared images which exist to this day.

In the place where Foe, having accomplished the law rested seven days to contemplate the tree and obtain the joy of extreme eternal beatitude ;—in that where he passed seven days under the tree *Pei to*, proceeding from the west to the east ;—in that where the gods, having created the edifice of the seven precious kings, waited on Foe seven days ;—in that where the blind dragon[9] with brilliant scales surrounded Foe for seven days ;—in that where Foe being seated under a tree, *Ni kiu liu*, and upon a square stone the god Bráhma[10] came to entreat him ;—in that where the four kings of the gods offered him a pot ;—in that where the chief of five hundred merchants persented him with parched rice and honey ;—in that where he converted *Kia se* and his brethren, master and disciples, to the number of a thousand ; in all these places have they erected towers. At the place where Foe obtained the law, there are three *seng kia lan ;* hard by are establishments for the clergy, who are there very numerous. The people supply them with abundance, so that they lack nothing. The precepts are rigidly followed ; the greatest gravity is observed in all their conduct,—in sitting down, in rising up, and in going forth. The four great towers erected in commemoration of all the holy acts that Foe performed while in the world are preserved to this moment since the *ni houan* of Foe. These four great towers are at the place where Foe was born, at the place where he obtained the law, at that where he turned the wheel of the law, and at that where he entered into *ni houan*."

NOTES.

(1) *Four yeou yans.*—About 18 or 20 miles.—J. W. L.

(2) *The town* of *Kia ye.*—*Kia ye*, sometimes *Kia ya*, is the transcription of the Sanscrit गय, *Gaya*. This town is not to be confounded with the modern one of the same name situated on the left bank of the river Phulgo. The ruins of the ancient Gaya, at present called *Buddha Gaya*, are situated in a vast plain a short distance west of the *Nilajan* or *Amánal* river, which forms the upper part of the Phulgo. These ruins present nothing but irregular heaps of bricks and stones, amongst which are here and there still to be detected the foundations of regular buildings. A vast quantity of building materials has been removed from these ruins, which have thus become more and more shapeless. The number of stone figures found dispersed within a distance of fifteen or twenty miles around the site, is truly astonishing. All appear however to have belonged to a great temple and its vicinity, and to have been transported thence to various places. At present there are no Buddhists in the vicinity of Buddha Gaya.*

Hiuan thsang states that this town was in a very strong position. He found few inhabitants and not more than a thousand bráhman families descended from the ancient saints.

The ruins of Buddha Gaya, was visited in February 1833, by the Burmese ambassador Mengy Maha Chesu and his suite, on their way to the Upper Provinces to visit the Governor General. In going over and carefully examining these ruins, they found an ancient inscription in the Páli character in a half buried condition, near the Maha bodhi gach, or sacred fig-tree, on the terrace of the temple. A copy of this inscription was transmitted to the Asiatic Society of Bengal, by whom the following translation was published in their Journal for May 1834 :

"This is one of the 84,000 shrines erected by Sri Dharm Asoka, ruler of the world (Jambudwíp), at the end of the year 218 of Buddha's annihilation, (B. C. 326) upon the holy spot in which Bhagawan (Buddha) having tasted milk and honey (*madhupyasa*). In lapse of time having fallen into

* *Hamilton, Desc. of Hindustan*, Vol. I. p. 267.

a state of disrepair, it was rebuilt by a priest named Naikmahanta. Again being ruined, it was restored by Rája Sado-Mang. After a long interval it was once more demolished, when Rája Sempyu-Sakhen-tara-Mengi appointed his Gúrú, Sri-Dhamma-Rája-Guna to superintend the building. He proceeded to the spot with his disciple, Sri Kásyapa, but they were unable to complete it although aided in every way by the Rája. Afterwards Varadasi-Naik-Thera petitioned the Rája to undertake it, to which he readily assented, commissioning prince Pyatasing to the work, who again deputed the younger Pyusakheng, and his minister Ratha, to cross over and repair the sacred building. It was thus constructed a fourth time, and finished on Friday, the 10th day of Pyadola, in the Sakkaraj year 667 (A. D. 1305). On Sunday the 8th day of Tachhaon-Mungla, 668 (A. D. 1306), it was consecrated with splendid ceremonies and offerings of food, perfumes, banners, lamps, and púja, of the famous ornamented tree called *Calpa vriksha*; and the poor (two ?) were treated with charity as the Rája's own children. Thus was completed this meritorious act, which will produce eternal reward and virtuous fruits. May the founders endure in fame, enjoy the tranquillity of *Nirbhan* and become *Arahanta* on the advent of Arya Mitri (the future Buddha)."—Kl.

Professor Wilson, in commenting on this part of Fa hian's route, says that *Kia ye* is Buddha Gaya, "of course." But if we adopt the bearing and distance of our traveller,—and I know not on what grounds we can reject them,—nothing can be clearer than that neither modern Gaya nor Buddha Gaya, is the place here spoken of as the scene of Sákya's mortifications. It would be idle on my part to speculate upon a point which can be determined only by local investigation; but I may briefly mention that there are several circumstances, besides the testimony of Fa hian and Hiuan thsang, that render it extremely probable that the *Kia ye* of these authors was considerably to the north of modern Gaya. In the first place, the distance from Pátaliputra to the Bo-tree, is stated in the Mahavansa (page 111) to be seven yojanas only. Now taking the yojana of the Mahavansa to be equal in length to that employed by Fa hian, who makes nine of them between Pátaliputra and Giriyek, this would make the position of the Bo-tree correspond very closely with that of *Ram Gaya*; and even giving it the extreme length assigned it by Alexander Cunningham from well determined positions in the north-west, namely 7 miles, the distance would still fall much short of Gaya, even though no allowance be made for the sinuosities of the road. Again;—Capt. Kittoe mentions that according to tradition all religious ceremonies were anciently performed at Ram Gaya; and Buchanan says that many affirm Hulasganj (in the same neighbourhood) to be the ancient Gaya. Now if we connect with all these circumstances the Burabur caves cut with prodigious labour in the solid granite of the adjoining hills, and the conspicuous traces of a very extensive ancient town,* I think we have grounds for enquiring whether this may not be the Gaya of our pilgrim. That the Hindus have appropriated and sanctified the site is rather in favor of the conjecture, being exactly what they have done in other Buddhist localities. See also Prinsep's version of the inscriptions in these caves and his remarks upon them in J. A. S. Vol. V. p. 657. These inscriptions are the oldest I believe hitherto discovered in any cave in India; a circumstance which also adds some weight to the claims of this neighbourhood to be the site in question. But, I repeat, this point cannot be settled by closet speculations; and I earnestly commend it to the attention of such as have local opportunities of deciding it.—J. W. L.

(3) *Spent six years in mortifications.*—The first of the tribulations that Sákya Muni had to undergo, was to live six entire years in mortification and privations, ere he attained the highest degree of sanctity. He thus himself explains the cause of this tribulation: "There was formerly in the city of *Pho lo naï* (Benares) the son of a bráhman named *Ho man*, and the son of a potter named *Hou hi;* these two were young and comported themselves very affectionately together. Hou hi said to Ho man; "Let us go see *Kia she Jou lai,*" (the Tathágatha Kásyapa). Ho man replied, "Where be the use of going to see this shaven-headed monk!" And thus it stood till the third day. Again Hou hi said, "We might go but one moment to see him." The other replied, "Wherefore visit this shaven monk? How should he have the doctrine of Buddha?" Thereupon Hou hi seized Ho man by the head, and said, "I desire that you come and see the Jou lai with me." Ho man, quite frightened, said within himself, "This is no trifling matter; there must be something good therein. He then said "Let go my head and I will accompany you." Arrived where the Buddha was, they saluted the feet of Kia she. Hou hi said to the Buddha that Ho man recognised not the Three Precious Ones, and beseeched him to expound them to him, and convert him. Ho man on seeing the Buddha loved him and was filled with joy; he embraced religious life and studied the doctrine. Ho man is myself; Hou hi is he who, while I was yet prince, induced me to issue forth from the town and embrace religious life, and it was the son of a manufacturer of flower vases who guided me. Nevertheless as I in a former birth spoke disparagingly of the Buddha *Kia she,* I had to suffer the retributive penalty; what remains of this penalty, I must now suffer when on the point of becoming Buddha, by six years of mortifications.

* *Kittoe, J. A. S.* Vol. XVI. p. 402.

As the whole of this chapter is filled with the adventures of Buddha, while yet Bodhisattwa, and during these six years of mortifications, I shall subjoin the sequel of the legend given in Note 8. Chap. XXIII. and which has thrown so much light upon this subject.

A. "The prince when on the eve of quitting common life, leapt with joy and proceeded in peace. He entered the town; the people of the country gazed on him with delight and never seemed wearied with doing so. The prince by separating himself from every object of attachment and affection, had removed the root of all passion and pain.

B. He wished to have his head shaved; but in his haste he had taken with him no instrument for the purpose. Indra came with a sword in his hand; the gods and the genii received the hair. He then resumed his route, and advanced into the country. The inhabitants followed and watched him. He then went forth from the kingdom; and having advanced somewhat, he came to the kingdom of Mo kie (Magadha). He entered it by the right, and left it by the left gate. The people of the country, men and women, great and small, seeing the prince, exclaimed "This must be Indra, or Brahma, or some celestial genius, or a king of the dragons;" and they abandoned themselves to joy, not knowing who of these he might be. The prince, who knew their thoughts, left the road and sat down beneath a tree. Then the king of the country, *Ping sha* (Bimbására), inquired of his ministers, "How happens it every thing is so quiet in the kingdom, that not a sound or a whisper is to be heard?" They replied, "There is a Doctor of Reason traversing the kingdom, and coming to the court. Wherever he goes, he leaves a trace of light, and inspires respect by his majestic bearing. It is a thing not seen in this age. The people of the country, great and small, have gone out to see and contemplate him, and even till now none have returned." The king then went forth with all his officers, and having approached the Doctor of Reason, he beheld the prince shining with marvellous light. He asked the latter, "What genius art thou?" "I am no genius" replied the prince. "If thou art not a genius," returned the king, "whence art thou and what is the name of thy family?" "I come," replied the prince, "from the east of the Perfumed Mountains, from the north of the Mountains of snow; my kingdom is named *Kia weï;* my father is *Pé thsing;* and my mother, *Mo ye.*" King Bimbására replied, "Are you not Siddharta, then?" "I am he," answered the prince. Struck with admiration, the king threw himself at his feet and worshipped him. "Prince, whose birth has been signalised by so many miracles, (said he) whose exterior proclaims by its lustre an immortal, the holy king causing the wheel of the four continents to revolve, the expected treasure of the genii whose heads were raised from the midst of the four seas, wherefore hast thou abandoned thy heavenly (royal) rank to conceal thyself in the midst of the mountains? Doubtless thou hast an admirable purpose; I would fain learn it." The prince replied: "From what I have seen, men and things both in heaven and on earth, are born but to die. The sufferings that attend them are old age, sickness, death, and pain. These cannot be evaded. The body is but the receptacle of pains. Affliction and fear are immense. If man attain a glorious eminence, lo! he falls into excess of pride. Instead of the joys so ardently sought for, the world is replete with sorrows. It is this that wearies me, it is for this that I would fly to the mountains." The grandees and the elders replied; "This old age, this sickness, this death,—have been in the world from all time. Why distress yourself by anticipation? and thus to reject a glorious title, and to withdraw to a profound retreat to mortify your body, what is it but to encounter evil?" The prince repeated these verses: "According to your sayings, Lords, I should not foresee evil and be sad: but were I a king, in becoming old, sickness would supervene, and when death came I must then have a successor. In meeting this calamity, it were as if I had no successor. How then forbid my sorrow? There are in the world a tender parent, and a pious son whose affection penetrates even the marrow of his bones. At the moment of death they cannot succeed each other. As for this illusory body, on the day when, though exalted in rank, pain reaches it, the six relatives are at its side, as if for a blind man you should light torches. Of what use were these to such as are deprived of eyesight? I have reflected that all acts whatever are subject to instability, and must fall back in error. There is little happiness and much sorrow. The body doth not exist of itself, and the world, which is all vacuity, cannot be inhabited long. Beings which are born, die. Things which are finished, decay. In quiet cometh danger: in possession, loss. All beings are in tumult and confusion; all must return to void. The soul is without form; its progress is in darkness, and so it reaches the calamity of birth and death. Nor does it attain these once for all; but its desires and affections retain it in the bonds of ignorance. It plunges into the river of birth and death; and can in no wise acquire the comprehension of these. For this reason would I fly to the mountains; all my thoughts are turned to the four voids, towards the salvation of purity, of repressed lusts, and of extinct anger; I shall seek to direct my reflections to that which attains void and annihilation; and not only this, but I shall re-ascend to the source, I shall return to the beginning. I shall begin to issue from the root, and thus I expect to attain the mighty rest."

The king Bimbására, and the elders, pleased with the explanation thus given them by the prince, inferred that he was one of those prodigies destined to obtain the doctrine of Buddha, and trusted to his saving them amongst the first.

C. The prince kept silence and pursued his way, and continuing his reflections, said, "Now that I am about to enter the mountains, of what use to me are these precious garments? It is for such treasures as these that the ignorant and stupid men of the world expose themselves to danger." He then saw a hunter pass by, dressed in the garment prescribed by the law. The prince joyfully said to himself, "Behold the genuine dress of a man, the dress of him who, of pity, shall save the world. O hunter, why hast thou put it on? If thou wilt exchange it, thou wilt fulfil my desires." He then gave the huntsman his gold-adorned vesture, and received in exchange that conformable to the law, *Chin yue*, and passed on quickly. The hunter was delighted, and not less so the Bodhisattwa. The prince put on the *Chin yue* in lieu of his soft and splendid raiment, and looking with a pure eye upon his *seng kia li* (religious cowl), entered among the mountains. Charmed at having found the garments prescribed by the law, the Bodhisattwa shed a light which illumined the mountains and the forests. Amongst the *Tao szu*, one named *A lan*, and another *Kia lan*, who had passed many years in the study and who had sufficed in the four contemplations and attained five supernatural faculties, seeing this light were struck with amazement and asked, "What signifieth this prodigy?" They went forth to investigate, and beholding the prince said, "Siddharta hath indeed quitted his home! Welcome Siddharta! Let him sit on this bed; he shall have a clear spring and pleasant fruit. Let him now eat!" They then added in verse, "The Sun-King hath begun to rise; he is even now above the mountain top, and the light of knowledge is seen of all beings. If any behold the face of his image, he shall no more know weariness; for his reason and his virtue are without peer; there is nothing equal with which to compare them!" Then the Bodhisattwa took up the verse; "Although ye have cultivated the four fixed ideas, your spirits do not conceive supreme intelligent reason (*Prajna bodhi*). The rectitude of the heart is the root of it; it consists not in the worship of perverse genii, in the observance of vulgar things, which may be truly called searching for Bráhma in a long night. It is thus that he who knoweth not reason falleth by the revolution of the wheel into life and death." Then the Bodhisattwa conceived a merciful thought; seeing how all beings are subject to old age and ignorance, and how they cannot assure themselves against infirmities and the pains of death, he desired to effect their deliverance in order to render their thoughts single; and permitting that all, without exception, should sustain hunger and thirst, cold and heat, gain and loss, the pains of sin and other afflictions, he sought to calm and soften (these evils) ; finally to *unify* their thoughts and give rise to feelings of joy. He considered how, in the three worlds, there were pains and sadness, fears and alarms, and the disappointments of society ; and he longed to soothe men and lead them to abstraction, in short to *unify* their thoughts and give birth to the sentiment of protection. He yearned to save from the five conditions and the eight ills, those beings who clouded with ignorance and darkened by stupidity, distinguish not true reason. He longed to effect their salvation, and so to arrange that they should experience no contradiction in *unifying* their thoughts ; that they should experience the good and not the ill, and should feel no regret in abandoning the eight actions of the age, profit, loss, destruction, exaltation, praise, injury, grief and joy, so that they be neither moved nor disturbed. It is this which produced the second contemplation.

D. He then set forth again upon his route, and came to the valley* of *Sse na.* This valley was level and straight ; there were many fruit trees of different kinds ; every where there were living springs and lakes for ablution. All was pure and serene. There were no spiders, flies, hornets, wasps, or flees. In this valley there was a *Tao szu* named *Sse na.* He instructed disciples to the number of five hundred and guided their conduct. The Bodhisattwa sat down under a *So lo* tree (साल or शाल, Sála, Shorea robusta), and for the sake of his intentions asked for the supreme *bodhi* of unsurpassed truth. The gods presented him with a sweet dew ; but the Bodhisattwa would not accept it ; and he constrained himself to take no more daily than a single grain of hemp seed and one of rice to sustain his existence. He remained seated thus for six years. His body became exceedingly emaciated, and his skin adhered to the bones. His original purity, his repose, his profound calm, his silence, occupied his whole soul ; but his thoughts tranquilly dwelt upon, 1st. number, 2d. consequence, 3d. judgment, 4th. sight, 5th. return, 6th. purity. He expressed his thoughts three or four times. He went out by the twelve gates, but without disseminating or communicating his thoughts. His divine faculties became excellent. He penetrated and rejected desires and evil. He entered no more into the five cloaks, and experienced no longer the five desires. All evils became extinct of themselves. His reflection weighed, distinguished, and and illustrated. His thoughts saw without effort. He was as a hero who hath conquered. It was thus that by dint of purity he arrived at the third contemplation.

* In the original *Chhouan ;* which signifies not merely a *mountain-torrent,* and in general *running water,* but a *valley* watered by a rivulet.

E. In traversing heaven, Indra reflected thus, and said: "Behold, six entire years hath the Bodhisattwa been seated under a tree: his person hath become exceedingly emaciated. We must now present to this *king causing the wheel to revolve*, wherewithal to compensate the abstinence of six years." He then influenced the two daughters of *Sse na* in such wise that they had a dream. The world was completely at an end, and there was on the water a flower which had the lustre of the seven precious things. Suddenly the flower dried up, and lost its original hue: but there came a man to water it, and it was restored as at first. Then began all the flowers that were in the water to put forth and grow, and their sprouts covered the water as if they would grow out of it. The two damsels having thus dreamed, awakened, and surprised at the prodigy, ran to narrate it to their father. The father was unable to expound it. He consulted all the old men, but none could say what the dream imported. Indra once more descended and transformed himself into a Brahmacharí to interpret the dream of the young damsels. "The flower which you have seen produced on the water, is the eldest son of King Be thsing. Behold him for six years beneath the tree; his body is extremely emaciated. The flower which is dried up, and the man who caused it to revive by watering it, signify that food must be offered him to eat. The little flowers, the stalks of which would come forth, are the men who live or die in the five conditions." Indra then pronounced the following *gatha*:—"For six years he hath neither reclined nor laid down. He hath not so much as thought of hunger or thirst. His efforts have as yet attained nothing. His body is emaciated: his skin and his bones are in contact. Arm yourself with a respectful spirit, and offer food to the Bodhisattwa. There shall be great happiness in the present age, while the fruit and the reward shall be in subsequent ages." The damsels replied, "What shall we do to present him with food?" The Brahmachari replied, "Take ye the milk of five hundred cows, and present it to him to drink in succession. Every time that the milk of a cow shall be milked, you shall take the milk of that cow, and use it in the preparation of boiled rice. When, in boiling, the rice and milk shall rise from the vessel, it shall rise fifty-six feet upwards to the left, downwards to the right, to the right above, and to the left below. You shall fill his pot with this rice by means of a ladle, that it be not soiled."

F. The two damsels presented (the boiled rice) to the Bodhisattwa. The latter wished first to bathe himself ere he partook of the rice. He proceeded therefore towards the running stream, and washed his person. When he had finished his ablutions, he came forth from the water, the gods and the genii sheltering him with branches of trees. The young damsels then presented him with the rice and milk. When he had eaten thereof his strength returned, and, in a formula, he vowed infinite happiness to the young damsels, saying, "May you return to the Three Honorable Ones!" Having finished his meal he washed his hands, rinsed his mouth, and washed out his pot. In going away, he threw the last into the river. It ascended against the current. It had not gone seven *li* ere the gods formed a Garuda which came flying, and seizing the pot, bore it as well as the hair, to the spot where they have erected a tower in their honor.

G. The Bodhisattwa then proceeded on his route, and when about to pass the river *Ni lian chhen*, he made a gátha, signifying, "In passing the *Ni lian chhen* (Nilajan) I am moved with compassion for all men. The three conditions and the three poisoned spots, I will remove them as if they were washed away with water." The Bodhisattwa then reflected: "All ignorant beings fall into darkness. I must lay hold on the eight right things, and by the washing of water, I shall efface the three poisoned spots." He then began to ascend the bank. Blue birds to the number of five hundred, flew thrice around the Bodhisattwa, and having sung dolorously, departed.

H. He again set forth, and as he passed the lake of the blind dragon, this dragon issued rejoicing, manifesting his delight at the sight of the Bodhisattwa, and pronouncing this *gatha.* "Oh what happiness! I behold Siddhárta, who comes to deliver us! How shall we delay offering him the juices of the sweet unsurpassed dew? When he walks, the earth trembles beneath his tread. Musical instruments emit sounds of their own accord. He is truly as the Buddhas of times past. On this point I for one have no doubts. Even now will he, as the sun of Buddha, enlighten all beings, and awaken them from their slumber!"

I. He then advanced once more, and beheld the hill *Sou lin.* The country was flat and regular, and on every side clear and delightful. It produced delicate and beautiful plants. Sweet rivulets flowed in abundance. The perfume of flowers was delicious and pure. In the midst there was a lofty and handsome tree, all the branches of which were disposed with regularity the one above the other: all the leaves were adjoined to each other, and the flowers thickly locked together as the ornament of the gods. A pennon was at the top of the tree. It was the king of all the forest, and of original happiness. Then (Buddha) advancing a little, beheld a man mowing grass. The Bodhisattwa asked, "What is now thy name?" "My name is '*Happy Omen*,' and I now cut the *grass of happy omen.*" "If thou give me of that grass, then shall the ten parts of the world possess a happy omen." Then *Happy Omen* pronounced the following gátha:" "He hath rejected the dignity of Holy King, the seven treasures, the damsel of jasper for a spouse, beds of gold and of silver, carpets, broidered and many coloured stuffs, the plaintive voice of the bird *Kan than*, the harmony of the eight concords, and his superiority over the God Brahma, and now he provides himself with grass." The Bodhisattwa replied with this gátha: "I have made a vow during an *asankya*; it is to save men of the five conditions. I now proceed to fulfil this vow. It is on this account that I desired that the mower of grass should give me a handful of the grass, that holding it out towards the king of the trees, worldly thoughts might be wholly dispersed. Now must I carry out these purposes." The mower then presented him with the grass, and spread it upon the ground as had been told him. The Bodhisattwa sat down, and received the present. The Bodhisattwa performed the three things necessary to be seated, and having come before the tree, said, "If I can obtain the doctrine, I shall not evade the three oaths; my sides shall dry up and become immobile. If it be so that I attain complete Buddhahood, and obtain the doctrine, every hour shall produce its thought." Thereupon the Bodhisattwa sat down, and entered extasy. He cast away sorrow and the idea of joy; without either sadness or the thoughts of pleasure, his heart neither rested upon good, nor directed itself to evil. He was truly in the mean. Like a man who bathes, and, purified, covers himself with white felt; without, he was all purity, within, a spotless augury. Annihilated in repose, he completed without change the four contemplations; and after finishing these, he obtained determinate thought without abating his great compassion; by his knowledge and procedure, he penetrated the prime wonders, and comprehended the operation of the thirty-seven classes of the doctrine. And what are the thirty-seven classes? They are, first, the four *stases* of ideas of the *mens*; secondly, the four interruption of the *mens*; thirdly, the four spiritual sufficiencies; fourthly, the five roots; fifthly, the five forces; sixthly, the seven intelligent *mens*; seventhly the eight right actions. After the having run these over, he recommenced the void of pain. Extraordinarily without form, without wish or *ego*, he thought of the world which, by avarice, love, gluttony, lust, falls into the pains of life and death. How few understand how to know themselves, all deriving their origin from the *twelve nidánas!* What are these twelve? Their origin is ignorance; ignorance in action produces knowledge; knowledge in action produces name and title; title in action, produces the six entrances; the six entrances in action produce desire; desire in action produces love; love in action produces *caption*; caption in action produces possession; possession in action produces birth; birth in action produces old age and death, pain and compassion, sorrow and suffering, which are the pains of the heart and the instrument, of great calamity. When the soul has fallen into the vicissitude of life and death, if it would obtain the doctrine, it must interrupt love, and extinguish and suppress passion and lust. When quietude comes, then is ignorance extinct; ignorance being extinct, then is action extinct; action becoming extinct, then is knowledge extinct; knowledge being extinct, then are name and title extinct; name and title extinct, then are the six entrances extinct; the six entrances extinct, then is renewed pleasure extinct; renewed pleasure extinct, then is desire extinct; desire extinct, then is love extinct; love extinct, *caption* is extinct; caption extinct then is possession extinct; possession extinct, then is birth extinct; birth extinct, then are ended old age and death, sadness, compassion, pain and sorrow, the afflictions of the heart and all great calamities; and by this is meant to *have the doctrine*.

K. The Bodhisattwa then said within himself: "Now must I submit to the ministers and descendants of the *Mára*." He then caused to issue from the space between his eyebrows a ray of light which struck the palace of the Mára. The Mára, greatly alarmed, could not tranquillize his heart; and seeing that the Bodhisattwa was already beneath the tree, pure, without desires, unremittingly occupied with subtile thoughts, and that in his heart the venom of the passions, and eating, and drinking had no attractions, and that he thought no longer of sexual pleasures, he thus reflected: "This is the accomplishment of the doctrine; truly will there be a great victory over me. Ere yet he become Buddha, I will go and lay waste his doctrine." The son of Mára, *Siu ma thi*, interrupted his father thus: "The Bodhisattwa practises purity. In the three worlds he hath no peer; of himself hath he attained purity. The Brahmas and all the gods, by hundreds of millions go to pay him homage and to gaze upon him; it is not him that men or gods may attack. In disturbing his quietude and giving rise to evil, let himself destroy his own happiness. Oh king of the Mára, if you listen to these reasons, call hither the three damsels of jasper, the first named *Gracious Love*, the second *Ever Happy*, and the third *Great Joy*. Trouble not yourself, Oh king, my father; let *us* interrupt the penitence of the Bodhisattwa, a matter not important enough to disturb you. Be not cast down, Oh king!" Then the three damsels, whose charms were exalted by their celestial raiment, approached the Bodhisattwa followed by five hundred damsels of jasper. The musical instruments which they played upon, their songs, their lewd language, were all directed to disturb his study of the doctrine. All three took up the strain: "Thy virtue and thy goodness are such, said they, that the gods venerate and would worship thee: and it is for this that we come before thee. We are beautiful and pure; our age is in its flower; we implore permission to serve you, and to attend you on the right and on the left, in rising in the morning, and in lying down at night."

The beauty and the blandishments of these damsels produced no effect upon the soul of the Bodhisattwa; by a single word he transformed them into grey-headed old women, their teeth fallen out, their eyes lustreless, and their backs so crooked that they were compelled to avail themselves of the help of staves to return to whence they came. The Mára seeing this, was exasperated with rage, and coming with his 1,800,000 demons surrounded the space of thirty-six yojanas. These demons assumed the shape of lions, bears, rhinoceroses, tigers, elephants, oxen, horses, dogs, hogs, and apes. Some were seen with the heads of animals upon human bodies; others who had the forms of venomous serpents and the heads of six-eyed tortoises. Some had several heads, with fangs and crooked claws: they bore mountains on their backs, and caused fire, thunder, and lightning to issue from their mouths. They came from four sides to attack the Bodhisattwa, with all manner of arms. But nothing could daunt the courage of the latter, who came off victorious from all the attacks of his enemies. Finally the Bodhisattwa having, by his supernatural power, overcome and subdued the Mára, all the gods, full of joy, descended from heaven and scattered flowers. The Bodhisattwa obtained the rank of Buddha under the name of *Shy kia wen Jou lai* (Sákya Muni Tathágata) with the honorific title of *Establisher of men and gods*, and *the venerable Buddha of the age.*—Kl.

(4) *Covering him as he issued from the bath.*—See note 3 letter F. According to Hiuan thsang, Sákya bathed in the river Ni lian chhen; in memory of which a tower was erected which existed at his day.—Kl.

(5.) *Offered Foe rice and milk.*—In Singalese books only one woman is mentioned as having contributed to the sustenance of Buddha with milk and rice. Her name was *Sujatawa (Sujata?)* During a million kalpas she had done a vast number of good works, in the hope of having it in her power one day or other to present rice and milk to a Buddha. Her wish was granted. She was the daughter of a *Sitawno* (wealthy man) of the country of *Senananam niangani*, and became wife of the principal *Sitawno* of *Barenessi* (Benares). She offered a golden pot worth a million *massa* of gold, full of rice and milk to Buddha the very day of his accomplishment; and after that accomplishment, having heard him preach, she entered upon eternal blessedness.*—Kl.

(6.) *Under the Pei to tree.*—That is the *Borassus flabelliformis*, or toddy tree, in Sanscrit ताल tála. According to the legend given in note 3. D. it was not under a *Pei to*, but under a *So lo* (शाल Sála) that Buddha remained six years in mortifications. The Mongol legend given by M. Schmidt makes it an Indian fig, *ficus religiosa;* "near the king of trees, a

* Upham, Vol. III. 56.

lofty *Bodhi,* he sat with his legs crossed and in a motionless posture; he vanquished and subjected the *shimnous* (demons) and on the morrow, became Buddha to open the exhaustible sources of life."* In the account of Hiuan thsang it is likewise under a *Bodhi* that Sákya Muni is said to have rested several years.—Kl.

It will be seen when we come to Chapter XXXVII. that from the mode of propagation ascribed to the *Pei to* tree by Fa hian, it could not possibly belong to any of the palm tribe. His account identifies it with the *Ficus indica.* This tree is often produced from the seeds that have been dropped by birds in the axils of the Borassus flabelliformis, where they grow, and extend their descending roots so as in time to embrace entirely the Palmyra, except its upper parts. "In very old ones the top thereof is just seen issuing from the trunk of the Banyan itself as if it grew from thence, whereas it runs down through its centre and has its roots in the ground, the Palm being oldest."† This sight is familiar to all who have been in India.—J..W. L.

(8) *Three beautiful girls.*—For further particulars of Sákya's temptations the reader may refer to the Asiatic Researches, Vol. XX. p. 301.—J. W. L.

(9.) *The blind dragon with brilliant scales.*—Hiuan thsang names this dragon *Mou chi lin tho.*—Kl.

The dragon, here called *Mou chi lin tho,* is the *Muchalindo* of the Páli Annals. He is said to have protected Buddha during a thunder storm by encircling him seven times; thus forming a dormitory in which, remote for all disturbance, the latter reposed for a week in the enjoyment of heavenly beatitude. See also *Notices of the Life of Sákya,* As. Res. XX. p. 293. —J. W. L.

(10) The circumstance here alluded to is detailed at large in the twenty-eighth volume of the M*do,* entitled འཛངས་བླུན། (H*dsangs* b*lun*). This work has been published at St. Petersburgh, with a German translation by that eminent orientalist, M. I. J. Schmidt. In the legend in question, Sákya is represented as hesitating, after his attainment of Buddhahood, whether he should engage in the promulgation of the Law, or, in consequence of the hopeless perversity of mankind, emancipate himself at once by entering nirvána. Brahma and the other gods of his mansion are represented as entreating Sákya to enter at once upon the good work; and as reminding him of his prodigious efforts in former births to attain the opportunity he then enjoyed. In this way several legends are narrated at length: how countless ages ago, when Sákya was *Kanashinipali,* a king of Jambudwíp, he made a thousand holes in his body and lit as many lamps, or wicks, in them, for the sake of the doctrine;—how in another birth, when he was a king named *Jiling Girali,*

* *Gesch. der Ost Mongolian.*

† *Voigt, Hort. Cal. Suburb.*

he, for the same object, had a thousand iron spikes driven into his body :—how countless kalpas ago, when he was *Damgama*, son and heir of the king of Jambudwípa, he threw himself into a pit of fire ;—how innumerable ages past, when at Benares, as Udpala, he tore his own skin for paper, broke his bones for a pen, and used his blood for ink, as the condition of hearing the doctrine ;—and how, at a period unspeakably and immeasurably distant, he existed as a king of Jambudwípa named *Shidshi*, and was put to the test by Indra and Vishwakarma, the former assuming the shape of a hawk and chasing the latter in the form of a dove into the arms of the king, who negociated for its rescue at the expense of his own flesh. On being reminded of all these events, Sákya's resolution is taken, and he proceeds to Benares to "turn the wheel of the Law." Schmidt, *Der Weise und der Thor*, Vol. II. pp. 3—20. Some of these legends the reader will remember have been referred to in the earlier part of this volume.*—J. W. L.

(11) *Offered him parched rice and honey.*—Buddha, says Hiuan thsang, being seated with his legs crossed, and having attained the joy of eternal beatitude, issued, after seven days, from his profound meditations. Two merchants passing through the forest at the time, were warned by the guardian genius, who said, "The prince of the race of the Sákyas is here, he has obtained the rank of Buddha, his spirit is absorbed in meditation, and during forty nine days he has eaten nothing." The two merchants approached Buddha and offered him some parched rice and honey. Buddha accepted their presents, but as he had no vessels to contain them, the four kings of heaven coming from the cardinal points, brought him each a golden pot. Buddha declined their acceptance, because vessels of such precious material were not suitable to the ecclesiastical condition which he had embraced. He refused besides other pots of valuable material, and eventually accepted one of a very ordinary kind, &c."—Kl.

The story of these merchants is otherwise told in Pali works ; but is not worth repeating here.—J. W. L.

(12) *Where he converted Kia she and his brethren.*—These are the three brothers of Kia she (Kásyapa) who were converted by Sákya Muni ; namely *Uruwilwa Kásyapa* (Kásyapa of the quince tree), *Nadi* Kásyapa (of the river), and *Gaya Kásyapa* (of Gaya). These three personages are not to be confounded with Mahá Kásyapa (*Kia she*) nor with one named in Chinese *Shy ly Kia she* (in Sanscrit *Dasawala*, the ten-fold strong) who was one of the first five persons converted by Sákya Muni. According to the *Fan y ming i* the word Kásyapa signifies *family of the great tortoise* : according to others, *imbibed splendor*. The ancestors having from generation to generation

* See pages 55, 62, &c.

applied themselves to the study of reason, a miraculous tortoise, carrying a divine table on its back, replied to the questions of these virtuous ancestors, and hence the family name. He was able to perform the superior acts of *self-excitation;* and therefore they gave him the name of the *first of the high action*. Compare Chap. XX. note 39.—Kl.

(13) *Four great towers.*—That is, at Kapilavastu, Gaya, Benares, and Kusinagara.—J. W. L.

CHAPTER XXXII.

A yu becomes King of the Iron Wheel, and reigns over Yan feou thi.—He visits Hell, and constructs a prison for the punishment of criminals.—History of a Pi khieou who entered that prison.—The King is converted.

The King *A yu*, while yet a lad,[1] was playing upon the road; he met *Shy kia foe*, who was going about begging his subsistence. The lad, greatly pleased, gave a handful of earth to Foe. Foe took it, returned it to the ground, and passed along. The earth in return for that made him (A yu) *King of the Wheel of Iron.*[2] He reigned over *Yan feou thi*, and mounted the Iron Wheel. In visiting *Yan feou thi* he saw Hell[3] situated between two mountains and entirely surrounded with a girdle of iron, where the damned are confined. He asked his ministers the meaning of this; they answered that that was the place where the King of the Demons, *Yan lo*,[4] imprisoned the guilty. The King reflected and said, "If the King of the Demons hath devised a hell for the punishment of the guilty, why should not I, who am the king of men, prepare a hell for the punishment of the guilty?" Then addressing his ministers, he asked, "Who is he that can prepare me a hell for the punishment of the guilty?" They replied, "None but an extremely wicked man can do so."[5] The King then sent his ministers every where in quest of a wicked man. They found on the banks of a river, a black giant, with yellow hair and green eyes, talons instead of feet, and the mouth of a fish. He whistled the birds and the quadrupeds, and when these came, killed them with arrows so that not one escaped. When they had found this man they returned to the King. The King summoned him privately and said to him; "Enclose a space with a lofty wall, and place within it all manner of flowers and fruits, also beautiful valleys, and lakes pleasing and lovely to look upon, alluring men to gaze on them with eagerness. Thou shalt make a gate to this prison, and if any come and enter, thou shalt seize him forthwith, and shalt punish the guilty according to their kinds, allowing none to escape; and should I, even, enter, slacken not the punishment of the guilty: I make thee prince of the hell." A *Pi khieou* begging his subsistence entered the gate. The keeper of the gate was about to punish him as a criminal. The terrified *Pi khieou* solicited some respite till he had taken his repast. Some time after a man entered. The keeper of the gate put him into a mortar and pounded him; a red froth came from him. The *Pi khieou* having witnessed this, was convinced that the body is perishable and subject to misery, empty as a water-bubble[6] or as froth, and became Arhan. When that was done, the gaoler put the froth into a pot; the *Pi khieou* was enraptured. The fire dried up the froth, and when it had cooled, there arose from it a water-lily. The *Pi khieou* sat down, and the gaoler went to the King to rehearse the marvels that had been performed in the prison. He desired that the king should go and behold them. The king replied, "I have first something urgent to do; I cannot go thither now." The gaoler replied, "This is no small matter; it behoves you, oh king, to come quickly, and that you postpone other matters." The king followed him and entered: the *Pi khieou* preached to him the doctrine. The king obtained the faith, and repented of all the wickedness he had hitherto done. From that time he believed in and honored the *Three Precious Ones.*[7] He habitually went to the tree *Pei to*[8] to repent himself of his sins, to chastise himself, and subject himself to the eight purifications. The king's wife asked whither the king daily repaired to promenade? The grandees replied, that he always went to the tree *Pei to.* The queen awaited the time when the king was not there, and sent people to cut and throw down the tree. When the king returned and beheld this, he was so troubled and afflicted that he fell to the earth. The nobles bathed his face with water, and after a long time he returned to his senses. He caused a brick wall to be built round the roots of the tree, and these to be watered with a hundred pitchers of cow's milk. He cast himself upon ground, and made oath never to rise again unless the tree were reproduced. Scarcely had he made this oath, than the tree began to sprout again from its roots, and from that time to the present it has become at least ten *chang*[9] high!

NOTES.

(1) *King A yu, while yet a lad.*—The legend here alluded to may be found in M. Schmidt's *Der Weise und der Thor*, Vol. II. p. 217. "Once upon a time the Victorious-Accomplished (Sákya) went abroad with *Kungawo* (Ananda) in quest of alms. Several children were diverting themselves by the road-side, erecting little buildings of earth. One of these saw Buddha afar off, and resolved to present him on his approach with alms. For this purpose he took a handful of the earth they were using to present to Buddha; but being very small, he was unable to reach the dish. "Stoop down," exclaimed he to his companion, "and getting on thy back, I will put my offering in the alms-dish." "Willingly," replied his companion; so getting upon his shoulders, the former stretched out the handful of earth to Buddha. Hereupon Buddha lowered the begging pot and received the earth. Having received it, he transferred it to Kungawo with this command; "Make of this earth a (fluid) mud, and besprinkle therewith the temple. *Kungawo!* in as much as the temple shall be sprinkled with the gift brought me by the impulse of a happy spirit, and so accepted by me, for this meritorious service, after the lapse of one hundred years from my emancipation from pain, shall this little boy, by the name of *Asoka*, reign over *Jambudwípa;* and after he shall have established the pre-eminence of the Three Jewels throughout all lands, he shall bring the *sarira* to the highest honor, and erect for these at one and the same time, eighty-four thousand *sthupa* throughout Jambudwíp," &c.

I give this short legend, not so much in illustration of the text, as for its assertion that Asoka was a contemporary of Sákya Muni; the only instance of such that I at present remember. It would be curious to ascertain if any counterpart of this legend exists in Páli. I fancy not, and strongly suspect that the present is a Trans-himalayan interpolation. M. de Körös mentions that in the copy of the *Kah ghyur* from which he made his analysis, the H*dsangs blun* is stated to have been translated from the Chinese.* The existence of a Chinese copy would account for Fa hian's familiarity with many of the legends narrated in that work.—J. W. L.

(2) *King of the Iron Wheel.*—See note 12 Chap. XVII. It is there explained that the *king of the iron wheel* would appear at the time when the life of man, after having attained its limit of brevity (ten years), should return by a succession of increments to twenty thousand years. Nevertheless, in the text quoted in the *San tsang fa sou*, and which M. Remusat had before him, it is stated that "According to the *Ta chi tou lun*, the age of man augments and decreases in the lesser kalpas. The life of man is first 84,000 years: at the end of every century this term is abridged by on year, decreasing thus to 10 years. After remaining thus one hundred years, it increases again by one year, till it attains twenty thousand; and in this course of time appears *the king of the iron wheel*," &c. As the Buddha Sákya Muni, with whom A yu or Asoka was contemporary, was born at a time when the duration of human life was but a hundred years, it is evident that the king of the iron wheel did not withhold his appearance in the world till this duration extended to twenty thousand years.—Kl.

(3) *He saw Hell.*—According to the Buddhist tracts collected in the *San tsang fa sou*, precisely at the southern extremity of Jambudwípa, at the depth of 500 *yojanas* is the abode of king Yan lo; that is the infernal regions. They are named *Ti yo* because they are beneath the earth. Some of these Hells are great and some small. Of the great eight are hot and eight cold: of the smaller ones, sixteen are situated at the gates of each of the great ones, and so disposed that the torments successively increase. Hence they are named *Yeou thseng yo* (hells of transmigration and reduplication). All living beings condemned to suffering pass through these hells; and when they have passed through their punishment in one they are transferred to another. The sixteen mansions of hell thus passed are,—

1st. *He sha ti yo* (the hell of black sand). A hot blast blows over this black sand, making it burning hot, and carrying it against the skin and bones of the damned, who, thus scorched, suffer frightful anguish.

2nd. *Fey shi ti yo.*—Balls of iron, crammed with burning excrements, shoot forward and press against the damned, who are thus compelled to lay hold of them. These burn the bodies and hands of the damned, who are then compelled to put them in their mouths and swallow them, so that, from the

* *Asiatic Researches*, vol. xx, p. 480.

gullet to the belly, there is nothing that is not burnt. Insects with iron beaks peck their flesh, penetrating even to the bones.

3rd. *Thi ting ti yo.*—The ministers of this hell stretch the damned upon red hot iron, and fix them there with nails; nailing their hands and feet, and all round their bodies with five hundred nails.

4th. *Kio ti yo,* the hell of hunger:—The demons pour into the mouths of the damned melted copper, which, descending from the gullet to the belly, causes intolerable anguish.

5th. *Ko ti yo,* the hell of thirst.—The ministers of this hell take balls of red hot iron and place them in the mouths of the damned, thereby burning their lips and tongue.

6th. *Toung ho ti yo.*—The damned are cast into caldrons where they are boiled, and where their bodies rise, and sink, and turn round till wholly destroyed.

7th. *To toung ho ti yo.*—The ministers of this hell plunge the damned into caldrons, seethe and destroy them, and then, taking them out with hooks, cast them into other caldrons.

8th. *Shy mo ti yo.*—The damned are laid upon a large hot stone; other red hot stones keep their feet and hands stretched out, bruising their bodies, and reducing their flesh and bones to a stew.

9th. *Nouing hiouei ti yo.*—The damned are bathed in blood and pus: which they are compelled also to swallow; their bodies, members, head, and face are smeared with these, and they are thus consumed.

10th. *Liang ho ti yo.*—In this hell there are mighty fires. The damned take iron measures to measure out the fire to consume their bodies. The pain of their burning extorts from them groans and loud cries.

11th. *Hoei ho ti yo.*—A river of ashes, 500 *yeou siun* long, and as many broad, exhaling pestilential vapours: its surges dash and strike against each other with a terrific noise. Above and below there are iron spikes; on the shores, forests of swords; the branches, leaves, flowers, and fruits, are all so many swords. The damned are carried along by the current: whether they sink or whether they float, the iron points penetrate their bodies, within and without, occasioning ten thousand pains. If they leave the stream and come to the shore, the swords there wound them, and panthers and wolves devour their living flesh. If they fly, and for shelter climb the trees, the blades turned downwards fall upon them, and those turned upwards lacerate their hands. If they support themselves upon their feet, their skin and flesh fall to the ground cut in a thousand pieces; their nerves and their veins hang together. A bird with an iron beak pecks their head and brains. They then return to the river of ashes, and follow the current;

but whether diving down or rising to the surface, the iron points penetrate their bodies, tearing the skin and the flesh. Blood and pus issue from the wounds, and nothing but the whitened bones remain floating on the surface. A cold wind then blows over and revives them; and they pass on to the hell of iron balls.

12th. *Thi wan ti yo.*—The damned are here compelled to hold in their hands red hot iron balls; their hands and their feet are thus destroyed; their bodies stand up blazing.

13th. *Yn fou ti yo.*—The ministers if this hell stretch the damned upon red hot iron, and with hatchets of the same material, hack their hands and feet, their ears, noses, and members, causing them unheard of tortures.

14th. *Chay lang ti yo.*—Panthers and terrific wolves gnaw and tear the damned. Their flesh falls off; the bones are laid bare; and pus and blood run like a river.

15th. *Khian chou ti yo.*—A violent wind shakes the leaves of the sword-tree, and the swords fall upon the bodies of the damned; whose heads and faces and members are thus wounded and torn. An iron-beaked bird plucks out their eyes.

16th. *Han ping ti yo.*—A strong cold wind blows over the bodies of the damned and stiffens them; frost attacks their skin and bones, and causes them to fall down. The pain thereof extorts from them loud cries. Now, after the close of life, all living beings who have committed wickedness fall into these different hells.*

These are the sixteen lesser hells. The names of the eight burning hells and the eight freezing ones, which are greater ones, equally express the nature of the punishment to which the damned are subjected. The eight burning hells are.

1st. *Siang ti yo.*—In this hell, long and sharp talons of iron grow upon the hands of living beings, who with inflamed eyes and hearts full of rage and hatred, tear the flesh from each other, rending it in a savage manner. They believe themselves now dead; but a cold wind passes over them, their skin and flesh are reproduced, and they revive. In the *She lun* this hell is called that of *the resuscitated* (*Teng ho ti yo.*)

2nd. *He ching ti yo.*—In this hell demons bind the damned with chains of burning iron, and then decapitate or saw them. Burning chains clasp their bodies, scorch their skin, penetrate their flesh, and calcine their bones, causing the marrow to flow out; thus inflicting a thousand tortures. This hell is hence called that of *black chains.* (*He*, black, in a metaphorical sense.)

* *San tsang fa sou*, B. XLV. pp. 19—21.

3rd. *Touy ya li yo.*—This hell is also called *Choung ho.* Here are great mountains of rock, which spontaneously fall upon the damned, whose body, bones and flesh, are thus reduced to a pulp. Hence it is called the hell of *compressed mountains.*

4th. *Kiao wen ti yo.*—Here the damned are cast into vast caldrons where they are boiled, and, suffering horribly, utter loud cries.

5th. *Ta kiao wen ti yo.*—When the damned have been in this manner boiled by the demons, a wind blows that causes them to revive. They are then conveyed to furnaces where they are roasted, and suffer such cruel agonies that they utter frightful cries; and hence its name.

6th. *Chao chy ti yo.*—Its walls are of iron. The fire which there burns produces whirlwinds of flame which consume the damned within and without, and burning their skin and their flesh, and roasting them, cause them ten thousand tortures: and hence its name.

7th. *Ta chao chy ti yo.*—The walls of iron, reddened by fire within and without, consume the damned. There are pits full of flames and fire, and on both sides of these pits are mountains all of fire. The damned are taken hold of with iron pitchforks and tossed into the fire. Their flesh is roasted, causing them ten thousand tortures; and hence the name.

8th. *Wou kian ti yo.*—The damned undergo in this hell sufferings without intermission. It is the most terrible of all the hells. The appearance (the body) *is there without interruption;* the damned are there born and there die: when dead, they are reproduced; their body experiences no interruption, and hence the name.

The eight cold hells are—

1st. The hell *'O feou to,* or *'O pou to,* in Sanscrit *Arbuda.* This word signifies *wrinkles,* because the damned, by the cold to which their skin and flesh are subject, are wrinkled and chapped.

2d. The hell *Ny lay feou to,* or *Ny tseu pou lo* (in Sanscrit, *Nirarbuda*) This word signifies in Sanscrit *chinks* or *chaps,* because these are experienced by the damned there exposed to the cold.

3rd. The hell *'O cha cha,* or *Ho ho.*—These words are not interpreted. The damned by reason of the extreme cold cannot move their lips, and can therefore only produce this sound.

4th. The hell *'O po po,* or *Hiao hiao po.*—The damned, by reason of the extreme cold, are unable to move their tongues, and can only produce this sound betwixt their lips.

5th. The hell *'Eou heou.*—The damned by reason of the extreme cold can move neither tongue nor lips,—but the air passing into their weasand, produces this sound.

6th. The hell *Yo pho lo* (in Sanscrit, *Utphala*), or *ming pho lo*. This Sanscrit word signifies *blue water lilly*, because the damned, by reason of extreme cold, have their skin blown (expanded) like this flower.

7th. The hell *Po teou mo*, or *Po the mo* (in Sanscrit *Padma*, and in Páli *Paduma*). This Sanscrit word signifies *red lotus*; because the damned by reason of excessive cold, have their flesh plaited and coloured like this flower.

8th. The hell *Fen to ly* (in Sanscrit Pundaríka). This Sanscrit word signifies *white lotus*, because the damned, from excessive cold behold their flesh detach itself and fall away, leaving their naked bones like this flower. It is also named *Ma ha po the mo* (Mahá padma) the great red lotus. The skin and the flesh are half opened and similar to this flower.—C. L.

The division of the hells is somewhat differently given in the Buddhist works of Ceylon. They admit eight principal ones, under the name of *Naraka*, or *Niraya*. Around each of these are placed four smaller hells; the number of these places of punishment being thus raised to forty. In the *Dharma-pradípeka*, or *Torch of the Law*, a Singalese work interspersed with ancient Pali and Sanscrit texts, there is a Sanscrit couplet in which the names of the eight principal hells are thus recapitulated: *Samjívam, Kála-sútramcha, Samgháto, Ráuravas tathá, Mahárauravatápákhyá, Pratápáchi-námakáh*. These eight hells, mentioned in Menu (IV. 88, 89), are named *Ashta mahánáraká*.—E. B.

(4) *The king of the demons, Yan lo.*—Also called *Yan mo lo*, or *Yan ma lo*; corresponding with यम in Sanscrit.—Kl.

(5) *None but a very wicked man can do so.*—To keep a prison is one of the twelve bad acts reproved by the law, and called *'O liu yi*.—C. L.

(6) *A bubble of water.*—Sákya Muni says in the *Seng yan king*: "The sea is originally motionless and clear; but when storms and whirlwinds vex it, they produce bubbles of water. To this may be compared the nature of the loftiest intelligence, which, like the sea is pure, bright, excellent, till moved by the vanities of the heart, which thus render the world void and without reality. This void and unreal world is absolutely analogous to the bubbles of the sea."*—Kl.

(7) *The three precious ones.*—*Foe, Fa, Seng*, (Buddha, Dharma, Sanga,) or the Supreme Triad. The *Hoa Yan King* says: "That which is called Buddha, Dharma, Sanga, although the name expresses their substances, is in truth of one sole nature and consubstantial. *Buddha* signifies *intelligence*, indicating that his nature and substance are intelligent and rational, that he has enlightened the laws, and that he is neither void, nor being. *Dharma*

* *San tsang fa sou*, B. XLV. pp. 19—21.

is the *law*, or that which regulates: designating the law of silence and of extinction, which serves as the rule of the natural virtues. *Sanga* signifies in Chinese *the united band*, indicating that the excellent virtues separate not in two modes, but remain united."*

Relatively, the *three precious ones* are distinct and dissimilar. 1st *Buddha*: when he began to fulfil the law under the *Po thi* (bodhi) tree, he displayed a body of but six *chang*: when he came to discourse of the book *Hoa yan*, he appeared as the body of the honorable *Lou she na*. 2. *The law*; that is the great revolution, the lesser revolution, the precepts, the discourses, and the compilations which have been revealed in the five times. (The five times are, that of the *Hoa yan*, that of the *Deer-park* (see Chap. XXXIV.), that of the *Fang teng*, that of the *Prajna*, and that of the *nirvána*.) 3. *Sanga*; this designates such as have received the doctrine, who regulate the causes, and gather the fruits; or the *Shing wen*, the *Youan kio*, and the Bodhisattwas. The *Shing wen*, are those who have obtained the understanding of doctrine by the discourses of Foe; the *Youan kio* are those who have obtained the same by the consideration of the twelve concatenations; the Bodhisattwas are intelligence with affection. C. L.

(8) *The tree Pei to*.—Hiuan thsang saw this tree two centuries after Fa hian, as also the wall built around it by King Asoka.—Kl.

(9) *Ten chang*.—About 100 English feet.

CHAPTER XXXIII.

Hill of the Cock's foot.—Sojourn of the great Kia she.—Abode of the Arhans in this hill.

Going thence three *li* to the south, you come to a hill called the *Cock's Foot*.[1] It is here that the *Great Kia she* is actually present. He perforated the foot of the hill that he might enter it, and prevented any other from entering by the same way. At a considerable distance thence, there is a lateral opening, in which is the entire body of *Kia she*. The earth outside of this opening is that over which *Kia she* washed his hands. When the

* *San tsang fa sou*, B. IV. p. 24.

people of that country suffer from headache, they rub themselves with this earth and the pain is removed. In the same hill, to the west, is the abode of the Arhans.[2] The Clergy of Reason,[3] of all kingdoms and countries, come here annually to adore *Kia she*. Those who come with perplexed minds, behold in the night Arhans who discourse with them, and resolve their doubts; and having done this, disappear forthwith. The woods which cover this hill are very dense and tangled. There are many lions, tigers, and wolves, so that you journey not without apprehension.

NOTES.

(1) *The Cock's Foot*,— in Sanscrit कुक्कुटपाद्, *Kukutapáda*; according to the transcription of Hiuan thsang, *Khiu khiu cha po tho.* He adds that this hill is also called *Kiu lou po tho*, or the *foot of the Venerable*, गुरुपाद्. He says that you arrive after travelling one hundred *li* from a woody plain to the east of the river *Mou ho*, which appears to be the Sone. He describes the hill as very steep and lofty, and crowned with three peaks. The venerable Great Kia she (Mahá Kásyapa) dwells there still, for he dared not let his nirvana be seen; and hence it is called the *Hill of the Foot of the Venerable*.*

According to the Chinese and Japanese Chronology *Wa khan kwo to fen nen gakf oun-no tsu*, Kia she, the third Buddha of the present age, retired to this mountain in the 53d year of the XXIX. cycle of sixty, corresponding with 905 B. C.†—Kl.

The identity of names here produces a confusion of persons and dates. It is important to bear in mind that the name *Kia she*, or Kasyapa, which is that of the Buddha immediately preceding Sákya, belongs also to several personages of Buddhic legends. It is that of one of the heresiarchs (p. 144); that of the three principal disciples of Sákya (p. 295) and that of one of the five ecclesiastics converted by the latter (Chap. XXXIV, n. 6.) But the very passage quoted by M. Klaproth, referring the retreat of Kasyapa into the mountain of the Cock's Foot to the year 905 B. C. sufficently shows that Fa hian does not here speak of the Buddha Kásyapa, whose relics he elsewhere mentions as being preserved in the kingdom of Kosala (Chap. XX). The Kásyapa here spoken of can only therefore be one of Sákya's

* *Pian i tian*, B. LXV. p. 43.
† *Nouveau Journal Asiatique*, T. XII. p. 418.

disciples to whom the epithet *great* was ordinarily given. He is the first of those holy personages or patriarchs among whom was perpetuated the secret of the mysteries disclosed to them by their dying master. May we not in like manner account for the discrepancy betwixt the narrative of our author, who makes Kosala the country of Kásyapa Buddha, and the opinions of other writers who make Benares his birthplace ?—C. L.

Were the position of *Kia ye* known with certainty there would be no difficulty in identifying the triple-peaked hill in question. Supposing the former to be, as I have conjectured, somewhere in the neighbourhood of *Rám Gaya*, there is a hill set down in Rennel's map of South Behar, which corresponds in situation with that given to *Kukutapáda* both by our author and by Hiuan thsang. I subjoin that portion of the itinerary of the latter describing his route eastward from this neighbourhood to Rájagriha, in the hope that it may enable some enquirer on the spot to clear up the difficulties of the subject. "To the east of the river *Mou ho*, a great forest ; 100 *li*, *Kukutapáda* (the Cock's foot), or *Kiu lo po tho* (Gurupáda). North-east of the Cock's Foot, 100 *li*, mount *Fo tho fa na ;* thence 30 *li* east, *Si se chi*, a forest ; thence 10 *li* south-west, a great hill ; thence 60 *li* east, the capital." The river *Mou ho* cannot be, as M. Klaproth conjectures, the Sone, which is at least thrice too distant to answer Hiuan thsang's description ; neither can it be the *Mohana*, which joins the Nilajan many miles too far south to correspond with his subsequent course. The river named in Rennel's map *Moorhur* in its upper course, and *Little Pompon* as it approaches the Ganges, answers well as to distance and position. But be that as it may ; if we protract the above route from *Kukutapáda* to *Rájagriha*, we shall find the direct bearing and distance of the former from the latter to be about W. S. W. 171 *li*, or in round numbers 24 miles ; and if we set this off from the well ascertained position of Rájagriha, it will very nearly correspond with the hill I mention, but not at all with any to the south of modern Gayá. I throw out these conjectures however only for the consideration of such as have local opportunities of investigating the point.—J. W. L.

(2) *The abode of the Arhans.*—These are supposed to be still in existence like their master, the great Kasyapa.—Kl.

(3) *The Clergy of Reason.*—The *Tao sse.* There are three grand systems of religion in China ; that of Confucius, that of Buddha (Foe), and that of Lao tsze. These are called respectively, the religion of the Literati (*Jou kiao*), that of Foe (*Shy kiao*), and that of the Tao sse (*Tao kiao*). The last mentioned invariably ascribe the origin of their doctrines to Lao tsze (or *Lao tseu*) who was born in the third year of the

emperor Ting wang of the *Cheou* dynasty, about 604 B. C., and died in 523. (See Stanisla's Julien, *Livre des Recompenses et des Peines*, preface p. vii.) "The doctrine of Lao tseu insists upon the suppression of every vehement desire and of every passion calculated to disturb the peace and tranquillity of the soul. According to him, it should be the aim of every wiseman to exist without pain or sorrow; and in order to attain that happy quietude, he inculcates the banishment of the *past* from the mind and of all vain and useless solicitude about the *future*. To plan extensive enterprises, to agitate one's self with the cares essential to success, to abandon one's self to the devouring anxieties of ambition and avarice, is, according to this philosopher, to labour less for one's self than for posterity. It is madness, therefore, to sacrifice personal comfort and happiness for the profit of sons and nephews. In acting for ourselves, Lao tseu recommends moderation both in our desires and in our efforts; for he regards not as desirable any good that is obtained by trouble and annoyance." Grosier, *Description de la Chine*, p. 571. This sect seems to have extended itself very rapidly; we meet with many allusions to it in Fa hian; and I may mention as an instance of anachronism in Chinese chronology, that a follower of Lao tseu a *Tao sse* named *A i* is said to have recognized by supernatural signs the birth of Buddha, whom Chinese historians affirm to have flourished some 500 years anterior to the founder of the *Tao sse*. Such inconsistences sufficiently establish the unsoundness of this department of Chinese chronology. —J. W. L.

CHAPTER XXXIV.

Return to Pa lian foe.—Temple of the Vast Solitude.—Town of Pho lo nai.—Deer-park.—The first five converts of Foe.—The kingdom of Keou than mi.—Temple of Kiu sse lo.

Fa hian, on returning to *Pa lian foe*[1] ascended the Heng towards the west. After travelling ten *yeou yans* he came to a temple called that of the *Vast Solitude*.[2] It is one of the stations of Foe. There are to this day ecclesiastics there. Following the course of the river Heng towards the west for twelve *yeou yans* more, he came to the town of *Pho lo nai*,[3] in the kingdom of *Kia shi*.[4] To the north-west of the town, at the distance of ten *li,* you come to the temple situated in the Deer-park of the Immortal :[5] this Deer-park was formerly the station of a *Py chi foe ;* there are constantly deer reposing there. When the Honorable of the Age was on the point of accomplishing the law, the Gods sang in the midst of space, "The son of the king *Pe tsing* embraced ecclesiastical life and studied the doctrine, and in seven days he will become Foe." The *Pi chi foe* having heard this entered *ni houan ;* it is on this account he called the place the Garden of the plain of the Deer of the Immortal. Since the Honorable of the Age accomplished the law, men of subsequent times have erected a chapel in this place.

Foe being desirous of converting *Keou lin* amongst the five men,[6] these five men said amongst themselves, "For six years past this *Sha men Kiu tan*[7] practises austerities, eats but one grain of hemp seed and one grain of rice daily, and has not yet accomplished the law. How much the less, then, shall those accomplish the law who live in the intercourse of the world, abandoned to the (pleasures of the) body, the mouth, and the thoughts? To-day, when he shall come, let us be careful not to speak to him." Foe having approached, the five men rose and worshipped him.

At the distance of sixty paces to the north of this place, Foe, looking towards the west, sat down and began to turn the wheel of the law. He converted *Keou lin*[8] amongst the five men. Twenty paces to the north is the place where Foe rehearsed his history to *Mi le.*[9] Fifty paces south, is the place where the dragon *I lo po* asked Foe, "After how long a time shall I be delivered from this dragon's body?" In all those places they have erected towers, amongst which there are two *seng kia lan* inhabited by ecclesiastics.

Thirteen *yeou yan* to the north-west of the Deer-park, there is a kingdom called *Keou than mi.*[10] Its temple bears the name of *Kiu sse lo.*[11] Foe formerly stayed in this place, and on this account there are now many ecclesiastics there, the principal part of whom are of the *Less Translation.* Thence eight *yeou yans* to the east, is the place where Foe converted the evil genii. There too, he had stations, and walked, and sat. In all these places they have erected towers; and there are monasteries in which may be a hundred clergy.

NOTES.

(1.) *In returning to Pa lian foe.*—Fa hian when Pa lian foe (Pátali putra) directed his course in the first place towards the south-east to visit the new and the ancient town of Rájagriha, the capital of the Kings of Magadha, as also the Peak of the Vulture. From this mountain, situated to the south of the present town of Behar, and forming part of the ridge between the rivers Dahder and Banoura, he went in a westerly direction, crossed the river *Ni lian* (Nilajan or Amanat), and arrived at *Kia ye,* Buddha Gayá. Having visited the wonderful and the sacred places which rendered that vicinity famous as the scene of Sakya Muni's austerities during six consecutive years, he was about to return to Pátaliputra to pursue his journey and embark at the mouths of the Ganges for Ceylon, and thence to China. He had not, however, visited the holy city of Benares and its neighbourhood, equally famous in the history of Sakya Muni, as the country in which the Honorable of the Age had begun his ministry. Fa hian proceeded thither accordingly by the Ganges, and returned by the same route to Pátaliputra.

The thirty-third sheet of this work, containing the Budddist legend of the origin of the town of Pataliputra had been printed off ere I fell in with an interesting brochure published at Leipsig by M. Hermaun Brockhaus in 1835, under the title of "*Foundation of the town of Pâtaliputra, and history of Upasoka,* in Sanscrit and German. M. Brockhaus has extracted these two pieces from a collection of historiettes of *Somadeva,* of which manuscripts exist in the Library of the East India Company in London. This account of the foundation of Pátaliputra, not by a Buddhist, but by a Brahmin sectary, differs entirely from that given by Hiuan thsang. According to it a person named *Putraka* finds in the Vindhya mountains two sons disputing about their paternal heritage, which consisted of a vase, a staff, and a pair of slippers, all possessing miraculous properties. By a strategem, Putraka becomes possessed of these three objects, and flies away with them in the air. These confer on him facilities for making love to the beautiful *Pátali* and enable him to carry her off from the palace of her father. Having arrived on the banks of the Ganges, he there, in compliance with the request of his beloved one, and by the miraculous virtue of his staff, built a city, which in honor of the Princess he calls Pátaliputra. He becomes a powerful monarch, is reconciled to his father-in-law, and governs the whole country as far as the sea. I am unwilling to omit this little narrative, although not equal in interest to that given by Hiuan thsang.*—Kl.

This is the legend to which I have referred in page 259. The reader may find it in the *Journal of the Asiatic Society*, Vol. XIV. p. 140 or 144. —J. W. L.

(2) *A temple named the Vast Solitude.*—The Sanscrit etymon of this word I have been unable to ascertain. The temple spoken of is that called in Páli books *Iswere patne rándyé, Issa patana ramaia*, or *Issi pattene*. It was situated eighteen yojanas south of the Banian tree of the continent of Jambudwípa. All the Buddhas are supposed to have there begun their ministry. It was formerly frequented by a great number of Magi, or sages, who had the power of flying in the air. It is for this reason, add the Páli books, that the temple is named *Issa patana ramaia* by those who have witnessed this.†—Kl.

The temple here mentioned by Fa hian cannot be the *Isipatanan* of the Páli Annals, which describe the latter as an edifice, or large hall, at or near Benares, for the accommodation of *Isi* (saints, or devotees). Sákya is stated in the *Buddhawanso* to have departed from the neighbourhood of the *bodhi* tree, on the day of the full moon of *ásalhi* (April-May, B. C. 588), saying, "Let me repair to Báránasi," and taking his dish and robes he performed a journey of 18 yojanas. On the road meeting an individual named *Upako*, travelling on his own affairs, he informed him of his attainment of Buddhahood, and on the evening of the same day reached *Isipatanan Báránasi*. The distance here given of 18 yojanas, or a little more for the last day's journey, corresponds very well with the actual distance from Benares to the neighbourhood of Gayá, say 130 or 140 miles; taking the yojana at Capt. Cunningham's valuation of 7 miles.—J. W. L.

(3) *The city of Pho lo nai*;—that is the famous city of Benares, called in Sanscrit वारणसी, वराणसी, or वरणसी. The first two of these are derived, according to Indian Lexicographers, from *Vara*, the best, and *anas*, water; that is to say, the *Ganges*, on the banks of which this town is seated. It would appear however that the last name is the primitive one, although its derivation be irregular, from *Varaná*, a river which runs to the north-east of Benares, and throws itself into the Ganges, and *Asi*, the name of another river to the south of the town. The Varaná is the present *Berna*, a name derived from *Vri*, to choose. The Chinese transcribe Varanasi *Pho lo nai*, and explain the name in two ways, first, '*Deer-park*,' and next, '*surrounded*

* *See M. Klaproth's Note 4 or* Chap. XXVII. p. 259 French, E. D.
† *Pian i tian*, B. LIV. p. 4 v.

by the river;' both of these etymologies appear faulty. Hiuan thsang, who also visited this town, names it *Pho lo na sse.* He describes it as a large capital situated to the west and near the Ganges, being 18 or 19 li in length and five or six in breadth. The dwellings of the lower orders are very numerous, the population very considerable, and the number of houses more than ten thousand. There is a great crowd of merchants. The manners of the people are gentle and polished. All study with zeal. The principal part put faith in the heterodox doctrines, and there are but few who honor the law of Buddha. The climate is temperate and the soil produces grain and fruits; the trees have an extraordinary growth, as also grasses and plants. There are more than thirty *Kia lan,* and about three thousand priests and disciples, who all follow the doctrines of the less translation. There are about one hundred temples, in which ten thousand heretics worship the self-existent God (*Iswara*). They cut their hair, or wear it knotted above the head. They go quite naked and cover their bodies with ashes. The most pious live in continual austerities and seek to abandon life for death. To the north of the town is the river *Pho lo na* (Varaná); on its bank, about ten li from the town, is the *Kia lan,* of the Deer-park; there are about fifteen hundred priests and disciples, who all pursue the doctrines of the *less translation.* In the midst of the great enclosure is a temple more than two hundred feet high; it is surmounted by a golden arrow. The foundations are built with the stone *An mou lo ko,* and the walls are of brick. This temple is surrounded by a hundred chapels; all have arrows, and the divine images are all gilt. In the midst of the temple are the statues of Buddha and of a great number of other Tathágatas, sculptured in the stone *Theou shy.* The images of all are in the attitude of turning the wheel of the law (preaching.)—Kl.

(4.) *The kingdom of Kia shi;* i. e. काशि, *Kasi,* a name still borne by the country and town of Benares, and signifying *resplendent.*—Kl.

(5) *The Park of the deer of Immortal.*—The site of this deer park is, I have little doubt, Sarnáth, in the neighbourhood of which there is to this day, as my friend Capt. Kittoe informs me, a rumna for antelopes. It is called in Páli *Migadáyo,* 'a place set apart for deer,' and was the site, as stated above, of the *Isipatanan* hall, famous as the scene where Sákya first *turned the wheel of the Law.* I do not know whether there may not be some allusion to the *Py chi foe* (*Pratyeka Buddha*) in the term 'Deer of the Immortal;' the Pratyekas being typified as the reader will remember (p. 10) by *deer.*—J. W. L.

(6) *Among the five men.*—The 'five men' here alluded to are the five *bhikshus* who attended upon Sákya Muni while the latter was for six years

practising austerities on the banks of the Nilajan river. They accompanied him from Rájagriha in the full persuasion that he was destined to accomplish Buddhahood; but when they found their emaciated master under the necessity of restoring his strength by food, their faith failed them, and pronouncing him "a glutton and a loose man," they repaired to Benares and led an ascetic life. (Csoma de Körös, *Analysis of the* Mdo, leaves 192-200). The Páli Annals supply the rest of the story. On his attainment of Buddhahood, Sákya resolves, in acknowledgment of their attentions to him for so long a period, to preach the *Dhammo* first to these five ascetics; and on enquiry finds that they are residing in the *Isipatanan* in the deer-park (*Migadáyo*, in Sanscrit मृग, a deer, and दाय, a place ?) at Benares. Thither he proceeds. On seeing him approach from a distance, the five *bhikhus* make some jeering remarks upon his improved personal appearance, and resolve to show him no manner of respect. Sákya however penetrates their design, compassionately prevents them carrying it into execution, and finally expounds the Law to them and converts them.* This is the legend alluded to in the text.—J. W. L.

(7) The *Sha men Kiu tan.*—*Kiu tan* is the Chinese transcription of the Sanscrit Gautama, one of the numerous surnames of Buddha, and that more particularly used in India beyond the Ganges, where it has helped to form the name of the principal divinity of the Siamese *Somonakodom*, by the addition of the epithet *Somona* (*Sramana*), Samanean. All Buddhist nations have this name in equal honor; in Tibet it is *Geoutam;* in Mandchou and Mongolian *Godam*. There is less agreement as to its proper signification; for each of the nations that adore Buddha have upon this, as well as so many other points, such obscure and varying traditions as it is hardly possible to reconcile. Although Chinese books contain nothing satisfactory on this head, it may be not altogether useless to indicate briefly what they do say. According to them *Shy kia*, is the honorable name of *Kiu tan*. All men know, say they, that *Jou lai* is descended from a *Cha ti li* (Kshatrya) prince; but they do not know that *Kiu tan* was formerly a name of Shy kia. In the beginning he had five names, which were indiscriminately given him: *Kiu tan*, *Kau che* (sugar-cane), *Jy choung* (descendent of the Sun), *She y* (tranquil abode), and lastly *Shy kia*, which is now-a-days almost the only remaining one.

Kiu tan is the family name of the *Cha ti li* kings; it signifies in Sanscrit *perfectly pure*, or *the Great Vanquisher of the earth*. At the beginning of the present age there was a king named *Ta mao thsao*. Having abandoned his

* Turnour, *Páli Buddhistical Annals*, *J. A. S.* Vol. VII. p. 815.

kingdom to his minister, he went to the sage *Kiu tan* to study the doctrine, and adopting the name of his master, he called himself the *little Kiu tan*.

The name *Shy kia* is interpreted in a less confused manner. In Sanscrit it signifies *capable of piety*. *Shen yen*, the principal wife of the king *Kan che*, had a son named *Chang sheou*, and the second wife had four. *Shen yen*, to favour her son, induced the king to banish from the kingdom the other four children. Having arrived at the north of the Snowy Mountains, *Pei ching*, who was the fourth of these sons, became a king, built a city, and founded a kingdom which he called *She y* (tranquil abode). His father, having repented of his exile, recalled the son, but the latter would not come; when the king sighing, exclaimed, "my son *Shy kia!*" and hence the name.

It is interesting to compare with this recital of the same circumstance, the extract from the Kah Gyur, by M. Ksoma de Körös, given in note 9 Chap. XXII.—C. L.

The Singalese have two, apparently contradictory, accounts of the origin of the name Gautama. According to Clough (Singhal. Dict.), Sákya Muni was so called because on entering upon religious life he followed the instructions of the sage Gótama, whom they suppose to be the same philosopher to whom the *Nyaya* system is referred. According to others, Gautama is the proper name of the family in which Sákya was born. This latter opinion is evidently identical with that entertamed by the Buddhists of China. Now these two traditions give rise to the following difficulties: the biographers of Sákya, as far as at present known, do not say positively that he received the instructions of Gautama; and even if he had, there is nothing to lead us to believe that for this single reason he adopted the title of *Gautama*, which signifies the *Gautamide*. Secondly, the name of Gautama, is that of a descendant of the family of Gotama, a family which is one of the Bráhmanical Gotras, or stocks. It would not appear that this could be that of a member of the warrior caste, as Indian jurisconsults affirm in the most positive manner that the *Kshatryas* have neither *Gotras* nor tutelary saints. It follows from this that Sákya could not bear a name which at once refers to the warlike tribe to which he belonged, and to the Bráhman caste. The only way to solve the latter difficulty is to suppose that the name Gautama belonged, not to Sákya Muni alone, but to the warrior tribe of the Sákyas, as the Chinese suppose. We know indeed that it is permited to the Kshatryas to adopt the family name of their domestic priest; and hence, to explain how the Sákyas came to be called Gautama, it is sufficient to suppose that they had a family priest or spiritual director, a descendant of Gotama. This purely Indian distinction betwixt the Bráhmans, who have the right of designating their family by the name of the saint at the head of it, and the Kshatriyas, who borrow this name from their religious patron, may have been overlooked by the Buddhists, who do not recognise the distinction of caste to the same extent as the Bráhmans. Ignorance of this prescription, which is so intimately blended with Brahmanical organisation, may have given rise to these Singhalese traditions. The one may have tended to reconcile the title of *Gautamide* with the existence of the celebrated philosopher *Gótama;* the other may have preserved the true tradition without comprehending, or at least without seeking to explain it.—E. B.

(8) *Converted Keou lin among the five men.—Keou lin* is generally styled *Keou li* in Chinese Buddhist works. The following are the names of these five celebrated personages, according to Chinese books and Mongolian legends, in which the Sanscrit names are translated into Tibetan.

1st. *A jo Kiao chhin ju*, in Tibetan *Yang shi Go di ni ya.—A jo*, says the *Fan y ming i*, is a surname which signifies *knowing; Kiao chhin ju* is the name of the family; signifying *fire-pan.* In Páli the name is transcribed *Aja Kondanjan.* He was of a Bráhman family, and had in preceding states of existence performed the service of fire, and hence his family name. It belonged to the maternal uncle of Buddha.

2d. *O pi*, or Asvájit.—The *Fan y ming i* translates this word '*one who, mounts on horseback*,' or '*master of the horse.*' It is rendered in Tibetan *Ta tol*, which signifies '*a caparisoned horse.*' O pi was of the family of Buddha.

3d. *Po thi*, explained in Chinese as '*the little sage;*' in Tibetan *Ngang zen*, or *Ming zan.* He was also of the family of Buddha.

4th. *Shy ly Kia ye*, that is, '*tenfold strong Kasyapa*,' in Sanscrit दशबलकाश्यप Dasabala Kásyapa, is also named in Chinese *Pho fou*, in Tibetan *Lang ba.* He was of the family of the maternal uncles of Buddha. The *Fan y ming i* observes, that we must not confound him either with Mahá Kásyapa, or with the three Kásyapas, *Uruwilva Kásyapa*, *Nadi Kásyapa*, and *Gaya Kásyapa.*

5th. *Keou li thaï tseu*, or the prince royal *Keou li*, called by Fa hian *Keou lin;* in Tibetan *Zang den.* He was the eldest son of king *Hou fan wang*, maternal uncle of Buddha.

These five personages are called in Singalese books *Paswaga Mahánunansi*, or *the five great priests.* They were very learned Bráhmans, and chiefly expert in preaching. Having recognised the characteristic marks upon the person of the last Buddha, to wit, the thirty-two *Assulakunu*, and the two hundred and sixteen symptoms called *Magullakunu*, they ascertained with certainty that he should become Buddha. Then adopted religious life, and followed and served him for the six years that preceded the date of his attaining Buddhahood. After having heard his first sermons in this condition, they entered upon eternal glory.

A Mongolian tract entitled a "*History of the origin of the four verities of the whole law*," narrates in the following terms the conversion of the five personages in question:

"On the fifteenth day of the last month of spring of the year *Brouh-ah*, or '*the iron cow*,' during evening twilight, Buddha terminated his spiritual occupations, which consisted in the entire subjection of the spirits of Nisbana (निष्पन्न, *Nishpanna*, birth) or the *Seduction of birth*. At midnight he obtained Dyan (ध्यान, Dhyána, *the most profound meditation*) or the *highest degree of the sanctity of anchorites*, and at sunrise he had attained the nature of a *veritable accomplished Buddha, existing of himself in supreme spirituality*.

The truly accomplished Buddha began then to turn the wheel of spiritual doctrine and to spread abroad the law, announcing that he had obtained victory over the depths of innate misery, that he had destroyed all the imperfections which oppress the soul, and that he had become Buddha, the restorer of the world. Many among the people were seized with consternation and exclaimed, "The king's son hath lost his reason!" Others pretended that he had quitted the throne and his country to marry a daughter of Sákya; but others proclaimed that the king's son had become a *truly accomplished Buddha*.

The Buddha then pronounced the following instructive discourse: "Of what avail is it to present the people with the nectar of spiritual doctrine when instruction is wanting? They have no ears to hear it, and it is useless to explain it." He therefore retired anew into solitude in the country of *Arshi*, where he remained forty-nine days and as many nights to obtain a new *Dyan*. As soon as this was obtained, *Esroun tegri* (Brahma) approached him, carrying in his hand a golden wheel with a thousand rays, the symbol of spiritual dominion, and said; "Truly thou hast not become Buddha for thine own welfare, but for that of all the creatures in the world; deign to follow up the work and to spread abroad the doctrine." But the Buddha accepted not the invitation. The Mahá Rajá tegri (great kings of spirits) holding in their hands the *Naïman takil* (the eight sacrifices) came then and said to him: "Master of tenfold strength! great hero that hast vanquished all the innate seductions of the creature! deemest thou not fit that thou shouldst undertake the salvation of all beings?" Their request was equally rejected. Finally *Khourmousda tegri* (Indra) himself accompanied by the thirty-two other *tegri*, approached Buddha to adore him, and rendered him all the honor meet for a Buddha, encircling the spot where he dwelt. Khourmousda, holding in his hand the *Doung erdeni* (the precious shell) said to him; "Oh thou creator of the nectar of spirituality, who like unto a precious medicament, purgest and cleansest the creature from the innate wickedness in which he slumbers, condescend to let us hear thy majestic spiritual voice!" At this invitation were present the five priests and disciples of the Buddha, to wit *Yang shi Go di ni ya*, r*Ta tol*, *Ngang zen*, *Lang ba*, and *Zang den*, who up to that moment had been unable to form a judgment of their master. Discoursing among themselves of the wisdom of Buddha, they said; "If *Goodam* hath become Buddha, we must necessarily adopt his spiritual doctrine; but if he have not yet arrived at the rank of Buddha, why should we worship him?" At the same instant *Yang shi Go di ni ya*, who perceived himself on the eve of recognising the Buddha, suddenly turned his eyes towards him and beheld his body shining with the lustre of gold, and encircled by a brilliant halo. Thoroughly convinced by this sign, he accomplished the first adoration due to the Buddha, and thus obtained the right of one day succeeding in his dignity. The four other disciples followed his example, and similarly adored Buddha. They said to him; "Since thou art become the veritable Buddha of the world, deign to proceed to Váránasí; for it is there that the throne of a thousand by-gone Buddhas hath been; and it is there that thou shouldst abide and turn the wheel of the doctrine." Whilst they thus addressed him in prayer, they did not quit the posture of adoration; a new halo surrounded the Buddha, and his entire body emitted rays of inexpressible splendor.

Yielding to the pressing importunities of his disciples, Sákya Muni arose and proceeded to Váránasí, to adore and occupy the throne of the thousand Buddhas; he chose for his principal seat that of the three Buddhas of the present age of the world, *Ortchilong ebdektchi* (*Krakuchchanda*), *Altan chidakchi* (Kanaka Muni) and *Gerel zakikchi* (Kasyapa).

In the same year, on the fourth day of the month of mid-summer, the Buddha received, as his first disciples, the five priests mentioned above and communicated to them the principles of the four spiritual verities. The existence of misery is the first; the second is that this immense misery extends its empire every where; final deliverance from this misery is the third; and lastly, the fourth is the infinite number of obstacles which oppose this deliverance. "Hence," he added, "you, who are priests, are equally subject to this misery, of which you should know the immensity; you should contribute to indicate to others the road of deliverance, and you should do all that you can to remove all obstructions."

(9) *Mi le.*—See note 8—Chap. VI.

(10) *Keou than mi.*—Hiuan thsang and the Chino-Japanese map append-

ed to this volume, call this country *Kiao chang mi*; in Sanscrit कौशाम्बी, Kausámbí. It is the name of an ancient town situated in the lower part of the Duab, and neighbourhood of *Kurrat*; it is also called *Vatsapattana*. The name of Kausámbí comes from its founder, *Kusamba* (Wilson, Sanscrit Dict. p. 255, Sec. ed.) Hiuan thsang makes this kingdom six thousand *li* in circuit, and describes it as very fertile. The climate is cold, the inhabitants are of a savage and ferocious character; they nevertheless love study, and occupy themselves with science and the arts. There are about half a score of *kia lan*, but in a state of extreme dilapidation; nor were there more than three hundred priests and disciples; these follow the doctrines of the Less Translation. There are fifty chapels belonging to the heretics, who are extremely numerous in that country. In the town there is a great temple more than sixty feet high, where may be seen an image of Buddha carved in sandal wood, and fixed high upon the stone. This temple was constructed by order of the king *Ou tho yan na*, whose name signifies '*Manifested love*.'—Kl.

M. Remusat observes that it may be doubted whether Fa hian personally visited this kingdom of *Keou than mi*. He speaks indeed but vaguely of it, and instead of his usual expression, "you arrive at such a place,"—"you reach such a town," he contents himself with simply stating "there is such a kingdom." The circumstances he reports are common to too great a number of places to enable us to fix its site with precision. The traveller's indications serve only to fix it at about 60 miles N. W. of Benares.—C. L.

(11) *Kiu sse lo*.—Hiuan thsang found the ruins of it in the south-east angle of the town itself. He says that the temple received its name from that of a chief named *Kiu sse lo* (Kusala ?) who founded it. In the interior is a chapel dedicated to Buddha.*

CHAPTER XXXV.

Kingdom of Tha thsen.—The Seng kia lan Pho lo yue.

Two hundred *yeou yan*[1] to the south, there is a kingdom called *Tha thsen*,[2] where there is a *seng kia lan* of the former Foe *Kia she*.[3] They have excavated a great mountain of rock to

* *Pian i tian*, B. LIV. p. 4.

construct it. It consists of five stories; the lowest, which hath the form of an elephant, includes five hundred stone chambers. The second which hath the form of a lion, contains four hundred chambers. The third, which hath the form of a horse, contains three hundred chambers. The fourth, which hath the form of an ox, contains two hundred chambers. The fifth, which has the form of a pigeon, contains one hundred chambers. At the uppermost story, there is a spring of water which follows the circumvolutions of the rock. It encircles the apartments in its descent, performing thus the tour of the edifice to the lowest floor, the apartments of which also it waters, and then passes out at the gate. In all the stories there are windows pierced through the rock for the admission of the light, so that every chamber is perfectly illuminated and there is no darkness there. At the four corners of the edifice, they have hewn the rock and formed steps for ascending; at present men ascend by means of small ladders to reach a place where formerly a man left the print of his foot. Here is the reason why they call this temple *Pho lo yue*. *Pho lo yue* in Indian signifies a *pigeon*.* In this temple there are always Arhans who dwell there. The little hill is waste and uninhabited; it is only at a very great distance that there are any villages. The inhabitants are a perverse race who do not recognise the law of Foe. The Samaneans, Brahmans, heretics, and all the people of the country have frequently seen men come flying to the temple. When therefore the Clergy of Reason of the other kingdoms would go thither and practice the rites, the natives said to them, "Why come you not flying? We have seen ecclesiastics arrive here on the wing!" The ecclesiastics answered, "Our wings are not yet formed."

The roads of the kingdom of *Tha thsen* are dangerous, toilsome, and not easy to know. Those who desire to proceed thither should first pay a certain sum of money to the king of the country, who will then appoint people to accompany them and show them the way. On their return, each points out the way to the others. Fahian was unable to proceed thither, and learnt what he has been able to report from the people of the country.

NOTES.

(1) *Two hundred yeou yan.*—About 270 leagues.

(2) *A kingdom named Thā thsen*, that is the दक्षिण, *Dakshina* (the south), a denomination applied to the vast country called at present the Deccan, which is the vulgar pronunciation of *Dakshina.*—Kl.

(3) *A seng kia lan of the former Foe kia she.*—The Buddha Kasyapa, whose religious epoch preceded that of Sákya Muni, is here spoken of. Kasyapa is the third of the Tathágatas who have appeared in the kalpa in which we live. He is considered therefore to have lived about two millions of years before Sákya Muni. (See Chap. XX. note 39.—Kl.)

(4) *Pho lo yue in Indian signifies pigeon.*—*Pho lo yue* is not the exact transcription of the Sanscrit word पारावत, Párávata ; it is nearer that of पारबा, Párabá, which in Mahratta and other dialects signifies *rock pigeon.* It would not be easy to determine in what part of the Deccan the *monastery of the pigeon* was situated ; this indication of Fa hian, who did not see it himself, is too vague to enable us to identify it among the numerous excavations met with among the hills in India. Nevertheless, the fact of the existence of such a monument in the fifth century of our era, is important and interesting, and may lead to a modification of the opinion of many English savans who have visited India, that we are not warranted in ascribing any considerable antiquity to these excavations. The celebrated H. H. Wilson, for instance, observes, "A review of the religious revolutions of the Peninsula would be incomplete without some notice of the numerous and celebrated cavern Temples with which it abounds, and its other monuments of a religious character. The collections of Colonel Mackenzie furnish no addition to our knowledge of the former ; the subject is indeed capable of little except graphic illustration, and there being few drawings or plans of any value relating to them. The omission is of little importance, for the topic has been handled in the Asiatic Researches, and in the transactions of the Bombay Literary Society, in the latter particularly by Mr. Erskine, in a manner that leaves nothing to desire. To extensive knowledge that writer adds sound judgment, discriminative observation, distinct conception, and perspicuous description, and his account of Elephanta, and his observations on the Bauddha remains in India, should be studied attentively by all who would investigate the history of the Bauddhas and Jains. The caverns in general are *Saiva* and *Baud-*

dha. There are a few Jain excavations at Ellora, but none at Elephanta or Keneri. There is no satisfactory clue to the date of any of these excavations, but there is reason to think that many of them bear a high antiquity. It may be questionable whether the *Saivas* or *Bauddhas* took the lead in these structures, but there is some reason to suppose the former, in which case the Saiva appropriation being consequent upon the downfall of the Bauddha faith, Mr. Erskine observes the Elephanta caves cannot be much more than eight centuries remote. The *Bauddhas* according to a tradition previously alluded to, came into the Peninsula only in the third century after Christianity and their excavations could not therefore have been made earlier than the fifth or sixth. The *Saivas* who formed similar caverns, were a particular sect, or that of the *Jogis*, as is proved by the sculptures, the large ear-rings, the emaciated penitents and the repetition of the details of *Daksha's* sacrifice, a favorite story in the *Saiva Puránas*, none of which are probably older than the eighth or ninth century." *Descrip. Catalogue of the Mackenzie Collection*, Vol. I. p. lxix.

The *Foe koue ki* completely refutes the hypotheses of those who affirm that the Buddhists made their appearance in India only in the third century of our era: a careful investigation of the environs of Patna, Gaya, and Benares would probably bring to light many of the monuments which Fa hian saw, and described. It is even probable that the monastery of the Pigeon still exists in the rock of the Deccan where it was originally cut, and that its discovery is reserved for some learned Englishman who shall traverse the country in the character of an able enquirer and a practised observer. —Kl.

The description given by our traveller of these cave temples is by far too vague to enable us to identify them; but the existence of such in the Dekhan at this early period is sufficiently established by this important chapter. Col. Sykes in his highly interesting *Notes on the Religious, Moral, and Political state of India*, is of opinion that Fa hian alludes to the caves of Ellora. "Those who have read, says he, my description of the caves of Ellora, may be induced to recognise in these stupendous and magnificent works, the originals of Fa hian's monastery and 1500 chambers. Considering the constant bias of human nature to enhance the value of that in which a personal interest is mixed up, I am surprised the travellers from the Dekhan did not lead Fa hian a little more astray than they appear to have done. My description of temples supported by Elephants and Lions, of a temple of three stories (Teen lokh), of windows pierced in the rock, of multitudinous chambers, of the course of rivulets down the mountain and over and into the caves of the uninhabited locality, and finally, even the name may be supposed to have originated in the flocks of blue pigeons which no doubt then, as now, inhabited the perforations in the mountains: my description, I repeat, offers so many matters of approximation to the general points of the inflated and distorted accounts given to Fa hian by the people from the Dekhan, that it may fairly be permitted to us to consider that Fa hian is describing Ellora. The excavations in Salsette would afford the next approximation, and after these the wonderous labours at Junir (Jooneer) and the Ajanta Ghat, Fa hian's silence with respect to the Linga caves at Ellora, which he would have designated as those of the heretics, offers to my mind satisfactory proof that in his day they were not in existence. Apparently for the preceding 1000 years there had not been Hindu dynasties or a Hindu population sufficiently wealthy, powerful, or numerous, to have produced them."—J. W. L.

(5) *Flying.*—See note 2 of the preceding Chapter.

CHAPTER XXXVI.

Books and Precepts collected by Fa hian.—Precepts of the Mo ho seng chhi.—Precepts of the Sa pho to.—The A pi tan.

Proceeding in an easterly direction from the kingdom of *Pho lo nai*, you return to the town of *Pa lian foe.*[1] Fa hian had from the first enquired for the Precepts; but all the masters of the kingdoms of India of the North had transmitted these from mouth to mouth, without ever reducing the volume to writing;[2] on this account he had come so far and had reached Mid-India. There, in a monastery of the *Mo ho yan*, he obtained a collection of the Precepts. This was the collection of the precepts of the *Mo ho seng chhi*,[3] which from the time when Foe was in the world has been followed by the majority. This book was communicated (to Fa hian) in the temple of *Chhi houan.*[4] As for the other eighteen collections,[5] each has its professor who maintains it. The great *Koueï*[6] differs not from the smaller; when the smaller is not conformable, custom explains it.[7] But Fa hian obtained the most authentic and copious, those which comprised most amply the traditions, in a collection in which are brought together the Precepts, forming perhaps seven thousand *kie*;[8] these are the collected precepts of the *Sa pho to*,[9] those observed by the ecclesiastics of the land of *Thsin*. But all these Precepts having been transmitted from master to master, by a uninterrupted tradition, have never been committed to writing in books.[10] There were also in this collection sundry extracts from the *A pi tan*,[11] forming about six thousand *Kie*. There was also a copy of the Sacred Books[12] in two thousand five hundred *Kie*, as also a copy of the sacred work on the means of attaining *Pan ni houan*, consisting of about five thousand *Kie*; and of the *A pi tan* of the *Mo ho seng chhi*.

On this account *Fa hian* dwelt here three years, studying the books and the *Fan*[13] language, and copying the precepts. *Tao chhing*,[14] when he arrived at the Kingdom of the Middle, and beheld the law of the *Sha men*, and all the clergy grave, decorous, and conducting themselves in a manner greatly to be admired, reflected, with a sigh, that the inhabitants of the frontiers of the kingdom of *Thsin* were deficient in the precepts, and transgressed their duties; and said that if hereafter he could become Foe, he wished that he might not be re-born in the country of the frontiers; on this account he remained and returned not. *Fa hian*, whose first desire was that the Precepts should be diffused and should penetrate into the land of Han, returned therefore alone.

NOTES.

(1) *Pa lian foe.*—Pátaliputra.

(2) *To writing.*—This would prove that in the northern part of India, which the Chinese call *Northern Hian thsu*, civilisation and the art of writing were not so extensively diffused as in Mid-India, situated on the banks of the Ganges, and its affluents.—Kl.

(3) *The precepts of the Mo po seng chhi*;—That is, of the monks of the Great Convocation who compiled the precepts of Sákya. The Singalese traditions contain extremely interesting particulars connected with this subject, and must be the more carefully studied as they exhibit certain differences

from the Mongol legends, and may on many points serve to modify and complete the extracts we have given of these.

According to these traditions, in the eighth year of *Ajassat* (Ajatasatru), three weeks after the death of Buddha, five hundred monks, having set out from the town of *Cusinanaw* (*Kusinagara*), arrived at that of *Rájagriha-murara* (Rájgriha). The king, apprised of their arrival and of their intention of promulgating the doctrine, prepared for them in the mount *Wabahara-park-wateye* a magnificently adorned dwelling. These monks, with Kasyapa at their head, took possession of it and sat down according to their eldership, leaving vacant the seat due to Ananda. The latter having attained the rank of Arhan made the same known to the assembly in an extraordinary manner: the earth having opened in the middle of the hall, Ananda came up from this opening, and took the seat that had been reserved for him.

Then Mahá Kasyapa, addressing the assembly, asked with what portion of the doctrine they would first engage themselves. They decided on the *Venna pittaka* (Vinaya pittaka), and Upálisthavira was charged to expound it. The care of commenting on the *Sutra pittaka*, which contain the discourses addressed to men, devolved upon Ananda, who explained all the passages upon which he was questioned by Kásyapa, and composed the *Dierganikáya* (Dírghanikáya) which contains the sixty-two bana-wara. (Each *bana-wara* consists of two hundred and fifty *gathas* or verses.) The *Maddimenikaya* (Madhyamanikáya) which is a portion of the *Sutra pittaka*, and contains eighty thousand bana-wara, having been compiled and set in order, the first disciple of *Damsenerviserrint-maha-Teroonwahansey*, was charged to prepare it for the remembrance of man. *Saninktenikáya* (Samyuktanikáya) which is another part of the *Sutra pittaka*, composed of a hundred *bana-wára*, was compiled and divided into two parts under the editorship of Maha Kasyapa and his disciples. The *Angotternikáya* (Angottaranikáya) containing two thousand bana-wara, and which also forms part of the *Sutra pittaka*, was distributed into two parts, of which Anurudda, assisted by his first disciple, undertook the compilation.

Next the *Abhidharma pittaka*, which contains the discourses preached to the gods, was compiled and divided into two. parts by the five hundred monks; who further collected in two classes, the inferior works, such as the *Soutternipata* (*Sútranipáta*) the *Dharmapadeya*, &c. This collection of precepts, also prepared by Mahá Kasyapa and his five hundred priestly confreres, was completed in seven months.*

A hundred years after the death of Buddha, the king Kalasoka invited *Sabba Kamy Yasa* (*Sarvakáme Yasa*) and other Arhans to the number of

* *Sac. and Hist. Books of Ceylon*; Vol. I. p. 32.

seven hundred, to a convocation at *Visalah* (Vaisáli) in the temple of *Walucaw*. There he interrogated them upon the *Istewir rewade* (Sthaviraváda) and the Vinaya, and charged them to set these in order: which was accomplished in six months.*

In the last place, the king Dharmasoka having asked *Moggali-putte-Tissemahastervira*, and a thousand other Arhans to make a new collection of the laws of Buddha, they assembled at *Pellelup* (Pátaliputra) in the temple of *Asocarahama* (Asokaráma), and completed this third collection in the space of nine months, the 235th year of Buddha, and the 17th of Dharmasoka.—C. L.

(4) *The temple of Chhi houan.*—At first sight one might infer from this passage that the temple here spoken of was in the town of *Pa lian foe;* it was however in the kingdom of Kosala. (See Chap. XX.) It is well to remark here, that for a moment our traveller interrupts the narration of his journey. He is not at the end of it; he has yet many fatigues to undergo, many dangers to encounter; but the religious purposes which encouraged him to undertake his long pilgrimage are fulfilled. He has reached the country where he can cultivate the sacred tongue, discourse of the precepts with enlightened ecclesiastics, meditate upon and collect them. No other land offers such resources; he sojourns therefore there, and having in a manner settled himself, recapitulates the results he had obtained up to that moment. India of the North which he first visited, was to him a land of little interest; a sterile and almost savage country, which he had rapidly traversed to reach that holy land, that classic scene where the monuments and traditions of his religion were preserved intact,—Mid-India. Scarcely has he entered it when he is every where received with tokens of interest and respect by his co-religionists, who applaud his courage and his zeal, and press him to satisfy their curiosity. Thenceforward temples and holy places succeed each other at short intervals, and it was in one of the most magnificent of all that he had seen, in the temple of *Chhi houan*, one of the most celebrated places of the worship of Buddha, that he for the first time obtained a copy of the Precepts.—C. L.

(5) *The eighteen collections.*—There are two ways of dividing the sacred books; either in twelve collections *(pou,* classes) which at once contain those of the *Great* and the *Less Translation;* or into eighteen classes, which are divided equally between these two doctrines. The nine classes of books devoted specially to the Great Translation are, the *Sútra*, the *Gaya*, the *Gáthá*, the *Itihása*, the *Játaka*, the *Abhutadharma*, the *Udána*, the *Vaipulya* and the *Vyákarna*. The *Nidána*, the *Avádána*, and the *Upadesa* are

* *Ibid.* p. 43.

not included, because, says the *Ta chi tou lan*, 1st, in the *Great Translation*, the supreme law is simply announced, without thence deducing motives (*Yin Youan*, Nidána); 2d, discourses and instructions (*Yeou pho ti che, Upadesa*) are suppressed as useless because perfect reason alone is addressed; 3d, eternal truth is alone exhibited without the necessity of metaphors or comparisons (*Pho tho, Váda*) for its illustration.*

The last three works are, on the contrary, suited for the Less Translation, which has not the *Vaipulya*, the *Vyákarana*, nor, the *Udána.* In the Less Translation the law of life and of extinction are alone treated of; there is therefore no *Py foe ho* (Vaipulya). As men of the Less Translation are unable to become Buddhas, there is no *Ho kia lo* (Vyákarana), nor any *Yeou tho na* (Udana), because they have need to borrow motives in order to speak.† The nine classes of books of the Less Translation are therefore the *Sutras*, the *Geyas*, the *Itihasas*, the *Játakas*, the *Abhutadharmas*, the *Avadánas*, and the *Upadesas.*

According to the Buddhists of Nepal, the original body of the holy scriptures amounts, when complete, to 84,000 volumes, which are designated, either collectively or separately, *Sútra* and *Dharma*, or by that of *Buddhavachna* (words of Buddha). Sákya Sinha first collected the doctrines of his predecessors, to which he added those peculiar to himself. The words *Tantra* and *Purána* are ordinarily employed, though in a very vague manner, to distinguish the esoteric and exoteric doctrines, and it would appear that they should be applied more particularly to those of the *Upadesa* and *Vyákarana;* the *Gáthas*, the *Játakas*, and the Avadánas would appear, according to Mr. Hodgson, rather to be subdivisions of the *Vyákarana*, than distinct classes.—C. L.

(6) *The great Koueï.*—The three *Koueï* correspond to the *three precious ones*, and in a manner complete the dogma of the triad, the basis of Samanean theology. *Jou laï*, when he began to perfect right intelligence, addressing himself to the chief among his disciples, opened to them the precepts of the three *Koueï*, to quit evil, to return to good, and to establish the root of entrance into reason. The commentary upon the *Hoa yan king* says; "The *three precious ones* are whatever is the most excellent and of the best omen. These are the three supports by means of which great matters are to be distinguished, all the roots of the virtues to be produced, the evils of life and death to be removed, and the joys of *Ni pan* to be obtained. They are called the *three stays* or *rests.*

1st. *Resting upon Buddha.* Koueï has the signification of *return*, i. e.

* *San tsang fa sou*, B. XXXIII. p. 26 v.

† *Ta chi tou lun*, quoted in the same, B. XXXIV. p. 20.

revolting against the master of evil and returning to the master of goodness. Resting upon the great intelligence of Buddha, you escape the three uncleannesses (that of the sword, of blood, and of fire), and free yourself from life and death in the three worlds. Hence the sacred text, " In resting upon Foe, you never more return to the other spirits whom the heretics adore."

2d. *Resting upon the Law.*—This signifies that what Foe hath said, instruction or teaching, may be set in action and should be practised by all men. Such is the doctrine of ancient traditions. To return, is to quit bad laws and attach one's-self to the true law. In resting upon what Foe has taught, you are enabled to come forth from the three uncleannesses, and are emancipated from the evil of birth and death in the three worlds. Hence the sacred text, " He who rests upon the Law is for ever incapable of killing or hurting."

3d. *Resting upon the Seng.*—Men of the three revolutions who leave their homes (i. e. embrace religious life), are heartily united in the law revealed by Foe, and are hence called *Seng.* Those who revolt against such sectaries as follow heretical practices ; those whose hearts are given up to the ecclesiastics of the three revolutions ; those who believe in the communion of men of right practice and rest upon it ; such succeed in escaping from the three unclean things, and from the pains of life and death in the three worlds. Hence it is written in the holy text, " He who returns to the ecclesiastics and rests upon them, never changes again and cannot rest upon men addicted to heresy."*—C. L.

(7) *Custom explains it.*—The passage is somewhat obscure, and according to M. Landresse may mean, " *the commentary explains it.*"

(8) *Kie.*—This is the abbreviated Chinese transcription of Gáthá गाथा, verses.—Kl.

(9) *The collected precepts of the Sa pho to.*—There are five classes of precepts which form the treasure of precepts taught by the Tathágata, and these have been divided in the following manner: When the venerable of the Age had attained his thirty-eighth year and had obtained the law, he proceeded to the town. The king having finished his lenten meal, directed Raholo to wash the platter. In doing so the latter carelessly let it fall, and thus broke it into five pieces. That very day many *bhikshus* said to Foe, " The platter is broken into five pieces." Foe replied ; " In the five hundred years immediating following my death, wicked *bhikshus* shall divide the treasure of the *Pi ni* (Vinaya) into five classes." It afterwards so happened that five disciples of the rank of *Yeou pho khieou to* (perhaps the Sanscrit उपगुप्त, *Upagupta*) divided the great treasure of the precepts of the Tathágata according to their own views, in the following manners :

* *San tsang fa sou,* B. IX. p. 16 v.

1st. *Tan wou te*, or *Tan mo khieou to.*—This word signifies the *destruction of darkness* (apparently तमोघ्न, Tamoghna). This class is also called the '*Treasure of the law*,' and the "*Precepts divided into four parts.*" It is said in the *Ta tsy king*; "After my Ni phan, all my disciples shall collect the twelve classes of the sacred books; they shall copy them, study them, bring them to the highest perfection, and shall publish the words thereof, which shall be called the *Destruction of darkness*. This class shall be that of *Tan wou te*." The four parts of these precepts are; 1st, the law of the *Pi khieou*; 2d, the law of the *Pi khieou ni*; 3d, the law of those who have received the prohibitions; and 4th, the law of the departed.

2d. *Sa pho to.*—This Sanscrit word signifies *the sum*, or the *precepts of the lectures* (of *Upasi*). This class is likewise called the *True Law of the three worlds*. It is said in the *Ta tsy king*; "After my Ni phan all my disciples shall collect the twelve classes of the sacred books; they shall unceasingly study them; and they shall add explanations and commentaries, so as entirely to solve all difficulties. This class shall be that of the *Sa pho to*."

3d. *Kia se Koueï.*—This Sanscrit word signifies '*contemplation of the double void*;' it is the rule of perfect existence. It is said in the *Ta tsy king*; "After my Ni phan all my disciples shall collect the twelve classes of the sacred books; they shall say that there is no more Ego, and shall thus cast away their errors as dead carcases.

4th. *Mi sha se.*—This Sanscrit word implies '*that which is not manifest and cannot be perceived*.' This class is also called that of "*the precepts divided into five parts*." It is said in the *Ta tsy king*; "After my Ni phan, all my disciples shall collect the twelve classes of sacred books. The similitudes of earth, water, fire, air, shall not exist; there shall be naught but empty space. This class shall be that of the *Mi sha se*." The five parts of these precepts are, 1st. The observances of the *Pi khieou*; 2d. Those of the *Pi khieou ni*. 3d. The law of received prohibitions; 4th. The law of the departed; 5th. The law of the monks.

5th. *Pho thso fou lo.*—This Sanscrit word signifies '*calf*.' It is said that in very remote antiquity there was an immortal who had sexual connexion with a calf. The latter produced a son, and hence the name *calf* remained in the family. In this class are discussed the vanity of Ego as well as the five collections (form, perception by the senses, reflection, action, and knowledge). It is said in the *Ta tsy king*; "After my *Ni phan* all my disciples shall collect the twelve classes of the sacred books. All shall proclaim that there is but one Ego, and they shall not explain the similitude of the void. This shall be called the class of the ***Pho thso fou lo.****—Kl.

(10) *Were not committed to writing.*—In Ceylon, from the time of the introduction of Buddhism in that island under king Deveny Paetissa (236 years after the death of Buddha) to the time of king Valagambu (643 years and 9 months after the same epoch), the Buddhist doctrines were transmitted only by tradition and preaching. But at this time thirty-six learned priests taking counsel together, and being of opinion that in after ages there might arise priests of inferior capacity, collected together by the authority of the king, five hundred priests of recognised learning and sanctity; and having assembled at a placed called Matula, began collecting and transcribing the sacred books.†—C. L.

(11) *A pi tan :*—A Sanscrit word *(Abhidharma)* signifying '*the peerless Law*;' it is one of the three *Tsang* or '*receptacles*,' that is, one of the three classes of books which contain the text and the sense of the laws. (See Chap. XVI. note 22).

According to another classification of the sacred books, there are ***eight containants*** which comprise the different kinds of ***king***, the ***liu***, the ***lun*** and the *cheou*. *King* signifies *law, a constant and unchanging thing.* Whatever the saints have ruled, is called law; that which the heretics can neither change nor destroy, is called constant, or invariable. ***Liu*** is the law; it is that which distinguishes the light and the weighty, and withstands sin. *Lun* are the discourses which expound the most profound meaning of the laws. *Cheou* signifies *vow;* it designates prayers and invocations. Amongst all these books there are different ones for the ***great*** and the ***less translation***, for the *Ching wen* (Srávaka) and the *Youan kio* (Pratyeka Buddha). Those of the *Ching wen* are; 1st. The '*receptacle of the king*,' which comprises the four *A han* (Agama). *A han* signifies '*the peerless law*,' because the law of the age admits of comparison with no other law. The four *A han* are; the *long A han* (dírgágama), the *mean A han* (madyamágama), the *mixed A han* (samyuktágama), and *the supplementary A han* (angottarágama), which, doubtless by mistake, the commentator in the *San tsang fa sou* quotes as the first. 2d. *The receptacle of the Precepts*, in which are comprised those of the four *Fen* (degrees), namely those of the *Pi kheou*, of the *Pi khieou ni*, of the *Cheou kiaï* (received prohibitions) and of the *Mieï chang* (terminated disputes); the ten *Soung* (lectures), of Foe's disciple *Yeou pho li* and others. 3d. *The receptacles of the discourses*, that is, the *Api tan* and others. 4th. The *receptacle of*

* *Fan y ming i*, quoted in the *San tsang fa sou*, B. XX. p. 17 and sequel.
† *Upham*, Vol. II. p. 43.

prayers; this includes the *Dharani*, to remove all sickness and avoïd all evil. *Dharani* is a Sanscrit word signifying *invocation*, or that which will promote good and restrain evil. The four *Tsang* are peculiar to the Pratyeka Buddhas. 5th. The *receptacle of the king*, in which are comprised the *Miao fa yun hoa king*, the *Ta fang Foe hoa yen*, and other *King*. 6th. The *receptacle of the precepts*, such as the *Shen kiaï king* of the Phou sas, the prohibitions of the *Fan wang* and others. 7th. The *receptacle of the discourses*, such as the *Ta chy tou lun*, the *Shy ty king*, and others. 8th. The *receptacle of the prayers*, such as the *Ling yen cheou*, the *Ta peï*, and other prayers.*—C. L.

(12) *A copy of the sacred books.*—We have seen that this word applies more particularly to the *Sutras*. (Chap. XVI. note 24). The enumeration which Fa hian here gives of the collection he had made is one of the most interesting points of his narrative; and the number of the *Gáthas* or verses he assigns to each book, proves that many of these works were very extensive. We have thought it right to enter upon some special details connected with this subject; but we must again refer to the more general classification given by M. Remusat, in the notes to Chap. XVI.—C. L.

(13) *The Fan language*; i. e. the Sanscrit.—Kl.

(14) *Ta chhing.*—The last of the little band who accompanied our pilgrim from *Chhang 'an*. See Chap. I.

CHAPTER XXXVII.

Kingdom of Chen pho.—Kingdom of To mo li ti.—Fa hian embarks.—He arrives at the kingdom of Lions.

Following the course of the Ganges towards the east the distance of eighteen *yeou yan*,[1] you arrive at the great kingdom *Chen pho*,[2] on the southern bank of the stream. In the chapels of Foe on our route, and in four places where Foe sat, they have erected towers which are apparently inhabited by ecclesiastics.[3] Thence proceeding easterly about fifty *yeou yan*,[4] you come to the kingdom of *To mo li ti*.[5] There is the embouchure into the sea.[6]

* *Hoa yen king*, quoted in the *San tsang fa sou*, B. XXXI. p. 6 v.

In this kingdom there are twenty-four *seng kia lan*, all peopled by the clergy, and the Law of Foe is flourishing.

Fa hian dwelt there two years, occupied in transcribing the sacred books and depicting the images. At this time some merchants putting to sea in large vessels, shaped their course to the south-west; and in the beginning of winter, the wind being then favourable, after a navigation of fourteen nights and as many days, he arrived at the *Kingdom of Lions*.[7] The people of the country (of *To mo li ti*) assert that this kingdom is about seven hundred *yeou yan*[8] distant from their's. It is situated on an island; it is fifty *yeou yan*[9] from east to west, and from north to south, thirty *yeou yan*.[10] To the right and to the left there are small islets to the number of a hundred; their distance from each other is in some cases ten *li*, in others from twenty to two hundred *li;* all are dependent upon the great island. Many precious things and pearls are procured there. There is a district which produces the jewel *Mo ni*,[11] and which may be about ten *li* square. The king sends thither people to protect it, and when they have gathered the jewels he takes three pieces out of every ten.

NOTES.

(1) *Eighteen yeou yans.* About 24 leagues.—Kl.

(2) *The great kingdom of Chen po.*—चम्पा *Champa* or चम्पापुरी *Champapuri*, is the name of the ancient capital of *Karna*, king of Anga desa, and elder brother, by his mother, of the *Pándu* princes, being the son of *Súrya* and *Kunti* before the marriage of the latter with *Pándu.* The town for this reason bore also the name of *Karnapura*, and it was situated on the site of the present Bhaghulpore, or at least not far from that place. We have seen that the kings of Anga, were for a long time the suzerains of the princes of Magadha, but that the latter emancipated themselves from their tributary condition under the reign of Máha Padma, who with his son Bimbásara overcame the kingdom of Anga and made it a province of their own.

Hiuan thsang places the kingdom of *Chen pho* in Mid-India, and gives it four thousand *li* in circumference. The capital was protected on the north by the Ganges, and was more than forty *li* in circuit. "The country, he adds, is fertile, the climate warm." In his time there were half a score of *kia lan*, for the most part in a state of dilapidation; and not more than two hundred monks. The heretics had about twenty temples.* The name Champa is still found on some maps, preserved in that of *Champanagar*. —Kl.

(3) *Inhabited by ecclesiastics.*—We may infer from this expression that Fa hian did not land from the vessel in which he descended the Ganges.—Kl.

(4) *Nearly fifty yeou yans.*—About 68 leagues.—Kl.

(5) *At the kingdom of To mo li ti.*—Hiuan thsang calls this kingdom *Tan mo ly ti.* "It belongs, says he, to Mid-India: it is fourteen hundred *li* in extent and its capital is ten *li* in circumference. It is situated on the sea shore, and great traffic is there carried on by land and by water." He found there ten *kia lan* inhabited by more than a thousand monks. The heretics had about fifty temples. Hard by the town was a tower erected by king Asoka in honor of a throne of the four past Buddhas, and of other memorials of their lives and acts, of which traces existed in the neighbourhood.† *To mo li ti* or *Tan mo ly ti*, is the transcription of ताम्रलिप्ती, *Támralipti*, which signifies "*spotted with copper*." The place which formerly bore this name is the modern Tumlook, on the right bank of the Hughli (more properly Rupnarain) not far from Calcutta. The Mahavansa calls it *Támalitti*, corresponding exactly with our author's transcription. This country enjoyed, according to the Buddhists, great renown in ancient times. At the close of the 5th century before our era, the king *Dharmásoka*, sovereign of all Jambudwípa, despatched to the king of Ceylon an ambassador who embarked at this port. According to the narratives of Fa hian and Hiuan thsang, this town was still of considerable importance in the 5th and 7th centuries.—Kl.

It is well to remark that, according to Wilson, the name of this province is Támalipti (affected with sorrow); whence it follows, if this orthography be correct, that there is no need to invent the form *Támraliptí* in order to infer from it the Páli *Támalitti*.—E. B.

(6) *The entrance to the sea:*—that is, of the Ganges. This circumstance leaves no doubt regarding the situation of this country, and we may further infer from the account of Fa hian, that the Hughli was in his time one of the principal branches of the Ganges.—Kl.

(7) *The kingdom of Lions.*—In Chinese, *Sse tseu koue*, which is the translation of the Sanscrit सिंहल, ('having lions'). Hiuan thsang writes the name *Seng kia lo*, and says that the country is comprised within the limits

* *Pian i tian*, B. LXXV. art. 13.
† *Ibid.* art. 18.

of India. He gives it seven thousand *li* in circumference; and the principal town 40 *li*. He adds that this island was formerly called that of '*Jewels*,' because of the number of precious things it produced.* Further details will be found in the notes to the following chapter.—Kl.

(8) *Seven hundred yeou yan.*—About 930 leagues.—Kl.

(9) *Fifty yeou yan.*—68 leagues.—Kl.

(10) *Thirty yeou yan:*—about forty leagues. As M. Remusat remarks, these distances and their proportions are accurate; but Fa hian is deceived precisely as Eratosthenes was in giving greater extent to Ceylon in longitude than in latitude. By the little islands grouped to the right and the left, it is evident that he means the Maldives.—C. L.

(11) *The jewel Mo ni.*—In the original *Mo ni chu; chu* properly signifying a *pearl*, but in the general sense to be here taken, a *jewel*. मणि, *Mani*, in Sanscrit, is a *jewel, precious stone;* and corresponds in some measure with the Chinese *chu*. Pearls are called मुक्ता *muktá*, in the same language; but a precious stone is called the *jewel of Mani;* pearls moreover are not here spoken of, but carbuncles, which are said to emit rays of light in the night time. The description of the *Mani* given in Buddhist works is fabulous.—Kl.

CHAPTER XXXVIII.

Description of the kingdom of Lions.—Prints of the feet of Foe.—Monastery of the Mountain without Fear.—The tree Peï to. The tooth of Foe.—Ceremonies performed in honor of it.—Chapel of Po thi.—The Samanean Tha mo kiu thi.

This kingdom[1] was originally uninhabited by man; only demons, genii,[2] and dragons dwelt there. Nevertheless, merchants of other countries trafficked with them. When the season for the traffic came, the genii and the demons appeared not, but set forward their precious commodities marked with the exact price; if these suited the merchants, they paid the price and took the goods.[3] As these traders went, and came, and sojourned, the inhabitants of other

* *Pian i tian*, B. LXVI. art. 4. p. 11 v.

kingdoms learnt that this country was very beautiful; these also came, and eventually established a great kingdom.

This country is temperate; the vicissitude of winter and summer is unknown. The grass and the trees are ever verdant. The sowing of the fields is at the pleasure of the people; there is no (fixed) time for that.

When Foe arrived in this country he was desirous of converting the wicked dragons.[4] By the strength of his divine foot, he left the print of one of his feet to the north of the royal city, and the print of the other on the summit of a mountain.[5] The two traces are at the distance of fifteen *yeou yan*[6] from each other. Over the mark of that to the north of the royal city, they have built a great tower forty *chang*[7] high. It is embellished with gold and silver, and the most precious materials are combined to form its walls. They have moreover erected a *seng kia lan,* called the *Mountain without Fear,*[8] where are five thousand ecclesiastics. They have erected a hall to Foe, with carvings in gold and in silver. Amongst all the precious things to be seen there, is an image of blue jasper, two *chang* high; its entire body is formed of the seven precious things. It sparkles with splendour, and is more majestic than can be described.

Many years had now elapsed since *Fa hian* left the *Land of Han*:[9] the people with whom he had mingled were men of foreign lands. The hills, the rivers, the plants, the trees,—every thing that had met his eyes, was strange to him. And what was more, those who had begun the journey with him were now separated from him; some had remained behind, and some had died. Ever reflecting on the past,[10] his heart was thougthful and dejected. Suddenly, while at the side of this jasper figure, he beheld a merchant presenting in homage to it a fan of white lute-string of the country of *Tsin.*[11] Without any one perceiving it, this excited so great an emotion that the tears flowed and filled his eyes.

The ancient kings of this country sent to the Kingdom of the Middle in quest of the seeds of the tree *Peï to.*[12] They planted these alongside the hall of Foe. When the tree was about twenty *chang*[13] high it leant to the south-east. The king, fearful that it would fall, caused it to be supported by eight or nine pillars, which formed an enclosure supporting it. The tree, in the centre of the place where it was propped up, put forth a branch which, perforating the pillar, descended to the earth, and took root. Its size was about four *wei.*[14] These pillars, although cleft in twain, and thrown down, have not been removed by the people. Beneath the tree they have erected a chapel in which there is a seated image. The Clergy of Reason habitually and unremittingly worship it.

In the city they have moreover erected an edifice for a Tooth of Foe. It is entirely constructed with the seven precious things. The king purifies himself and abstains from the observance of bráhmanical rites. The inhabitants of the city possess faith and reverence, and are firm in their convictions. From the earliest times of this kingdom, they have never experienced famine, scarcity, calamity, or trouble. The clergy have in their treasury an infinity of precious things, and *Mo ni* beyond price. The king having entered into this treasury, beheld a jewel *Mo ni,* and immediately felt a desire to carry it away. Three days after he made amends. He sent for the clergy, and prostrating himself before them, repented. Opening his heart to them, he said, "I desire that you should enact a law, forbidding future kings to enter your treasury; at least, until they shall have accomplished forty sacrifices in the character of mendicants; then let it be lawful for them to enter."

The town is inhabited by many magistrates and grandees, and the merchants *Sa pho.*[15] The houses are beautiful, and the public edifices well adorned. The streets and the roads are level and straight. In all the crossways there are halls built for preaching. On the eighth, the fourteenth, and the fifteenth day of the moon, they erect a lofty pulpit, and a great multitude of the four castes assembles to listen to the Law. The natives of the country assert that they may have amongst them altogether from fifty to sixty thousand ecclesiastics, who that all eat in common. The king, moreover, has in the town, five or six thousand whom he supplies with food in common. When these are hungry, each takes his own pot, and goes in quest of what he requires. They only take as much as their pots will contain quite full, and return.

The tooth of Foe[16] is commonly exposed to the public in the middle of the third moon. Ten days beforehand, the king, having selected a large elephant with great care, sends a preacher, who, clad in royal robes and mounted on the elephant, beats a drum and calls out, saying, "The *Phou sa,* in the course of three *A seng ki,*[17] practised mortifications without regard to his person or his life. He relinquished the queen his wife; he tore out his eyes to give them to a man; he cut his own flesh to redeem a pigeon; he sacrificed his head to present it in alms; he cast his body to a famished tiger, and spared not even the marrow of his bones.[18] Thus, by such austerities, and by the practice of mortifications for the good of all living beings, even thus did he become Foe. During the forty nine years that he continued in the world, he preached the law, and converted by the doctrine. Those who were unsettled, he confirmed; those who knew not the rules, knew them. All living creatures were thus saved, and he entered into *Ni houan;* since his *Ni houan* 1497 years[19] have elapsed. When the Eyes of the World were quenched, all living beings experienced deep sorrow." Ten days after this, the tooth of Foe is conveyed to the chapel of the *Mountain without Fear.* Every man in the kingdom, enlightened by the doctrine, and anxious to promote happiness, comes from his quarter, to level the roads, to adorn the highways and streets, to scatter all sorts of flowers and perfumes. Then, after the chaunts, the king causes to be displayed on both sides of the road, representations of the five hundred successive manifestations[20] in which the *Phou sa* assumed different forms; such as that of *Siu ta nou,* the transformation into lightning,[21] that of the king of the elephants,[22] and that of the stag-horse.[23] These figures, painted in various colours, are carefully executed and appear living. At last the tooth of Foe is carried through the midst of the road, and is adored wherever it passes. Arrived at the chapel of the *Mountain without Fear*, they ascend into the hall of Foe; they burn there perfumes, making accumulated clouds; they perform religious acts without intermission night and day the whole of the ninety days. The tooth is then conveyed back to the chapel in the town. This chapel is very elegant; during the day, they open the gates and perform the ceremonies according to the law.

To the east of the *Chapel without Fear* there is a hill on which is a chapel named *Po thi*,[24] where there may be two thousand ecclesiastics. Amongst their number is a Samanean of great virtue, named *Tha mo kiu ti*, whom the people of the country hold in great veneration. He hath dwelt in a stone house near forty years, constantly occupied in charitable acts. He has succeeded in domesticating in the same house serpents and rats, without either doing injury to the other.

NOTES.

(1) *This kingdom.*—The fubulous origin of Ceylon, as detailed by Hiuan thsang, is evidently borrowed from traditions collected in the place itself, or drawn up from the originals, although differing in some notable respects from the accounts of the Singhalese. According to the Chinese traveller, the daughter of a king of southern India, set out on a lucky day, to marry the prince of a neighbouring country. Her escort fled at the sight of a lion, leaving her exposed to his attack. But the king of the lions, placing her upon his back, bore her away to his den, situated in a remote part of the mountains. There he caught deer for her, and brought her fruits, and furnished all her wants according to the season. For months and years that princess lived with him, and eventually becoming enceinte, she brought forth a son and a daughter, who in form were human, although begotten by a being of so different a nature. The son grew apace, and soon acquired strength equal to his father. Having attained puberty, and become sensible of his manly virtue, he inquired of his mother, "How can a beast of the forest be my sire, when my mother is human? Not being of the same species how can they copulate?" The mother having apprised him of what had

formerly happened,—"Men and beasts, he added, are of natures wholly distinct; let us immediately fly from this place and return no more." "Before fleeing," rejoined the mother, "let us be sure that we can." The son then began to follow the lion; he climbed the mountains with him; traversed the defiles, and examined the passes with care: then one day when his sire was far away, he took his mother and sister in his arms and reached the places of human habitation. The mother said; "Let us carefully conceal our secrets, and avoid repeating our history; for if it become known, men will despise us. Let us go hence to the kingdom of my father; we are insecure in a land where the religion of the people is different from our own." The inhabitants having asked them whence they came, they replied, "We are originally of these countries; exiled into far-away parts, children and mother, we mutually aid each other and seek our homes again." The people of the country, touched with compassion, immediately hastened to provide them with whatever they required. Meanwhile the king of the lions, returning to his cave, and finding neither his dear son nor daughter, issued furiously from the depths of the mountains and sought the dwellings of men. The earth shook with his roar. He attacked both man and beast, destroying every thing that had life. The inhabitants came out immediately to take and destroy him. They beat the drums, sounded the great conchs, and armed with cross-bows and spears, formed themselves into bands the better to resist the danger. The king commanded them to keep together, and putting himself at their head, they gradually stole through the forest and passed the hills. The roaring of the enraged lion struck terror into man and beast, who fled away in alarm. The king proclaimed that whoever should capture the lion and so deliver the kingdom from the calamity which afflicted it, should be rewarded with all manner of honors and rewards. On hearing this proclamation of the king, the son, addressing his mother, said to her; "Our wretchedness is extreme! I know not how to alleviate it. I must answer this appeal." "Say not so" replied his mother; "though this be a savage beast, he is not the less thy father; and our misfortunes are no sufficient reason that you should destroy him." The son rejoined; "Men and beasts are of different natures; what relations of justice can exist between them? Our right is that of resistance; what hope can he entertain in his breast?" Thus said, he armed himself with a dagger, and offered to fulfill the king's command. A numerous band accompanied him. The lion was couching in the forest; not a man dared to approach him. As soon as the son appeared the lion fell upon him and threw him to the ground; when the latter, full of rage and forgetting their relationship, plunged his dagger into the lion's belly. The lion suffered great anguish from the wound, and died, still preserving his tender love for his son as if the latter had done him no injury. The king then asked, "Who is this man? if there be aught supernatural in him, we must give him the rewards, but punish him also severely." The son having narrated his history, "Approach," said the king; "thy sire was savage and could have no paternal affection. The nature of wild animals is difficult to subdue, and wicked sentiments are easily produced in their hearts. To destroy that which is noxious to a people, is a noble action; to take the life of one's father is to do violence to the heart. Rewards of every kind shall honor this action, but exile shall punish the transgression. Thus shall the law of the state be respected, and the word of the king be free of duplicity." He then equipped two large vessels, which he loaded with provisions and necessaries, and unwilling that the son of the lion should remain longer in the kingdom; he gave him young men and young damsels for his reward, who set sail in different vessels according to their sex. That on which the young men embarked reached the Island of Jewels; and, as many precious things were found there, there these remained. In the sequel, some merchants having landed on that island, the inhabitants killed the chief of them, retained their wives and had many children. They elected chiefs to govern and magistrates for the regulation of affairs; they founded towns, built villages, and in memory of the daring action of their ancestor, called the kingdom they had established by his name. The vessel on which the damsels embarked, arrived at the western part of Persia, in a country inhabited by genii: those who landed had children by their intercourse with the genii, and established the "*Great Occidental kingdom of Women.*"

The natives of the Kingdom of Lions have oval faces, dark complexions, square chins, and lofty foreheads; they are robust and bold; their temper is hot and passionate. How can they, who are the descendants of a savage beast, endure insult?*—C. L.

(2) *Only demons and genii.*—The greater number of travellers who have been led to investigate the religious and historical traditions of Ceylon, make mention of these supernatural beings, with whom the first colonists from India for a long time struggled ere they obtained quiet possession of the entire island. According to the Rájavali, demons possessed Ceylon during 1844 years, namely, from the time of its depopulation consequent upon the famous wars betwixt Ráma and Rávana, to the time when Sákya Muni, desirous of establishing his religion in that island, created an extensive fire which destroyed the whole country and compelled the demons to flee to the ocean and take refuge in the island of *Yakgiri dewina.*† Accord-

* *Pian i tian*, B. LXVI. p. 11. et seq.
† *Upham, Sacred and Hist. Books of Ceylon*, Vol. II. p. 16 and p. 168 et seq.

ing to the computation of some authors, this happened when Buddha was 35 years of age ; 588 B. C. and 45 before the *Nirvána*.*

Hiuan thsang repeats, with that pretentious prolixity which is common with him, those Buddhist legends which relate how *Seng kia lo* (Sinhala) effected the riddance of Ceylon for ever from the demons who had withdrawn before the power of Sákya, at the time when he had subjected the rest of their race. In this narrative, which we shall greatly abridge, it is stated that formerly in the Isle of Jewels there was an iron town inhahabited by five hundred *Lo sha* women, (Rakshasi), or female demons, whose craftiness was equalled by their cruelty. Some merchants having come to the island for commercial purposes, the *Lo sha*, bringing perfumes and playing upon various instruments, advanced to meet them and invite them to enter the town for repose and amusement. Seduced by the beauty and conversation of these women, the merchants had (sexual) commerce with them, and each of them brought forth a son. The chief of these strangers was *Seng kia*, and his son was named *Seng kia lo*. The latter having in a dream had a revelation of the dangers which threatened him, he and his companions secretly gained the seashore, and with the assistance of a celestial steed escaped from the island. The queen of the *Lo sha* flew in pursuit of *Seng kia lo*, and endeavoured by her charms and carresses to seduce him to return : but, immoveable, *Seng kia lo* pronounced curses upon her and menaced her with his sword,—saying, " Thou art a *Lo sha*, I am a man ; being of different natures, we should never unite ; if we do so, we shall be mutually wretched. It must be that your destiny should fulfil itself!" Then the *Lo sha* publicly reproaching *Seng kia lo* with his conduct and his ingratitude, accused him of having abandoned her, rejected her, and overwhelmed her with maledictions and insults after having taken her to wife and accepted her presents. The king touched with her complaints and blinded by her beauty, protected her against *Seng kia lo*, and, despising the cautions of the latter, took her to wife. But in the middle of the night she flew back to the Isle of Jewels and returned instanter with five hundred other *Lo sha*, carrying desolation and slaughter into the palace of the king. She laid hold of all who were there, and glutting themselves with the flesh and blood of some, and bearing off the carcasses of others, returned to the Isle. Next morning, by daylight, the magistrates and the courtiers assembled for the royal audience, and awaited long the opening of the palace gates. Seeing none, and hearing none, they crossed the threshold, and found in the halls nought but piles of bones ! Turning away from the sight, they uttered loud cries, and wept in ignorance of the cause of such so great a misfortune. *Seng kia lo* apprised

* *Trans. As. Society*, Vol. III. p. 58.

them of the whole, and having narrated what had happened to himself, they, struck with his courage and wisdom, elected him for king. He then prepared arms, and having collected troops embarked to defy the power of the *Lo sha.* Having overcome these he compelled them to throw themselves into the sea, and take refuge in a neighbouring island; and then destroyed the iron town. Presently people from all sides flocked to the island, and a kingdom was established which bore the name of the king, *Seng kia lo.**

The Singhalese books state that it was *Vijiya* (Vijaya), son of Sinhala, who at the head of seven hundred warriors, and with the aid of *Cawany*, effected the destruction of the supernatural beings that remained in the island after the expedition of Sákya Muni amongst them.†—C. L.

(3) *They took the goods.*—This account exhibits a curious analogy with the well known passage in Pliny, which ascribes the same mode of traffic to the Seres: *Fluminis ulteriore ripâ merces positas juxtá venalia tolli ab his, si placeat permutatio.*‡—R.

(4) *Converted the wicked dragons.*—The dragons and the genii which originally inhabited Ceylon, were called, the former *Nágas*, and the second *Yakshas*, in Páli *Yakka.* Their conversion by Sákya Muni has furnished Singhalese writers with numerous legends which, with the traditions relating to *Vijaya*, form the heroic age in the history of Ceylon. Every thing is supernatural in these legends; the journey of Sákya from central India through the air, his discussions with the *Yakshas*, the miracles he performed to convince them, and the circumstances attending their final expulsion from the island, which ever after adhered to the faith of Sákya. Side by side with these legends are those referring to *Vijaya Sinhabáhu*, who came from Kalinga, with seven hundred men, and occupied at first but a limited extent of coast. If there be any thing historical in these incoherent and often contradictory narratives, it is rather in the legends relating to *Vijaya* than in those detailing the pretended journey of Sákya. These several recitals may be consulted in the compilation of Upham. We may remark that the account given of the arrival of *Mahinda* in Ceylon, and the conversion of the king *Devenipaetissa*, would seem to prove that it was only under this prince, that is to say, if Ceylonese chronology be correct, about the fourth century before our era, that Buddhism was established in Ceylon.§ —E. B.

According to the Chinese, one century after the Nirvána, *Mo hi yn ti lo*

* *Pian i tian*, B. LXVI. art. 4, pp. 13—16 v.
† *Upham, Sac. and Hist. Books of Ceylon*, Vol. I. p. 69, and Vol. II. p. 171, et seq.
‡ *Hist. Nat.* B. VI. ch. XXIV.
§ *Sac. and Hist. Books of Ceylon*, Vol. I. p. 84 et seq.

(Mahendra), younger brother of king Asoka, abandoned the world and proceeded to diffuse the doctrine among the inhabitants of Ceylon. These changed their customs and were converted to the true faith. Two centuries later, the doctrines of Foe were divided into two classes, denominated *Mo ho pi ho lo* (Mahávihára), and the other *A po ye chi li* (Abhayashri).*—C. L.

(5) *The print of his feet on the top of a mountain.*—This mountain, from its height and the veneration with which it is regarded, has ever attracted the attention of travellers, to whom it is known as *Adam's Peak*. At the time of Sákya's third visit to Ceylon, fifteen years subsequent to his first, Saman-deva Rája came to adore him, and said, "Behold, O Buddha, that lofty mountain, whose name is *Samana kuta*, blue as a rock of sapphire, its summit concealed in the clouds! Many Buddhas have there left their relics, by means of which the memory of their transit through the world is preserved among men. Deign to add one jewel to these, and leave there the impress of thy foot, which shall be to this islea precious blessing." On this Buddha raised himself to the clouds, and hovering above the mountain, the latter sprung from its base to receive in the air the impress of the blessed foot, and then fell back again to the place it occupies to this day.†

Buddhists mention a great many prints of this kind; the veneration these receive, scarcely inferior to that paid to Buddha himself, has no doubt conted to augment the number. It is quite plain that every country must have its own, and that each sect pretend to honor in it the divinty it adores, or the head of the doctrine it has embraced. All therefore do not belong to Sákya Muni; indeed the Páli texts recognise but five genuine ones, named *Pancha pra patha*, 'the five divine feet.' Capt. Low has devoted an article to this subject in the Transactions of the Royal Asiatic Society of London.—C. L.

The Singhalese name this impression and the mountain on which it exists, *Hammanelle Siripade*, or more exactly, *Samadhela Sripáda*, that is, 'the sacred foot of the mountain of Samana.' *Samana*, or *Saman*, is the tutelary God of this mountain. In the Mahávansa this mountain is called *Samanta kúta parvata*, and it is very probable that *Samanta kuta* is the primitive form of *Samanhela*. Valentyn has given a minute and exact account of this mountain and the images found on the summit of Adam's Peak, in his description of Ceylon; a work of which Weston has made extensive use in his compilation of Singhalese History. This mountain, according to Valentyn, is situated about fourteen German miles from Colombo. Its summit

* *Pian i tian*, B. LXVI.

† *Upham*, Vol. II. p. 23.

can be reached only by means of an iron chain fixed to the rock, the links of which serve as steps. The summit forms an area of a hundred and fifty paces in length and a hundred and ten in breadth. In the centre of this space is a stone seven or eight feet long and projecting about three feet from the soil. It is there that devotees imagine that they recognise the print, some of Sákya Muni's foot, others of Adam's.

The Singhalese however admit of only one print on the mountain *Samanhela;* a few traditions only affirm that Sákya Muni placed one of his feet upon *Samanhela* and another upon that of the Madura. What may have given rise to the tradition of the twofold impress mentioned by Fa hian is that the mountain is divided into two summits, upon one of which is to be seen the Sripada ; but the distance of fifteen *yeou yans* which according to our author, separates these footprints, is certainly exaggerated. Lastly, as we have just had occasion to see, there is nothing more common amongst Buddhist nations than the existence of such prints of the feet of Sákya. Even in Ceylon it is stated that he left such memorials in other parts of the island, and in particular in the bed of the river Calamy.*—E. B.

(6) *Fifteen yeou yans.*—60 or 70 English miles.

(7) *Forty chang.*—A *chang* is a measure of ten Chinese feet ; and the Chinese foot is eight lines shorter than ours. Taking the *chang* as equal to three metres and sixty centimetres, the height of this tower would be twenty-two metres.—C. L.

(8) *The Mountain without Fear;*—in Chinese, *Wou 'weï.* Hiuan thsang appears not to have known this building ; in fact he does not mention the temple of the *Tooth of Foe*, of which we shall speak immediately, nor of another smaller temple near it, in the vicinity of the king's palace. Both were sumptuously adorned.†—C. L.

The Sanscrit name of this *Seng kia lan* is *Abhayagiri*, a word which means exactly 'the mountain of security.' The Mahávansa and the Rájaratnákari state, that the king Walakanabhaya, or according to the latter work, Deveny Paetissa, caused the temple of a heathen named Girrie (doubtless Giri) to be destroyed, and caused to be constructed upon its site twelve temples consecrated to Sákya, which communicated with each other ; and in the midst of which was erected an immense *vihara.* He then combined his own name *Abhaya* with that of *Giri*, so that the entire monument was named *Abhaya Giri.*‡ According to the *Mahávansa*, this event took place about the year 456 of Buddha, or about eighty-seven years before our era. Possibly the explanation thus given by Singhalese authorities is somewhat

* *Upham*, Vol. I. p. 7, and Vol. II. p. 22, 23.
† *Pian i tian*, B. LXVI. art. 4. p. 17.
‡ *Upham*, Vol. I. p. 219, Vol. II. p. 43.

strained; for by holding to the sense of the word *Abhaya Giri*, which is regularly rendered '*Mountain of Security*,' there is no need to have recourse to the history of the priest *Giri*, and the more so as this name does not appear suitable for a man. It is as well to note that Fa hian understood this word in the sense in which we have just explained it, so that he had more accurate information than is to be found in Singhalese legends. —E. B.

(9) *The land of Han*,—or China. According to the practice of the Chinese, their country is designated after the dynasties which have ruled it with the greatest glory, even after they have long ceased to reign.

(10) *Reflecting upon the past*;—in the text, *looking back upon the shadow*.

(11) *The land of Thsin*.—The name of a celebrated dynasty which is ordinarily applied to all China, but which here more particularly designates the province of *Shen si* of which Fa hian was a native.—C. L.

(12) *The tree Pei to*.—In Sanscrit, *Bodhi*, a name given from the circumstance of Buddha having acquired supreme intelligence under its shadow. According to Singhalese tradition it wasfrom Central India that the kings of Ceylon obtain a branch of this tree. The Rájavali states that Mahindo Kumára, son of Dharmásoka, one of the successors of Chandragupta, drew around the right branch of the Bodhi tree a yellow line, and that he entreated the gods that that branch should be transported to Ceylon. In an instant the branch detached itself from the tree as if it had been cut with a saw, and rising in the air, it sped to Ceylon, where it was received in a golden vase and afterwards planted in consecrated ground.* This event took place in the reign of the Singhalese king Deweny Paetissa. Now the year 236 corresponds with our 307 B. C. if we admit the Singhalese computation, which if I am not mistaken, must be reduced by some fifty years to make it synchronise with other indications drawn from Bráhmanical sources. A passage from the *Rájanatnakari* proves that the *bodhi* was planted near Anaradhapura, that at least to which Fa hian refers, and which was still flourishing in his time. Moreover the narratives of our traveller is much more copious than the *Rájávali*. According to the *Mahávansa*, which narrates the fact as detailed in the works quoted, the branch of the holy tree was conveyed to Ceylon in a less miraculous manner, that is, on a ship.—E. B.

(13) *Twenty chang*.—About 200 English feet.

(14) *Four Wei*.—About 234 English inches.

(15) *Sa pho merchants*.—*Sa pho* is the Chinese form of perhaps a Sin-

* *Upham*, Vol. II. p. 184.

ghalese expression; but our historical and philological information connected with Ceylon, is not so circumstantial as to enable us on every occasion to restore with certainty such words and expressions as present themselves, more especially when a secondary interest attaches to them as in this instance would appear to be the case.

(16) *The tooth of Foe.*—Buddhists recognise the authenticity of several relics of this kind, (see Chap. V. note 5. and Chap. XIII. note 8;) but none is so celebrated as that here spoken of, nor has any been subject to such variety of fortune. The Singhalese name it the *Dulada wahanse* (the honorable tooth). According to their accounts, Mahasana, who ascended the throne of Ceylon 818 years after the death of Buddha, despatched an ambassador with rich presents to *Guhásíha*, king of *Kalinga rata* (Kalinga désa) in the south of Bengal, to obtain from him this precious relic, then in his possession. The king of Kalinga consented to yield it up; but Mahasana dying in the interval, it was received with the greatest solemnity by his son *Kiertissry mayawarna*, who built a temple for its reception. Fourteen hundred years after the death of Buddha, the Malabars came from the coast of Coromandel to the attack of Ceylon, and having seized that country, persecuted the faith, and carried off the sacred tooth to the banks of the Ganges (perhaps the Godavery). Eighty-six years afterwards, *Mahalu Wijayaba* expelled the Malabars, and some years subsequently *Parákramabahu* brought back again to Ceylon the tooth of Buddha. In the latter part of the 16th Century, the Portuguese carried it off in their turn, when Constantino of Braganza, refused considerable sums for its redemption, and animated with religious zeal, publicly reduced it to ashes. Next morning however the priest of Buddha found another tooth in the corolla of a lotus, in every respect similar: and it is this that is now in the possession of the English, and for the restoration of which the late king of Burmah sent two embassies to Calcutta.

On comparing the first of these particulars with the date discussed above, we may infer that our traveller visited Ceylon not long after the king of Kalinga had sent thither the tooth of Buddha.—C. L.

For a very ample account of this celebrated relic and its fortunes the reader may refer to the late Hon. Mr. Turnour's account in the Journal of the Asiatic Society, Vol. VI. p. 856, et seq., an account which he concludes by mentioning that he had held official custody of the relic since 1828; it having been found necessary for the tranquillity of the country that the British Government should retain so precious an object in its own possession. "During that period," says Mr. Turnour, "the six-fold caskets in which it is enshrined have been twice opened; once in May 1828, at the request of the natives, when a magnificent festival was celebrated, which lasted a fortnight; and once in 1834, to admit of Sir Robert and Lady Horton seeing it, on which occasion the scientific Austrian traveller, Baron Von Hugel was also present. The keys of the sanctuary are never absent from my library, excepting during the actual performance of the daily religious ceremonies, and at night a military guard is posted at the temple."

I fear, however, that there are good grounds for believing that this object of idle curiosity and miserable superstition, guarded with so much pomp and care, has no pretensions whatever to a higher antiquity than the 16th century at furthest; and that we cannot boast with Col. Sykes, that "this celebrated relic, after falling into the hands of the Malabars and Portuguese is now *safely* lodged under the lock and key of the English." The circumstances under which it was destroyed, not by order of the Viceroy, D. Constantino de Braganza, as stated by M. Landresse, but in direct opposition to his wishes, are thus detailed by the Portuguese historian, Diogo de Couto. "As soon as the king of Pegu heard of the capture of Jafnapatam and the seizure of the tooth-relic by the Viceroy, he despatched ambassadors to the latter, offering unlimited sums of gold for its redemption, and making promises of eternal friendship and alliance in the event of compliance with his wishes. The Viceroy consulted his captains and counsellors, who were unanimous in thinking that so magnificent an offer should not be rejected. Meanwhile the rumour of this negociation reached the ears of the Archbishop, D. Gaspar, who immediately went to the Viceroy, expostulated with him upon a traffic so dishonoring to God, and forbade him to sell for any amount of gold, an object which contributed to the perpetuation of idolatry among the heathen. The Viceroy was too good a Catholic to act upon his own responsibility in opposition to the wishes of the Archbishop; but having summoned a council, to which the latter and all the clergy were invited, he laid before them the urgent necessities of the state, which might at once be relieved by so splendid a ransom. The subject was fully discussed by the assembly, and it was finally determined that the ransom, were it even the whole world, could not be accepted, as being offensive to God." The historian mentions by name the whole of the clergy who came to this honorable determination, and proceeds; "This being agreed to, and a resolution being drawn out and signed by all present, a copy of which may be seen in the record-office (*torre do tombo*), the Viceroy commanded the treasurer to bring forth the tooth, and then transferred it to the Archbishop. The latter, in the presence of all, with his own hands, put the tooth into a metal mortar, and having broken it into pieces, cast the fragments into a chaffingdish, which he then caused to be thrown, ashes, coals and all, into the middle of the river, in the presence of all the people, who looked on from their windows and verandahs. The Viceroy murmured greatly at this transaction, saying that the heathen had no scarcity of other idols, would easily fashion another tooth as substitute for that which had been destroyed, and would pay it the same veneration; while so great a sum of money would have been a substantial benefit to the state in its present need. To soothe the Viceroy, and serve as a memorial of this event, the ecclesiastics had a shield prepared, having in the centre a painting representing himself and the Archbishop at a table, around which were the other prelates and clergy who had been actually present on the occasion, and in the midst a blazing chaffer; while the heathen were standing by holding in their hands bags of money which they threw upon the fire, with these five letters, the initial of Constantino's name, CCCCC; and underneath the words *Constantinus cœli cupidine cremavit crumenas;* implying that Constantino, intent upon heaven, despised worldly treasures," &c. De Couto, *Da historia da India*, Dec. VII. B. 9. Chap. XVII. On referring to a subsequent volume of the same history, I find that notwithstanding its complete destruction as here recorded, this miraculous tooth was sold some years afterwards to the king of Pegu, who celebrated its arrival in his kingdom with extravagant festivals and rejoicings!—J. W. L.

(17) *In the course of three A seng ki.*—This is the transcription of the Sanscrit *Asankhya*, which signifies innumerable and which is the first of the ten great numbers explained by Foe to indicate how boundless and inexhaustible are the virtues of the Buddhas, the acts of the Bodhisattwas, the ocean of their desires, and infinite laws of mundane developments.* The *Asankhya* is equivalent to a hundred quadrillions. "Asankhya signifies an infinite number; with what propriety speak ye of three *Asankhyas?* asks the *Kiu che lun.*" "Because," it is retorted, "*Wou sou* signifies *innumerable*, and not *without number.*"

Sákya Muni led the life of a Bodhisattwa during three *Asankhyas.* The first comprises the existence of three score and fifteen thousand Buddhas, (or three score and fifteen ages of the world, as a thousand Buddhas must appear in every age of the world) from Sákya, surnamed the *ancient*, to *Shi khi Foe* (Sikhí Buddha). In his earlier births Sákya Muni was a manufacturer of tiles, and was named *Ta kouang ming.* Sákya the *ancient* having come to lodge with the tiler, the latter rendered him the triple service of preparing him a seat of grass, of enlightening him with a lantern, and of giving him to drink. He worshipped Foe, and conceived the wish, if in

* *Hoa yan king*, quoted in the *San tsang fa sou*, B. XLIII. p. 16.

time to come he should become Foe, he should bear the name of his guest. Hence he is now called *Shy kia wen.*

The second *Asankhya* begins with *Shi khi Foe*, and presents a succession of seventy-six thousand Buddhas, up to the advent of *Jan teng Foe* (Dipankara Buddha). When *Jan teng Foe* was born, his body shone like a lamp; and hence he took this name on attaining Buddhahood. Sákya, who was then named *Jou toung*, presented him with three lotus stalks; he took off the deer skin with which he was clad and placed it under the feet of the Buddha to protect them from the mud and spread out his hair upon the ground. For this *Jan teng* said to him, "In ninety-one Kalpas thou shalt become Buddha and shall be called *Shy kia wen.*"

Finally the third *Asankhya* embraces the lives of seventy-seven thousand Buddhas from *Jan teng Foe* to *Pi pho shi* (Vipasyi), the first of the seven Buddhas generally named together, and to whom invocations are collectively addressed.*—C. L.

(18) *He spared not the marrow of his bones.*—These different acts of Sákya Muni while yet a Bodhisattwa, have been detailed elsewhere. See particularly Chaps. IX. X. XI.

Full particulars of many of these fabulous events, referred to Sákya's anterior existences, may be found in M. Schmidt's *Weiser und Thor*, as I have before intimated.—J. W. L.

(19) 1497 *years have elapsed.*—There is too little agreement between the various dates given by Fa hian, as well as too little uniformity in his manner of computation to enable us to establish any well determined point of departure in his chronology. Nevertheless we may see that he here reckons after the Chinese Buddhic era most generally admitted (950 B. C.) which differs by nearly five centuries from that of the Singhalese (543 B. C.) and according to which the year of the nirvána would correspond with 410 A. D., a date which is also very certainly that of the abode of our traveller in Ceylon. A great religious movement at that time agitated the country; the struggle which ensued between Bráhmanism and Buddhism, and which ended, somewhat later, in the overthrow of the latter cult in the lands of its birth, had not yet exercised its baneful influence in Ceylon. On the contrary, this island presented to unhappy proselytes, a refuge from the intolerance of the Bráhmans: and as happens in such cases, zeal redoubled with persecution. A learned priest from the continent of India, named *Buddhaghosa*, after having to a great extent revived the religion of which he was a zealous partisan, had hardly left Ceylon to spread the doctrine beyond the Ganges in Ava, and among the Burmans, (Crawford, Embassy to Ava,

* *Thian taï sse kiao yi*, cited in the *San tsang fa sou*, B. XII. p. 27.

p. 491; and Bournouf and Lassen Essai Sur le Páli, p. 62) when Fa hian arrived there under circumstance highly favourable for the objects of his voyage, as the account of the pompous ceremonies he witnessed testifies. "Since the origin of this kingdom, he observes, there has been no famine or scarcity, no calamity or troubles;" which shows that he was there before the pestilence which desolated this island under *Upatissa* at the beginning of the fifth century; and, especially, that he was there before the invasion of the Malabars, which occurred shortly afterwards. Thus it is in the interval between these events and the time when the tooth of Foe was imported from the Peninsula, that we must fix the arrival of Fa hian in Ceylon. We shall see further on that he returned to his own country in 414; now as he dwelt two years in Ceylon and was seven months on his voyage to China, the year 412 must be the true date corresponding with 1497; an era which coincides perfectly with the historical circumstances we have mentioned, and which places the death of Buddha in the year 1084 or 1085 B. C. This is a new date to collate with those already gathered of this event, and may be compared with the other Singhalese dates discussed by M. M. Bournouf and Lassen in their researches on the sacred language of the Buddhists.—C. L.

(20) *Five hundred successive manifestations.*—The *Játaka*, births or manifestations of Buddha, to which the Chinese sometimes, but improperly, apply the term *incarnation* (avatára) are apparently spoken of here. However many of these births succeed each other, the being who is their subject, hath still no divine character; he is subject to *avidyá*, that is, to all the imperfections attached to individual existence, to the errors, the affections,—in a word, to the illusions of every kind which constitute the sensible world' and of which we have had frequent occasion to speak in the course of these notes. It is not till he has attained the point of absolute perfection essential to Buddhahood, that he is commingled with infinite intelligence and is for ever freed from individuality, and consequently, according to M. Remusat's expression, from the vicissitudes of the phenomenal world.

Fa hian speaks of only five hundred manifestations; but five hundred and fifty are generally spoken of as principal ones, and the doctrines of transmigration admit that Buddha passed through the entire scale of creation, that he passed through every state of existence in the sea, earth, and air, and underwent every condition of human life. "When one body was destroyed, said Buddha himself, I received another; and the number of my births and deaths can only be compared to that of all the trees and plants in the entire universe. It is impossible to reckon the bodies I have possessed."*

* *Sieou hing pen kei king*, quoted in the *San tsang fa sou*, B. LXXVII. p. 8.

These five hundred and fifty *Játaka* are the subjects of pictures and emblems piously preserved in temples for the veneration of the people on the occasion of grand ceremonials, such as Fa hian describes. To each of these manifestations belongs a legend or recital of the events of which Buddha was the subject under the different forms in which he figures, and which serves as a practical discourse upon the conduct to be observed in analogous conditions. Mr. Upham has published four of these legends, accompanied by figures, as also a Singhalese list of the five hundred and fifty Játakas.—C. L.

(20) *That of Siu ta nou.*—This is the transcription of the Sanscrit *Sútanu*, 'fair-bodied,' which is found in the Singhalese list of the *Játaka.*—C. L.

(21) *Transformation into lightning.*—There is nothing impossible in this transformation according to Buddhist notions, which admit of the gods and saints assuming every form of body, and even similating several at once. Buddha, say Chinese authors, by his supernatural power, assumed various forms appertaining to no created being with a material body. To save living creatures and overwhelm then with benign influences, he accommodates himself to their understandings, and manifests himself in all manner of bodies, as the light of the one moon reflects itself on many waters. He can become lightning, as well as a plant or tree; but this manifestation is not included among the five hundred and fifty *játakas;* at least the Singhalese list of Upham contains nothing analogous.

The *Rája Ratnákari* narrates that when the tooth of Buddha reached Ceylon, it appeared self-raised in the sky in the similitude of a planet; and having taken its place in the firmament shone with six brilliant colours.* Might not the painted figure seen by Fa hian be a memorial of this prodigy, and that he mistook it for one of the manifestations of Buddha amongst which it was placed?—C. L.

(22) *That of the king of elephants.*—This játaka may be the one which figures in the Singhalese list under the name of *Matanga*, or perhaps that of *Hatty pála.*†—C. L.

(23) *That of the stag-horse.*—This is no doubt the játaka named *Rooroomaga;* that is the *Gazelle called Ruru.*—C. L.

(24) *A chapel named Po thi.*—Hiuan thsang makes no mention of this chapel, but he speaks of the mountain upon which it was situated, and which is in the south-east corner of the kingdom. He calls it *Ling kia.* Jou laï formerly inhabited it, and it was there that he expounded the *Ling kïa king.*‡—C. L.

* *Upham*, Vol. II. p. 72.
† *Upham*, Vol. III. p. 277.
‡ *Pian i tian*, B. LXVI. art 4. p. 180.

CHAPTER XXXIX.

Chapel of Mo ho pi ho lo.—Cremation of the body of a Samanean.—Destiny of Foe's Pot.

At seven *li* to the south of the town, there is a chapel called *Mo ho pi ho lo*,[1] where three thousand ecclesiastics reside. There was there a Samanean of exalted virtue, one who observed the precepts with exactitude, and lived in the greatest purity. The people of the country all believed that he was an *Arhan*. When his end was approaching, the king visited him, and in conformity with the law, assembled the ecclesiastics and asked them if the mendicant had obtained the doctrine. They answered, that in reality he was an *Arhan*. When he was dead, the king, having consulted the rituals and the sacred books, conducted his funeral as beseemed an *Arhan*. To the east of the chapel, at the distance of four or five *li*, they piled up wood upon a space of about three *chang*, and to the same height; above it they placed sandal-wood, the essence of aloe-wood, and all sorts of odoriferous woods. On the four sides they made steps, and covered the whole with a beautiful tissue of very pure white wool. On this pile they raised a bed similar to a funeral car, but without *loung iu*. At the instant of the *she weï*,[2] the king and the four castes of the inhabitants of the country unitedly offered up flowers and perfumes. When the car was brought to the place of sepulture, the king himself offered flowers and perfumes. This oblation ended, they placed the car upon the pile which was sprinkled all over with storax, and applied fire. Whilst it burnt, every one had his heart filled with recollections; every one, having taken off his upper garments, waved from afar a kind of parasol of feathers[3] to assist the *she weï*. When the *she weï* was finished, they sought for and collected together the bones, and erected a tower over them. Fa hian on his arrival found not this Samanean alive; he was able only to assist at his funeral.

The king firmly believes in the Law of Foe. As he was desirous of building a new chapel for the ecclesiastics, he began by giving these a grand entertainment. After they had eaten, he selected two fine field-oxen whose horns he ornamented with gold, and silver, and precious things. They made a beautiful plough[4] of gold, and the king himself ploughed the four sides of an arpent;[5] and when he had disseized himself of it, he gave them its inhabitants, its families, its fields and its houses. He wrote the deed upon iron, importing that now and from generation to generation, this property should be transmitted without any one daring to alter or to change it.

Whilst Fa hian was in these parts he heard the Clergy of Reason declare from a lofty throne where they read the Sacred Books, that the pot of Foe was at first at *Phi she li*,[6] and that it has now been nearly some 1100 years, at *Kian tho weï*[7] (Fa hian when he heard this discourse knew précisely the number of years, but now he has forgotten it). It must return to the kingdom of the western *Yue ti.*[8] At the end of eleven hundred years it will go to the kingdom of *Yu thian*,[9] and will there remain eleven hundred years. Thence it will go to the kingdom of *Khiu thse.*[10] After eleven hundred years it must go anew to the *Country of Han* for eleven hundred years; then it will return to the *Kingdom of Lions*. After eleven hundred years it will return to Mid-India. From Mid-India it will rise to the heaven *Teou shou.*[11] When *Mi le phou sa*[12] shall behold it, he will exclaim, sighing, "The pot of *Shy kia wen Foe* hath come!" Then, with all the gods, he will offer it flowers and perfumes for seven days. The seven days expired, the pot will return to *Yan feou thi*. The king of the sea-dragons will take it to his dragon-palace. When *Mi le* shall be on the eve of completing the law, the pot, divided into four (parts), will return to its original place on mount *Phin na*. *Mi le* having accomplished the law, the four kings of heaven shall meditate afresh on Foe, conformably to the law of antecedent

Foes. The thousand Foes of the Age of the Sages[13] shall all make use of this pot. When the pot shall be no more, the law of Foe will be insensibly extinguished. When the law of Foe is extinct, the age of man shall become again short, so that its duration shall be no more than from five to ten years. Rice and butter will disappear. Men, become extremely wicked, will arm themselves with clubs that shall become swords ; each will attack the other, and they shall fight and kill each other. There shall be amongst their number some so fortunate as to escape, and fly to the mountains. When the destruction of the wicked shall be complete, these men shall come forth and re-appear, saying to each other, "They of the olden time lived long ; but they committed every kind of wickedness and transgressed the law ; and therefore hath our life been gradually abridged and reduced to ten years. Let us now do that which is right : let us raise our penitent hearts to charity, and cultivate deeds of humanity and justice. Each thus exhibiting faith and justice, the duration of our lives will increase and reach to four score thousand years." When *Mi le* shall appear in the world, and shall begin to turn the wheel of the doctrine, he shall first convert the disciples adhering faithfully to the law of *Shy kia,* men out of their homes,[14] those who shall have received the three *Koueï*[15] and the five precepts,[16] and those who shall have kept the law, and observed the worship of the *three precious ones.* The second and the third converted in this order, are the protegés of Foe. Fa hian would that instant have copied the book which contained this, but the people said, "This is not written ; we know it by oral tradition."

NOTES.

(1) *Chapel of Mo ho pi ho lo.*—This is the Sanscrit word ***Mahávihára,*** the great temple, or rather the great monastery—for according to the definition given by Mr. Upham (Hist. and Doct. of Buddhism, p. 19) vihára does not properly mean a temple, but a habitation of monks with a chapel; called by the Chinese *Seng kia lan.* Fa hian has it all to himself here ; Hiuan thsang makes no mention of this building.

(2) *At the moment of the she weï.*—She weï is a *Fan* word which it is impossible to restore with certainty, either because the transcription is

formed in a manner too irregular, or because it has long fallen into disuse.* The *San tsang fa sou*, (B. V. p. 3,) explains it by *fen shao*, to consume, to burn, the act of burning. It may be the transcription of the two first syllables of *Shavadáha*, the cremation of a body. The *she weï* is one of the *four sepultures*, that of fire. The others are that of water, that of earth, and that of forests.†—C. L.

(3) *Parasol of feathers.*—In Ceylon the fan-like leaves of the Palmyra tree (*Borassus flabelliformis*) are to this day used as parasols; and it is perhaps to an imitation of these, formed of feathers, that our pilgrim here alludes.—J. W. L.

(4) The ceremony here described by Fa hian is precisely that adopted by Dewananpiyatisso on founding the Mahawiharo. The details are given at length in the fifteenth Chapter of the Mahawanso, to which work I must refer the reader for many illustrations of Fa hian's account of Ceylon, which want of space compels me to omit here.—J. W. L.

(5.) *An arpent.*—A measuse of land containg 100 perches of 18 ft. each.

(6) *Pi she li.*—Vaisali. (See Chapt. XXV. note 2.)

(7) *Kian tho weï.*—This country, named also *Kian tho* aund *Kan tho lo*, is Gandhara (See Chap. X. note).—According to the Account of Western Countries, it is situated to the west of Udyána, and was namd at first *Ye pho lo;* but being subjected by the *Ye tha* (Getœ) it changed its name. Udyána and Kandahar are the countries of northern India which in the time of Fa hian preserved most of the important traditions of Buddhism; but their neighborhood to each other, and the demarcation so difficult to establish among so many petty states always at war with each other and alternately conquering and conquered, occasion sometimes slight discrepancies if not in the site of the particular scenes of Foe's actions, at least in the precise determination of the kingdoms to which they belonged. It is thus that many memorable circumstances narrated by Fa hian and Hiuan thsang as having occurred in Udyána, may, according to other travellers, have taken place in Kandahar and vice versá, without any fair ground of accusing these narratives of contradiction to each other.

At the commencement of the 6th century two Chinese Buddhist monks, *Soung yun tse* and *Hoeï seng*, came to Gandhara, impelled by the same motives which actuated Fa hian a century earlier. The narrative they have given deserves on sundry accounts to be compared with that of the Foe Koue ki. At the time of their arrival the country had been at war with the Khi pin on the question of the boundaries of the two states.

* *Fa youan chou lin*, quoted in the *San tsang fa sou*, B. XIX. p. 14 v.
† *Pian i tian*, B. LXIII. art. 7, p. 8.

The king was a cruel tyrant, delighting in murder and blood, a disbeliever in the law of Foe, a worshipper of genii, and dependent entirely on his own strength and courage. He had seven hundred war elephants, each mounting ten men armed with swords and lances, and to the trunk of each elephant was affixed a sabre to smite the enemy. The king constantly dwelt on the frontiers in the midst of the mountains, so that the people suffered greatly, and their families murmured. Soung yun joined the camp to deliver the imperial letter. The king received it seated. * * * Soung yun said to him, "Of mountains, some are high and others low; among rivers some are great and others small; and so in the world there are exalted men and there are humble ones. The Ye tha and the king of Ou chang both received the imperial missive with respect; how hath the great king alone received it otherwise?" The king replied, "Were I to see in person the great king of the Weï, I would salute him; but what is there surprising in that I should peruse his letters seated? When men receive a letter from father or mother, they read it seated; the Lord of the Weï is father and mother to me; and I read his letter also seated. In this, what is there contrary to propriety?" Yun could not move him from this * * *

After journeying five days to the west, the travellers reached the place where Jou lai made an alms-gift of his head; in that place there was a tower inhabited by twenty monks. According to Fa hian this took place in the kingdom of *Chu sha si lo* (Chap. XI.), situated seven days' journey to the east of Kian tho weï, which doubtless no longer existed as an independent kingdom in the time of Soung yun's journey. Three days further journey to the west is the river *Sou theou*, on the western bank of which is the place where Jou laï, having assumed the form of the fish, ***Ma kieï*** (Makara?) came out of the river and during twelve years fed men on his flesh. A tower was erected in memory of this event, and the impression of the scales of a fish are still to be seen upon a rock.

Further west, three day's journey, you come to the town of ***Foe sha fou.*** There are both within and without this town, ancient temples for which devotees have peculiar veneration. One *li* north of the town is the palace of the white elephant. It is a temple dedicated to Foe. It is adorned with statues of stone covered with precious ornaments: these have many heads to each body and are covered with leaves of gold which dazzle the eyes. In front of the temple is the tree of the white elephant. Its flowers and leaves resemble those of the jujube tree; it bears fruit at the close of winter. Old men repeat from tradition, that when this tree shall die, the law of Foe will die also. * * *

At one day's journey further west is the spot where Jou laï tore out an eye to present it to a man. (See Chap. X.) A tower and a temple have been there erected. On a stone is the impress of the foot of Kia she Foe.

Continuing farther west Soung yun arrives at the town of *Kan tho lo;* seven *li* to the south-east of which is the *feou tou*, built by king *Kia ni sse kia*, and which must be the same edifice which Fa hian places in Beluchistan. (*Foe leou sha*, that is, *Purushapura*, *Peshawur*.—J. W. L.) (Chap. XII.) The legend regarding the king Kia ni sse kia is related in pretty nearly the same terms by these two travellers and Hiuan thsang,* who concurs with Soung yun in stating that this temple is in Kandahar. Both dwell upon its magnificence. "Amongst the *Feou thou* of western countries," says Soung yun, "this is the first. When they began to build it, they used pearls to form the trellis work destined to cover it. But some years after, the king, observing that this tissue of pearls being worth more than ten thousand pieces of gold, feared that after his death it might be abstracted, and that if the great tower should fall, no one would seek to restore it, took down the pearl tissue lattice, and placed it in a copper vase, which he caused to be buried one hundred paces north-west of the tower; and over it he planted a tree. This tree is named *Pho thi;* its branches spread out on all sides and its foliage shuts out the sight of the sky. Beneath it are four seated statues, each five toises high."

Proceeding seven days' journey further north, and passing a great river, you arrive at the place where Jou lai released the pigeon. According to Fa hian it was in the country called *So ho to* that the Bodhisattwa accomplished this act of charity. (Chap. IX.) Soung yun knew not this name, which had probably disappeared with the little state to which it belonged.

On leaving this point, the travellers neglect to note the distances as well as the direction of their march. They arrive successively in the kingdom of *Na kia lo ho*, which is identical with *Na kie*, placed by Fa hian sixteen yojanas west of *Foe leou sha*. (Chap. XII.) In that place was the skull-bone of Foe. It was four inches in circumference, and of a yellowish-white; below was a cavity which might receive a man's thumb, resembling a bee's hive. In the town is the temple *Khi ho lan*, where there are thirteen fragments of the *Kia sha* (mantle) of Foe. It is probably the chapel of the *Seng kia li* mentioned in the Foe koue ki. There is also the brass staff of Foe, seven *chang* in length (about 21 metres) it is washed with tubes filled with water. It is entirely covered with leaves of gold. The weight of this staff varies; there are times when it is so heavy that a hundred men cannot raise it; again, at other times, it is so light that a single man may carry it away. In the same town are also the tooth and the hair of Foe; these

* *Pian i tian*, B. LXIII. art. 7, p. 1.

relics are preciously enshrined, and morning and evening offerings are presented to them.

At *Kiu lo lo lòu*, fifteen paces in the mountain, is the cave of the shadow of Foe. When seen far off the shadow is distinctly perceived; but on a nearer approach, it is seen just as if the eyes were dizzied; if you stretch out the hand nothing more is felt than the stone wall. On retiring again, gradually the figure re-appears. It is one of the most singular things in the world. In front of the stone there is a square stone on which is a print of the foot of Foe. At a hundred paces south-west of the cave is the spot where Foe washed his clothes; and one *li* north-east is the cave of *Mou lian*. To the north of this cave is a mountain at the foot of which is a great temple with a *Feou thou* ten toises high. There are still seven other towers, to the south of which there is a stone with an inscription said to be made by the hand of Jou laï himself; and which is still very well understood.*

On comparing the above with the narrative of Fa hian, it will be seen that they do not differ from each other in any essential point, and that the former contains some particulars of which the other traveller seems to have been ignorant, or to have neglected to record. Of these is the curious tradition ascribing to Sákya Tathágatha the inscription here mentioned. As to what refers to the pot of Foe, Hiuan thsang relates that after the nirvána it was in *Kian tho weï*, where it was worshipped for several centuries; but that it subsequently passed into various kingdoms, and was at that time in Persia.||—C. L.

(8) *The western Yue ti.*—These are the great Yue ti, who, driven to the westward, first by the northern Hioung, and then by the Ousun, quitted the Tangut where they led a wandering life, and becoming masters of Transoxania, founded there an empire, long powerful, and extended their conquests to Cabul, Kandahar, and the countries situated on both banks of the Indus. See note 9 to Chap. XII.—C. L.

(9) *The kingdom of Yu thian.*—Khotan. See Chap. III.

(10) *The kingdom of Khiu thse.*—M. Remusat thought that this country might be that of Beshbalik; may not rather *Koutche*, which was moreover a part of Beshbalik, be more particularly indicated here?—C. L.

(11) *The Heaven Teou shou—Tushita* in Sanscrit. It is the fourth of the six heavens situated one above another and constituting the world of desires. It is there that beings arrived at the state immediately preceding that of absolute perfection, that is to say, that of Bodhisattwa, await the moment of their return to the earth in the character of Buddhas.—C. L.

(12) *Mi le Phou sa.*—Maïtreya Buddha. See note 8, Chap. VI.

* *Pian i tian*, B. LXIII. art. 7, p. 7. v.

(13) ***The age of ages,***—in Sanscrit *Bhadra kalpa.* It is the present age in which we live, and one of those periods assigned for the formation, continnance, and destruction of the world. It is to last 236 millions of years, of which 151,200,000 have already elapsed, and during which one thousand Buddhas must successively appear for the salvation all creatures. There have already appeared but four of these, and the life of man is on the decrease, seeing that from 84,000 years it is reduced to 100. Calamities of different kinds successively overtake all parts of the universe. When the age of man shall have decreased to 30 years, the rain of heaven shall cease; the drought which shall succeed will prevent the reproduction of plants and vegetables; there will be no more water and an immense number of men will die. When the life of man is further reduced to twenty years, epidemics and all kinds of sickness shall arise, and carry off an infinity of victims. Finally when the average of life shall be but 10 years, man shall be given up to strife and war. Trees and plants even shall become weapons in their hands, and be the means of mutual destruction, so that immense numbers shall perish thus. Then, according to the tradition preserved by Fa hian, ***Mi le*** (Maïtreya) shall appear in the character of Buddha to regenerate the world; and the life of man shall be extended once more to 80,000 years.—C. L.

(14) ***Men out of their homes.***—This expression, as we have often seen, implies men who have adopted religious life and who live in solitude.

(15) ***The three Koueï.*** See Chap. XXXVI. note 7.

(16) ***The five precepts.*** See Chap. XVI. note 12.

CHAPTER XL.

Departure from the Kingdom of Lions.—Kingdom of Ye pho ti.—Lao mountain —Town of Thsing cheou.—Return to Chhang an.—Conclusion.

Fa hian sojourned two years in this kingdom. He there sought for and obtained the volume which contains the precepts of *Mi sha se.* He obtained the long *A han* and the miscellaneous *A han;* at length he had a collection of the different *Tsang,*[1] all of them books which were wanting in the land of Han. When in possession of these volumes in the *fan* language, he placed them aboard a large trading vessel capable of accommodating more than two hundred men. Astern was fastened a small vessel to provide against the dangers of a sea voyage, and injury to the larger one. With a favorable wind they proceeded easterly for two days, when they were overtaken by a hurricane. The ship took in water, and the merchants were anxious to board the small vessel; but the crew of the latter, fearful of overloading her, cut the cable. The merchants were extremely alarmed for their lives, and, expecting every moment that the vessel would go to the bottom, they took the heaviest objects and cast them into the sea. Fa hian worked with the crew in pumping out the water; all that was superfluous of his own he, too, threw into the sea. But he dreaded lest the merchants would cast over board his books and his images! His sole resource was then to pray *Kouan shi in,*[2] to allow all the ecclesiastics to return alive to the land of Han. "As for me, said he, I undertook this distant journey to seek for the Law; I trust to the gods to protect this ship and enable me to reach the haven."

The hurricane having lasted thirteen days and thirteen nights, they came to the shore of an island; and when the tide had ebbed, having discovered the place of the leak, they stopped it up, and again put to sea. There are many pirates there, from whom when taken there is no escape. The sea was vast, immense, shoreless; neither the east nor the west were known; the course was regulated by the sun, the moon, and the stars.[3] When the weather was cloudy or rainy, there was no help but follow the wind. During the night when the weather was dark, they saw nothing but huge waves dashing against each other, fire-coloured lightnings, tortoises, crocodiles, sea-monsters, and other prodigies. The merchants were much troubled, as they knew not whither they were drifting. The sea was bottomless, and there was not even a rock at which they could stop. When the sky had become serene, they then knew to steer easterly, and they proceeded afresh on their route; but had they come upon any hidden rock there was no means of saving their lives. Thus was it with them for ninety days, when they arrived in the kingdom of *Ye pho thi.*[4] Heretics and Bráhmans are numerous there, and there the law of Foe is in no wise entertained.

After a sojourn of six months in this kingdom, Fa hian proceeded anew with certain merchants in a large vessel capable of holding two hundred men. They took with them provisions for fifty days. They set sail on the sixteenth day of the fourth moon. Fa hian was very happy aboard this vessel. They proceeded north-east towards *Kouang cheou.*[5] At the end of about a month they encountered a frightful wind, and violent rain. The merchants and the passengers were equally alarmed. Fa hian at this juncture prayed with all his heart to *Kouan shi in,* as did all the ecclesiastics of the land of Han, beseeching the gods to succour them and to calm the heavens. When calm was restored, the Bráhmans took counsel among themselves, and said, "It is the presence of this Samanean on board that has drawn down upon us this calamity; we must land this mendicant upon the shore of some island of the sea. It must not be that for one man we be all exposed to such danger." The chief benefactor[6] of Fa hian said, "If you set ashore this Samanean, I will denounce you to the king on our arrival in the land of Han. The king of the land of Han is himself an adherent of the law of Foe; he reveres mendicants and ecclesiastics." The merchants hesitating, dared not to set him ashore. Still the sky was very threatening; the pilots mutually looked at each other, and were greatly embarrassed. They had now been seventy days on the passage. Provisions and water were exhausted; they used salt water for cooking and they divided the fresh water; each person had two *shing.*[7] As it was drawing towards its end, the merchants took counsel together and said, "The time (calculated) for this long passage may be fifty days to reach *Kouang cheou;* now many days have elapsed since that term was passed; our resources are expended; it were better for us to steer to the north-west in quest of land."

In twelve days and nights they arrived at the south of the mountain *Lao*[8] situated on the confines of *Chhang kouang kian,*[9] and found there fresh water and vegetables. After so perilous a navigation, after so many fatigues and apprehensions for so many days, when they went ashore and beheld the plant *Li ho thsai,* they verily believed they were in the land of Han! Still they saw neither inhabitants nor traces of man, and they knew not in what place they were. Some said that they were not yet at *Kouang cheou;* others that they had passed it; none knew what to determine upon. They went into a little boat to enter the mouth of the river, in order to find some one of whom to enquire of the place at which they had arrived. They found two hunters returning home, and directed Fa hian to act as interpreter and interrogate them. Fa hian began by encouraging them; he then asked, "What people are you?" They answered, "We are adherents of Foe." He asked again, "What went ye in quest of in the hills?" They answered us deceitfully, "To-morrow is the 15th day of the seventh moon; we sought for something to offer in sacrifice to Foe." He asked again "What kingdom is this?" They answered "It is *Thsing cheou,*[10] on the confines of *Chhang kouan kiun* which belongs to the family of the *Lieou.*" The merchants having heard this were greatly rejoiced; they demanded their merchandise immediately, and sent some one to *Chhang kouang. Li yng,* who was governor there, and believed in and honored the law of Foe, learning that there were Samaneans aboard with books and images, entered a boat and came out to the sea; he then sent people beforehand, to the shore, and having received the books and the images, returned to the town. The merchants set out for *Yang cheou.*[11] The people of *Thsing cheou,* who are under the dominion of the *Lieou,* invited Fa hian to remain a winter and a summer. At the end of the summer's rest,[12] Fa hian left his masters. He longed ardently to see *Chhang 'an* again; but that which he had at heart being a weighty matter, he halted in the south, where the masters published the Sacred Books and the Precepts.

Fa hian, after leaving *Chhang 'an,*[13] was six years in reaching the *Kingdom of the Middle:* he sojourned there six years; and took another three in returning to *Thsing cheou*. The kingdoms which he traversed amount to the number of at least thirty. After passing the River of Sand in the west, he arrived in India. The decency, the gravity, the piety of the clergy are admirable; they cannot be described. The present is a mere summary: not having been hitherto heard by the masters, he casts not his eyes retrospectively on details. He crossed the sea, and hath returned after having overcome every manner of fatigue, and has enjoyed the happiness of receiving many high and noble favors. He has been in dangers and has escaped them; and now therefore he puts upon the bambu[15] what has happened to him, anxious to communicate to the wise what he hath seen and heard.

This year *Kya yn*, the twelfth of the years *I yi*[16] of the *Tsin*, being the year of the star of longevity, at the end of the summer rest they went out to meet Fa hian the traveller.[17] On his arrival, they detained him to pass the festivals of the winter. They discoursed with him; they interrogated him on his travels. His good faith lent confidence to his recitals; so that what was known but imperfectly before, was now better explained. He hath set in order the beginning and the end. He himself said, "In recapitulating what I have experienced, my heart is involuntarily moved. The sweat that hath flowed in my perils, is not the cause of present emotion. This body hath been preserved by the sentiments which animated me. It was the end that induced me to hazard my life in countries where there is no certainty of its preservation, and to attain that at every risk was the object of my hopes."

They were touched with these words; they were touched to behold such a man: they observed among themselves, that a very few had indeed expatriated themselves for the sake of the Doctrine; but no one had ever forgotten self in quest of the law as Fa hian had done. One must know the conviction which truth produces, otherwise one cannot partake of the zeal which produces earnestness. Without merit and without activity nothing is achieved. On accomplishing aught with merit and activity, how shall one be abandoned to oblivion? To lose what is esteemed—to esteem what mankind forget,—oh!

NOTES.

(1) *A collection of the different Tsang.*—For explanations of the precepts of *Mi cha se*, the four *A han* (Agama) and various other works comprised under the title *Tsang* (collection), see Chap. XXXVI. notes 10 and 12.

(2) *Kouan shi in.*—Avalokiteswara, a well-known personage in Buddhic mythology. (See Chap. XVI. note 30.) Fa hian, in his distress, invokes him as the god whose power is exercised over animated creatures, who, according to the theological system developed by Mr. Hodgson, owe to him their origin, as the creation of the different mansions composing the material world is considered the work of Manjusri. Buddhists have consecrated to *Kouan shi in* one of the ten consecutive days into which each month is divided, namely the 24th. On this day the four kings of the gods descend among mortals to weigh their good and evil actions. By pronouncing the name *Kouan shi in Phou sa*, all sorrows are extinguished and all virtue nourished and enlarged.*—C. L.

(3) *Their course was regulated by the sun, moon, and stars.*—This important passage would lead us to infer that the mariner's compass was unknown, even in China, at the time of Fa hian, who otherwise would scarcely have omitted some reference to that instrument in speaking of his perilous situation in this hurricane. Chinese writers refer this invention, some to the fabulous ages of their history, others to the reign of *Ching Wang* of the *Chow* dynasty, that is 1121—1114 B. C. It is remarkable, however, that Marco Polo makes no mention of the compass, the use of which was wholly unknown in Europe at the time of his travels.—J. W. L.

(4) *A kingdom named Ye pho ti,—Yava dwipa.*—This is the first mention of the Island of Java found in Chinese authors; but it was not till some years after the return of Fa hian that they possessed details of its geographical position, of the productions of its soil and the manners of its inhabitants. An embassy which the king of this country despatched to the emperor of China in the twelfth year *yuen kia* (436) under the dynasty of the *Soung*, originated that intercourse which, occasional at first and interrupted by long intervals, increased towards the middle of the 10th century in consequence of establishments formed there by the Chinese. Those who were settled there were called *Tang*, from the name of the dynasty under which

* *Fa youen chou lin*, quoted in the *San tsang fa sou*, B. XLII. p. 3.

this colonisation was effected. It was about this time that they adopted the form *Che pho* to represent the name *Java*; a transcription which prevailed for a long time. Under the dominion of the Mongols, several military expeditions were sent against the Javanese, whose country then received the name of *Koua wa* ('sound of gourd') which was given in consequence of the resemblance observed between the voice of the inhabitants and that of a gourd when struck. Lastly, modern annalists and geographers have applied to Java the names peculiar to other islands and districts situated in its neighbourhood, or dependent upon it. Such is that of *Pou kia loung* which belongs to an isle (Borneo?) said to be eight days sail from *Che pho*; and *Kiao lieou pa*, which is perhaps the province of *Sheri bon* in the isle of Java itself. The *San tsai tou hoeï*, quoted in the Japanese Encyclopedia, says: "*Pou kia loung*, *Ta che pho*, and *Koua wa* are three distinct kingdoms; formerly they constituted but one.*

The number and variety of ancient monuments found in Java have led to the belief that this island was colonised by different people of the continent of Asia; but the religion, institutions, and literature of Hindustan do not appear to have been generally diffused in this island till towards the middle of the 9th Century, and it is only from this era that any dependance can be placed in the traditions of the Japanese. All that precedes it is confused, obscure, contradictory, and interpolated with the fabulous and heroic history of continental India. The sectaries of Buddha, repelled by the Bráhmans to the extremities of Asia and to the adjacent isles, took refuge in Java as they did in Ceylon, Ava, and Siam; but it is probable that if Buddhism was not generally diffused there till about this period, it was at all events introduced earlier. It is seen from Fa hian's account that at the beginning of the 5th century that religion numbered there neither many proselytes, nor important monuments; Bráhmanism predominated there. According to a description of Java written in Chinese and which forms part of the precious library left by M. Klaproth, we must assign to the introduction of Buddhism in this island a date much older than is usually supposed. It was in the reign of the emperor *Koung wou ti* of the *Han* (from 24 to 57 A. D.) that the natives of *Ou In tou* (India) crossed the sea and went to Java. Having beheld the precious things produced on this island, they arranged with the inhabitants a traffic of exchange, and introduced among them the art of building houses, that of writing, and the Law of Buddha.† In truth however, the book from which we extract these particulars, printed at Batavia and compiled almost entirely from European sources, is not to

* *Encyc. Japan.* B. XIV. pp. 10—12.
† *Kiao lieou pa tsoung lun*, p. 58 v.

be taken as an independent authority. But the quotation of the name of an Emperor of China, seems to give some weight to this passage as indicating that the opinion there advanced had been taken from Chinese annals. However improbable this date may appear, and however contradictory to the narrative of Fa hian and unconfirmed by other Chinese works, I have deemed it right to insert it here in order to attract the attention of such as are desirous of testing its authenticity by comparison with the traditions preserved by Raffles and Crawford.

In the same work the name of Java is transcribed *Chao ya*, and the author states that this name was given to the country by reason of the quantity of millet (*panicum italicum*) which it produces. (The Isle of Barley of Ptolemy.) He adds that the *Tang* named this kingdom *Kiao lieou pa*, without knowing the origin of this name which is peculiar to a particular locality, while *Chao ya* is the general name of the whole Island.—C. L.

(5) *Towards Kouang cheou.*—This is the town named Canton by Europeans, the capital of the province of *Kouang toung.*—C. L.

(6) *The principal benefactor*:—in Chinese *tan youeï.* I concur with M. Remusat, in the meaning of this word borrowed from the *Fan* language, as given in an early part of this work. (See Chap. I. note 12.)—C. L.

(7) *Two shing.*—The *shing* is the twentieth part of the *shi* or Chinese bushel, and its capacity is calculated to contain a hundred and twenty thousand grains of millet.—C. L.

(8) *Lao.*—A mountain in the district of *Laï cheou fou*, in *Shan toung*, on the borders of the sea. It is said to be twenty *li* in height and to have a circumference of eighty *li*. It extends throughout the Peninsula, to the north of which is situated the present town of *Tsy me hian*, and is sixty *li* south-east of this town. It is distinguished into the great and the small *Lao shan.* These two mountains formerly formed but one. The river *Pe sha* has its rise there.—C. L.

(9) *Chang kouang kiun.*—The present town of *Ping ten cheou*, in the department of *Laï cheou fou* of the *Shan toung*, bore under the first dynasty of the *Soung* the name of *Shang kouang kiun*, which was changed by the Weï into that of *Shang kouang hian*, and ceased entirely to be used under the Souï.*—C. L.

(10) *Thsing cheou.*—This is the present town of *Thsing cheou fou* in the *Shan toung.*—C. L.

(11) *Yang cheou.*—At the period when Fa hian wrote, the *Yang cheou* comprised all *Kiang nan*, a part of *Honan* and the northern angle of *Kiang si.* At present *Yang cheou* is no more than a department of the

* *Ta tsing y toung chi*, B. CVII. p. 7 v. † *Ibid.* p. 2.

province of *Kiang sou*, which again is but a dismemberment of the eastern part of the ancient *Kiang nan*. The present *Yang cheou* is two hundred *li* north-east of *Kiang ning fou* (Nankin) on the great canal. Its position constitutes it one of the most commercial towns in China, and the greater part of its immense population consists of traders.†—C. L.

(12) *At the end of the summer rest.*—For, '*this sojourn being ended.*' This mode of speech which frequently recurs in Fa hian has been explained elsewhere. (Chap. I. note 8.)—C. L.

I think it very probable that the *summer rest* here spoken of, is the *Wasso*, or period of sacred repose of the Buddhists, during which priests were permitted and even enjoined to abstain from pilgrimages and to devote themselves to stationary religious observances. It began with the full moon of July, and ended with that of November, thus including the whole of the rainy season. Fa hian mentions this rest elsewhere, and no doubt felt it incumbent upon him to halt at the time enjoined by his religion. In addition to what I have observed upon the subject of the festival of Jaganath (pages 21 and 261), I may here mention that the Rev. Dr. Stevenson has suggested,* that the Rath Játrá may possibly be the remains of a triumphant entry with which the sages were welcomed on returning from their peregrinations to hold the Wasso.—J. W. L.

(13) *Chhang an:* Otherwise *Si'an fou* in *Chen si*, the native country of Fa hian.—C. L.

(14) *He halted in the south.*—That is to say at Nanking, where he published the religious books he had brought with him. This was the important duty that Fa hian had imposed upon himself before returning to his native country.—C. L.

(15) *He hath put upon the bambu.*—More exactly *bambu taffetas* (*chou py*). This expression designates the substance, or part of the bambu upon which men wrote before the invention of paper, whether this was done by engraving the characters with a style, or by tracing them with some kind of varnish; but it here refers to paper the invention of which dates several centuries before Fa hian.—C. L.

(16) *The twelfth of the years I yi.*—That is, 414 A. D., the eighteenth year of the reign of *'An ty*. The *star of longevity* (*Sheou sing*) is one of the twelve divisions of the Chinese zodiac as it was figured in the times of the Han. It corresponds with the *Balance*, and thus indicates that the year had already reached the autumnal equinox.—C. L.

(17) *Fa hian the traveller.*—This is the same expression *tao jin*, already used in Chapter IV. which M. Remusat, had translated *priest* and which

* Journ. Royal Asiatic Society, Vol. VII. p. 8.

M. Klaproth, regarded as synonymous with *Tao sse*, or the doctors of reason. It appears to me that from the manner of using it in this place there can be no doubt as to its true meaning. The figurative sense of the word *tao*, for *reason*, *doctrine*, ought to be here set aside, although consecrated by ordinary usage, and its primitive and natural meaning, a *road*, preferred : *Tao jin*, a man of the road, a traveller.—C. L.

On showing the original characters to an intelligent Chinese, he at once interpreted them "priest," and denied that they bear the meaning assigned to them by M. Landresse.—J. W. L.

INDEX.

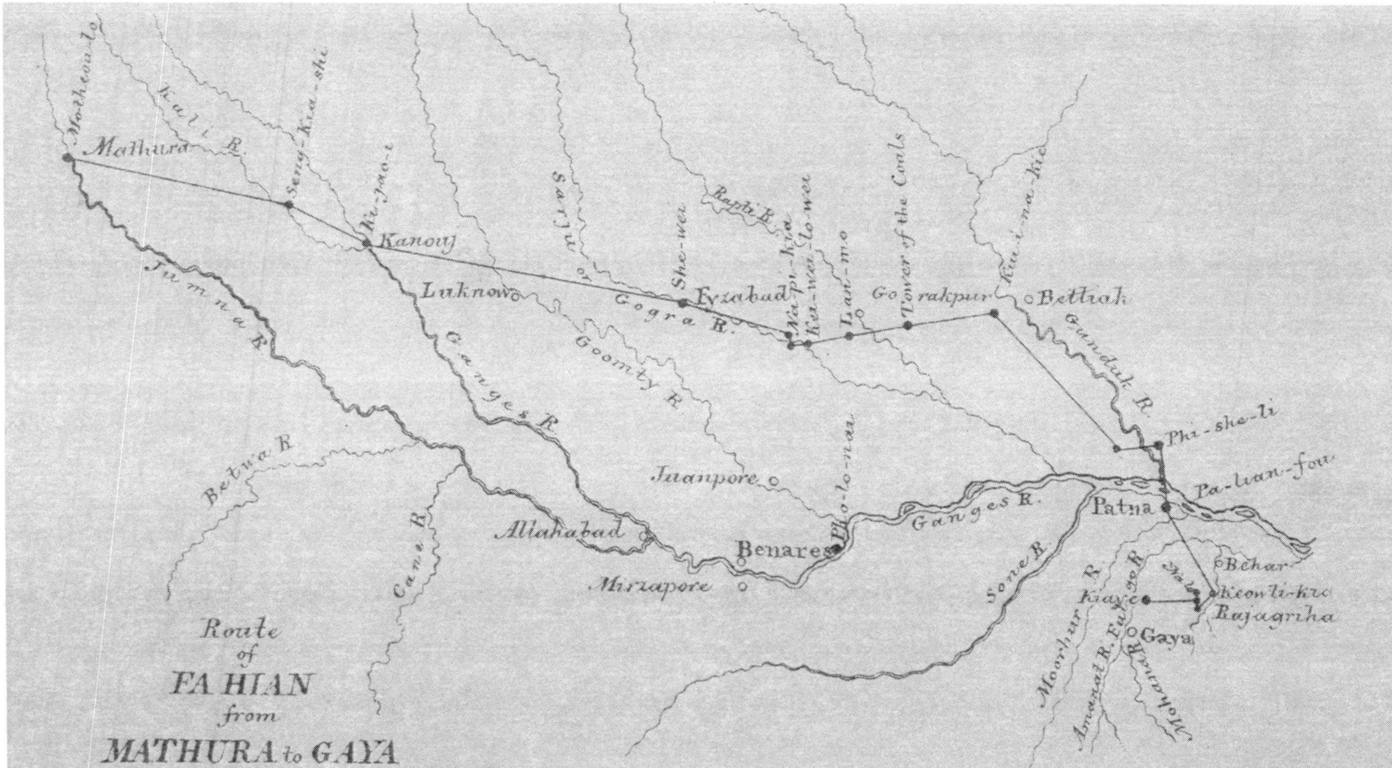

Route of FA HIAN from MATHURA to GAYA
Mo-theou-lo
Mathura
Kali R.
Seng-Kia-shi
Ki-jao-i
Kanouj
Jumna R.
Luknow
Ganges R.
Sarju or Gogra R.
Goomty R.
She-wei
Fyzabad
Rapti R.
Na-pi-kia
Kia-wei-lo-wei
Lan-mo
Gorakpur
Tower of the Coals
Kiu-i-na-kie
Bettiah
Gunduk R.
Phi-she-li
Pa-lian-fou
Patna
Betwa R.
Cane R.
Juanpore
Allahabad
Benares
Pho-lo-nai
Mirzapore
Ganges R.
Sone R.
Behar
Keowli-kio
Rajagriha
Kiaye
Gaya
Moorhur R.
Amanat R.
Eufgo R.
Mohana R.

CHINESE MAP OF INDIA

Shewing the route of Hiouen-thsang

Pl. II

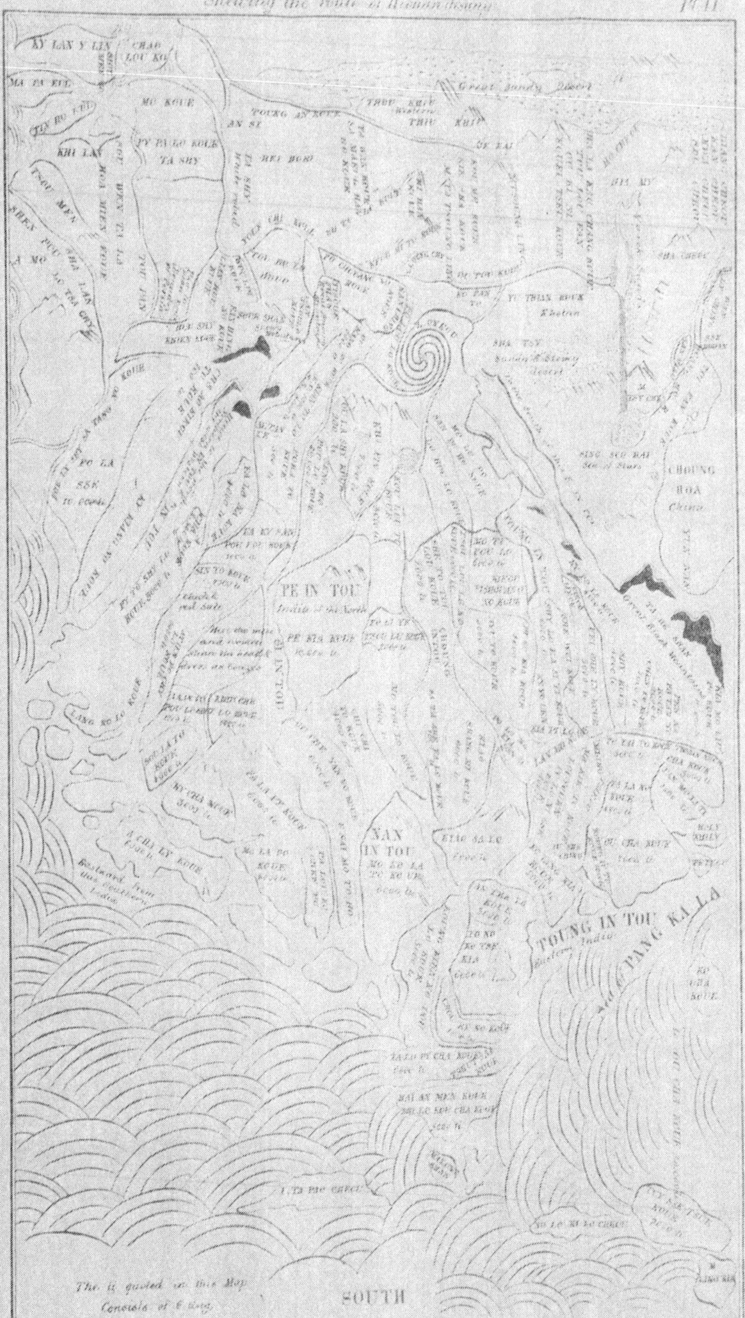

Incarnation of Sakya Muni

Birth of Sákya Muni